DEMOGRAPHY
FROM SCANTY EVIDENCE

DEMOGRAPHY
FROM SCANTY EVIDENCE

Central Africa
in the Colonial Era

edited by
Bruce Fetter

Lynne Rienner Publishers • Boulder and London

Published in the United States of America in 1990 by
Lynne Rienner Publishers, Inc.
1800 30th Street, Boulder, Colorado 80301

and in the United Kingdom by
Lynne Rienner Publishers, Inc.
3 Henrietta Street, Covent Garden, London WC2E 8LU

Library of Congress Cataloging-in-Publication Data
Demography from scanty evidence : central Africa in the colonial era /
edited by Bruce Fetter.
    p. cm.
  Includes bibliographical references.
  ISBN 1-55587-199-2 (alk. paper)
   1. Africa, Central—Population—History—Statistical methods.
I. Fetter, Bruce.
  HB3664.3.A3D46 1990
  304.6'0967—dc20   90-33585
                                                         CIP

British Cataloguing in Publication Data
A Cataloguing in Publication record for this book
is available from the British Library.

Printed and bound in the United States of America

The paper used in this publication meets the requirements
of the American National Standard for Permanence of
Paper for Printed Library Materials Z39.48-1984.

To the memory of

Rita Headrick

A courageous pioneer in the
historical demography of Central Africa

Contents

PART 2 INNOVATIONS IN METHOD

PART 3 CASE STUDIES

Maps, Figures, and Tables

MAPS

FIGURES

TABLES

Acknowledgments

This book was made possible by grants from the National Science Foundation (Geography and Regional Sciences Program and Measurement Methods and Data Resources Program, proposal SES-8520051) and the University of Wisconsin–Milwaukee Foundation, which supplemented the NSF grant. The book evolved from the Conference on the Analysis of Census Data from Colonial Central Africa held at the University of Wisconsin, Milwaukee, Golda Meir Library, 18–22 August 1986. This evolution would not have happened without the enthusiastic support of Golda Meir Library successive heads William C. Roselle (now director of libraries at the University of Pittsburgh) and William D. Moritz (formerly associate director and then acting director). The conference they organized was memorable, and staff members too numerous to mention individually contributed to arrangements at every stage of operations. The conference itself was held in the American Geographic Society Collection with the gracious support of Director Roman Drazniowski, Howard Deller, Chris Baruth, and the entire staff.

Travel, lodging, and amenities for participants were organized by Lisa Jensen. Nicole Chandler assembled a magnificent team of simultaneous interpreters and was subsequently responsible for translation of Chapters 9, 10, 20, and 21 from French. Our special thanks to Vice Chancellor John Schroeder, Dean William Halloran, and Associate Dean Richard Meadows for supervision of the conference and the resultant publication.

The conference was enlivened by the participation of, in addition to the authors of this book, William Brass, Kusum Datta, John Thornton, Linda Heywood, Issac Lamba, Jane Parpart, Bucyalimwe Mararo, Nungisa ya Bulongo, Jan Vansina, Hans Panofsky, Scott Pollard, and Verena Fjermestad.

The book benefited enormously from the critical support of Pat Manning. Other suggestions came from David Healy and Osei-Mensah Aborampah. Donna Genzmer-Schenstrom and Jean Zamorsky, of the University of Wisconsin–Milwaukee Cartographic Services Laboratory, organized the production of maps and graphs, and Robert Van Alstine, Jim Hicks, Julia Fletcher, Brad Javenkoski, and Christel Syrrakos put the finishing touches on them. Claudia Sullivan of the university's Social Science Research Facility typed the final manuscript—a major undertaking—with help from Antoinette Newell and Peggy Kleiber of the Department of History. Mistakes have been provided courtesy of the editor.

B.F.

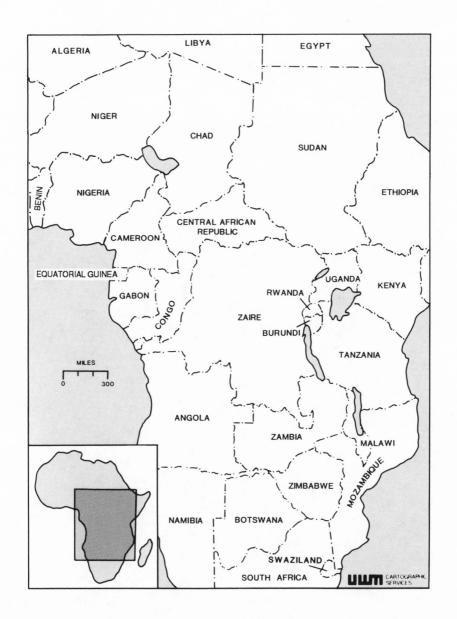

CENTRAL AFRICA

Demography in the Reconstruction of African Colonial History

BRUCE FETTER

If the human experience is to be measured rather than simply described, demography is its most basic indicator. No discipline treats phenomena more essential to our lives than birth, death, and migration. The power of demography lies in the possibilities of comparison across time and space. Are the inhabitants of a given region having more children than the generation of their parents? Are they dying younger than their neighbors? Through comparisons such as these we can assess the welfare of any population we can enumerate.

Therein lies the rub. Improvements during the last hundred years in the technology of counting people have made possible unprecedented accuracy in our demographic knowledge. We can, for example, measure the collective fecundity of women at every point in their fertility cycle or the probability of death for tiny subsections of the population. This precision, however, has given professional demographers unrealistic expectations as to what they need to know in order to produce significant observations about the societies they study. Many dismiss as unscientific the analysis of data that does not conform to the standards of statistics currently collected in industrialized countries.

This limitation of analysis to "modern" data removes much of human history from the demographer's domain. It precludes, moreover, the study of the recent past of areas like Africa, where scientific surveys are a recent innovation, thereby depriving those addressing current problems of any sense of historical continuity. As a result, scholars and policymakers are often left to choose between two equally undesirable assumptions: that current conditions are much the same as those of the past or that they cannot be known at all.

The irony of this dilemma is that population statistics exist for most of Africa—and, indeed, for the rest of the tropical world—for most of the twentieth century. Unfortunately, they have been largely disregarded because of their universally acknowledged shortcomings. National censuses in the scientifically accepted sense of the term, for example, were not conducted in Central Africa until well after World War II. After independence, moreover, even these enumerations were found to be seriously underestimated. In focusing on the deficiencies of these aggregate data, moreover, researchers frequently overlooked careful investigations of subnational regions.[1]

Nonetheless, a case can be made for analyzing defective data. Blurred vision is preferable to blindness. In that sense, the demographic evidence that survives constitutes shadows, much like those described by Plato in his myth of the cave. Each set of colonial population statistics is only the reflection of the demographic processes it purports to measure. In the absence of more accurate information, however, scholars can interpret these data provided that they remember that they are dealing with the shadows of objects rather than the objects themselves.

This intellectual enterprise requires double courage. Scholars must be prepared to deal with dubious and ambivalent data that must be interrogated like unreliable witnesses in a court of law.[2] On the basis of that evidence they must go beyond their initial observations to identify as far as possible prevailing trends in fertility, mortality, and migration. In the absence of the precision of modern social surveys the task of such historical reconstruction rests on the interpretation of phenomena that we cannot measure directly. Nonetheless, since the understanding of the colonial experience is a necessary component in providing African decisionmakers with background to Africa's current problems, dealing with uncertainties is well worth the effort. As Maimonides put it, "He whose father did not have him taught, is obliged to teach himself when he reaches the age of discernment. Learning precedes action; action does not necessarily lead to learning."[3]

Knowledge of the colonial past can help contemporary leaders make decisions regarding the future of their countries because of the complex relationship between the most basic conditions in societies and demographic variables, which interact with the environment, famines, diseases, family values, warfare, and governmental demands. If we can identify, for example, colonial policies that led to famines, contemporary leaders might know at least some policies to avoid. By the same token, knowledge of the policies that most effectively *did* reduce mortality and morbidity rates can help current public officials decide how best to spend their limited funds.

APPROACHES AND SOURCES IN DEMOGRAPHY

Colonial demography, like any historical field, involves investigation on two scales. Before embarking on detailed research the scholar should have a general idea of what specialists in other regions have learned about their parts of the world. To use the cartographic analogy, we need to construct a small-scale map with a great deal of generalization that can provide a broad notion of the patterns found elsewhere, before larger-scale, more detailed maps can be drawn.

Needless to say, scholars and policymakers interested in the demography of colonial Africa are not acting in an absolute vacuum; but the literature is diffuse and contradictory. Contributors to this volume will discuss the monographic literature relating to Central Africa in detail, but those writings must be seen in the context of the wide variety of approaches to historical demography in general.

Across the relevant disciplines (which include archeology, geography, history, and sociology) two major approaches are discernible: the holistic, which describes an entire population, and the partial, which surveys only a segment of it. Demographers frequently generalize about entire populations, but most of the data relating to historical populations is partial rather than holistic. As indicated above, holistic data relating to even subnational regions are (outside of China) a relatively recent phenomenon. The sources for retrospective surveys of parts of the population, by contrast, are venerable and diverse.

Archeologists, with some help from geographers, have led the search for demographic information based on physical remains. These investigations have, of necessity, been based on partial evidence, based on either regional analyses of microenvironment or the discovery of surviving sites of human occupation. These efforts have focused on two techniques of reconstruction: estimation of the ability of a given historical population to live in a defined environment and analysis of human skeletal remains. The environmental approach is basically economic, involving either the calculation of a carrying capacity—the population that any region can support, given a particular technology—or a cost comparison model that assesses the relative social costs to a population of exploiting a given set of resources.[4]

The analysis of skeletal remains falls under the general rubric of paleodemography. This approach stresses the analysis of human bones found at a particular site, through which archeologists can estimate the age at death of the historical population. This technique is not particularly adaptable to tropical climates, where acidic soils destroy osseous materials, but it can be used in temperate climates with spectacular results.[5]

Physical evidence from the natural environment or of human remains is necessarily impersonal; verbal evidence, by contrast, permits the demographic researcher to know populations as individuals. These sources, which are also partial, are those most often explored by historians and also fall into two categories: *lists*, compiled at a single moment, and *registers*, maintained over a number of years.

Lists are related to modern censuses in that they contain one or more pieces of information about specific individuals. In the best of cases they can reveal sex, age, social standing, and ethnic background, crucial components of any social analysis. Earlier lists are seldom so systematic, but they nonetheless constitute social snapshots that are our best demographic source for the period from the last Roman times until the end of the Middle Ages.[6]

Registers, by contrast, provide the raw material for producing moving pictures of demographic change. By recording the baptisms, burials, and residence of local populations over time they allow the researcher to establish measures of nuptuality, fertility, mortality, and even migration and to learn how these measures changed through the years. Historians of Europe, North America, and the tropics have, with the help of computers, studied a large number of communities for the period dating roughly from the sixteenth to the nineteenth centuries.[7]

Since the nineteenth century these sources on the lives of individual communities have given way to national ones, which represent the first true holistic sources for historical demography. Population registry, rather than being left in the hands of religious authorities, has become the province of the industrial state. Legally, at least, all births and deaths must be reported to public officials; and in many countries, the requirement also applies to changes of domicile. The analysis of these statistics is at the base of most demography carried out on a national level. The large number of vital events recorded allows the early detection of changes in vital rates and makes possible the comparison of subsections of the population with each other and with the general population.

These analyses, alas, are predicated on the assumption that all relevant events have been reported to the authorities—while in reality many escape the legal record. To manage this discrepancy demographers have distinguished between de jure counts, which describe the population as it is legally recorded, and de facto counts, which describe the population as it actually is. The earliest censuses in colonial Africa were usually de jure.

Although vital records are systematic, they are not necessarily detailed enough to satisfy the curiosity of modern researchers. Indeed, the information required by a researcher would be prohibitively expensive to collect for the population as a whole. This economic reality has given rise to the modern sample survey—which in a certain sense is a return to partial sources. Its use rests on the argument that a carefully chosen sample can stand as a surrogate for the population as a whole. It can, moreover, be more exact than a census because each investigator can decide precisely which questions to ask of the subjects. Using it, unfortunately, involves some loss of historical perspective in that information is limited to responses given at the moment or moments when the survey is taken. This is the technique preferred by contemporary demographic researchers, who can ask women a detailed and varied array of questions about their childbearing.

Even the most exacting survey, however, covers only a fraction of the entire population of any given geographical unit; real aggregate data depends on modern censuses. Since their invention in Western Europe during the eighteenth century, censuses have become increasingly detailed and, in most cases, increasingly accurate. They are, moreover, the most commonly available source of demographic information.

The historical demography of modern industrial societies depends on an analysis of surveys, censuses, and vital registers. Everyone agrees that demographic indicators measure the health of societies, but scholars and policymakers alike disagree on what constitutes a healthy society. Is a country undergoing rapid population increase better or worse off than one whose population is in equilibrium? Experts since Thomas Henry Malthus have argued the respective merits of high and low rates of natural increase.

THE DEMOGRAPHIC TRANSITION MODEL

Since World War II Western Europe and North America have been acknowledged as a cynosure for the rest of the world. Initially, demographers believed that these regions had gone through a uniform set of phases, which they called "the demographic transition." This theory holds that before the industrial revolution these regions, like the rest of the world, were characterized by high deathrates and high birthrates. Deathrates began to fall before birthrates, so populations grew rapidly. Eventually birthrates also fell, and the most developed societies reached a new equilibrium of low birthrates and low deathrates. These stages of population change were seen as concomitant to the stages of economic development, to which all "self-respecting" nations were to aspire. The historical demographers' job was to see just how this happy state had come about.[8]

Transition theory provided the rationale for the massive Princeton European Fertility Project, funded by the United Nations and a number of private and national foundations. Since 1963 this project has brought together many of the most talented demographers in the world together with social and economic historians concerned with the origins of modern European societies. In the course of their investigations, however, project members discovered that the demographic reality did not coincide with the transition theory as it was originally framed. In some countries the decline in fertility actually preceded the decline in mortality. Demographic changes, moreover, did not necessarily coincide with economic development and industrialization. To give one example, fertility decline began in France at the end of the eighteenth century, some eighty years before it began in Great Britain and Germany, countries of at least equal economic development. Studies based on family reconstruction from local population registers showed enormous variation within countries and between Eastern and Western Europe. Ultimately, the members of the project arrived at a more modest consensus: the nations of Europe had undergone a decline in fertility that more or less coincided with the decline in mortality, spreading from France in the late eighteenth century to the Soviet Union in the twentieth. Seven books and many articles have been published so far, with much research still to be done.[9]

The results of the Princeton survey notwithstanding, transition theory is still alive and well. The lead section of the 1988 *Annales de démographie historique*, official journal of the Société de Démographie Historique, insists on the importance of the notion, although conceding that societies with differing fertility patterns might undergo different kinds of transition. At the time of this writing, however, the group most likely to undermine transition theory are the zoologists. T. H. Clutton-Brock has recently brought together a study of fertility variations within twenty-five species ranging from insects to humans. This work, *Reproductive Success: Studies of Variation in Contrasting Breeding Systems*, highlights the range of variation in fertility and survival to adulthood, thereby implicitly calling into question the uniqueness of the population for which transition theory was devised—Western countries since the Industrial Revolution. Another question raised is whether an emphasis on differences *within* societies (or species, for that matter) will diminish the interest in differences *between* them.[10]

The interpretation of European demography during the last two hundred years, then, is still in flux. The lack of closure on relatively well documented regions of the world has fortunately not prevented scholars from examining less well documented ones. An international group, for example, has examined the censuses conducted under British rule in India in the late nineteenth and twentieth centuries, analyzing the demographic changes that took place on that subcontinent. N. Gerald Barrier's edited volume, *The Census in British India: New Perspectives*, contains essays on a number of potentially cross-cultural topics: how censuses can be used to examine political, religious, and social change; the effect of imperial policies on the colonial population; and an analysis of the categories devised by the colonial government to measure its subjects.[11] One might therefore conclude that there is much in the general literature that can be applied to the study of the tropical world.

THE STUDY OF DEMOGRAPHY IN TWENTIETH-CENTURY AFRICA

Before proceeding to our particular subdivision of Africa let us examine the scholarship relating to the historical demography of the continent as a whole. Africa, after all, developed its own demographic traditions under colonial rule, practices that were inevitably shaped by political considerations. The earliest sources for these inquiries were population counts and surveys conducted by colonial authorities, but effective vital registration did not come in tropical areas of the continent until the 1930s. Indeed, many governments did not have an accurate estimate of their populations until the 1960s—after independence.[12]

Analyses of the available data reflect the concerns of the governments of the time. The earliest studies were an extension of the colonial reconnaissance of newly conquered territories. They sought to ascertain the whereabouts of the indigenous populations to assess how they were faring under European rule. Although some studies were concerned with the question of whether or not the new rulers were killing off their charges, the major concern before World War II was to locate able-bodied men who could be taxed and thus forced to work for the government and for European entrepreneurs. During the 1930s the League of Nations began to amass data on colonial fertility, mortality, and migration without much effect on the policies of colonial powers.[13]

The agenda of policymakers also included a set of demographic issues related to the allocation of public funds. In those days missions and private corporations played a relatively larger role in public health than at present, while governments spent most of their health budgets on campaigns to eradicate particular diseases.[14] The demographic area on which colonial governments spent most time and effort was migration, encouraging men to seek work in distant mines and discouraging women and children from joining them at the work sites.

World War II brought greater concern for the welfare of the populations as a whole. German mastery of Europe imperiled the existing empires, detaching French and Belgian colonies from their metropoles and thrusting on British colonies a substantial role in the war effort. Systematic surveys of colonial censuses conducted after the war were part of a wider concern for assessing imperial assets and reorganizing colonial governments after the independence of most of the former colonies in Asia.

This tightening of colonial supervision involved an understanding of entire populations rather than just the number of able-bodied men available for work. National censuses arrived at more realistic population estimates and approximations of vital rates. Another relatively new demographic concern was the effect of urbanization, in that colonial regimes were beginning to lift restrictions on urban residence. Surveys show these city populations to be healthier, better nourished, and more fertile than rural ones.[15]

The population counts that have survived from the colonial period thus encompass a broad gamut of investigations ranging from superficial estimates of taxpayers to be dunned to scientific surveys that are still used by demographers. Censuses and surveys conducted since independence are often more accurate, and invariably more detailed, than their predecessors. The interpretation of these inquiries, however, requires a political element not needed for dealing with colonial data. The former were designed almost exclusively by members or agents of the colonial ruling elite. Nowadays, although most instruments have some local input, the impetus often comes from outside agencies.

After independence the United Nations, former colonizers, and the United

States encouraged the new regimes to conduct still more rigorous censuses and surveys conforming to the standards established in developed areas. By the 1970s some thirty African countries had conducted censuses under the United Nations' African Population Census Program. The censuses, however, disquieted many Western analysts by showing that African populations were larger than previously believed and that they were growing at an enormous rate.[16] In the 1960s and early 1970s many still felt that there was a single developmental model to which the new states should conform in order to prosper. With the global economic downturn of the middle 1970s, however, many foreign observers began to doubt whether Africa would ever grow along Western lines. Droughts, famines, and wars suggested that Africa might be permanently caught in a web of poverty. The decline in mortality coupled with continuing high birthrates led many to the conclusion that Africa might remain poor for the foreseeable future.[17]

In response, scholars concerned with Africa adopted two contrasting attitudes. One group set about to study African fertility patterns in order to discover means of curbing population growth. These scholars followed what John Iliffe has called a "natalist interpretation of African history . . . [that] sees the roots of Africa's present population problem in the high fertility of precolonial societies and the positive impact of colonial rule on mortality rates." The main implication of this position is that governments ought to be curbing the birthrate. Although some governments responded to this analysis with antinatalist policies, others were offended, arguing that children were exclusively a national asset.[18]

In support of African resistance to natalism many Marxists argued that Africa's problem was not an autochthonous one of overpopulation but the result of colonial and neocolonial exploitation by agents of world capitalism as they affect local production and family relations. As Dennis Cordell and the late Joel Gregory put it, "The demographic regime of a society is the sum of dialectical class-specific demographic strategies developed within contradictory as well as cooperative sex and age specific domestic units." If that is the case, independent governments can do little to affect fertility practices beyond insisting that their population be protected from the depredations of international capital.[19]

This dialogue between natalists and Marxists, although producing no definitive solutions to African population problems, did stimulate a renewed interest in the demography of the colonial period.[20] Partisans of both positions combed the surviving sources to answer such questions as whether African fertility had always been as high as it was now and whether capitalist projects had indeed raised mortality levels.

Indeed, one might go beyond the debates of foreign scholars to ask how African decisionmakers, demographers, and even historians might best make use of colonial demographic statistics. Such analyses can demonstrate the effect of policies on demography in a context quite different from today's. The broad range of choices thus revealed—and the consequences of policies or even of inaction—could well provide object lessons for African rulers who must choose among policy alternatives. Their decisions, of course, are made in the light of local conditions; let us now turn to Central Africa itself.

CENTRAL AFRICA UNDER COLONIAL RULE

Except for coastal regions, the boundaries of Central Africa are quite arbitrary. (See frontispiece.) No natural obstacles divide this land mass from West, East, or Southern Africa. David Birmingham and Phyllis Martin, the editors of the definitive Longman history of the region, define it as extending from the northern savanna in the Central African Republic and Zaire through the rain forest and southern savanna to the edge of the Kalahari Desert in the west and the Limpopo River in the east.[21] The authors of our collection accept that general definition, although following colonial lines (which exclude Cameroon and Equatorial Guinea to the west and include Rwanda and Burundi in the east).

Despite this geographical diversity, human settlement patterns have given Central Africa a coherence that allows it to be treated as a single unit. Most of the peoples of this region (the main exceptions being inhabitants of the Central African Republic and northern Zaire) speak Bantu languages, which are closely related both to each other and to languages spoken in neighboring countries to the west, east, and south. The vast majority were hoe-cultivators, whose settlements were clustered in river valleys and volcanic highlands. Women did much of the farming, which accounts for a dowry system through which the family of a woman about to be married was compensated for the loss of her labor—the reverse of the nuptual exchange arrangements found in most of Europe and Asia.

Although political institutions were less homogeneous than marriage patterns and cultivation systems, the constellation as a whole can be considered a coherent society. Political organization varied from long-lasting centralized kingdoms with well-defined core areas to fragmentation zones where political authority extended for only a few miles in any direction. These disparate units, however, were held together by a network of religious cults, exogamous clans, and trading networks, which fostered regional cohesion.[22]

The most extensive commercial network in precolonial times was that of the slave trade, which had enormous ramifications for the lives of the local population. Beginning on the coast in the sixteenth century, the Atlantic slave trade forced existing political entities into a wide variety of strategies to protect their populations from immediate death and hereditary servitude. Most groups fled to defensible locales; others amalgamated to resist predators; others, after living as victims, became traders themselves. During the eighteenth century a new trade began to spread eastward from the Indian Ocean, and by the nineteenth century raiders from the east were confronting raiders from the west. Indeed, European powers justified their invasions of the area as intended to put an end to the slave trade.[23]

Beginning in the 1880s, the inhabitants of Central Africa were forcibly incorporated by European powers into four competing empires, whose boundaries were as arbitrary as those of the region itself. The oldest of these belonged to the Portuguese, who had established bases on the Atlantic and Indian Ocean coasts as early as the sixteenth century. Although subsequent expansion up the valleys of the Cuanza and Zambezi Rivers allowed the Portuguese to claim large sections of the region, their colonies of Angola and Mozambique encompassed only a small proportion of the land they once sought.

North of the Portuguese possessions lay the territories claimed by the French and King Léopold II of Belgium. The Congo River more or less divided these two empires, with the French obtaining most of the land watered by tributaries that flow into the river from the north and the Belgians most of the land watered by southern tributaries. The French soon created a federation (French Equatorial Africa) consisting of what is now Gabon, the Congo Republic, and the Central African Republic, to which they added Chad, which extends northward into the Sahara Desert. The Belgian state took over what is today Zaire from King Léopold in 1908. The empire was extended after World War I, when Belgium received a League of Nations mandate to govern the kingdoms of Rwanda and Burundi, which had been previously attached to German East Africa.

The British established their Central African empire a few years later than the French and Belgians. Rather than beginning with claims to the Atlantic coast, the British possessions were an extension of holdings in South Africa. In 1889 they proclaimed a protectorate over what is today Malawi and established a chartered company that came to govern what is today Zimbabwe and Zambia. After 1924 the administration of Zimbabwe (then Southern Rhodesia) was delegated to the local white settlers, while that of the other two territories (then known as Northern Rhodesia and Nyasaland) was left to imperial civil servants.

Indeed, Southern Rhodesia after 1924 was the only colony in the region that was not governed by a bureaucracy directed from an imperial capital in Europe. None of these regimes were accountable to the indigenous inhabitants. Their very boundaries were determined by European diplomats concerned solely with rivalries for territory among competing nation-states. Thus, in no way can the new governments be said to represent the will of the governed.

Within each colony the European conquerors established a hierarchy of administrative units with a variety of names—most commonly, *provinces*, *districts*, and *chiefdoms*. These colonial subdivisions served as the units of administration, socialization, and recordkeeping. Although the colonizers made some effort to administer Africans from important precolonial kingdoms within the same unit, internal boundaries were extremely fluid, being altered for the convenience of the imperial administrators.[24]

These boundaries came to divide Africans who had previously had close contacts with one another. The divisions that arose were often more cultural than physical; for most of the colonial period Africans could pass from one European domain to another with relative ease, despite government efforts to restrict African freedom of movement. In another way, however, European administrations created linguistic barriers to African communication. Each power administered its colonies in its own dominant language—English, French, and Portuguese—which Africans had to master in order to advance in colonial society. Even after independence, which was gained in the 1960s and 1970s, the languages imposed by the colonizers still inhibit communication among African leaders whose native languages are often closer together than their European languages of adoption.

Despite linguistic differences, the colonial regimes employed similar administrative strategies to reduce their African subjects to obedience. Often this process involved three stages: conquest, pacification, and the imposition of taxation. During the earliest stage, when colonial regimes sought to expand their territories to maximum size, they used their armies primarily to suppress Africans who resisted their control of waterways, paths, and intended boundaries with other European powers. Once these boundaries had been ratified by diplomatic accord, the colonizers turned to the pacification of Africans who had not been subdued in the initial conquest. When this process was complete in any given area, the administration levied hut taxes, first payable in labor or local products, then payable only in colonial currency.

These levies were intended to force Africans to pay for the colonial governments imposed on them. Some taxpayers were able to acquit their obligation by producing or transporting goods that could be sold on export markets, but little that was grown actually found buyers abroad. More commonly, the colonizers insisted that able-bodied men sell their labor to the small number of European employers able to pay wages. This brought large numbers of recently colonized Africans into competition for the limited number of available jobs, thereby driving down wage rates.

In order to minimize the number of taxpayers (predominantly men, for most of the colonial period) who escaped taxation, colonial administrations were obliged to develop accounting systems so that officials could distinguish between those who had paid their tax and those who had not.[25] To record individual payments they issued receipts—either bits of paper, which rapidly deteriorated under tropical conditions, or metal tokens, which could be tied together with fiber and worn around the wrist or neck.

Although invaluable for helping an administrator determine whether or not an individual had paid his tax, receipt records were of little use in estimating the revenue potential of a given area. To obtain this information colonial governments conducted their first censuses, which were intended to gauge the potential for tax collection for each district. This estimate could also be used by the administration to determine just how effective individual officers were in collecting taxes. As a result, the officers soon realized that they were playing a delicate game. If their estimates of population were too low, their districts might be amalgamated with surrounding ones to produce a more viable economic unit, as Jeffrey Stone (Chapter 7) shows for the Mapanza District in what is today Zambia. If their estimates were too high, they might be dismissed for failing to apprehend a sufficient proportion of eligible taxpayers! Higher authorities soon took steps to decouple the counting process from tax collection, although in many areas the same individuals were responsible for both tasks.

The earliest censuses were, in any event, extremely imprecise instruments. Many of them actually counted only tax-eligible men, extrapolating estimates for women and children from tiny surveys by means of fixed formulas. As David Beach (Chapter 5) shows for what is today Zimbabwe, censuses were really only annual updates of tax records, while in other colonies (what is today Malawi was one of the earliest), as Justice Mlia (Chapter 8) demonstrates, the government eventually attempted to carry out independent periodic enumerations. The autonomy of these investigations was ultimately assured by increasingly generalized tax payment. As fewer Africans evaded the tax collector, population estimates lost their function of determining how well European administrators were performing their fiscal tasks.

This diminished urgency coincided in most colonies with the high colonial period between the wars, when primary resistance to European rule had subsided and effective nationalist pressures for independence had not yet begun. Official enumerations became more comprehensive, measuring the numbers, distribution, and age-sex composition of African populations. In the Belgian Congo (now Zaire) in particular, as Léon de St. Moulin (Chapter 20) argues, officials began to conduct surveys intended to measure fertility (out of fear that African women were not having enough children to ensure survival),[26] mortality (for workers and small children), and migration (so that managers of large enterprises could judge where to look for additional workers).

Elsewhere, systematic surveys were not taken until after World War II or even after independence. Because of the centrality of the Zambian copper mines to the economy of what was then Northern Rhodesia, the British administration authorized a survey of urban Africans, which was conducted between 1950 and 1955 by J. Clyde Mitchell, one of the contributors to this collection (Chapter 17). Comparable statistics for rural Zambians, however, were not compiled until the census of 1969. The only comprehensive investigation of an entire territory was the Belgians' Enquêtes Démographiques, conducted in what is now Zaire between 1955 and 1957.[27]

The results of these enumerations were far more comforting to the administrators who conducted them. The late Rita Headrick (Chapter 19) shows that fertility rates were, as feared by colonial critics, actually falling among peoples of the rain forest in what was then French Equatorial Africa. Léon de St. Moulin suggests that the same was true for Zairians until the 1930s.

Another domain in which colonial policies did not meet their goals was control of migration. Authorities hoped to restrict urban residence to able-bodied males, but some women and children nonetheless did manage to migrate to the mines and towns. Sharon Stichter (Chapter 15) discusses the conditions within rural households that led, and still lead, women to migrate to urban areas. Karen Tranberg Hansen (Chapter 16) shows how children came to work in urban areas. In sum, a study of colonial censuses can help us examine the gap between colonial policy and practice.

ORGANIZATION

Given the novelty and diversity of the field, we cannot anticipate the needs of all potential readers. We have therefore devised a straightforward topical organizational strategy. We divide the essays into three parts: the first assesses the enumerations performed by various colonial entities. The second part examines methodological innovations in analyzing the available data, and the third consists of case studies relating to individual colonies or subregions. For readers who do not have great experience in formal demography these parts can serve as a manual for approaching the discipline.

Part 1 begins with a general disquisition on how to approach censuses by Jean Stengers, doyen of Belgian historians, whose writings range from the Middle Ages to contemporary times, including work on emigration from Belgium itself.[28] Stengers establishes the vital distinction between *dénombrements* (the French term for enumerations, population counts collected without statistical rigor) and the more modern *recensements* (censuses)—a distinction that is followed in this book.

This chapter is followed by a bibliographic essay by two of the best practitioners of that craft, David Henige and David Gardinier. Henige,[29] editor of the methods journal *History in Africa*, and Gardinier,[30] who compiles the Africa section of the American Historical Association's *Recently Published Articles*, suggest how African historians can obtain insights from other disciplines and research on other continents.

Following these general essays, we present a series of essays relating to censuses conducted in individual territories. David Beach, of the University of Zimbabwe, calls into question a venerable axiom of colonial wisdom. Beach's work on his country's population before colonial rule has enabled him to identify a preferred environment, a massif he calls Zimbabwe's Fertile

Crescent.[31] Until recently, most scholars have held that the indigenous African populations were driven from that environment, first by Nguni invaders from the south and then by Rhodesian whites. Beach shows, to the contrary, that the indigenous Africans continued to live in that massif, despite expropriations of large parts of their land.

Djilali Sari, of the Université d'Alger, shows the limits of applying *retrojection* of late colonial or early independence censuses to colonial conditions in his native Algeria. The justification for using this technique is that in the absence of comprehensive data from the period under study, the best substitute is a careful analysis of the earliest available data. That territory, although beyond the limits of Central Africa, should have been most accurately counted in Africa. For most of the colonial period, Algeria was treated as an integral part of France, a country whose censuses were conducted to exacting professional standards. Sari[32] shows that French population estimates for their colonized territory must be viewed with considerable suspicion. As late as the 1950s vital registration and census counts seriously underestimated the Algerian Muslim population.

Two of our contributors, Mwelwa Musambachime and Jeffrey Stone, provide insights into enumerations of Zambia at two very different periods under colonial rule. Musambachime, dean of the School of Education at the University of Zambia's Lusaka campus,[33] describes population counts during the early years of colonial administration, showing how haphazard approximations were enough to satisfy administrators between 1900 and 1930.

Stone, by contrast, discusses a period in which he personally participated in the counts. As a district officer in the very last years of colonial rule, this accomplished historian of cartography recounts his own experience in the collecting of information on population as part of his touring reports.[34]

Justice Mlia shows the power of retrojection in his approach to neighboring Malawi. Thus, Mlia, head of the Department of Geography at the University of Malawi,[35] shows how the 1966 census of his country throws light on colonial enumerations dating back to the turn of the century.

Daniel Nyambariza, former chair of the Université de Burundi's department of history,[36] broaches a general theme touched on in different ways by a number of the other contributors: the role of changing administrative demands in determining the nature of materials contained in official enumerations. In particular, the Belgian mandatory power sought estimates of the kingdom's production potential in foodstuffs and of clandestine labor migrations. Nyambariza rightly concludes that African welfare was often missing from administrative priorities.

Nyambariza's former colleague, Gaëtan Feltz, a historian who has just left the Université de Burundi for Madagascar, deals with quite a different subset of an African population: the Roman Catholic Burundians. Feltz, who has also written extensively about Roman Catholics in Zaire,[37] describes the wealth of material relating to the demography of Burundi available from missionary archives. These sources contain not only a wide variety of aggregated statistics but also roll books of baptisms, marriages, and deaths, which can provide detailed information about the vital rates of Burundians under colonial rule.

In Part 2, turning from sources to methods, Kenneth Hill, an experienced demographer of Africa now teaching at Johns Hopkins,[38] describes the techniques used by the profession to extract demographic statistics from Stengers' *recensements*. Hill suggests ways of augmenting estimates of fertility, mortality, and migration by a number of ingenious methods, which include conducting surveys, transforming known indicators into other ones, and examining age distributions of both the living and the dead.

Mansell Prothero writes on colonial migrations, addressing the most general problem of ascertaining the number of migrants, given the permeability of colonial borders. Prothero, who has published classical studies of migration in West Africa as well as in Central Africa,[39] despairs that much can be gleaned from enumerations conducted before World War II but gives a number of examples from postwar investigations and shows how a careful reading of censuses and surveys can help scholars reconstruct migratory patterns. Methodologically, he advocates a combination of contemporary investigations and retrospective inquiries.

Other geographers have developed approaches to extrapolating demographic indicators that are, sadly, little known and less used by historians. Jeffrey Stone, who went from district administration to a distinguished career in historical cartography, shows how explorers' reference maps can reveal population patterns in late precolonial and early colonial times. Stone discusses a number of early maps and then subjects a single map of short-lived Mapanza District to intensive analysis, revealing both settlement patterns and colonial criteria for the location of administrative centers.

Another geographer, Frank Stetzer, whose work has been primarily quantitative,[40] demonstrates a technique that is delicate but has enormous potential for understanding the geographical aspects of colonial occupation. Stetzer describes how spatial autocorrelation can enable researchers to juxtapose location with more usual quantitative indicators to test hypotheses relating to the causes of demographic differences. In effect, Stetzer is describing not tomorrow's agenda but that of the day after, when researchers, having established patterns of demography for colonial Africa, will proceed to discuss causes for those patterns.

Yet another question arises when we consider migrants who were systematically excluded from colonial records. As mentioned above, colonial administrations actively discouraged cityward migration by women and children. In this respect, British administrations tended to be the harshest, out of a mixture of fear that women and children were an unnecessary distraction to urban workers and a paternalistic distrust of "detribalized" Africans.[41]

These official attitudes resulted in not only an underestimation of the number of women and children living in urban areas but also a lack of research into the circumstances of their departure. Sharon Stichter, chair of the Department of Sociology at the University of Massachusetts, Boston suggests an investigation of family relations that led women to leave rural areas. Stichter, who has written the volume on migrant workers in the new Cambridge University Press series,[42] suggests that the study of women migrants begin with a household-level analysis of their situation in rural areas before they left home. In this way the economic pressures on African women can be separated from those on African men.

Karen Tranberg Hansen is concerned with the use of child labor in city society.[43] She discovers that the employers of child migrants were often other Africans and the work roles the children performed often seemed to be an extension of family relationships from their rural homes, but in reality they were being absorbed into a new, urban labor system.

The fate of urban women and children, although frequently unstated in the censuses, can be found in surveys. Clyde Mitchell, who trained a generation of social scientists at Harare, Manchester, and Oxford, returned to Zambia to find statistics on infant mortality based on the survey of the Zambian Copperbelt, which he supervised from 1950 to 1955.[44] Having earlier written on fertility and migration among these pioneering urban Africans, Mitchell reanalyzes his data to ascertain levels and possible determinants of infant mortality.

In addition to surveys, retrospective inquiries can look beyond the direction of demographic change to the factors that produced the change. This has given rise to a most interesting exercise and critique of the population changes revealed by the 1963 census of Zambia. The initial analysis, written by Patrick Ohadike, a UN population specialist of Nigerian origin,[45] attempts to identify the social and organizational determinants of various demographic indicators taken from the census. In a critique of Ohadike's analysis Osei-Mensah Aborampah, a demographer of Ghanaian origin teaching at the University of Wisconsin, Milwaukee,[46] reminds us of the role also played by family values in determining family size.

Part 3 demonstrates how new methods of analysis can be applied to particular case studies. The late Rita Headrick, to whom this book is dedicated, shows the great historical depth that can be obtained from the use of a carefully constructed population survey taken at the end of the colonial period. Headrick[47] uses surveys done by the French for Gabon, the Congo, and the Central African Republic to bring order to a motley array of archival statistics, revealing regional trends within each of the three territories she studied. Thus, fertility tended to fall in forest areas while it remained level in the savannas.

Similar regional patterns can be found in Léon de St. Moulin's analysis of district-level demographic change in Zaire. St. Moulin, associate dean of the Faculté Théologique de Kinshasa, shows the insights gained during twenty years of analyzing colonial censuses and training a generation of Zairian demographers.[48] His exegesis of three censuses taken between 1938 and 1957, predicated on stable population tables, constitutes the most comprehensive available estimate of demographic trends during the last thirty years of colonial rule in Zaire. In it he shows an increasingly precipitous rise in fertility, accompanied by a decline in infant mortality and cityward migration.

Quite different results are found in Sabakinu Kivilu's essay on the Roman Catholics of the Zairian city of Matadi. Sabakinu, chair of the Department of Demography at the Université de Kinshasa, has been writing on the demography of his country for over fifteen years.[49] His essay, based on missionary roll books, shows the extent to which mission records can be used to establish rates of crude mortality and fertility.

Historical demography, as the essays in this collection amply show, can open the way to a variety of new perspectives on the effects of colonial rule. These essays, however, rather than constituting the last word on the subject, are in reality an invitation to further investigation. In this way they mark a new departure in the historiography of colonial Africa. The first generation after independence has made substantial inroads into the surviving verbal evidence. We know far more than before about resistance movements, administrative organization, and colonial policy. In the generation ahead we hope to speak with a new clarity when we discuss the births, deaths, and migrations of Africans living under colonial rule.

NOTES

1. Robert R. Kuczynski, *Demographic Survey of the British Colonial Empire*, 3 vols. (London, 1948–1949), 528; J. Boutte and L. de St. Moulin, "Zaïre," in Groupe de Démographie Africaine, *L'évaluation des effectifs de la population des pays africains*, Vol. 1 (Paris, 1982).

2. Bruce Fetter, "Decoding and Interpreting African Census Data: Vital Evidence from an Unsavory Witness," *Cahiers d'études africaines* 27 (1987), 83–105.

3. Talmud Torah 1.3, quoted in Philip Cohen, *Rambam on the Torah: An Anthology of Maimonides, Commentaries on Verses of the Torah* (Jerusalem, 1985), 143.

4. Michael B. Schiffer, *Advances in Archaeological Method and Theory*, vol. 1 (New York, 1978), 31–103; Ester Boserup, *Population and Technological Change* (Chicago, 1981); Robert I. Gilbert, Jr., and James H. Mielke, *The Analysis of Prehistoric Diets* (Orlando, 1985).

5. Jane Buikstra and Lyle Konigsberg, "Paleodemography: Critiques and Controversies," *American Anthropologist* 87 (1985), 316–333; Stig Wellider, *Prehistoric Demography*, Acta Archeologica Lundensis, serie in 8 minore, no. 8 (Lund, 1979), 46–55; Kenneth M. Weiss, *Demographic Models for Anthropology*, Memoirs of the Society for American Archaeology, no. 27 (Washington, 1973); Alan C. Swedlund, ed., *Population Studies in*

Archaeology and Biological Anthropology, Memoirs of the SAA, no. 30 (Washington, 1975).

6. David Herlihy, *Medieval Households* (Cambridge, MA, 1985); S. D. Goitein, *A Mediterranean Society: The Jewish Communities of the Arab World as Portrayed in the Documents of the Cairo Geniza*, vol. 2 (Berkeley, 1971), 139–143.

7. Michael Flinn, *The European Demographic System, 1500–1820* (Baltimore, 1981); E. A. Wrigley and R. S. Schofield, *The Population History of England, 1511–1871* (London, 1981). For an isolated African example, see John L. Thornton, "An Eighteenth Century Baptismal Register and the Demographic History of Manguenzo," in *African Historical Demography*, vol. 1 (Edinburgh, 1977), 405–415. See also P. C. Smith (Xenos) and Shui-meng Ng, *The Components of Population Change in Nineteenth-Century Southeast Asia: Village Data from the Philippines*, Papers of the East-West Population Institute, no. 6 (Honolulu, 1981); Commission Internationale d'Histoire des Mouvements Sociaux et des Structures Sociales, *Les migrations internationales de la fin du XVIIIᵉ siècle à nos jours* (Paris, 1980); Ira Glazer and Luigi de Rosa, *Migration Across Time and Nations: Population Mobility in Historical Contexts* (New York, 1986).

8. Demographic transition was the subject of the Société de Démographie Historique's 1987 "Entretiens de Malher," to which the first two hundred pages of the *Annales de démographie historique 1988* were devoted. See especially the articles by Alfred Perrenoud, Etienne van de Walle, and Henri Leridon. See also Dennis Cordell, Joel Gregory, and Victor Piché, "African Historical Demography: The Search for a Theoretical Framework," in Cordell and Gregory, eds., *African Population and Capitalism: Historical Perspectives* (Boulder, 1987), 14–32.

9. For a history and summary of the current state of the project, see Ansley J. Coale and Susan Cott Watkins, *The Decline of Fertility in Europe: The Revised Proceedings of a Conference on the Princeton European Fertility Project* (Princeton, 1986). For a compilation of criticism of transition theory, see W. Penn Handwerker, *Culture and Transition: An Anthropological Critique of Demographic Transition Theory* (Boulder, 1986).

10. T. H. Clutton-Brock, *Reproductive Success: Studies of Individual Variation in Contrasting Breeding Systems* (Chicago, 1988).

11. N. Gerald Barrier, *The Census in British India: New Perspectives* (Manohar, 1981); Rama Deb Roy, "Glimpses on the History of Calcutta, 1600–1800," *Annales de démographie historique 1988*, 243–257.

12. Sabakinu Kivilu, "Les sources de l'histoire démographique au Zaire," *Etudes d'histoire africaine* 6 (1974), 119–136; Gilroy Coleman, "The African Population of Malawi: An Analysis of the Censuses Between 1901 and 1966," *Society of Malawi Journal* 27, no. 1 (1974), 27–41 and no. 3 (1974), 37–46; Kuczynski, *Demographic Survey*; Djilali Sari, *Le désastre démographique (de 1867–1868) en Algérie* (Algiers, 1982).

13. L. Legrand, "La dépopulation du Congo belge et les recensements de 1917," *Congo* 1 (1921), 202–210; R. van Nitsen, *L'hygiène des travailleurs noirs dans les camps industriels du Haut-Katanga* (Brussels, 1933); L. Mottoulle, *Politique sociale de l'Union Minière du Haut-Katanga pour sa main d'oeuvre indigène et ses resultats au cours de 20 années d'application* (Brussels, 1946); G. St. J. Orde Browne, *The African Labourer* (London, 1933); Margaret Read, "Migrant Labour in Africa and Its Effects on Tribal Life," *International Labour Review* 45 (1942), 605–631; S. J. K. Baker and R. T. White, "The Distribution of Native Population over South-East Central Africa," *Africa* 10

(1946), 37–54; Richard Symonds and Michael Carder, *The United Nations and the Population Question, 1945–1970* (London, 1973).

14. David Arnold, ed., *Imperial Medicine and Indigenous Societies* (New York, 1988); Roy Macleod and Milton Lewis, *Disease, Medicine, and Empire: Perspectives on Western Medicine and the Experience of European Expansion* (New York, 1988), esp. the articles by Maryinez Lyons; Gwyn Prins, "But What Was the Disease? The Present State of Health and Healing in African Studies," *Past and Present* 124 (1989), 159–179.

15. Pierre Gourou, *La densité de la population rurale au Congo belge* (Brussels, 1954); Glenn Trewartha and Wilbur Zelinsky, "The Population Geography of Belgian Africa," *Annals of the Association of American Geographers* 44, no. 2 (1954), 135–162. Anatole Romaniuk, *La fécondité des populations congolaises* (Paris, 1967); J. Clyde Mitchell, "Differential Fertility Amongst Urban Africans in Zambia," *Rhodes-Livingstone Journal* 37 (1965), 1–25.

16. The best postindependence statement of the progress of African demography was William Brass et al., eds., *The Demography of Tropical Africa* (Princeton, 1968). For the developmentalist point of view, see Peter R. Gould, "Tanzania 1920–63: The Spatial Impress of the Modernization Process," *World Politics* 27 (1970), 149–170; Wilbur Zelinsky, "The Hypothesis of the Mobility Transition," *Geographical Review* 61 (1971), 219–249; and Anatole Romaniuk, "Increase in Natural Fertility During the Early Stages of Modernization: Evidence from an African Case Study, Zaire," *Population Studies* 34 (1980), 293–310.

17. John Cleland and Chris Scott, *The World Fertility Survey: An Assessment* (Oxford, 1987); Symonds and Carder, *The United Nations and the Population Question*; Etienne van de Walle et al., eds. *The State of African Demography* (Liège, 1988); John Knodel and Etienne van de Walle, "Lessons from the Past: Policy Implications of Historical Fertility Studies," *Population and Development Review* 5 (1979), 217–246; A. S. Oberai, ed., *State Policies and Internal Migration* (New York, 1983).

18. John Iliffe ("The Origins of African Population Growth," *Journal of African History* 30 [1989], 165–169) suggests that the leading statement of the position is John Caldwell's "The Social Repercussions of Colonial Rule: Demographic Aspects," in A. Adu Boahen, ed., *Unesco General History of Africa*, vol. 7 (Berkeley, 1985), 458–486.

19. Cordell and Gregory, *African Population*, 32, and Joel Gregory, Dennis Cordell, and Raymond Gervais, *African Historical Demography: A Multidisciplinary Approach* (Los Angeles, 1984), the best available bibliography on the subject. See also Joel Gregory and Victor Piché, "African Population: Reproduction for Whom?" *Daedalus* 52, no. 1 (1982), 179–209.

20. The current interest in African historical demography is signaled by conferences held at Edinburgh (*African Historical Demography*, vols. 1 and 2), Paris (*Histoire démographique, concept d'ethnie, recherches diverses*, Groupe "Afrique Noire," no. 8, [Paris, 1985] and the 7th "Entretiens de Malher," 1985), and Montreal (Workshop on African Population and Capitalism: Historical Perspectives, 1985).

Representative current articles include Léon de St. Moulin, "L'organisation de l'espace en Afrique centrale à la fin du XIXe siècle," *Cultures et développement* 14 (1982), 259–296; idem, *Atlas des Collectivités du Zaïre* (Kinshasa, 1976); Christian Thibon, "Fécondité et transition démographique au Burundi," *Cahiers d'histoire* 1 (1983), 23–56; Patrick Ohadike, *Demographic*

Perspectives in Zambia (Manchester, 1981). On the demography of Africa in general, see, John Caldwell *Theory of Fertility Decline* (New York, 1982); John Caldwell and Pat Caldwell, "The Demographic Evidence for the Incidence and Cause of Abnormally Low Fertility in Tropical Africa," *World Health Statistics Quarterly* 36, no. 1 (1983), 2–34; Sharon Stichter, *Migrant Laborers* (Cambridge, 1985); and John I. Clarke and Leszek Kosinski, *Redistribution of Population in Africa* (London, 1982).

21. David Birmingham and Phyllis Martin, eds., *History of Central Africa*, vol. 1 (New York, 1983), viii.

22. Jan Vansina, *Kingdoms of the Savanna* (Madison, 1966), 19–33.

23. Joseph C. Miller, *Way of Death: Merchant Capitalism and the Angola Slave Trade* (Madison, 1988). See also Vansina, *Kingdoms of the Savanna*; Paul Lovejoy, *Transformations in Slavery: A History of Slavery in Africa* (Cambridge, 1983); and Ralph Austen, *African Economic History: Internal Development and External Dependency* (Portsmouth, 1987).

24. Bruce Fetter, *Colonial Rule and Regional Imbalance in Central Africa* (Boulder, 1983), 15.

25. Jeffrey Stone, "Northern Rhodesia: Early Pictorial Fiscal Marks," *Cinderella Philatelist* (January 1977), 15–16.

26. Bruce Fetter, "Relocating Central Africa's Biological Reproduction, 1923–1963," *International Journal of African Historical Studies* 19 (1986), 463–478.

27. See, e.g., Mitchell, "Differential Fertility," 1–25; République Démocratique du Congo, Bureau de la Démographie, *Tableau général de la démographie congolaise: Enquête démographique par la sondage 1955–57— Analyse générale des resultats statistiques* (Léopoldville, 1961).

28. Jean Stengers, "Les mouvements migratoires en Belgique aux XIXe et XXe siècles," in *Les migrations internationales de la fin du XVIIIe siècle à nos jours* (Paris, 1980).

29. David Henige, "Their Numbers Become Thick: Native American Historical Demography As Expiation," in James A. Clifton, ed., *The Invented Indian: Iconoclastic Essays* (Chicago, 1989); idem, "Primary Source by Primary Source? On the Role of Epidemics in New World Depopulation," *Ethnohistory* 33 (1986), 293–312; idem, "Measuring the Immeasurable: The Slave Trade, West African Population, and the Pyrrhonist Critic," *Journal of African History* 27 (1986), 295–313; idem, "If Pigs Could Fly: Timucuan Population and Native American Historical Demography," *Journal of Interdisciplinary History* 16 (1985–1986), 701–720; idem, "On the Contact Population of Hispaniola: History as Higher Mathematics," *Hispanic-American Historical Review* 58 (1978), 217–237, 700–712.

30. David E. Gardinier, "Decolonization in French, Belgian, Portuguese, and Italian Africa: Bibliography," in Prosser Gifford and William Roger Louis, eds., *Decolonization and African Independence: The Transfer of Power, 1960– 1980* (New Haven, 1988), 573–635; idem, "Decolonization in French, Belgian, and Portuguese Africa: A Bibliographical Essay," in Gifford and Louis, eds., *Transfer of Power in Africa: Decolonization, 1940–1960* (New Haven, 1982), 515–566; idem, "French Colonial Rule in Africa: A Bibliographical Essay," in Gifford and Louis, eds., *France and Britain in Africa: Imperial Rivalry and Colonial Rule* (New Haven, 1971), 787–950.

31. David Beach, *The Shona and Zimbabwe 900–1850* (Gweru, 1984); idem, *War and Politics in Zimbabwe 1840–1900* (Gweru, 1986).

32. Djilali Sari's magnum opus is *Le désastre démographique de 1867– 1868 en Algérie* (Algiers, 1982).

33. Mwelwa Musambachime, "Protest Migrations in Mweru-Luapula 1900–1940," *African Studies* 47 (1988), 19–34.

34. Jeffrey Stone, "The District Map: An Episode in British Colonial Cartography in Africa, with Particular Reference to Northern Rhodesia," *Cartographic Journal* 19 (1982), 104–112; idem, "The British Association Essays on the Human Geography of Northern Rhodesia, 1931–35," *Zambian Geographic Journal* 33–34 (1977–78), 31–48; idem, "Early Maps as Demographic Sources: The Case of Zambia," in *African Historical Demography*, vol. 1 (Edinburgh, 1977), 453–473.

35. Justice R. R. Mlia, *Public Decision-Making and the Spatial Organization of Development in Malawi* (Ann Arbor, 1978).

36. Daniel Nyambariza, "L'occupation des terres de la plaine de Bujumbura par les Swahili," *Cahiers d'histoire* 3 (1985), 53–80. See also Christian Thibon, "Fecondité et transition démographique au Burundi," *Cahiers d'histoire* 1 (1983), 23–56; idem, "Crise démographique et mise en dépendance au Burundi et dans la région des Grands Lacs, 1880–1910," *Cahiers d'histoire* 2 (1984), 19–40; idem, "Un siècle de croissance démographique au Burundi (1850–1960)," *Cahiers d'histoire* 3 (1985), 5–21; Jean Pierre Chrétien and Emile Mworoha, "Les migrations du XXe siècle en Afrique Orientale: Le cas de l'émigration des Banyarwanda et des Barundi vers l'Uganda," in *Les migrations internationales de la fin du XVIIIe siècle à nos jours* (Paris, 1980).

37. Gaëtan Feltz, "La problématique de l'histoire ou du choix d'une historiographie au Burundi," *History in Africa* 15 (1988), 229–252; idem, "Monseigneur de Hemptinne pendant la Seconde Guerre Mondiale," in Académie Royale des Sciences d'Outremer, *Le Congo belge durant la Seconde Guerre Mondiale: Recueil d'études* (Brussels, 1983), 419–437; idem, "Histoire des mentalités et histoire des missions au Burundi, ca. 1880–1960," *History in Africa* 12 (1985), 51–63; idem, "Une introduction à l'histoire de l'enseignement en Afrique Centrale (XIXe–XXe siècles): idéologies, pouvoirs, sociétés," *Bulletin de l'Institut Historique Belge de Rome* 51 (1981), 351–399.

38. Kenneth Hill, "Estimating Adult Mortality Levels from Information on Widowhood," *Population Studies* 31 (1977), 75–84; Kenneth Hill and J. Trussell, "Further Developments in Indirect Mortality Estimation," *Population Studies* 31 (1977), 313–334; Kenneth Hill and William Brass, *Estimating Adult Mortality from Orphanhood* (Liège, 1973).

39. R. Mansell Prothero, *Migrant and Malaria in Africa* (London, 1965); R. Mansell Prothero and K. Michael Barbour, *Essays on African Population* (London, 1961); R Mansell Prothero and Murray Chapman, *Circulation in Third World Countries* (London, 1985).

40. Frank Stetzer and Bruce Fetter, *Determinants of Natural Increase Migration in Central Africa 1921–1966*, Studies on the Interrelationships between Migration and Development in Third World Settings, no. 18 (Columbus, 1986); Frank Stetzer, "Specifying Weights in Spatial Forecasting Models: The Results of Some Experiments," *Environment and Planning A* 14 (1982), 571–584; idem, "The Analysis of Spatial Parameter Variation with Jackknifed Parameters," *Journal of Regional Science* 22 (1982), 177–189.

41. Helmuth Heisler, *Urbanization and the Government of Migration* (New York, 1974), 98–100; Karen Tranberg Hansen, "Negotiating Sex and Gender in Urban Zambia," *Journal of Southern African Studies* 10 (1984), 219–238; George Chauncey, Jr., "The Locus of Reproduction: Women's Labour in the Zambian Copperbelt, 1921–1953," *Journal of Southern African Studies* 7 (1981), 135–164.

42. Sharon Stichter, *Migrant Laborers* (Cambridge, 1985); idem, *Migrant Labour in Kenya: Capitalism and African Response, 1895–1975* (London, 1982); Sharon Stichter and Jane Parpart, eds., *Patriarchy and Class: African Women in the Home and Workforce* (Boulder, 1988).

43. Karen Tranberg Hansen, *Distant Companions: Servants and Employers in Zambia, 1900–1985* (Ithaca, 1989); idem, "Urban Women and Work in Africa," *Transafrica Forum* 4, no. 3 (1987), 9–24; Karen Tranberg Hansen and Margaret Strobel, "Family History in Africa," 3, nos. 3–4 (1985), 127–149.

44. J. Clyde Mitchell, *Cities, Society, and Social Perception: Central African Perspectives* (Oxford, 1987); idem, "Differential Fertility Amongst Urban Africans in Zambia"; idem, "Wage Labour and African Population Movements in Central Africa," in Barbour and Prothero, *Essays on African Population*, 193–248; idem, "An Estimate of Fertility in some Yao Hamlets in Liwonde District, Nyasaland," *Africa* 19 (1949), 293–308.

45. Patrick Ohadike and H. Tesfaghiorghis, *The Population of Zambia* (Gap, 1974); *Development of, and Factors in, the Employment of African Migrants in the Copper Mines of Zambia, 1940–1966*, Zambian Papers, no. 4 (Lusaka, 1969); Patrick Ohadike, "Counting Heads in Africa: The Experience of Zambia, 1963 and 1969," *Journal of Administration Overseas* 9 (1970), 248; idem, "Urbanization: Growth, Transition, and Problems of a Premier West African City (Lagos, Nigeria)," *Urban Affairs Quarterly* 3 (1968), 69–90. Ohadike is also coeditor of *The State of African Demography* cited in note 17.

46. Osei-Mensah Aborampah, "Determinants of Breast-Feeding and Post-Partum Sexual Abstinence: Analysis of a Sample of Yoruba Women, Western Nigeria," *Journal of Biosocial Science* 17 (1985), 461–469; idem, "Plural Marriage and Fertility Differentials: A Study of the Yoruba of Western Nigeria," *Human Organization* 46 (1987), 29–38.

47. Ralph A. Austen and Rita Headrick, "Equatorial Africa Under Colonial Rule," in Birmingham and Martin, *History of Central Africa* 2: 27–94.

48. Léon de St. Moulin, "La répartition par région du Produit Intérieur Brut du Zaïre du 1957 à 1984," *Zaïre-Afrique* (1987), 451–477; idem, "Essai d'histoire de la population du Zaïre," *Zaïre-Afrique* (1987), 389–407; idem, "La population du Congo pendant la Seconde Guerre Mondiale," in Académie Royale des Sciences d'Outremer, *Le Congo belge durant la Seconde Guerre Mondiale*, 15–50; idem, "L'organisation de l'espace en Afrique Centrale"; Léon de St. Moulin and Josephe Boute, *Perspectives démographiques régionales 1975–1985* (Kinshasa, 1982); de St. Moulin, *Atlas de collectivités du Zaïre*.

49. Sabakinu Kivilu, "Population and Health in Zaire during the Colonial Period from the End of the Nineteenth Century to 1960," *Transafrican Journal of History* 13 (1984), 92–109; idem, "Les sources de l'histoire démographique du Zaïre," *Etudes d'histoire africaine* 6 (1974), 119–136.

PART 1

SOURCES

Some Methodological Reflections

JEAN STENGERS

The word *census* is often used in a rather equivocal way to cover two types of operations that deserve a separate treatment: the *census stricto sensu* (based on the individual answers given by the members of the aggregate, whether the population as a whole or a sample of the population) and the *enumeration*, or count of the population (the operation actually practiced in all countries of the world before a census was taken). The French words for these two kinds of operation are perhaps clearer than the English: *recensements* and *dénombrements*.

However, even French historians and demographers frequently confuse the two. They often speak, for instance, of the *recensements de l'Empire*, when actually, at the time of Napoleon, France still stuck to the old system of the *dénombrements*. This corresponds to a strong tendency to use the word *dénombrements* for the Old Regime and to consider the nineteenth and the twentieth centuries as the age of the *recensements*, putting all operations in Colonial Africa under the latter heading.

But what is crucial is not the *time*, but the *nature*, of the operation. As regards Africa, the first real census was taken in Ruanda-Urundi (now Rwanda and Burundi) in 1952. It involved only a sample of the population, chosen by the system of random numbers, but the method was that of a *census* in the proper meaning of the word: every single house or hut was visited by the commissioners.[1] A little later that method was extended to the Belgian Congo and formed the basis of the major demographic inquiry of 1955–1957.[2]

There is often a great illusion in the history of enumerations and censuses: the illusion of progress. One tends to believe that as the years pass, the results of such operations must become better and better. The contrary is sometimes true. In Southern Rhodesia for instance, as David Beach (Chapter 5) points out, in the 1920s the accuracy of the figures of the counts tended to decline. The native commissioners previously went from village to village and tried to ascertain on the spot the number of inhabitants. When their work became more sedentary and they began to prefer the car for their travels, they came to rely more and more on information provided by their messengers, which was of poorer quality. In the case of Zaire (the former Belgian Congo) the 1970 census, ten years after independence, was not nearly as reliable as the preindependence operation of 1955–1957.[3]

And when methods *do* improve over time (as often happened) even this can be a problem for historians; for if they do not clearly measure the impact of the change in methods, they may be led to build up a discontinuous *series* of figures and draw conclusions from it as if it were continuous. Before the age of the censuses, in the Belgian Congo, the figures provided by the population counts often vary much more according to the methods used than according to the change in the population itself.[4]

When we try to ascertain the value of a population count or a census, the questions asked must center on two main notions: *ability* and *will*. *Ability* and *will* are the two key words of any critical examination.

The ability may be that of the author or authors of the count. In some cases this is a quite flagrant factor. Henry Morton Stanley was evidently unable in 1884–1885 to make any serious count of the population of the Congo basin. The "method" he used was farcical. He took as a basis for his calculations the density of population he had observed along the banks of the Congo River and some of its tributaries and bluntly attributed the same density to the whole of the Upper Congo basin. In spite of that (and in spite of a stupid blunder in his calculation that passed unnoticed),[5] the figure he gave was taken seriously and was repeated over and over again by later authors. It formed the basis of many comments and accusations about the "depopulation" of the Congo under the regime of King Léopold II.[6]

In other cases, however, the factor of ability is less visible. As Rita Headrick (Chapter 19) points out, population counts in French Equatorial Africa suffered for a rather long time from the fact that the authorities were unable to give any serious figure for the population of regions that they did not control.

But the question of ability also concerns those who furnish the basic data. The classical example is that of the Africans who did not know their precise age—hence their tendency to give ages ending with five or zero and, as a result, when ages are tabulated by single years, the clustering of reported ages into figures ending with five or zero. This was often observed by O. E. Umoh in Nigeria,[7] Rita Headrick in French Central Africa, and others. It reminds the demographer of a situation that existed in Europe in medieval times.[8]

The *will* (to try and discover the reality or not, to tell the truth or not) is often still more important than the ability. It obeys all kinds of feelings, interests, and objectives. It works at all levels. It concerns the individual, the chief, the administrator, the higher authorities.

Individuals may be moved by such feelings as the unwillingness to speak of dead children or (a question of material interest) by the tendency to misrepresent the age of adolescent boys: their age is underestimated so as to avoid the head tax. Both phenomena have been observed in Africa. The African chief who knows that corvée labor and military recruitment may depend on the figure of population of his village may also be strongly tempted to reduce the figure. The administrator may give that which he considers will be good—or at least not bad—for his career. The best solution is often to give an annual figure that is just a little higher than the former one; if it is not, the administrator risks being asked a lot of questions. Such an attitude on the part of an administrator was not infrequent in the Belgian Congo.[9]

The most amusing story in that respect concerns the officers in the service of agronomy in Rwanda and Burundi. They had to declare to the international authorities the average value in calories of the daily ration of the inhabitants of the two territories. The initial figures had been much more optimistic in Burundi than in Rwanda. As there was after that an annual improvement (without a regular improvement the efficiency of the Belgian regime and of the agronomists themselves would have been questioned) the inhabitants of Burundi, according to the official figures, finished by eating like ogres—twice as much as the inhabitants of Rwanda.[10]

However, the most striking decisions on figures (they are no longer calculations but decisions) occur at the highest level. Giving an arbitrary figure spares work and trouble. The Belgian government, after World War II, was asked to provide the International Labour Office in Geneva with information respecting the "active population" of the Belgian Congo. They had (among other figures) to indicate the number of "active" women in the sector of agriculture. The solution was quite simple: the figure sent to Geneva (which was officially published in the Year Book of Labour Statistics) was simply the total number of women living in the rural areas.[11] This was rather innocuous, but in other cases a decision may have definite political implications.[12] Experts are convinced that in the Republic of Cameroon, when Ahmadou Ahidjo served as president (1960–1982) the northern part of the country, from which the president originated, was provided with a population figure substantially greater than the reality so as to allow the allocation of larger subsidies.[13]

The worst occurs when there is a "general will," from top to bottom, to distort the facts. This happened in Nigeria at the time of the 1962 enumeration, an operation that had great political importance, since the population of the various regions of the country would form the basis for their number of seats in Parliament. This led to all kinds of ameliorations of the figures: people making sure that they were counted twice, the "discovery" of villages that had been overlooked in previous enumerations, and administrative officers accepting counts that had been made in a most generous spirit.[14] The case of Nigeria is a caricature, but a caricature often helps to understand what can happen elsewhere on a smaller scale.

The great lesson for demographers is that they must not, when they try to evaluate enumerations or censuses, limit themselves to the question of *how* the figures were arrived at: *why* is sometimes more important.

NOTES

1. V. Neesen, "Le premier recensement par échantillonnage au Ruanda-Urundi," in *Zaïre* (May 1953), pp. 469–488.

2. See Anatole Romaniuk, *La Fécondité des populations congolaises* (Paris, 1967), 34–39.

3. I refer here to the severe criticisms of Henri Nicolai, "Progrès dans la connaissance géographique au Zaïre, au Rwanda et au Burundi en 1967, 1968, 1969 et 1970," *Bulletin de la Société Belge d'Etudes Géographiques* 40 (1971), 281–283.

4. As the great specialist J. van Wing said for the interwar period, "Les chiffres fournis annuellement dans les rapports du Gouvernement n'accusaient pas un accroissement réel de la population, mais une amélioration des recensements" ("Démographie congolaise," *Courrier d'Afrique*, 19 May 1945.

5. His observations along the Congo and its tributaries extended to 1,515 miles of river. This meant, he wrote, "river banks of twice 1,515 miles or . . . *2,030* miles" (Henry Morton Stanley, *The Congo and the Founding of Its Free State*, vol. 2 (London, 1885), 350. This figure of 2,030 served for all his further calculations.

6. See Roger Louis and Jean Stengers, *E. D. Morel's History of the Congo Reform Movement* (Oxford, 1968), 252–256.

7. O. E. Umoh, "Demographic Statistics in Nigeria," in S. H. Ominde and C. N. Ejiogu, eds., *Population Growth and Economic Development in Africa* (London, 1972), 21.

8. Josiah Cox Russell, *British Medieval Population* (Albuquerque, 1948), and my review, *Revue belge de philologie et d'histoire* 28 (1950), 600–606.

9. "Quand on connaît la valeur des recensements, quand on sait, par exemple, que des administrateurs territoriaux—et je ne leur jette pas la pierre car je sais qu'on leur demande bien plus de rapports qu'ils n'en pourraient fournir—forcent sciemment les chiffres pour éviter qu'en haut lieu on ne leur endosse, injustement d'ailleurs, la responsabilité de la situation" (Guy Malengreau, "Le Congo à la croisée des chemins," *Revue nouvelle* [15 January 1947], p. 10).

10. Jean-Paul Harroy, *Rwanda: De la féodalité à la démocratie, 1955–1962* (Brussels, 1984), 170.

11. Jean Stengers, "L'historien devant l'abondance statistique," *Revue de l'Institut, de Sociologie* 43 (1970), 444–445.

12. See e.g., Pierre Péan, *Affaires africaines* (Verviers, 1984), 189–190.

13. Information provided by Pierre Salmon, who worked in the country.

14. Among a vast literature, see R. K. Udo, "Population and Politics in Nigeria," in John C. Caldwell and Chukuka Okonjo, eds., *The Population of Tropical Africa* (New York, 1968), 97–101; T. M. Yesufu, "The Politics and Economics of Nigeria's Population Census," in Caldwell and Okonjo, *Population of Tropical Africa*, 106–116.

3 _____

Bibliographic Aids for the Historical Demographer

DAVID HENIGE
DAVID GARDINIER

As its name reminds us forcibly enough if we take the time to contemplate it, *historical demography* is a hybrid discipline, whose success depends on effectively uniting two disciplines with very different conceptions of goals and methods. This is particularly the case with respect to the evidence itself, which historians are likely to treat somewhat differently than are demographers. Beyond that, there is the matter of gaining efficient access to information on work done in, and evidence about, past populations.

Given the exiguity of the evidential base for Africanist historical demographers, much is to be gained by being aware of historical demographic work done elsewhere, both in areas with much more evidence (for that provides a sense of the character of the evidence that may be missing for Africa) and in areas similar to Africa, such as the New World in the first few centuries after contact (for gaining understanding about how others cope with defective data). With this view in mind, the following bibliographical aids are included in order to present as broad a picture as possible of work done both in Africa and elsewhere. While it does not pretend to be comprehensive, it does assume that the proper study of historical demography is best when it is comparative, drawing into it the gains and losses made in the field in all parts of the world.

SERIAL BIBLIOGRAPHIES:
DEMOGRAPHY AND RELATED FIELDS

More than ever, knowledge has a way of proliferating these days, rendering effective access to the best of it all the more difficult—indeed, probably a labor of Sisyphus. Even so, making use of serial bibliographies is the best single way to maintain a currency in this, as in any, field. The following bibliographies appear regularly (or did as of 1986). For information on other serial bibliographies in history (broadly defined) see David Henige, *Serial Bibliographies and Abstracts in History* (Westport, CT: Greenwood, 1986).

- *Bibliographie der Wirtschaftswissenschaften*. Published in Kiel, this bibliography appears twice each year and includes some nine to ten thousand items. Each number is divided into eighteen categories, one of which is *demography*. As is to be expected, its greatest strength lies in reporting East German and Russian publications.
- *Bibliographie internationale de démographie historique (BIDH)*. The demographer marooned in the proverbial desert island would want this bibliography if there were room for no others. Once published as part of *Annales de démographie historique*, this now appears separately once a year, a year or two after the fact. *BIDH* is, as its name implies, devoted entirely to the past, and its typical complement of seven hundred to one thousand entries is briefly annotated and arranged in several fairly refined categories, which are clearly indicated in a detailed table of contents. It includes a good index, making it easy to consult with very specific ends in mind.
- Bibliography in *Population Index (PI)*. *PI* appears several times a year. It is published by the Office of Population Research at Princeton University and reflects in its some three thousand entries each year the acquisitions of the library of the Office of Population Research as well as several others. Entries are arranged in some twenty categories, many further subdivided and featuring brief abstracts. Coverage is largely on contemporary demographic issues, but a fair amount of historical material is included. Each issue has author and geographical indexes, which are cumulated annually. In the annual index is a list of about five hundred journals canvassed. The currency of this listing is probably the best of all the serial bibliographies.
- *Bibliographie géographique internationale*. This is published in the popular *Bulletin Signaletique* format by the Centre National de la Recherche Scientifique, Paris and is cumulated and indexed annually. In recent years between six and seven thousand items have been included, each with an abstract. Demographic materials are included. Although these usually are not demarcated from other materials, the indexing is among the best in the field, as is currency.
- *Current Geographical Publications (CGP)*. This encompasses additions to the catalog of the American Geographical Society's library, now located at the University of Wisconsin–Milwaukee. About ten thousand items appear in the ten numbers that are published during each year; these are arranged in fifteen thematic, and twelve regional, categories. *CGP* is current and an annual index is published.
- *Geo Abstracts*. There are various series of this bimonthly. The two likely to be of most interest are C, Economic Geography, and D, Social and Historical Geography. Between the two from five to six thousand items appear annually, many of them of relevance to

historical demography. Author and geographical indexes are published annually but do not appear first in individual issues. Foreign titles are translated into English.

- *Social Sciences Citation Index (SSCI)*. This monster is one of the first fruits of the electronic age so far as bibliographical tools are concerned. It appears three time a year, with the third number being an annual cumulation (also available in five-year cumulations). It is divided into three parts, one of which is a key word index with paired words, easing specific access. Each year about fifteen hundred journals are analyzed fully and another three-thousand-plus selectively. As might be expected, currency is outstanding. All titles are translated into English. Publication details and authors' addresses are provided, as is a leaven of other information, particularly relating to the citational aspects of scholarly literature. Using *SSCI* can prove hard at first, but it is also fascinating.

SERIAL BIBLIOGRAPHIES: AFRICA AND THE MIDDLE EAST

- *Africa Index to Continental Periodical Literature*. This performs a valuable service by canvassing the local publications in Africa, materials that frequently escape the attention of the compilers of bibliographies who might be located outside Africa. It appears annually and lately has included nearly four thousand items each time, drawn from nearly two hundred journals. Needless to say, not many demographic items per se are included, but what there are are likely to escape notice in most or all of the other bibliographies.
- *Africa Bibliography*. This now appears (since its inauguration in 1985) as a separate number of *Africa*. Each year about three thousand items are to be included, covering all of Africa and arranged thematically and geographically. If this sounds a lot like the *IAB* discussed below, it is, although the overlap between the two is not quite total.
- *Annuaire de l'Afrique du Nord (AAN)*. In *AAN* two bibliographies appear each year, one entitled "Bibliographie systématique: Langue arabe," the other "Bibliographie systématique: Langues européenes." Between them they seem to provide extraordinarily comprehensive coverage of North Africa, less Egypt. The coverage of the notoriously elusive field of government publications is among the best and should provide good data for the historical demographers of the future. In a typical year about two thousand items are encompassed in the two bibliographies, about three-quarters of them in European languages. They are divided into a number of categories and provided with cross-reference and author indexes.

- *Annuaire des pays de l'Océan Indien.* In each number appears a section called "Information Bibliographiques" dealing with the Indian Ocean islands and, less thoroughly, the East African countries. The seven hundred or so items are arranged geographically and then by format (theses and memoires, books, articles studies and reports, colloquia). There are no indexes, but coverage of ephemera seems to be good.
- *Annuaire du Tiers Monde.* The bibliography in each number includes about fifteen hundred items concerned with the Third World *en gros* and with specific regions, including Africa. Perhaps its most valuable characteristic is its list of about 650 journals devoted in whole or part to the Third World, a useful quarry to mine for a quick sense of the range of serial materials in this field.
- *Bibliographie de l'Afrique sub-saharienne: Sciences humaines et sociales.* Despite its inclusive title, the *Bibliographie*, published at the Musée Royal de l'Afrique Centrale in Tervuren, is concerned primarily with Central Africa, the ex-Belgian possessions in particular. It is arranged in the difficult and inefficient *fiche* format and is about four years in arrears. Even so, with its good index and list of journals and collective works, it provides the best entrée in the areas of Africa it covers best. Otherwise, though, it is unlikely to be of much use.
- *Bibliographie des travaux en langue française sur l'Afrique au sud de Sahara (sciences sociales et humaines).* If one accepts the unlikely premise that language is a legitimate way to demarcate the world of publication, then, within its proclaimed scope, this bibliography is very good, particularly (of course) for the former French African colonies. Lately, each volume (published annually) has included about three thousand items arranged into some twenty general and geographical categories. Of value, too, is the listing of some three hundred French language journals covering all fields in the humanities and social sciences as they relate to Africa.
- *Current Bibliography on African Affairs (CBAA).* Normally published twice a year, *CBAA* is strongest on contemporary political and social matters and on materials that appear in nonscholarly journals not well covered by other continuing Africanist bibliographies.
- *Documentatieblad.* Published quarterly by the Afrika Studiecentrum in Leiden, each number includes five to six hundred abstracts arranged in broad geographical classifications and drawn from some two hundred journals. All disciplines are covered, history being the largest.
- *International African Bibliography (IAB).* Now the senior serial Africanist bibliography, *IAB* is compiled by the Library of the School of Oriental and African Studies and is published quarterly,

with an annual index appearing as part of the fourth number each year. Materials are grouped into several general and geographical categories by author, and all fields of study are covered. Apparently, about one thousand journals are canvassed; but no list of these is provided.

- *Middle East Journal.* Each quarterly number contains a "Bibliography of Periodical Literature," whose items total some three thousand each year. North Africa and the Sudan are included; but since the arrangement is exclusively by subject, it may be difficult to identify materials on these areas. Coverage of popular periodicals and Arabic language journals is particularly good. There are no indexes, again rendering specific access poor.

- *Quarterly Index Islamicus (QII).* *QII* covers all aspects of the Islamic world, including the parts of Africa influenced by Islam and Arabic culture. Recently some forty-five hundred items have been included over the year, divided into some forty regional and topical classifications. Each issue includes a subject index, cumulated annually, and there is also an author index included in the fourth number each year.

- *Recently Published Articles (RPA).* Behind its innocuous title lurks the best serial bibliography in history now being published. Appearing under the auspices of the American Historical Association, *RPA* is divided into nearly twenty broad categories, each prepared by a specialist in the field. *RPA* is published three times a year, with each number including about five thousand items. Africa and the ancient world are the most thoroughly covered fields, but the good overall coverage permits the user interested in comparative study to have a field day. Unfortunately, there are no indexes of any kind and the abbreviations used to identify journals can occasionally be mystifying. Withal, this is *the* tool to consult, on grounds both of its broad coverage and its good currency. Although less focused than *BIDH*, it will reward the user who applies himself.

RETROSPECTIVE BIBLIOGRAPHIES

Although there are many of these in various geographical areas, both for Africa and for other parts of the world, access to them is relatively simple through library card catalogs, electronic data bases, or the current bibliographies just mentioned. Here we mention only one.

- Gregory, Joel W., Dennis D. Cordell, and Raymond Gervais, *African Historical Demography: A Multidisciplinary Bibliography.* Los Angeles: Crossroads, 1984.

More than twenty-five hundred items are listed and arranged in various topical and geographical categories; it includes an author index as well as a subject-geographical index. A supplement is in preparation.

BIBLIOGRAPHIES OF BIBLIOGRAPHIES

The infrastructure of Africanist bibliography has become developed to the point where it is now necessary to compile lists of the various bibliographies that have appeared here and there, sometimes in the most unexpected places. To date, this work has been done by Yvette Scheven in the following three publications:

- *Bibliographies for African Studies, 1970–1975*. Waltham, MA: Crossroads, 1977.
- *Bibliographies for African Studies, 1976–1979*. Waltham, MA: Crossroads, 1980.
- *Bibliographies for African Studies, 1980–1983*. Oxford: Hans Zell, 1984.

Together, these works include nearly 3,500 bibliographies, or an average of about 250 each year, which emphasizes starkly both the work in African studies and the attempts to harness that work bibliographically. Each of these three works is organized on a topical-cum-geographical basis, with author and subject indexes. In the most recent of these, there are more than twenty bibliographies listed under *demography* in the index, as well as numerous others under such related topics as *censuses*. Scheven is presently preparing a consolidated, updated bibliography to cover the period through 1985.

CENSUSES

Getting a bibliographical grip on censuses is no easier than it is for any other type of government publication. Fortunately, the task has been mitigated by a series of bibliographies published by the Bureau of Business Research at the University of Texas with the Population Research Center, also at the University of Texas. Entitled *International Population Census Bibliography*, each of the major world areas is covered by a separate volume. The volume for Africa and Asia is Elaine Domschke and Doreen Goyer's *The Handbook of National Population Censuses* (Westport, CT: Greenwood, 1986).

Even better news is that based on (but also updating) these bibliographies, Research Publications, Woodbridge, CT, is issuing censuses (both published and unpublished) of about three hundred political entities. These appear in three series: before 1945, 1945–1967, and 1968 to the present. A guide to these microfilm sets is available from the publisher. In any event, it is fair to assume that most research libraries with area studies emphases will purchase part or all of this material.

Finally, there is John R. Pinfold, ed., *African Population Census Reports: A Bibliography and Checklist* (Oxford: Hans Zell, 1985). Arranged alphabetically by political entity, this serves as a union list for holdings of African census materials in the United Kingdom. A U.S. counterpart is Victoria K. Evalds, *Union List of African Censuses, Development Plans, and Statistical Abstracts* (Oxford: Hans Zell, 1985). See also Maidel Cason, *Censuses in the Melville J. Herskovits Library of African Studies* (Evanston, 1987). However, both these compilations (particularly that of Evalds) are likely to become obsolete with the publication of the microfilm sets mentioned above, which will certainly mean that many more libraries will acquire many more African census records.

4

The Limits of Colonial Statistics:
A Lesson from Algeria

DJILALI SARI

Historians of settler colonies inevitably face a paucity of statistics, particularly those relating to the demography of the dominant population. The process of settlement causes the conquered society, at the very least, to be underestimated and marginalized—if not subjected to outright repression and the utter denial of its existence.

The aim of the colonizer to suppress the truth remains unchanged; but the methods vary over time—from destruction of preexisting archives at the moment of conquest to transfer of recent materials to the metropole at the end of the War of Liberation. Indeed, in the final months before independence much that could not be removed from Algeria was destroyed. In these circumstances, what is the value of surviving demographic statistics?

To examine this important question, I propose to discuss three problems: the fate of the archives that existed before colonial conquest, pitfalls in using colonial statistics, and controversies concerning major events in the demographic history of Algeria under colonial rule.

THE FATE OF PREEXISTING ARCHIVES

The reconstruction of Algeria's population history, especially during the nineteenth century, involves many difficulties. The two major obstacles are the near-total destruction of archives and the disruption caused by the prolonged war of conquest.

Indeed, the army of occupation was the principal agent in the destruction of documents, both public and private. French officers themselves testify to the destruction, scattering, and disappearance of records, particularly in Algiers[1] but also in other towns. As to the latter, the case of Constantine is particularly revealing. Berbrugger, keeper of the colonial library in Algiers, was unable, for want of a means of transport, to complete his mission to Constantine to collect the archives and documents remaining after the siege (i.e., after the destruction of much of the material). Moreover, on the return journey, he was obliged to abandon a number of packing cases containing documents.

What sort of records were destroyed? Even though the regency of Algiers did not possess a system of public archives comparable to those of European countries, the government did collect data reflecting the sociodemographic and economic organization of the territory. These records, like those in all Muslim countries, included documents concerning relations between private persons and public authorities and among private persons. Public documents included records of individual and communal taxes, registers of real property including the *habous* lands (special foundations for religious purposes),[2] and name lists from diverse public bodies, including the army. These data could provide the raw material for studying numerous aspects of the country's socioeconomic life and demography.

Of a more private nature—but also having a public side that can corroborate and enlarge the official archives—are the *mahakma* (official pronouncements) of the *cadis* (Muslim judges). These decisions establish, in the event of the death of the head of a family, the *freda* testament, which lists the members of the family in order of birth and ancestry with the shares of all of the interested parties, together with a list of the possessions of the deceased. All this constitutes an important source of information concerning the family, the society, the economy, and individual relations in general—all of which is of considerable importance in the social sciences.[3]

Beyond the loss of preexisting archives, the historian faces another obstacle to the reconstruction of nineteenth-century conditions: prolonged warfare throughout the country. The conquest, with its many consequences for socioeconomic life, went on practically uninterrupted for over forty years, from 1830 until the nearly general insurrection of 1871–1872.[4] More accurately, the process encompassed not one conquest but a series of conquests, which spread progressively across the country, particularly during the period 1834–1847, when Emir Abd el Kader subjected the invaders to sporadic combat rather than continuous attack. As a result, soldiers and civilians moved in and out of the Western and Central Tell, causing considerable disruption of economic and social life. Some tribes retreated either definitively or temporarily westward toward Morocco and southward into the Sahara—often suffering substantial losses.[5] In the east, Bey Hadj Ahmed's resistance to the French in Kabylia and the High Plains led to similar population movements, whose effects were exacerbated by the occupier's policy of "scorched earth."

All this resulted in the loss of archives, mostly private documents. Certain towns were completely occupied by the French forces: Tlemcen, for instance, remained empty for a few months in 1836 and again in 1842; when it was reoccupied by Algerians, it was covered with ruins. In 1849 there was a huge fire, in spite of the presence of a garrison equal in number to the civilian population.[6]

For a long time after the cessation of hostilities—throughout the nineteenth century and even into the twentieth century—the population of many urban centers continued to diminish. In the process still more archives were lost, especially property deeds, whose absence facilitated dispossessions under the laws concerning real property first promulgated in 1873.[7] Indeed, the destruction of deeds also facilitated expropriations in nearby rural areas.[8]

Other documents disappeared in the same process, notably the genealogies so dear to Algerian families, which gave accounts of the network of social relations necessary for the analysis of a society. These are incalculable losses for research.

The end result of the loss of these documents and archives and of the many and profound changes ensuing from the prolongation of the war was that the views of colonial administrators prevailed at all levels in the discussion of the colonial population estimates. Their views colored the perception of the very character of the country in precolonial times. Their analyses conveyed the impression of an empty land, sparsely populated. After the first forty years of occupation, which were accompanied by a series of natural calamities, they also spoke of a "degeneration of the Arab people."[9] It was in this context and atmosphere that the colonial government designed its population enumerations and, not coincidentally, the redistribution of real property.

THE PITFALLS IN USING COLONIAL STATISTICS

The quantitative approach is based mainly on two sources: censuses of the population and vital statistics registers. Cross-checking is sometimes possible where other statistics are available.

The government conducted its first enumeration of the Algerian population in 1845 during the resistance of Abd el Kader and performed other counts when necessity dictated. By 1881 their aim was to conduct a general census every five years, a frequency that they maintained except for the two world wars. During this time, however, the country was only partly occupied; and a state of war continued. Indeed, the data collected are open to a number of criticisms and must be treated with reservations, given the difficulties in gathering information. The large rates of increase recorded during the nineteenth century reflect general undercounts in the earlier figures rather than real growth.[10]

In any case, the earlier reports must be discounted because they were collected in wartime from only a fraction of the Algerian population. Even after the war subsided, Algerians remained deeply suspicious of the colonial administration. Officials, moreover, lived in isolation. Up to the outbreak of the War of Liberation in 1954, some regions quite near the coast (Bou Maad near Miliana) and others further inland (some sections of Hodna) lived almost completely free of government authority.[11] In other regions pastoralists moving with their herds were practically uncontrollable.

These flaws in coverage call into question the elevated growth rates reported in the nineteenth century. The annual rates range from a high of 4 percent between 1872 and 1876 and 1.1 percent between 1891 and 1896. Of course, this evolution points to an improvement in the methods of counting "on the ground." Even rates such as 1.1 percent are not credible if one puts them in the socioeconomic context of the time, one of great mortality due, in part, to famine.[12]

If the rates of increase seem to be more realistic in the last censuses, there still remains an underestimation: a certain fringe of the population always escapes the enumeration, as is shown by the deficiencies of the official registers.

Compared with other countries in Africa, Algeria is in a privileged position regarding population registration. By 1882 the whole country was covered, the principal towns even earlier than that.[13] These data are useful, but their limits must be taken into account. As I have worked on these data for a long time in different localities, I feel entitled to observe that the gaps are numerous, especially in the rural areas and small towns and that discrepancies appear in numbers reported for the sexes and between the coast and the interior. Indeed, the colonial authorities overtly recognized these shortcomings.[14]

The calculation of certain demographic indicators—total population change, fertility and mortality rates, and rates of natural increase—provides proof of these deficiencies in census figures. The gaps are most apparent regarding age and sex classification. Generally speaking, there is a clear undercounting of females. In all cases, too, reported mortality rates are negligible where they should be high, given prevailing economic and sanitary conditions. Typically, families avoided making "unnecessary" declarations to the government; few, for example, would have reported a stillbirth. Official registers must therefore be treated with caution.

Cross-checking is the best way to approach the statistics, since it can illuminate their deficiencies. The following example is instructive, as it comes from official sources.[15] It concerns the men's age cohort of twenty-year-olds. In 1956 ninety-four thousand young men reported for induction into the army, whereas in 1936 there were only eighty-three thousand registered male births. In spite of this increase of 12.7 percent, the figure is *still* below the reality: in 1956 the War of Liberation was on, and a sizeable proportion of that age group was in hiding in the mountains or among the refugees. The divergence between the registrations in 1936 and the actual births was at least 20 percent.

The conclusion to be drawn is that of *a general underestimation in all official demographic data*. That underestimation, perhaps, throws some light on the paradoxically large increase of the population in the census of 1966, which tends to mask the effects of the War of Liberation. But the quantification of the losses occasioned by that war is itself still unsolved.

CONTROVERSIES CONCERNING MAJOR EVENTS
IN THE DEMOGRAPHIC HISTORY OF ALGERIA

Four major demographic events are still the object of debate among historians of Algeria, as X. Yacono points out:[16] estimation of the national population at the time of the invasion of 1830, the deathrate during the famine of 1867–1868, the number killed in the uprisings of 1945, and the number who fell during the War of Liberation between 1954 and 1962.

My estimate of the national population in 1830 comes from my research on the famine of 1867–1868.[17] Until investigating that event, I had accepted Yacono's estimate of three million, which had been repeated by almost all observers.[18] That number, however, appeared too low when I calculated, on the basis of eyewitness testimony, documents, and cross-checking, the number of victims of the famine. Nearly a million people died then, practically twice as many as earlier estimated. I therefore increased my estimate of the total population in 1830 to five million.

The next estimate I reexamined was that for the insurrection of 1945. In spite of the fact that it is a fairly recent event of which all the objective data were known to the French authorities in Algiers and in Paris, silence was well kept. Reference to this event is not superfluous: it fits well into the *strategy of the colonial administration from 1830 to 1962.* The great differences noted by differeni observers recall, curiously, those of 1830, 1867–1868, and 1954–1962. (Incidentally, the estimated number of European victims varies from 98 to 103.)

Without entering into details, it is to be noted that the figures vary from five hundred on the Algerian side to three times that figure from official sources and goes up to thirty-five thousand according to the U.S. consul quoted by other sources (Confédération Générale du Travail et Parti Communiste Français) and as much as eighty thousand according to the Ulémas. The figure most currently advanced is forty-five thousand.[19]

These very large oscillations are linked to two factors: the intensity of the aerial and naval bombardments following the riots of 1945 and the dense population of the bombarded region, a compact mountain mass. And so, *in spite of its being a politicomilitary event of limited dimensions* in time and space, the consequences, both human and statistical, are impossible to evaluate.

Such also is the problem of 1954–1962 except that this time what is in question is a war covering the whole country and lasting practically eight years. Considering that the total of Algerian lives lost was never established on a basis of undeniable statistics and taking into account the demographic growth during the period from 1954 to 1962 of 3.1 per hundred (pseudo?), evidence emerged, strengthened by the passage of time and the silence on the part of the Algerians. Indeed, if that 3.1 growth rate was to be taken into account, the total had to be reduced to much less than the estimations advanced by the Algerians (about a million victims). This coherent reasoning resulted in the justification of all the colonial arguments of the past and of those who imposed war on the people. All this shows the dimensions of the problem and the size of the task confronting students engaged in the objective research for true historical reality.

Consequently, I do not propose to modify the actual data, but I desire to situate the facts in their proper context and so facilitate research, taking for my basis the restatement of the situation by Yacono.[20] To refute the Algerian estimation of the losses, he based his argument on two facts: a comparison with other combats on the international plane and an examination of certain demographic data based on the statistics of the French military sources.

First, it is very difficult to compare losses in the Algerian war with those of conflicts of an entirely different nature. The Algerian war was a revolutionary war waged by the mass of the population—who were often reduced, in the rural districts, to hunger and malnutrition—against a powerful army of more than 500 thousand regular soldiers, well trained, well armed, and using all means to both crush all armed resistance and obtain the collaboration of the majority of the nonclandestine population in the towns and the countryside.

Nor does the second argument stand up to a critical examination. The author thought he could calculate the losses fairly accurately. It suffices, according to him, to determine the difference between the population as counted in 1962 and that counted in 1954, adding the natural increase between the two dates; for he accepts the second-mentioned census as "precise data." But *I have pointed out the general underestimation of official censuses.*[21]

Again, he takes as his basis a rate of growth for the period 1954–1962 that no demographer can accept: 3.4 percent, *a rate not only superior to the succeeding years but incompatible with the facts of the economic and demographic situation.* The infant mortality alone had reached alarming proportions.[22] The author should have taken account of the natural demographic changes given by the civil registers between 1954 and 1962, even though these data, too, were less than the actual fact. In such conditions the total number of losses would not be 256 thousand but 125 thousand. Recognizing that this estimation of 256 thousand was very low, the author pushes it up to 300 thousand, and esteems that this solves the problem of quantifying the Algerian losses. To quell any doubts he refers to another observer, whom he describes as a "specialist," whose analysis is based essentially on the abundant literature about the war in Algeria mostly composed by supporters of the French Army.[23] The observer in question is G. Pervillé: his estimations oscillate between 300 and 400 thousand.[24]

In actual fact these estimates, which remain close to military sources and show up the bias in many details, are far from accurate reflections of the historical facts. The dissemination of such accounts constitutes a clear manipulation of the statistics, the more so as on the Algerian side no research has been undertaken, and in any case such research is confronted with the grave problem of the lost archives—the same problem as in 1830.

In no case can these estimations be accepted: they ignore completely the state of affairs on the ground. They are close to the official statements of the army, which ignore the realities on the ground, namely, the context of the war in its two main forms: the military operations properly so called and their unavowed consequences on the civilian population.

It may be impossible to fix the broad outlines of a methodology for research in this limited framework. But one must at least *start with observations at ground level* in order to a arrive at certain relations and proportions taken from observations in the most representative regions of the country. The data collected after consultation of both sides, cross-checking, and comparison of diverse statistics[25] by one very attentive observer (who donned a French uniform but had a strong desire to understand the opponent) constitute such an approach. One of the conclusions, formulated by a French officer in one of the least affected areas, is worth noting: "For one victim of the FLN there are 25 victims of the 'forces of order.'"[26]

This kind of precision is not possible in regions very affected, such as Kabylia, and the rest of the eastern parts of the county. In Kabylia indeed, the estimation by one of the leaders of the Third Wilaya, can easily be accepted by all observers: "In Kabylia there is not a single family that does not weep for two or three of its members killed by the French."[27] These two observations suffice by themselves to justify the rejection of the totals we are examining, but also the review and correction (that is, increase) of the figures of the census of 1954. In the last analysis it amounts to a *confirmation of the underestimation in general of all statistics*. On the basis of one death per family, the lowest estimation possible, the total of one million can be exceeded.

In consequence, it is only by repeated investigations—cross-checked, methodical, and above all regionalized and even localized—that history can be served. For the present one must surrender to the evidence and take into account the manifest underestimation of the statistical data diffused by the other side.[28]

Since 1830 one constant phenomenon affects the principal sources of Algerian demography, notably in regard to the three major landmarks of its history (the catastrophe of 1867–1868, the repression of the uprising in 1945, and most of all the War of Liberation): in each case there is an undeniable underestimation. No doubt at the beginning there were real obstacles; but later, in spite of a certain improvement, there remained a desire to hide reality by minimizing the losses of human life, so rendering the history of a whole people difficult to analyze, principally in the ultimate phase of the War of Liberation.

It is therefore advisable to examine with very critical attention all demographic material concerning the period under study: it is the only way to approach the historical reality in all its complexity.

NOTES

1. Pellissier de Reynaud, *Annales* (Paris, 1864).

2. A. Tammini, who has done considerable work on these documents, points out their importance, notably in the case of the Beylic of Constantine and the Great Mosque of Algiers.

3. D. Sari, "Le démantèlement de la propriété foncière," *Revue historique* 505 (1973), 47–76.

4. The insurrections were often fatal to private archives, which often included manuscripts vital to local and regional history.

5. In these conditions the effect on the conservation of archives was even worse than in the preceding case. Nevertheless, the "collective memory" manages sometimes to retain and transmit certain significant details, as we have observed when investigating communities settled outside of the national borders. On this particular question, see C. R. Ageron, *Les Algériens musulmans et la France* (Paris, 1968).

6. Y. Lacoste, A. Nouschi, and A. Prenant, *L'Algérie, passé et présent* (Paris, 1960).

7. This regression of the urban population touches many problems. The case of Tlemcen is exemplary. Observers in the middle of the nineteenth century have noted the extent of the ruins. It also contained a population of some ten thousand with a garrison of approximately the same number. See L. Baudricourt, *Histoire de la colonisation de l'Algérie* (Paris, 1860).

8. Sari, "Le démantèlement."

9. D. Sari, *Le désastre démographique de 1867–68* (Algiers, 1982).

10. This phenomenon affects even the latest censuses. See L. Chevalier, *Le problème démographique nord-africain* (Paris, 1948).

11. Y. Courrière, *L'heure des colonels* (Paris, 1970). The author mentions these regions. Furthermore, the example given on p. 489 clearly indicates the relation between the *supposed* population and the *real* population, given as 1:8, even though that sector was of no special interest to the French army, given its *strategic importance*.

12. Boyer-Banse, "Les populations agricoles indigènes dans le département d'Alger," *Bulletin de la Société de Géographie d'Alger* (1906), 196.

13. The general situation at this time must not be forgotten. See C. A. Julien, *Histoire de l'Algérie contemporaine*, vol. 2 (Paris, 1979).

14. *Résultats statistiques du dénombrement de la population de 1954*, vol. 1 (Algiers, 1956), xxxiii.

15. *Résultats statistiques* 1. It is to be noted that it was in 1956 that the strike of schoolboys and students took place: it included the same age group.

16. X. Yacono, "Peut-on évaluer la population de l'Algérie en 1830?" *Revue Africaine* 95 (1954), 277–307.

17. Sari, "Le désastre démographique."

18. X. Yacono, "Les pertes algériennes de 1954 à 1962," *Revue de l'occident musulman et la Méditerranée* 2 (1982), .

19. Ainat-Tabet, *Le 8 Mai 1945 en Algérie* (Algiers, 1985).

20. Yacono, "Les pertes."

21. Vidal Naquet, *La raison d'état* (Paris, 1972).

22. See the case of the Bessembourg camp on Collo Peninsula described in *Le Monde*, 7 July 1959.

23. See the regular reports in *L'annuaire de l'Afrique du Nord.*

24. In a work destined for the general public, G. Pervillé claims he can give a new account of the war, with photographs to support it. He tries to demonstrate that there was a "concurrent civil war: among the Algerians themselves alongside the Franco-Algerian war" (*Revue Histoire* [1983], 89–92).

25. M. Launay, *Paysans algériens, la terre, la vigne, et les hommes* (Paris, 1963).

26. This was in Ain Temouchent, a district of low hills and easy terrain, where the war lasted from 1956 until 1960, "one of the calmest and most pacified regions in Algeria."

27. Quoted by Courrière, *L'heure des colonels,* 521.

28. It is to be noted that in practically all the works on the period the figure of one million Algerian victims is maintained. So in the book of a former parachutist, P. Montagnon, involved in the hostilities from the beginning in 1954, seven times mentioned in dispatches, and twice wounded. He mentions, in passing, certain circumstances that render the quantification of losses difficult, or even impossible. However, his book, which won an award from the Académie Française, is full of errors—even in the locating of certain places that were quite famous during the war. See Gerart Watelet, *La guerre d'Algérie* (Paris, 1985).

5

First Steps in the Demographic History of Zimbabwe: The Colonial Period from 1895 to 1922

DAVID N. BEACH

The first census of the population of what is now Zimbabwe was taken in 1962. Prior to that true censuses had only been taken for the non-African minority population, and the number of the African majority had only been estimated overall. Since much of the modern history of the country has been concerned with the domination of the majority by the minority, it is curious that so little attention has been paid by historians to the numbers, distribution, and nature of the majority of the population. Geographers, economists, and demographers have tended to concentrate on the period since 1962 when reasonably reliable data have been available; but very few such researchers have looked at the crucially important decades between the coming of colonial rule in 1890 and the 1962 census, when the dramatic modern population increase was already well advanced.[1]

This contribution arises out of an interest in the precolonial population of the country and a growing realization that an essential first step toward the study of the late precolonial population must be a study of the early colonial period.[2] The colonial government's estimates of the African rural population in each of the thirty-two districts of the country during the years 1895–1922 (with comments on reliability), assembled, as far as I know, for the first time, is being published elsewhere.[3] The year 1922 was chosen as the closing date of the study because until then, the numbers, distribution, and composition of the population were more like those of the precolonial era than those of the later decades, when urbanization, forced removals of people from alienated land, and the immigration of Africans from other colonies increasingly complicated the picture. Moreover, it was in the period from 1913 to 1922 that the population estimates began to approach, but not to reach, reliability. The analysis of the data throws a great deal of light on precolonial Zimbabwean history in the nineteenth century, but it also illuminates the early colonial period and, in some cases, compels us to reexamine some aspects of the question of land.

THE DATA

The available figures are represented in Figures 5.1–5.3. They come from estimates supplied by the local administrative officers in their annual reports and in six partial or general surveys of the African population. The 1895–1899 figures are too fragmentary to be of any use; but the 1900–1922 figures for the thirty-two districts are reasonably complete as far as the "total indigenous" population estimates were concerned; at times attempts were made to show the age, sex, marital status, and location of the population, as well as to calculate the numbers of immigrant Africans. The officials quite often commented on the figures that they were supplying and referred to such factors as infant mortality, polygamy, and the numbers and causes of deaths.

Since the initial and continuing reason for the enumerating of the population was the collection of tax and labor, it is not surprising that the graphs for each district tend to show a steep rise in the first decade, as more and more villages and individuals were added to the tax registers, especially in the larger and more remote districts. In the second decade, however, it had become more difficult for taxable men to escape detection by the officials, though children and taxable women continued to be undercounted. Moreover, the different officials used very varying methods of estimating the population, ranging from blatant guesswork to raising of the numbers of adult male taxpayers by various factors to actual attempts at counting the population or taking sample surveys. From 1913 attempts were made to force the officials to estimate the total population by raising the adult male taxpayer figure by a factor of 3.5 and by 1920 twenty-three districts out of thirty-two were using this method, though it is not always clear whether the remainder were doing so or not. Knowledgeable officials knew that the figures underestimated the number of women and children, but on the whole very few thought that the real figure was more than 20 percent higher than their estimates. On that basis the real 1920 figure would have been in the vicinity of 880 thousand, rising to 947 thousand by 1922; but at present it is not possible to tell how much further this figure should be increased to approach the mirage of "reliability." Between 1953–1955 and the 1962 census the difference between estimates and the de facto total was about 17 percent.[4]

However, the main emphasis of this chapter is the conclusions that can be drawn from the distribution of the population and from the individual district graphs, as opposed to the estimated "national" total.

THE MAP

The map begins with the district boundaries. These remained remarkably consistent throughout the colonial period, with subdivision of existing

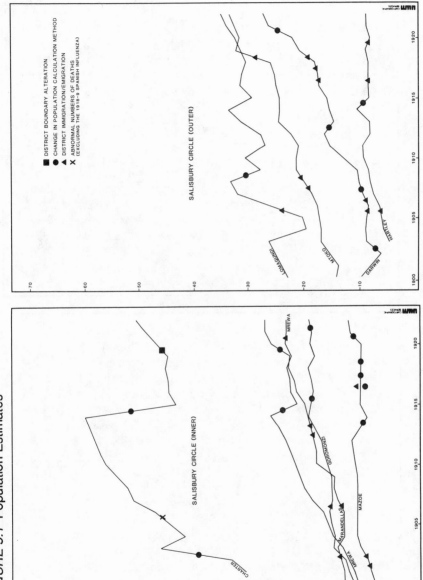

FIGURE 5.1 Population Estimates

FIGURE 5.2 Population Estimates

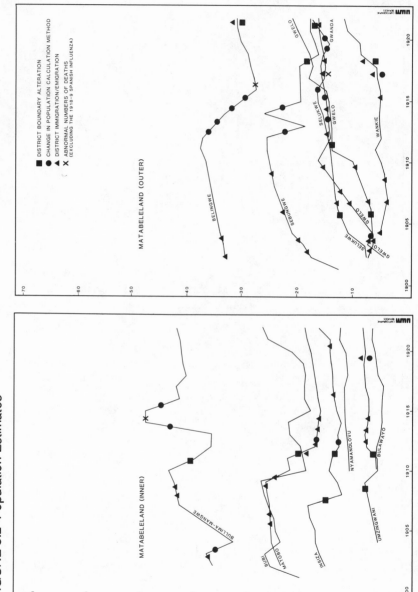

FIGURE 5.3 Population Estimates

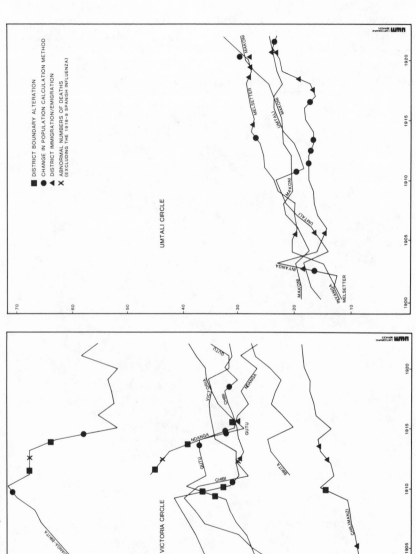

districts being the rule, rather than the complete redrawing of boundaries. Modifications of district boundaries did take place between 1900 and 1922; but most of these were minor, and the population involved was merely transferred from the tax registers of one district to the next without actually moving. See Map 5.1.

MAP 5.1 Zimbabwe (Southern Rhodesia) Population, 1920

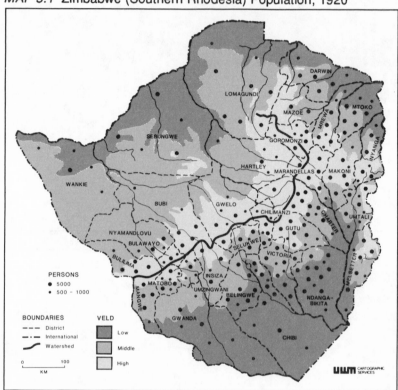

I then locate on the map the population of 1920, a year chosen because it is the earliest in which the 3.5 raising factor can be applied to the majority of districts.[5] Pending the production of a detailed population map of each district area in the late nineteenth and early twentieth centuries (which is almost certainly possible but will take time to complete) basic units of 5,000 and 500–1,000 are marked. Wherever possible, they are located according to the known distribution of population as given by reference to the entire documentation of the period. (Regional shifts between the late nineteenth century and 1920 will be discussed below, but on a national scale they are minor.) Even in the big and thinly populated districts of the northwest and south-southeast, a unit of 5,000 is located in the middle of what was actually a much more scattered group of smaller units, but it is done in relation to known subdistrict figures in nearly every case. (District names have *not* displaced population units but rather the reverse.)

The result gives us a remarkably uneven distribution of population in the country. It is worth noting that a map based on the 1911 figures that was used in predecessors to this work gave a very similar picture, though based on even less accurate data.

THE ENVIRONMENT

Until recently, historians have tended to follow the conventional division of Zimbabwe by geographers into *highveld, middleveld,* and *lowveld* zones, with the eastern highlands and the dry, rain-shadowed middle Save valley providing a special case of complex microenvironments.[6] The distribution of the population in the early twentieth century suggests that the people themselves, with two millennia of experience of the country, saw things rather differently. If we mark on the population map the main watershed from the right bank of the middle Mhanyame to the far southwest of the country, dividing the middle Zambezi catchment area on the one hand from the catchment areas of the Limpopo, Save, and Mazowe-Ruenya on the other, we can see a dramatic difference between the distribution east and west of the watershed.

West of the watershed and above the 1,333-meter contour we find some settlement, especially in the southwest of the plateau, but below that contour the population was very thin and scattered, with what concentrations there were being along the rivers, especially the middle Zambezi. East of the watershed, we find a Great Crescent of relatively dense population with its inner edge marked by the main watershed and its outer limits confined by the dry southeast lowveld. Inside the Great Crescent the distinction between highveld and middleveld in terms of population distribution is not obvious, though the distinction between these and the lowveld is. This distribution (as will be shown) was not the result of either the coming of colonial rule or of the Nguni incursions of the nineteenth century but dates back to at least the eighteenth century and has parallels before about 1300.

Using the actual preferences of the people in choosing settlement sites to highlight the environmental picture, we can easily explain the differences between the Great Crescent and the rest of the country. West of the watershed, much of the soil is sandy or sodic, and surface water tends to be confined to the bigger rivers. In the southeast lowveld and the middle Save valley, as well as the fringes of the lower Zambezi valley in the far north and northeast, conditions are extremely dry. But in the Great Crescent extensive erosion over geological time has produced, in between granite dome mountains, valleys in which a rich variety of arable, grazing, and wooded lands were available for a population roughly one-tenth the size of that of today. Moreover, west of the watershed the land tends to be very flat or undulating overall, and the few hills do not often lend themselves to defense, whereas in the Great Crescent the granite dome formations supply superb natural strongholds, some with caves for use as a last resort. Historical studies confirm that settlements in the Great Crescent were nearly always on defensible sites in the eighteenth and nineteenth centuries and that this was not so much due to the coming of the Nguni as to the incessant cross-raiding that went on between neighbors.[7] The main exceptions to this were in the southwest, where the powerful Changamire and Ndebele states rarely faced actual invasion and villages were built in more open country.

In short, it was the Great Crescent that provided the preferred environment of the majority of the precolonial people of Zimbabwe. This is not to underplay the factor of the population in the other areas, which made a skillful use of a harsh environment. Nor should one expect the watershed to show up as dramatically on district maps as it does on the national map: the watershed itself is physically inconspicuous on the ground, and people often lived close to it on both sides, but the density of population to the west fell off rapidly.

PRECOLONIAL CORRELATIONS

Computer analyses of archeological sites of "Iron Age" people from about 200 to about 1300 show a broad correlation with the Great Crescent, though this is less obvious for the stone buildings of the Great Zimbabwe and Kame "cultures," which were built for an elite between about 1200 and 1700.[8] Documentary evidence from 1500 is not adequate for this kind of study until the nineteenth century;[9] and until we have a countrywide archeological record for the ordinary people in this period it will be difficult to check the picture given by traditions of a rather depopulated south in the seventeenth and early eighteenth centuries leading in due course to reoccupation in the 1750–1850 period.[10]

The distribution map throws a good deal of light on the nineteenth century. Firstly, the long-established myth that the Ndebele depopulated a broad zone around their state by raiding and incorporating the Shona is clearly untrue. North, west, and south of their state the Ndebele had naturally thinly populated areas (indeed, this may be one reason why they chose to settle there); but to the east the heavily populated Belingwe and Selukwe Districts of the colonial era adjoined the independent southern Shona areas without any such depopulated zone. Since the southern Shona area experienced the most raiding by the Ndebele from the 1850s to the 1890s, it can only be concluded that depopulation was not a major aim or effect of Ndebele raiders.[11] The relatively thinly populated zone on the Insiza-Belingwe borders lay within the area of Ndebele control, and probably derived from local microenvironmental factors. Traditions and documents indicate some depopulation in the thinly peopled Wankie and Hartley and western Charter districts, but it is difficult to see these as having ever approached Great Crescent densities. The impact of the other Nguni state, that of the Gaza, who occupied the Melsetter District from 1862 to 1889, is more difficult to assess: there was a major emigration when the Gaza left in 1889, and colonial figures and notes show repeated moves back and forth over the colonial frontier up to 1922, but the overall trend was that Melsetter began as the least populated eastern district in that period and ended as the most populated. So the question of depopulation under Gaza rule remains to be examined. The Inyanga District, on the other hand, had a larger population than earlier studies have suggested.[12]

Without going into detail, it is worth mentioning for the sake of comparison with other chapters that evidence for any export slave trade from the Zimbabwean plateau is virtually nonexistent and that on the contrary, there was a slight but noticeable import of slaves from the Zambezi valley and beyond in the north and northeast.

THE COLONIAL IMPACT

Ndebele losses in 1893 are unlikely to have exceeded two thousand, and total Ndebele and Shona losses in 1896–1897, conservatively estimated at five thousand, are unlikely to have doubled that, at least as a result of battle.[13] In the Ndebele state war-induced famine killed an unknown number in 1896–1897, but actual deaths from the same cause in the rest of the country at that time were probably few.[14] The Ndebele losses, whatever they were, may not have been made up: from 1910 the population figures show very little increase, while increases before that are probably illusory.[15] No comparable losses seem to have occurred in the non-Ndebele areas.

The immediate effects of the 1896–1897 fighting in terms of the movement of population seem to have been limited. Matobo District experienced a 50 percent increase of its population in 1896 as Ndebele took refuge there; and thereafter there was a steady drainage to other districts, partly due to evictions from white-owned farms from 1906. Refugees from Hartley who went to Lomagundi in 1897 had mostly returned by the early 1900s.

As colonial rule continued, movements of population from district to district were surprisingly limited up to 1922: making a generous estimate from the available figures, nineteen districts gained or lost less than 4 percent of their population, nine gained or lost 5–10 percent, and four gained or lost more than 10 percent.[16] Matobo's massive loss of 56 percent is almost certainly higher than the real figure;[17] but Insiza's loss of 18 percent, which was also due to evictions from farms, is probably a reflection of reality. The other two cases of major population movements occurred in Mtoko (+36 percent) and Inyanga (+20 percent), as people fled from the Portuguese in neighboring Mozambique in 1908 and 1917–1918. In short, the first three decades of colonial rule involved much less movement of the population from one district to another than might have been expected, though the next sixty years were to see considerable movement.

The situation within the districts requires a much more detailed analysis, but this cannot yet be supplied for the pre-1923 period. However, the broad generalization accepted in some quarters—that the creation of settler farms and African "reserves" in this early period involved the movement of the people from a highveld to a middleveld or lowveld environment—requires some modification. The alienation of the Ndebele lands in the southwest *did* involve such a process, and the alienation of parts of Inyanga and Melsetter were equally flagrant examples, but if one looks at the early twentieth-century population distribution and the African-owned areas of the 1960s, it can be seen that quite a lot of the Great Crescent to the northeast of the old Ndebele state did stay in African hands. This is not to underplay the serious nature of land alienation: great, irregular chunks of settler farmland *had* been carved out of the Great Crescent. These lay in the best land in the country and included not just the areas where the people had been living before 1896–1897 but land within the territory of each dynasty that had not been effectively occupied until then because it lacked defensive sites. Even in the areas outside the Great Crescent, alienation created relative land shortage. Given the fact that the population increased tenfold in the six decades from 1920 to 1980, the people in 1980 had 10 percent of the land available to them in 1920, discounting land alienation, allowing for it, they had only five percent.[18]

THE POPULATION OF ZIMBABWE BEFORE 1923

In view of the fact that so little work has been carried out on the pre-1962 population, anything written about the pre-1923 population has to be regarded as extremely tentative. On the other hand, even the simplest observations and suggestions have some value in that they are better than nothing at all.

The colonial government's estimate for the African population in 1901 was 561,927. It is clear from the evidence that this was a wild underestimate, so that the apparent increase in the population based on estimates over the next decade was illusory. Yet as the estimates continued over the years until 1962, they overtook the real population figure of the early twentieth century and began to reflect the real *increase* even if they were underestimating the real *annual figures* by as much as 20 percent. There is probably no precise point at which the estimates begin to reflect reality, but the decade 1913–1922 is almost certainly the crucial one.

One thing is clear: there is no evidence that the population had ever been higher than it was in 1913–1922, so we have either a stable population or one experiencing a slight growth that either existed under precolonial conditions or resulted from colonial rule.[19] This contrasts with the massive losses of population in lands north of the Zambezi. It is not difficult to see why this should have been so: with virtually no export slave trade, with the Ndebele state interested in increasing rather than reducing the population,[20] and comparatively short and localized colonial wars,[21] the Zimbabwean plateau was then, as it is now, a remarkably healthy part of Africa. The best-recorded deaths (those of adult males) show that the most common reason for death was pneumonia in the winter months, the second being dysentery in the hot months before the summer rains and the third, malaria. The latter was less important and was often noted as being deadly only if "complications" set in. Smallpox was endemic but not usually deadly: in 1903 in Ndanga it was reckoned that only 6–7 percent of smallpox sufferers died. Even the "Spanish" influenza of 1918–1919, though spectacular, hardly dented the population graphs at the time, though losses of children might have affected the growth of the visible population in later years. Most of the country was too high and cold to allow sleeping sickness to be a significant factor.

What is surprising about the precolonial and early colonial population is not that it rose after 1900 but that it did not rise higher before then. Oral traditions spoke of thousands of deaths during famines, but recent research has shown that in directly observed cases in the nineteenth century the people often became very hungry indeed during famines but rarely actually died of starvation. (Presumably, however, their resistance to pneumonia and dysentery would have been much lowered by hunger.) This was because when famine did strike, it was just possible for the people to get by on gathering and hunting.[22] But this means that factors were keeping the population down to a point just below what could be sustained by gathering and hunting in an emergency. Here, there were a number of factors that did or might apply, some involuntary and some voluntary, and it is difficult to tell from the data so far available just which were important.

The available reports agree that about 50 percent of babies died not long after birth, with a total of six births for each woman being regarded as average by Gutu women in 1915. However, infant mortality and the effects of polygamy have yet to be assessed in detail. Another factor might have been the shortage of land in the precolonial period. This looks paradoxical in view of the apparent availability of land in the early years and the tremendous growth of the population that accompanied increasing land shortage in the last six decades. However, oral traditions did not mislead when they spoke of shortages of land in the past: arable and grazing land that was out of running distance of a defensive site when neighborly or more remote raiders descended was simply unusable, and the number of defensive sites was limited. (This factor almost certainly accounts for the explosive growth of livestock herds from an artificial low point caused by the 1896 rinderpest pandemic.) In other words, there may have been a deliberate limitation of the population by such methods as prolonged suckling of infants, but this factor, too, remains to be researched in detail.

But here speculation is beginning to run ahead of the solid evidence. It will take a great deal of work before the historical demography of Zimbabwe before 1962 can approach the levels of sophistication already reached in the other areas covered by this collection. However, it seems to be clear already that the Zimbabwean case is sufficiently different from the territories farther north to put the researcher on guard against applying "northern" experiences to the south without due caution.

NOTES

1. L. Zinyama and R. Whitlow ("Changing Patterns of Population Distribution in Zimbabwe," *GeoJournal* 13, no. 4 [1986], 365–384) summarize Zimbabwean demography from a geographer's perspective. R. W. M. Johnson ("African Population Estimates—Myth or Reality?" *Rhodesian Journal of Economics* 3, no. 1 [1969], 5–16) examines estimates and national figures. P. Mosley (*The Settler Economies* [Cambridge, 1983], 111–113) discusses population as an element in an analysis of the economy. The main historians who have examined population factors are R. H. Palmer (*Land and Racial Domination in Rhodesia* [London, 1977], 2–4, 12); R. M. G. Mtetwa ("The 'Political' and Economic History of the Duma People of South-Eastern Rhodesia from the Early Eighteenth Century to 1945," [Ph.D. diss., University of Rhodesia, 1976], 300–350); J. R. D. Cobbing ("The Ndebele Under the Khumalos, 1820–1896," [Ph.D. diss., University of Lancaster, 1976], 466–469); I. R. Phimister ("The 'Spanish' Influenza Pandemic of 1918 and Its Impact on the Southern Rhodesian Mining Industry," *Central African Journal of Medicine* 19, no. 7 [1973], 143–148).

2. D. N. Beach, "Towards a Population History of Pre-Colonial Zimbabwe," Department of History Seminar Paper no. 59 (University of Zimbabwe, 1984).

3. D. N. Beach, "Zimbabwean Demography: Early Colonial Data," *Zambezia*, in press. Unless otherwise stated, all of the data in this chapter come from the text and tables in this article.

4. Johnson, "African Population Estimates," 12.

5. Beach ("Zimbabwean Demography") points out that a gap in the data for the South Mazoe District prevents the use of an earlier date. In addition, 1920 was the year in which the alterations to reserves by the 1914–1915 Native Reserves Commission became law.

6. E.g., Palmer, *Land and Racial Domination*, 5–8.

7. D. N. Beach, "From Heroism to History: Mapondera and the Northern Zimbabwean Plateau," *History in Africa* 15 (1988).

8. P. J. J. Sinclair, *Space, Time, and Social Formation: A Territorial Approach to the Archaeology and Anthropology of Zimbabwe and Mozambique Pre-1700 A.D.* (Uppsala, 1987).

9. D. N. Beach, "Documents and African Society on the Zimbabwean Plateau Before 1890," *Paideuma* 23 (1987), 129–145.

10. D. N. Beach, *The Shona and Zimbabwe 900–1850* (Mambo, 1984), 203–209, 293–317.

11. D. N. Beach, *War and Politics in Zimbabwe 1840–1900*, (Mambo, 1986), 13–44.

12. This is so even allowing for the immigration from Mozambique noted below.

13. J. R. D. Cobbing, "Ndebele Under the Khumalos," 367; A. Gava, "The First Chimurenga 1896–7: An Insight into African Casualties" (University of Zimbabwe, 1987).

14. J. Iliffe, *Famine in Zimbabwe 1890–1960* (Gweru: Mambo, in press).

15. This applies to the districts that saw the heaviest fighting, Bulawayo-Bubi-Nyamandlovu, Matobo, Umzingwani, and Insiza.

16. The number of those crossing district or colonial borders are often merged with losses or gains from other causes, while some movements out of districts are covered by a general increase.

17. Matobo's losses of population to other districts were undoubtedly great, but the total loss from the estimates is almost certainly due to changing methods of calculation, and it is not fully reflected in the figures from neighboring districts.

18. For the whole twentieth century, see Zinyama and Whitlow, "Changing Patterns."

19. It is not known just how and when the population reached its nineteenth-century level and probably is not knowable until more detailed archeology of the previous two millennia becomes available.

20. Compare Cobbing, "Ndebele Under the Khumalos," 84–114 with J. Guy, *The Destruction of the Zulu Kingdom* (London, 1979), 11–12 on differing Nguni attitudes toward early marriage.

21. Seven months was the longest period in which continuous fighting took place in any district.

22. Iliffe, *Famine in Zimbabwe*.

6

Factors Affecting Census Reliability in Colonial Zambia, 1900-1930

MWELWA C. MUSAMBACHIME

In an introduction to a monograph on the study of a population map of Luapula-Bangweulu Region of Northern Rhodesia (now Zambia), George Kay quotes a district officer, who complained that "a dearth of basic population data presents a handy perennial problem in Northern Rhodesia. . . . No accurate and comprehensive count of the country's population has ever been made and no detailed surveys of population distribution are yet available."[1]

This was the position during much of the colonial period in Zambia.[2] Whereas the administration was able to keep an "accurate" census of the small European population from 1911 on, no census of the African population was undertaken.[3] This was only done in 1963, a year before independence. Prior to this event population statistics were compiled from the estimates provided by administrative officers and statistics on labor population and employment.[4] All of these were unreliable, yet they formed a valuable source for compiling African population statistics in colonial Zambia. I shall concentrate on the period 1890–1930, when there was hardly any scientific enumeration.

ESTABLISHMENT OF COLONIAL RULE

Between 1890 and 1900, the British South Africa Company (BSAC) was preoccupied with establishing its own administration. In North-Eastern Rhodesia (NER) the administration had to use force to defeat the Ngoni in 1897 and the Lunda of Mwata Kazembe in 1893 and 1899.[5] In North-Western Rhodesia (NWR) the population was submissive and accepted the company administration without resistance. During this period the BSAC established administrative stations (*bomas*) under the control of native commissioners (later changed to *district commissioners*). A number of the *bomas* were grouped together to form a magisterial district (later called *province*) under the jurisdiction of a magisterial district commissioner (later *provincial commissioner*), who in turn was under the authority of the administrator. The territory of NER was first divided into nine districts (later reduced to eight) with fourteen *bomas*. North-Western Rhodesia was initially divided into six districts (later reduced to five) with twenty *bomas*.[6]

Among the duties of the native commissioner were to maintain law and order in the subdistrict. For this purpose he toured his district each year. Cullen Gouldsbury and J. W. Sheane explain

> The main object of the tour is to get into closer touch with the people, [and] the subsidiary matters are checking of the census, the enumeration of stock, inquiring into the conditions of crops, the consideration of applications to move from village to village, and in general the promulgation of administrative decrees which may not be operative since the last visit.[7]

After 1900 the duties also included the collection of taxes, which made censustaking imperative. The unit of calculation was the *village*, composed of several families. Some were large, others were small.[8] Initially, very little censustaking was done in NWR. In NER the exercise began in 1898, confined to the "vicinity of the administration stations." As such, it was not possible to give "accurate information regarding the number of natives inhabiting the territory."[9] In 1902 the administrator of NER echoed the same difficulty. He went on to caution that censustaking was "a long and difficult task" and that it had to be understood that the figures given were of no real value but were given for the purpose of conveying an *idea* of the approximate number of people in the country.[10] This notion changed with the introduction of the hut tax in 1901. The administration had to take census of taxpayers and estimate their tax revenue from it. One native commissioner informs us how this was done:

> The only part of census actually counted are the taxable huts. The total number of huts and the population are estimated. . . . In a number of villages I count the number of taxable huts and population . . . and find that the average is: To every taxable hut there is one untaxable; To every hut the average is three people. For example 5 taxable huts multiply by 2 = 10 huts; multiply 10 by 3 = 30. The usual occupants of a taxable hut is the owner and a child. The usual occupants of an untaxable hut is an old couple with a young nephew or niece or an old woman and her daughter who is often the wife of a man in the village or 3 to 4 young boys or a couple of old women with a niece or nephew. . . . The above method will for this District Fort Rosebery be found very reliable and I believe if one had time to go and actually count every hut the total would be very near as stated; the same applies to the population.[11]

Using this principle, the administrator of NER estimated the African population to be 256,000 in 1900, though he admitted that "the true number is certain to be larger than the figures here given."[12] For 1901 he gave "300,000 as an approximate figure."[13] In 1902, based on the census returns made by native commissioners, the population was given as 338,878, which the administrator thought was "approximately correct."[14] It was put at 345,961 in March 1903,[15] 398,000 in 1907, 406,375 in 1908, 438,500 in 1910, and 448,930 in 1911.[16]

For NWR the census began rather late. Initally, its area was uncertain because of the boundary dispute with Portuguese West Africa, which was settled in 1905 by the king of Italy. The settlement removed a large area from NWR reducing the population. Before the settlement the population was put at 400,000 in 1904. After the settlement the population was given as being 500,000 in 1906, 322,000 in 1907, and 500,000 in 1908 and 1909. Another source put the figures at 320,000 in 1907, 357,586 in 1908, and 370,055 in 1911.[17]

1900–1911: CONSTRAINTS ON CENSUS IN NORTH-EASTERN RHODESIA

While the population of NWR was stable, that of NER was not. In fact, between 1900 and 1910, it registered a decrease each year[18] due to a number of factors, among which were (1) the proliferation of *mitanda* (sg. *umutanda*, small huts built close to gardens to facilitate tending crops and protecting them from ravaging wild animals and birds), (2) flights across the international boundaries, (3) tax collection methods, (4) labor migration, and (5) the appearance of sleeping sickness, followed by the introduction of tough regulations to control its spread.[19]

Mitanda

Mitanda became a feature of life after the establishment of colonial rule in NER. Before that inhabitants lived in large stockaded villages, providing security from attacks by East African traders or by warring ethnic groups (such as the Bemba or Ngoni) looking for slaves, foodstuffs, or merely the fun of conquering. After 1900, when the BSAC adminis-tration was firmly established and the threat of insecurity removed, stockaded villages began to break up. People began to settle where they liked. In Mpika District, where it was common sight to see villages of two hundred to five hundred huts at the end of the nineteenth century, by 1904 such villages were nowhere to be seen.[20] (See Map 6.1.) The number of huts in the largest settlement dwindled to not more than twenty. In Luwingu between 1900 and 1903 a population of eighteen thousand split into small groups covering an area of about 10,000 km^2.[21] Villages consisted of ten to fifteen able-bodied men with their families.

One administrative official complained that "many villages are in the process of disintegration by the formation of smaller vilages out in the bush by the younger people. The population is nearly everywhere far smaller."[22]

MAP 6.1 Republic of Zambia Administrative Districts

The proliferation of *mitanda* was seen as being in "conflict with the orderly system of district administration." Supervision and maintenance of law and order were impossible if each "family was permitted to construct Mitanda when and where they please."[23] *Mitanda* also interfered with the collection of hut tax by enabling many taxpayers to evade payment and also with the censustaking, in that there were no villages any longer.[24] As such, *mitanda* made the work of the administration very difficult and could not be allowed to continue. At a meeting of the acting administrator of NER and the Bemba chiefs held in Kasama a directive proscribing *mitanda* was issued. And at another meeting of chiefs held in Kasama in 1907 the acting undersecretary for native affairs directed chiefs "not to cut gardens in the forest country far away from the village since those who do so will disperse in Mitanda: which the Administrator had 'forbidden.'"[25] People found living in *mitanda* were arrested, fined, or imprisoned for two months. Others had their grain bins burned down. Even with these measures, it took the administration many years to break up the *mitanda*.[26]

Flights Across International Borders

Between 1890 and 1900, when the BSAC was establishing its rule over the Rhodesias, the *Compagnie du Katanga* was doing the same with Congo. It established a number of administrative posts (*postes*), each headed by a *chef du poste*. Besides maintaining law and order, he was also required to deliver ivory and rubber collected from the Africans.[27] In collecting rubber as payment for tax, a lot of brutal force was used.[28] Each village was given a quota to fulfill. If it failed, the villagers were arrested, beaten up, imprisoned, and even killed by the *Force Publique* (a quasi-military force) for failing to meet the quota.[29] These activities forced a large number of Congolese villages built along the Luapula River to cross into NER. Their flight helped to increase the population figures temporarily.[30] After the exposure in Europe in 1903 of maladministration of the Congo, these activities were stopped, enabling the displaced people to return to the Congo[31]—which in turn led to a decrease in the population.[32]

Payment of Tax

Another cause for the decrease in the census figures was due to the methods of collecting tax. Hut tax was introduced in 1901, initially paid in kind but later changed to poll tax and paid in money.[33] To ensure that most of the taxpayers were accounted for, each native commissioner "had a complete map of his district with positions of villages and a complete census of the adult male population."[34] Collection of tax was accompanied by a series of coercive measures such as imprisonment of defaulters and the burning of their huts and grain bins.[35] During each tour by a native commissioner, these measures forced many defaulters to miss the count by hiding in the bush for several days to escape arrest or passing for dead. Others deceived the administration with the multiple presentation of the few tax receipts available. Others migrated to neighboring countries such as Congo and German East Africa (and Angola for those in NWR) where the demands for payment of tax were less excessive.[36] In a number of cases whole villages built along the borders "decamped" into neighboring countries to avoid the payment of tax.[37] In a number of cases defaulters crisscrossed the boundary to avoid paying tax to any administration. Chief Kaputa described what happened in his area: "When Rhodesian officials chased after them, they ran over the border and when the Belgians came, they ran back into Northern Rhodesia, consequently they pay no tax nowhere."[38] And J. C. Moore, a cotton expert sent by the colonial office to Northern Rhodesia in 1924 to assess the country's ability and potential to grow cotton, noted during his tour of Mporokoso District that "when the time comes to pay his tax, the Northern Rhodesian African migrates to the Congo or elsewhere . . . leaving his village for months at a time to return later."[39] This was reported in other border areas as well. These flights naturally caused a decrease in the amounts of tax revenue collected and the number of people counted.

Labor Migration

The demand for tax brought with it the phenomenon of labor migration. In NWR many taxpayers were able to pay their taxes through sales of cattle and grain.[40] In most areas of NER very few people were able to raise money locally. Faced with few employment opportunities, many taxpayers elected to migrate to Katanga, Southern Rhodesia, and South Africa to earn their tax money. Some migrants were recruited on contracts varying from six months to two years by recruiting agencies such as the Witwatersrand Native Labour Bureau for South Africa mines, the Rhodesia Native Labour Bureau for Southern Rhodesian mines and farms, and the Tanganyika Concessions Limited (and later the Robert Williams and Company) for the Katangan mines.[41] Some of the migrants never returned.[42]

Due to the migration of able-bodied men, the birthrate declined. Girls of marriageable age could not find husbands. Those who were married waited for the return of their husbands.[43] Cases of adultery and divorce increased as is evidenced in the cases brought before the magistrates.[44]

Sleeping Sickness

Another reason for the decrease in population was the appearance of sleeping sickness in NER in 1906, spread from the Congo. As soon as its presence was known, the principal medical officer, Dr. Spillane, took a tour of the areas bordering the Congo. He found the presence of the vector tsetse fly (*Glossina palpalis*) along the Lower Luapula and Kalungwishi Rivers. Immediately, measures were taken to contain the spread of the disease: the area was quarantined, tough regulations were introduced in 1907 to curb the movement of the people, and to reduce contact between the Congo (the source of the disease) and NER all dugout canoes were confiscated and destroyed without compensation.[45] All the villages lying along the banks of the Luapula and Kalungwishi Rivers were moved to higher ground.[46] Fishing was proscribed.[47]

As a reaction to these measures, whole villages moved across the border into the Congo, where the regulations were less stringent. Fort Rosebery reported a loss of between seven and ten thousand people, while in Kawambwa "over 3,000 families"[48] crossed into the Congo. In Tanganyika hundreds of people left to live in German East Africa.[49] The BSAC admitted to a "shortage of hut tax revenue" in the affected areas owing to the inability of the people to earn money locally.[50] For Fort Rosebery and Mweru-Luapula Districts attempts to stop these migrations proved futile. Each year the administrative officials sent disconcerting reports to the administrator. For example, in 1909 Dr. Storrs reported that "the opposite bank of the Luapula is thick with villages and more are being built (unfortunately it must be admitted that some of these are at least our people . . . from this side) and as long as these villages are allowed to remain with the facilities for fishing and the like, they will be a continual temptation . . . to our people."[51]

The temptation to cross to the west bank continued. Some of those who crossed went to seek wage employment in the mines of Katanga. In 1909 Arthur Pearson, medical officer for the Union Minière du Haut-Katanga, estimated that twenty-eight hundred men had "surreptitiously crossed" the Luapula to seek work as voluntary laborers in the mines of Katanga.[52] In 1910 Averay Jones, the native commissioner for Fort Rosebery, commented on the futility of stopping the crossings. He wrote,

> Though the natives have been moved away from the precincts of Luapula River and have no canoes, there is no doubt that a good number cross every year and [it] is a matter of great difficulty to prevent this. There is a great incentive for natives to cross. They have relations living on the Congo side right on the banks of the rivers who, they see are not succumbing to sleeping sickness and who are ready at any time to bring a canoe across to fetch their friends and relatives.[53]

Although there were no new cases reported, the regulations continued to be strictly enforced. More and more people crossed into the Congo to settle or to seek wage employment. Each year, the native commissioner sent despondent reports on how futile it was to try to stop these migrations. In 1913 the native commissioner of Fort Rosebery wrote the following report:

> 28 guards have been maintained along the sleeping sickness boundary to prevent natives from entering the area and crossing into Congo Territory. In spite of this and frequent prosecutions many natives go into the area for purposes of hunting, fishing etc., others abandon their homes altogether in this side and settle in Congo Territory. It is extremely doubtful whether these guards do any good at all and the whole operations of the regulations simply tend to drive our natives over to the Belgians, where apparently sleeping sickness regulations can be easily evaded or are not strictly imposed.

The native commissioner for Kawambwa had this to say: "The same number of sleeping sickness guards are maintained along the western border of the district, but these are powerless to prevent a large number of our natives from crossing to the Congo to obtain work." And the native commissioner for Chienge reports that "natives still continue to dribble over the border into small parties when they can evade the patrols, and until some means is found to enable us to regain these people . . . nothing can be done to stop the migration."[54]

These migrations created a lot of disenchantment among the Northern Rhodesian authorities. In this they were joined by the *Livingstone Mail*. Its editor, Leopold Moore, spared no effort in criticizing the Belgians. He complained bitterly that "all the laws we make and the money and energy which we extend this country to prevent the spread of sleeping sickness are practically valueless as we have no cooperation from the authorities from the Congo."

During the period of World War I the regulations were relaxed to allow the recruitment of porters for the war effort. After the war there was a further relaxation. Finally, the regulations were suspended in 1922, and the displaced people were allowed to return to their original villages. Even those who migrated to the Congo side returned.[55]

1911–1920

In 1911 NER and NWR amalgamated under the name Northern Rhodesia. And from 1911 the company administration began to give composite territorial figures for Africans in its annual reports. In the first year of administering the territory the secretary for native affairs estimated the population of the territory as 824,756: 376,254 for NWR and 448,502 for NER. The secretary was quick to caution that when a complete census of all districts have been taken, the population "will be found to exceed 900,000." He further added, "A complete census is very necessary for successful administration not only for the purposes of tax collection but it is a most useful instrument in the hands of District Officers."[56] This was to gauge the potential of the district in terms of the manpower available for recruitment by recruiting agencies, farmers, traders, missionaries, prospectors, and the administration itself.

In 1913 the population of Northern Rhodesia was estimated at 822,337—22,319 less than the preceding year.[57] The decrease was attributed to the fact that the population was "revised" downward in a number of districts. Why this was done was not disclosed. In some districts the reduction was partly due to migrations and in others to diseases that ravaged the country. One of these was smallpox.

Smallpox epidemics appeared from time to time in many parts of the country and left hundreds of deaths in its train, while thousands were left behind.[58] In 1902 almost all the districts of NER reported the presence of a severe smallpox epidemic in which thousands lost their lives.[59] In 1913 the disease again reached epidemic proportions.[60] Many of those who contracted the disease were segregated and quarantined in camps built outside or far away from the village to avoid the spread of the disease. Here they were attended to by those who had contracted the disease earlier and had acquired some immunity.[61] But even with these precautions, smallpox was "responsible for a large number of deaths" in many districts. In Kawambwa alone, 1,700 deaths were reported; in Chienge 1,674 died.[62] Hundreds of deaths went unreported: "People died like flies," recalls one informant.[63] The administration spent large sums on vaccinations to contain the disease. For example, the native commissioner for Mporokoso spent £66 3s. 5 1/2d. in six months.[64] The effect of the disease in the affected parts was best summed by Dr. MacFarlane, a missionary doctor at Mporkoso, who reported that "the smallpox epidemic put a stop to every branch of our work for a period of nearly three months. . . . Our school was closed for a long time and excepting for a service in the open air, the ordinary services and meetings were abandoned."[65] In such a situation no proper census could be taken, and the figures given were very rough estimates.

In late 1914 World War I broke out in Europe. It was quickly extended to the African empires. As Northern Rhodesia shared a common border with German East Africa, thousands of able-bodied men were recruited as soldiers. Others were recruited for "carrier work." According to Kenneth Bradley, "probably every able-bodied man in the country was away from his village on carrier work for 6 months at one time or another and most more than once."[66] The services of the carriers and soldiers were in R. W. Langham's words "beyond praise and it must be remembered that without their assistance, the campaign against the Germans in Tanganyika could not have been possibly carried on."[67] Those who remained at home were encouraged to grow more food to produce enough surplus to sell to the administration, which needed as much food as it could get to feed the soldiers at the front.[68]

The conditions under which the African soldiers and carriers served were appalling. Sanitary conditions were inadequate, if not simply absent. As a result, thousands of people contracted dysentery and diarrhea, from which a large percentage died.[69] Those who survived dodged rerecruitment by either migrating to employment centers or dodging the tax collector by passing for dead.[70]

Another result of the war was famine, which affected several parts of NER from 1917. Due to heavy demands by the administration, too much food was extracted from the people, causing food shortages in the villages. Many survived on roots and wild fruits. By the time the war ended, food production was very, very low.[71] To avert further deterioration, the administration ordered hoes to be distributed for a very small fee. Cultivation of large gardens was encouraged in order to increase food production. These efforts were, however, thwarted by the appearance of a drought in the 1918/1919 and 1919/1920 rainy seasons. Many people, especially in the eastern side of Fort Rosebery District, lost their lives.[72] All these factors affected the collection of reliable statistics.

Influenza

Another consequence of the war was the appearance of Spanish influenza. Its virulence varied from district to district. The hardest hit appears to have been Kawambwa, where eleven thousand are reported to have died. Forty-seven died in Chienge.[73] Fort Rosebery reported "comparatively few" deaths.[74] Mortality in Mporokoso District Mission of the London Missionary Society reported that "nothing like it has been known in the history of the country."[75] Many people left the villages to try and escape the epidemic. In the process hundreds died in the bush—some from the disease, others from hunger and wild animals.[76] There is no doubt that the epidemic did affect the collection of census statistics in the affected areas.

1920–1930

In 1920, following the recession that appeared after the war, the Northern Administration increased hut tax from five to ten shillings per taxpayer.[77] As employment was still scarce, more and more taxpayers left the country to seek employment opportunities in the employment centers of Katanga, Southern Rhodesia, and South Africa.

Before the war the flow of migrants from NWR was very thin, as many were able to meet their tax and other obligations from the sale of cattle. In 1914 and 1915 the industry was hit by two diseases—first anthrax and later pleuropneumonia—introduced from Angola. The two wiped out the cattle trade, forcing more and more people to offer themselves for recruitment with Witwatersrand Native Labour Association (WNLA). Many became the "lost ones" and never returned.[78]

Around 1925 the Copperbelt was developed. By 1930 over twenty-two thousand men were working in the mines at Luanshya, Nkana, Chingola, and Mufulira. Within the rural areas, there was great population movement, which affected the census. For example, in 1920 the fishing industry developed in the Bangweulu and Mweru fisheries.[79] In 1922 the sleeping sickness regulations were removed, allowing people displaced in 1910 to return to their former villages along the banks of the Lower Luapula and Kalungwishi Rivers. Many of these became absorbed in the fishing industry, supplying dry and fresh fish to the Katanga mines.[80] The prosperity generated by this industry attracted migrants from the neighboring areas.[81] In many cases whole villages migrated, depopulating the plateau areas.[82]

CONCLUSION

We have established that the method of collecting population statistics during the period 1900–1930 was very crude, largely based on unverifiable estimates. This fact was acknowledged by the secretary of native affairs in 1926, who prefaced his report with the following remark:

> The figures given are obtained from a census taken by Native Commissioners in the course of their journeys among the villages in the sub-districts and from reports of births, deaths, and removals. Where it has been impossible to visit all villages in any given sub-district in the course of the year the factor obtained from those which have been visited is applied to the remainder and a fairly accurate result for the whole sub-district is thus arrived at.[83]

In 1920 he had this to say:

> The Native population of the Territory is estimated on the basis of the ratio of increase (or decrease) over the past five years. . . . This system of estimating the population is an innovation, and cannot be used indefinitely, as it cannot reasonably be applied to those districts that attract immigrants from adjoining Territories. It is often impossible for a District Officer to carry out a complete check of the population throughout his district during the year, but in most districts it is possible to visit about two-thirds of the villages. It would therefore seem better to base the estimate of population on the results actually obtained in the villages visited.[84]

In reports that followed, he was more detailed. In 1930 he reported that

> it has not been possible for District Officers to visit more than an average of 60 per cent of the villages in the territory. In compiling statistics, District Commissioners have used new figures in respect of villages visited, but have usually repeated 1929 figures in respect of villages unvisited. The more correct method would have been to estimate an increase in unvisited areas proportionate to that found exactly in visited areas.[85]

Even this was completely unsatisfactory. In one district, for example, the calculation was based on each hut's containing 2.5 persons, in another 2.34 persons, and in another as low as 1.33 persons per adult female. In another method used, the estimated figures were arrived at "by taking twenty per thousand as the average increase in child population and allowing for an adult death rate of fifteen per thousand and a small increase due to immigration."[86] In 1934 the secretary of native affairs openly admitted that the methods of obtaining statistics varied "considerably." Statistics were obtained or calculated based on "an actual count at one or two villages."[87] In other words, the administration did not employ a systematic way of collecting and verifying the population statistics in the country. During much of colonial rule no accurate figures were given. Statistics based on the count in one or two villages and applied to the whole district were most unsatisfactory. In the first place, the size of the village varied depending on social relations, availability of resources, and the status of the village (chief's capital, important ritual center, or village close to an exploitable resource). Similarly, the population of each village varied from year to year due to migrations, immigration, epidemics, famine, drought and presence or absence of a viable economic activity. Application of this method produced unreliable statistics.

Thus, although annual population statistics were compiled for the Africans of Northern Rhodesia, these were in no way accurate. They were at best estimated figures intended to give a very rough idea of the population of each district. In a report for 1927, the secretary of native affairs warned that "the totals given are not of course precisely accurate but having been based upon the same system for a number of years, it is contended that they furnish a reasonable approximation of the rate of increase or decrease of the population and the relative proportions of classes into which the people are divided for statistical purposes."[88] Nobody cared whether the approximation was accurate or not, as long as it served administrative purposes.

NOTES

1. George Kay, *A Population Map of the Luapula-Bangweulu Region of Northern Rhodesia with Notes on the Population*, Rhodes-Livingstone Communication, no. 26 (Manchester, 1962), i.

2. George Kay, *A Social Geography of Zambia* (London, 1967), 26; Frank Lorimer, *Demographic Information on Tropical Africa* (Boston, 1961), 167.

3. R. R. Kuczynski, *Demographic Survey of the British Colonial Empire*, vol. 2 (Oxford, 1949), 402–403.

4. *Reports on Censuses of Population and Employees in Northern Rhodesia, 1921, 1931, 1946, 1951.* Before the 1963 census the federal government published two publications on population census. These were *Census Population, 1956* (Salisbury, 1960) and *Reports on Northern Rhodesia African Demographic Surveys May to August 1960* (Salisbury, 1961).

5. For two good studies, see Fergus MacPherson, *Anatomy of a Conquest: The British Occupation of Zambia 1884–1924* (London, 1981), 57–147; Henry S. Meebelo, *Reaction to Colonialism: A Prelude to the Politics of Independence in Northern Rhodesia 1893–1939* (Lusaka, 1971).

6. British South Africa Company (BSAC), *Reports on the Administration of Rhodesia 1898–1900*, p. 61.

7. C. Gouldsbury and H. Sheane, *The Great Plateau of Northern Rhodesia* (London, 1911), 148.

8. Gouldsbury and Sheane, *Great Plateau*, 149; MacPherson, *Anatomy*, 111.

9. BSAC, *Administration of Rhodesia 1898–1900*, p. 63.

10. Ibid.

11. National Archives of Zambia (NAZ) KDF/3/1, vol. 1, s.v. "Fort Rosebery."

12. BSAC, *Administration of Rhodesia 1898–1900*, p. 63.

13. BSAC, *Directors' Reports and Accounts, 31 March 1899 and 31 March 1900*, p. 38.

14. BSAC, *Reports on the Administration of Rhodesia 1900–1902*, p. 433. Codrington added, "This figure may be taken as being approximately correct, but probable that several groups of villages have not been enumerated." See also H. Duff's comment on these figures (*Nyasaland Under the Foreign Office* [New York, 1903], 393).

15. BSAC, *Directors' Reports and Accounts 1902–3*, pp. 9, 11; "Careful census returns are being made from every Native Division and the following figures may be taken to represent very approximately the number of natives in the country . . . Total 345,961."

16. BSAC, *Directors' Reports and Accounts 1907–8, pp. 50, 61; idem, Directors' Reports and Accounts 1910–11*, p. 56.

17. MacPherson, *Anatomy*.

18. Kuczynski, *Demographic Survey*, 415.

19. BSAC, *Administration of Rhodesia 1900–1902*, p. 63; Meebelo, *Reaction*, 102.

20. Meebelo, *Reaction*, 103; NAZ/BS1/31: Francis Bertie to secretary, BSAC London, 3 May 1904.

21. Meebelo, *Reaction* 103; NAZ/KDF/1/1, vol. 3; Minutes of *ichaka* (meeting of chiefs and headmen) held at Fort Rosebery, 20 October 1906.

22. Meebelo, *Reaction*, 103; BSAC, *Report on Native Affairs*, years ending 31 March 1909 and 1910.

23. Meebelo, *Reaction*, 103; NAZ/KDF/1/1, vol. 1.3; Minutes of *ichaka* held at Fort Rosebery, 20 October 1906.

24. Meebelo, *Reaction*, 103; BSAC, *Native Affairs*, years ending 31 March 1909 and 1910.

25. NAZ/KDH/d/1: Minutes of *ichaka* held at Kasama, 7 August 1907; NAZ/KDF3/1, vol. 1, p. 251, *Indaba* for 1906.

26. NAZ/KDH/3/1: Report on *mitanda*; NAZ/KDF3/1, vol. 1, p. 251, *Indaba* for 1906. See *Indaba* for 1914.

27. Interview with Pink Chola, Kulwesa, Mwense District, 9 May, 1975; *A Manual of Belgian Congo*, Compilation of Naval Intelligence Division Geographical Section (London, 1920), 175.

28. *Livingstone Mail*, 27 July 1912.

29. J. M. Moubray, *In South Central Africa* (London, 1912), 129.

30. E. D. Morel, *King Leopold's Rule in Africa* (London, 1904), 210–213; idem, *Red Rubber* (London, 1907), 45; Raymond Buell, *The Native Problem of Africa*, vol. 2 (London, 1965), 496.

31. George Martelli, *From Leopold to Lumumba* (London, 1966), 161–162; Mwelwa Musambachime, "Protest Migrations in Mweru-Luapula 1900–1920," *African Studies Review* 47 (1988), 19–34.

32. The native commissioner for Fort Rosebery had this to say: "Large numbers of natives have left this District and gone across the Luapula to Belgian Territory. The Natives have not done this on account of any grievance against the administration, they simply returned to their own country from which they fled when the Belgian regime was not as human as at present" (NAZ/KDF/3/1, vol. 1, p. 396).

33. BSAC, *Administration of Rhodesia 1898–1900*, p. 100.

34. Tanganyika Concessions (TC) Archives, London; 137: Watson to Williams, 24 May 1910.

35. See the cases tried at Kawambwa and Kalungwishi *bomas*:

NAZ/NE/KTL/1/1; NAZ,KSG2/1/1; BSAC, *Native Affairs*, year ending 31 March 1905, p. 197.

36. Interview with Chisanga Mulenga Paulo, Mununga, 14 August 1970; MacPherson, *Anatomy*, 112–128.

37. MacPherson, *Anatomy*, 115.

38. NAZ/KSW/2/1: Minutes of *ichaka* held at Chiengi, 4 March 1918.

39. PRO/CO795/10: J. C. Moore, "Reports on the Possibilities of Developing of Cotton Industry in North East Rhodesia: Report on the Tour Undertaken in the Neighborhood of Lake Tanganyika."

40. NAZ/BS2/134: North-Western Rhodesia, General report for the year 1910.

41. BSAC, *Native Affairs*, year ending 31 March 1905, 197.

42. Chisanga; TC 139: Watson to Robert Williams and Company, 18 January 1919; TC 138/1: Watson to Williams, 10 April 1912.

43. In his report for the year ending 31 December 1929, the secretary for native affairs reported signs of a "decline in Juvenile birth rate due to the prolonged absence at work of a large proportion of the males." The lowest birthrate was recorded in Tanganyika (later Abercorn, now Mbala) District, where 44 percent of the taxable males were away.

District	Birthrate/1,000
NER	
Tanganyika	48
Mweru-Luapula	53
Awemba	48
East Luangwa	81
NWR	
Kafue	67
Barotse	60
Luangwa	72
Kasempa	97
Batoka	85

See Northern Rhodesia, *Native Affairs*, year ending 31 December 1929, pp. 7–9.

44. NAZ/KSG/2/1. See the cases brought to the Kawambwa magistrate's court.

45. Musambachime, "Protest," 7–8; William Lammond, "Luapula Valley," *Northern Rhodesia Journal* 2, no. 5 (1952), 53; Allan Kinghorn and Eustace Montgomery, "Report on the Sleeping Sickness Expedition to the Zambezi for the years 1907 to 1908," *Annals of Tropical Medicine and Parasitology* 12 (1908/1909), 85; NAZ/KDF/3/1, vol. 2, 87: Oral interviews.

46. NAZ/BS1/65: Administrator, "Report on Sleeping Sickness"; J. Cameron Scott, "Deserted Villages," *Chronicles of the London Missionary Society (CLMS)*, January 1911, 17–19.

47. Interview with Maxim Nkomba, Kashiba, 17 August 1979.

48. NAZ/KDF/3/1, vol. 1; NAZ/ZA7/1/1/8; Annual Report for the year ending 31 March 1913.

49. J. Cameron Scott, "Flight from the Fly," *CMLS* 896 (1910), 17.

50. NAZ/ZA7/1/1/8; Annual Report for 1913.

51. NAZ/BS1/65: W. H. T. Storrs, Fort Rosebery to principal medical officer, Fort Jameson, 10 April 1909.

52. TC Union Minière: A. Pearson to Halewyck, 29 March 1910; A. Pearson to acting administrator, NWR, 4 April 1910.

53. NAZ/BS1/65: Averay Jones to administrator, 10 August 1910.

54. NAZ/ZA7/3/1: Quarterly reports 1913 for Fort Rosebery, Kawambwa, and Chienge.

55. Interviews with Muyembe Besa, Kilwa Island, 13 May 1975.

56. NAZ/BS3/143: *Annual Report upon Native Affairs (ARUNA)*, year ending 31 March 1912.

57. NAZ/BS3/143: *ARUNA*, year ending 31 March 1914.

58. Andrew Roberts, *A History of Zambia* (London, 1981), 171; Dugald Campbell, *In the Heart of Bantuland* (London, 1922), 242; Gouldsbury and Sheane, *Great Plateau*, 295; Daniel Crawford, *Thinking Black* (London, 1912), 441.

59. BSAC, *Administration of Rhodesia 1900–1902*, 406–411, 420–427.

60. ACWM/LMS/CA/box 2, no. 482: Annual report for Mbereshi for 1913; Annual report for Mporokoso; NAZ/ZA7/1/1/8: Annual report for Kawambwa for the year ending 31 March 1914; NAZ/ZA7/3/1: Quarterly report for Chienge for quarter ending 31 December 1913.

61. Shingwe.

62. NAZ/ZA1/1/1/8: Annual report for Kawambwa; Annual report of Chienge; ACWM/LMS/CA/box 2, no. 482: Annual report for Mbereshi and Mporokoso for 1913.

63. Besa.

64. NAZ/ZA1/1/1/8: Annual report for Kawambwa.

65. ACWM/LM/CA/box 2, no. 482: Annual report for Mporokoso for 1913.

66. Kenneth Bradley, "Company Days: The Rule of the British South African Company in Northern Rhodesia," *Northern Rhodesia Journal (NRJ)* 5 (1962), 446.

67. R. W. Langham, "Memories of the 1914–1918 Campaign with Northern Rhodesia Forces," pt. 1, *NRJ* 2, no. 1 (1953), 59–60.

68. Chisanga

69. Ibid.

70. Many were caught and prosecuted. See court cases in NAZ/KSG/2/1/1.

71. NAZ/1/3/8: Annual report, year ending 31 March 1917; Brian Garvey, "The Development of the White Fathers' Mission Among the Bemba-Speaking People 1891–1964" (Ph.D. diss., London, 1979).

72. NAZ/ZA7/1/4/8: Annual report for Mweru-Luapula, year ending 31 March 1920. Reports stated that crops were "poor and there was a great scarcity of food" and that "the Natives survived on roots and wild fruit for food."

73. NAZ/ZA7/4/8: Annual reports for Kawambwa and Chienge, year ending 31 March 1920.

74. NAZ/ZA7/4/8: Annual report for Fort Rosebery, year ending 31 March 1920.

75. ACWM/LMS/CA/box 3, no. 488: decennial report 1910–1920.

76. Besa; Chisanga.

77. NAZ/ZA1/5/6: Annual report for Mweru-Luapula, year ending 31 March 1921; BSAC, *Directors' Reports and Accounts for the year ending 31 March 1916*, 1; NAZ/BS3/420: Inspector of Rhodesia Native Labour in Katanga, report for the year ending 31 March 1915, Government Notice no. 21, 4 April 1914.

78. Roberts, *A History*, 186.

79. See my "Development and Growth of the Fishing Industry in Mweru-Luapula 1920–1964" (Ph.D. diss., University of Wisconsin, 1981).

80. Ibid., 131–134.

81. Ibid., 150–152, 186–188.

82. Ibid., 189–192.

83. *Report upon Native Affairs for 1926*, 33.

84. *Report upon Native Affairs for 1928*, 5.

85. *Report upon Native Affairs for 1930*, 10.

86. *Report upon Native Affairs for 1932*, 14; *Report upon Native Affairs for 1933*, 16.

87. *Report Upon Native Affairs for 1934*, 12.

88. Ibid.

7

Recollections of the Annual Population Count in Late Colonial Zambia

JEFFREY C. STONE

This is an appropriate place to record my recollections (without recourse to any official records and entirely from memory) of how population counts were regularly conducted in one small part of central Africa. In case the practices that I shall describe were peculiar to a particular time and place, I will preface them by stating that I held the posts of cadet, district officer, district commissioner, and district secretary from 1959 to 1964, in Choma, Kalomo, and Gwembe Districts in Northern Rhodesia and was stationed at Choma, Sinazongwe, Kalomo, Lusitu, Gwembe, and Siavonga.

The population count took place during the annual round of village-to-village touring. The intention was that every chief's area should be toured by one of the district's administrative officers every year. During the course of a tour (which in my experience lasted from one to three weeks) every village was visited either on foot or by bicycle. Vehicles (usually a five-ton truck) were only used to transport the party between the *boma* and the points of origin and completion of the tour. Vehicles were not used to visit villages. The touring officer lived under canvas and removed camp every two or three days, depending on the density of villages. The villagers did not come to the camp, except for occasional individual cases; the touring officer went to the villages, thereby fulfilling his primary role of observing what was happening in the area and making himself available to the populace. He would observe the state of the crops and village hygiene and would interest himself in any local economic activity. He would hear complaints ranging from crop damage by wildlife to the need for a local dispensary or relations with a nearby Crown Land farmer. He would make a particular point of visiting schools, dispensaries, or any other development, where he would be asked to sign the visitors book. Tours to meet special needs were in addition to the annual round of village-to-village touring. For example, I recall a walking tour along the Ngwezi River to assess the problem of erosion.

The touring officer would normally be accompanied throughout the tour by the chief, his court assessors, and court clerk, plus *kapasus*, district messengers, carriers proportional in number to the duration of the tour in accordance with "standing orders," and a personal servant. All grades of permanent staff received per diem touring allowances plus a monthly cycle allowance. A district messenger would be sent out in advance to ensure that the party had gathered by the appointed day, while *kapasus* would notify village headmen of the days of their particular visits. A touring officer might occasionally visit the same chief's area in successive years. Sometimes district officers were detailed to concern themselves with particular chiefs' areas and handled all matters concerned with those areas, so that they became well acquainted with them, but in other cases the district commissioner took first choice and allocated tours to his staff. The conduct and purpose of village-to-village touring can be seen in the tour reports submitted on conclusion of every tour, many of which are extant in the national archives of Zambia.

The population count was accomplished utilizing tax registers, which were maintained in duplicate. The court clerk retained one set and the *boma* retained the other. However, it should be stressed that the purpose of the tour was not to collect tax, although the convenience of the presence of the court clerk in the village meant that tax was often paid at that time. However, the court clerk made his own independent tours for purposes of tax collection and the issue of licenses. Identity certificates (as well as tax exemption certificates at no cost) were issued on tour by the touring officer, so that he did return to the *boma* with a very small amount of revenue to account for.

The population count was made soon after arrival in each village. The villagers would normally be gathered with chairs and tables set out for the visitors. After the formal greetings, the touring officer would read out each name in turn from his register. If the person concerned was present, he would then be asked how many wives he had and the number and sex of their children. If the person concerned was absent, the headman would say where he believed him to be and the size of his family, a potential source of error if he had not visited his village recently. The list of names included men who were exempt from tax. Young men who acquired an identification certificate for the first time then became new entries for that village in both sets of tax registers, and their identification certificate number was entered in the *boma* register. "Individual dwellers" under native authority legislation were nominally registered under a proximate village. It should be appreciated that tax register sheets were designed to remain in use for a number of years, as preparing new sets was a time-consuming task for a clerk and another potential source of errors that would become apparent at the next tour. The touring officer thus had before him the figures recorded by the officer touring in the previous year and would therefore be inclined to query a number that was greatly different. The fact that next year another touring officer would be comparing his figures with yours implied that modest amount of care went into the compilation, although I recall checking my own figures in successive tours of the area of Chief Chikanta.

The reading of the register constituted something of a ritual, with no immediate purpose for the touring officer. It was a ritual during which contact was made with the assembled company. It was normally conducted in the vernacular, because the questions were so oft repeated that they quickly became known even to a touring officer whose linguistic proficiency was limited or who had a working knowledge only of some other local language, obtained in service elsewhere in the territory. The questions broke the ice, and afterwards matters could more eaily be raised that were of concern at that time or in that area. Also, it was proper to relax a little after reading the register to afford the opportunity for the villagers to raise questions with the touring officer or the chiefly retinue.

At the completion of each tour the figures were added up and submitted on a printed form along with the tour report. The year's touring figures were combined in the district annual report submitted to the provincial commissioner. I have no recollection of any customary practice in the case of an area that for some reason had not been toured, although I do recall that low touring returns would lead to a sharp inquiry from the provincial commissioner's office, so that there was official pressure to maintain the annual round, which was thought to be very much at the heart of the district officer's duties. Touring took place throughout the year, although the dry season was obviously favored. Hence, the annual total for the district was compiled over the year; and the totals did not represent a particular day. Also, tours to a particular chief's areas did not necessarily take place at the same time of the year, so that the duration between population counts in particular areas may vary by six to eighteen months.

A note on the inaccuracies inherent in this crude process of data collection has been compiled by a contemporary observer (G. Kay, in Rhodes-Livingstone Communication 26, 1962, 2–5). I would concur with his suggestion that we were "not primarily concerned with the accurate counting of heads" if by that he means that the population count was a by-product of the tour and not its primary purpose. Sometimes officers remained on tour for an extra day at the final camp, with official encouragement, to draft the tour report. The arithmetic would also be done at the same time. It was a simple task that took little time to complete. I can think of no reason why returns should not normally have been as accurate as the mode of data collection permitted. It would be interesting to know whether any tax registers are extant. If so, they could possibly be analyzed to explore further the reasons for the errors that were revealed by the first full census of the African population in 1963.

8

Demographic Data Resources for Colonial Malawi

JUSTICE R. NGOLEKA MLIA

The importance of adequate and reliable demographic data as a tool for efficient administration and planning can hardly be overemphasized. In Malawi since independence the government has devoted a significant proportion of its meager resources to the collection of such data. It conducted its first comprehensive census in 1966, followed by another in 1977, and a third census in 1987, which covered not only population but also housing.[1] Between 1970 and 1972 the government also conducted a major demographic sample survey aimed at providing a more accurate figure on the rate of population growth; and the information collected included general population characteristics, births, deaths, and migration.[2] These postindependence censuses and surveys have yielded data that has greatly improved our knowledge of the population situation in Malawi. However, the recent data is by itself inadequate unless seen as an extension of data resources available from the colonial period.

During the seventy-three years of British colonial rule between 1891 and 1964, for most of which period the country was known by the name Nyasaland, the colonial administration indulged, on a regular basis, in the "ritual" of censustaking. Population data also resulted from other administrative exercises. However, in common with the experience in most parts of Africa, the data collected by the colonial administration generally suffered from a variety of serious weaknesses. Some of the data is of such dubious validity that it is hazardous to draw any definite conclusions about past population trends from it. But this data is all that we have for the preindependence period (little is known about the *precolonial* population situation except in a vague, general, and speculative way); and notwithstanding its numerous deficiencies, we have to accept it as at least providing a rough indicator of past population changes and characteristics. The recent population censuses give us the advantage of hindsight, and we can examine and assess this data in the light of better-known, if not perfectly understood, recent demographic trends.

I shall describe the range of demographic data available from Malawi's colonial past; highlight its limitations; and show, in the light of recently available demographic material, its relative usefulness. This task has been partly accomplished by R. R. Kuczynski and G. Coleman, who have critically examined from different perspectives the census data up to 1945 and 1966, respectively.[3] But since 1966 new demographic data has become available that might help cast some further light on the demographic situation during the colonial period.

SOURCES OF POPULATION DATA

Sources of primary demographic data for the colonial period are scanty and generally associated with the colonial administration's censustaking activities. The censuses are unquestionably the most valuable and readily accessible source of demographic data, and my discussion will justifiably focus on this source.

The History of Censustaking

Prior to World War II the history of censustaking in Malawi closely followed the pattern common in many other British dependencies in Africa.[4] The first count of population was in 1891, as soon as a British protectorate was declared over the country. This count was, however, confined to Europeans and Asians only and was primarily intended to serve as a basis for a roster of certificates of claim to land by the non-African population.[5] Africans were included in a population count (more correctly, estimate) for the first time in 1901, after which there were counts decennially in 1911 and 1921.[6] After 1921 the administration flirted with the idea of conducting censuses quinquennially (as was happening in what is now Zimbabwe)[7] and did have population counts in 1926 and 1931.[8] However, with the financial difficulties of the depression years, it was decided to return to decennial censuses; and then because of the war, the next census, instead of being held in 1941, was postponed to 1945. The next census after that was conducted in 1956 by the Central Statistical Office of the now defunct Federation of Rhodesia and Nyasaland, of which Malawi was a constituent part between 1953 and 1961.[9] This was the last official census before Malawi became fully independent, although a less-known, and probably less-formal, census appears to have been conducted by the Ministry of Education and Social Development in 1963,[10] when Malawi was already self-governing but still under British rule. Reference has already been made to the postindependence censuses.

It is debatable whether all the population counts conducted between 1891 and 1956 are really worthy of the name *censuses*. The United Nations has defined a census as "the total process of collecting, compiling and publishing demographic, economic and social data pertaining, at a specified time or times, to all persons in a country or delimited territory."[11] Two of the essential characteristics of a census are universality and personal enumeration: it should include every person in the area without omission or duplication, and the data should be recorded separately for each individual.[12] As will soon be obvious, not all the above-mentioned counts were truly censuses, although I shall continue refer to them thus.

The Methodology of Censuses

The methodology used in the censuses varied, thus rendering the comparison of data between censuses difficult. The first notable difference in methodology is that while the pre–World War II censuses were basically de jure, nearly all subsequent censuses—including those for the postindependence period—have been conducted on a de facto basis. The 1963 census, being de jure, is the only misfit.

Little is known about the methods used in the pre-1911 censuses apart from the fact that in the 1901 census administrative officers were asked to establish the number of Africans liable to pay hut tax. How the tax returns were converted into estimates of total population is not clear. The 1911 census was similarly based on hut tax returns. On this occasion an estimate of the total population of each district was arrived at by multiplying the number of registered hut tax payers by a constant of 2.8 persons. This figure, used as a conversion factor from taxpayers to total population, was derived from a survey of selected villages in which all inhabitants were actually counted, which revealed that there were, on average, 2.8 persons per hut. An allowance had to be made for aged or infirm persons or persons otherwise exempted from the payment of hut tax. The breakdown of the population by gender was similarly arrived at by an estimate based on persons actually counted in the selected villages. How these "sample" villages were selected is not particularly clear, but it is apparent that established statistical principles were not necessarily followed.

Further methodological improvements were introduced in 1921. For the first time, instead of using tax returns as a basis for estimating population, the census of the African population was conducted by dividing each of districts into smaller areal units, each of which was assigned an *enumerator*, who visited each village within his enumeration area and counted all persons permanently domiciled in the village, whether present or away at the time. A separate form was used for each village; and the completed forms were checked by administrative officers at the district level, who then submitted them to the superintendent of census at census headquarters for further checking and compilation into a country report. The actual enumeration lasted two to three weeks during the month of April.

The methods introduced in 1921 were closely followed in 1926 and 1931, thus facilitating, within limits, the comparison of data for these three censuses. The similarity in the methods used in the three censuses was stressed (with a sense of satisfaction and pride) in the 1931 census report, which noted that not only were the forms used, the questions asked, and the season at which the censuses were taken the same, but even the enumerators employed were in many cases the same.

The census methods of 1945 were essentially the same as those of the previous three censuses except that it was a de facto census. As in the previous censuses, enumerators actually visited villages within enumeration areas assigned to them; and information was recorded on the basis of villages, as opposed to individuals. Although the enumeration was only of those physically living within the village at the time of the census, for each village an estimate of absentees who were outside the country was obtained by asking the village headman.

The 1956 census was a census in the true sense of the word only with respect to non-Africans and Africans working for them in urban areas, government stations, estates, and mission centers. This category of the population was actually enumerated, the working Africans being enumerated through their non-African employers. But the rural non-wage-earning majority of Africans were merely estimated based on a survey of adult men, reminiscent of the pre-1921 censuses. Like the 1945 census, it was conducted on a de facto principle.

Detailed information is not readily available on the 1963 "census." This census does not seem to have been conducted under the provisions of any census ordinance (as most of the earlier censuses had been), and we may safely assume that for the African population there was no actual enumeration.

In all the colonial censuses the non-African population, composed mainly of Europeans and Asians, was enumerated through the self-survey method, with questionnaires being sent to respondents by mail or delivered by hand. The questionnaires were channeled through district administrative officers, who (it was assumed) knew the whereabouts of all non-Africans in their areas. Besides furnishing information for themselves, the Europeans and Asians, as employers, were also expected to provide information regarding their African workers.

We may note in passing that in the postindependence censuses all races have been treated in a similar manner in terms of the methods used in collecting the data and analyzing it. These censuses have been based on modern census techniques, all data being recorded by trained enumerators and with a clear distinction made between de facto and de jure population.

The Content of Censuses

Just as the methods of the censuses used have changed over time, so have the contents. Given the nature of the methods used, there was an obvious limitation to the kind of demographic characteristics of the African population that could be reported prior to the 1921 census. In the 1911 census report an attempt was made to break down the population by sex and religion at the district level and by occupation and level of educational attainment at the countrywide level, but the figures cannot be anything more than crude estimates (if not wild guesses). For Europeans and Asians one can have more faith in the figures, since they were based on actual counts (though it is worth remembering that the smaller the numbers involved, the greater the implications of any inaccuracies in the data). For these racial groups the population is broken down even at the district level by sex, age, nationality, occupation, and religion.

The forms used in the 1921, 1926, and 1931 censuses allowed enumerators to record, for each village, children under five by sex, children from five to marriageable age by sex, adults by sex and marital status, religious beliefs by three major categories (Christian, Muslim, and pagan), ethnic affiliation, literacy (ability to read, write, and speak English), and infirmity (e.g., blindness or deafness). By 1931 nearly all this information was being recorded in the census reports by districts. Also reported by districts was information on Africans residing on private estates. Information on the occupations of Africans, however, continued to be reported only at the areal level of the country as a whole because, according to the 1931 census report, it was "not yet practicable to compile accurate statistics of industries and occupations of the native population." Starting in 1926, there was also an attempt to report by district the number of Africans working in Zimbabwe; but the figures were incomplete. Military statistics were featured in all the 1921, 1926, and 1931 censuses, as in the earlier censuses.

For non-Africans these three censuses continued to afford opportunities for a fairly detailed breakdown of the population by various characteristics. One interesting new development that occurred in 1931 was the reporting of the industries (not only the occupations) in which the non-Africans were engaged; and even at this early state as many as fourteen major industrial sectors and seventy-four subsectors were differentiated. Another interesting innovation introduced in 1931 was the reporting, separately, of the European and Asian population residing in the emerging urban centers of Blantyre, Limbe (now part of Blantyre), and Zomba. At this time no figures (except an estimate for Zomba) were given of the African urban population, on the grounds that only domestic servants resided in the townships.

One major (albeit not fully successful) improvement introduced in 1945 for the African population was the attempt to classify children under one year of age separately from those under five years. The five-years-to-marriageable-age group was also defined more precisely by stating an exact upper age of eighteen years, which also happened to be the taxable age. In this census infirmity was restricted to blindness. For the first time there was a more serious attempt to estimate the African population living in urban areas.

Also, although it was a de facto census, the information collected on labor migrants temporarily absent from the country is more complete than that of earlier censuses.

Although the 1956 and 1963 "censuses" may have provided useful district-by-district population estimates, their value as a source of other demographic data is severely limited. As noted by Bruce Fetter,[13] the district population estimates for 1956 are not even broken down by gender.

In contrast, the 1966 and 1977 censuses have yielded much more detailed information than any of the colonial censuses. Perhaps their biggest asset is that besides containing most of the information found in the earlier censuses, they feature finer breakdown of the population by age, generally based on five-year age groups. On the whole, they provide a better data base for studying past fertility and mortality patterns, particularly the 1977 census. The 1977 census may also be considered an appropriate precursor to the 1987 population and housing census insofar as it covered a number of nondemographic characteristics, such as number of dwellings, sources of drinking water, and radio ownership. But while being more comprehensive in certain areas, researchers interested in ethnic or religious affiliation may find the 1966 and 1972 censuses, especially the latter, disappointing, because these attributes are either not covered at all or are only indirectly covered. As for labor migration to neighboring countries, this was covered only in 1966.

Reliability of the Census Data

When we compare colonial and postcolonial census data, it is clearly evident that the biggest limitation with the former is not so much its content as its reliability. The reliability of any census data is, of course, a matter of degree. As aptly emphasized by E. van de Walle,[14] all demographic data are necessarily influenced by the psychological and administrative processes involved in collection and organization and are therefore subject to various kinds of systematic errors—some almost universal, others limited to specific cultural or administrative conditions. From the description of the methods used it should be evident that most of the colonial censuses in Malawi are fraught with inaccuracies. But apart from the methodological limitations, the cultural setting makes certain inaccuracies inevitable even in modern censuses. For instance, in Malawi (as in most parts of Africa) many people do not know—and probably are not really eager to know—their exact age; hence, census data on age is generally unreliable.

The authors of the 1921, 1926, and 1931 census reports made elaborate attempts to prove the completeness and accuracy of the census returns. But, Kuczynski observed, although these censuses were comparable to those of some other British dependencies, their accuracy with respect not only to age but even to the actual size of the population, marital status, and migration is dubious. The 1945 census was a significant improvement on these earlier censuses; but, regrettably, the 1956 census was a step backward, leading R. W. Stephens to observe in 1959 that Malawi was among the British African dependencies with the least reliable census data at the time.[15] These statements, of course, relate more to the African population than to the European population.

The postindependence censuses represent a big improvement on the colonial censuses. The more recent censuses have been conducted at a time when the political and socioeconomic climate has significantly changed, with people less suspicious of censuses and more parts of the country more readily accessible. With foreign financial and technical assistance, more resources and better expertise have also been available for these three censuses than for the earlier ones. Not allowing for inflation, the 1977 census, for instance, cost in cash terms over seven hundred times more per enumerated person than the 1931 census; and even allowing for inflation, the difference must be substantial. Improved circumstances do not, of course, necessarily guarantee perfect data; but there is little doubt that the recent censuses have yielded appreciably more reliable data than those of the colonial era. In the 1966 census a postenumeration survey estimated a margin of error in the census of less than 5 percent at a 95 percent confidence level.

Other Sources of Data

Although unquestionably the most valuable source, the censuses are not the sole source of demographic data. Some basic population figures may be obtained from such documents as the Nyasaland bluebooks, native welfare reports, annual colonial reports, reports of the various government departments (Medical Department, Education and Labour Department), and reports of specially appointed committees (the Committee Appointed To Enquire into Migrant Labour, the Post-War Development Committee). However, such figures are often either derived directly from the census reports or are estimates or projections based on earlier censuses or current tax returns; and their reliability is no better than their sources. If anything, as J. G. Pike and G. T. Rimmington and Kuczynski have observed,[16] they have tended to underestimate the total population. Their value is further limited by the fact that such figures are commonly not broken down by gender, age, or any other important demographic characteristic. For these reasons my analysis will be primarily based on census data, especially for the years 1921–1945.

Like many other countries in Africa, the vital registration system in Malawi does not provide an adequate data base for a nationwide demographic analysis. The registration of births and deaths is compulsory only to people of non-African origin, who constituted less than one-quarter of a percent of the total population in 1977. For Europeans a vital registration system was instituted under the 1904 Births and Deaths Registration Ordinance, which was applied to Asians soon afterwards (1905 for deaths, 1912 for births). For the African majority it appears that the colonial administration was contemplating introducing a scheme in the late 1940s; but it does not seem to have succeeded, and in any case, as noted by J. Clyde Mitchell,[17] the forms for registration did not include all the information necessary for the calculation of gross and net reproduction rates.

If Malawi did not have a viable vital registration system during the colonial days, neither did it have good sample demographic surveys comparable to those conducted in nearby Zimbabwe and Zambia in the late 1940s and early 1950s.[18] An interesting study of fertility was conducted by Mitchell between 1946 and 1947, but he was at pains to explain that "the sample is not a random one (in the statistical sense) and it is unsafe to generalize from it."[19] The Medical Department and administrative officers acting in their capacity as census officers also attempted to collect vital statistics on a sample basis in 1926 and in the 1930s; but these efforts were not particularly successful, and the information collected was of only limited value. On migration, one interesting primary study undertaken during the colonial period was that of M. Read in 1939, focusing on a number of selected villages in the present-day Central and Northern Regions.[20]

For the postindependence period the demographic data base has been significantly improved not only by the two censuses but also by the Malawi Population Change Survey of February 1970–January 1972. This major demographic sample survey provided the first reasonably reliable basis for estimating vital rates in the country.

THE COLONIAL DEMOGRAPHIC SETTING

Clearly, special care must necessarily be exercised in any attempt to interpret colonial demographic data; in particular, misplaced *concreteness* should be avoided as much as possible. But although the colonial data base has many limitations, it is by no means utterly useless; and I shall discuss the patterns or trends it suggests and wherever possible relate these to recent findings. This discussion also offers us the opportunity to explore further some specific limitations inherent in the data.

It should be mentioned at the outset that the geographical dimension of various demographic characteristics is not as fully explored as could be wished. Malawi is presently divided into three administrative regions, which are in turn divided into districts, twenty-four in all (see Map 8.1). Each district comprises several traditional authority areas, which in turn contain scores of villages. These administrative units, which have commonly been used to serve as a basis for reporting demographic data, have witnessed frequent and sometimes drastic changes in the past. The regional boundaries have been subjected to relatively few changes since their creation in 1921, but boundaries at district level and lower levels have been changed more

MAP 8.1 Malawi Population Density by Districts (based on 1966 census)

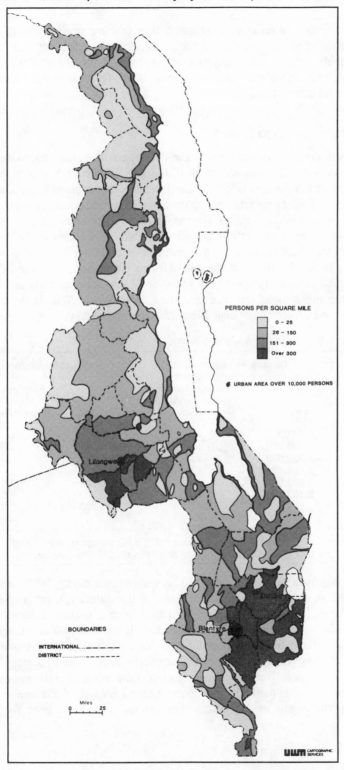

PERSONS PER SQUARE MILE

0 – 25
26 – 150
151 – 300
Over 300

URBAN AREA OVER 10,000 PERSONS

Lilongwe

Blantyre

BOUNDARIES

INTERNATIONAL
DISTRICT

Miles
0   25

UWM CARTOGRAPHIC
SERVICES

frequently and often more drastically, thus making any attempt to study population changes over time in geographical space a daunting task. In the present discussion geographical comparison will largely be confined to *regions*, with the boundary changes that have taken place over time largely (if not totally) allowed for.

Population Size and Growth

The total population ascertained at the various colonial censuses, rounded to the nearest hundred, is shown in Table 8.1. Whatever inaccuracies are inherent in the data, it is clear from the table that Malawi experienced a moderately high growth rate during the colonial period, generally in excess of 2 percent per annum except for the 1921–1926 intercensal period. The increase in population is primarily attributable to increases in the African population, which constituted an overwhelming majority; but these increases were matched by those of the non-African population. The non-African population increased from 429 to just over 15,000 between 1901 and 1956, with the most rapid increase occurring after World War II, when the population increased more than threefold in eleven years.

TABLE 8.1 Growth of Total Population, 1901–1963

	De Jure Population		De Facto Population	
Year	Population	Average Annual Intercensal Growth Rate (%)	Population	Average Annual Intercensal Growth Rate (%)
1901	737,200	—	—	—
1911	970,400	2.8	—	—
1921	1,202,000	2.2	—	—
1926	1,293,400	1.5	1,263,300	—
1931	1,603,500	4.4	1,573,500	4.5
1945	2,183,200	2.2	2,049,500	1.9
1956	—	—	2,770,200	2.5
1963	3,751,556	—	—	—

Source: Total population figures from census reports, except for 1963, which is derived from J. G. Pike, *Malawi: A Political and Economic History* (London, 1968), 22.

The growth rates in the table display marked irregularity. While ordinary changes in the vital rates could offer a possible explanation for the irregularity, they are inadequate to provide a full explanation. It seems more likely that an irregularity of such magnitude is the result of inaccuracies in the data and may be partly attributable to changes in censustaking techniques. As aptly observed by the National Statistical Office,[21] the 1926 population figure, although arrived at by methods supposedly exactly the same as used in 1921 and 1931, is particularly suspect. It seems unlikely that a period of as low a growth rate as 1.5 percent per annum could have been followed immediately by a period of a growth rate of 4.4 percent unless the population were recovering from a major disaster like famine, epidemic, or war. While, in common with other African countries, all the colonial censuses in Malawi may have underestimated the total population, the 1926 census may have done so in a gross manner, unless of course both the 1921 and 1931 censuses are to blame. Kuczynski argues that either the 1921 and 1926 censuses understated the population or the 1931 census overstated it. A closer analysis of the 1901–1945 census data (excluding that for 1926) and data for the postindependence period has led the National Statistical Office to conclude that during the colonial period as a whole the population must have grown at about 2.5 percent per annum.[22]

This growth rate is fairly close to the 2.6 percent officially accepted as the country's population growth rate in the early 1970s based on the results of the 1970–1972 population change survey. However, the unadjusted intercensal growth rates for 1945–1966 and 1966–1977 were 3.3 percent and 2.9 percent, respectively. The population, estimated at 7.06 million in 1985, is believed to be currently growing at about 3.2 percent per annum, a belief that may be justified in view of the improved medical facilities.

It should be evident from Table 8.2 that the population during the 1911–1945 period did not grow evenly among the regions. Generally speaking, the Southern Region experienced the fastest growth, while the North had the slowest. But, as in the case of the national annual growth rates (and probably for the same reasons), the regional intercensal percentage growth rates show marked instability. In this regard it may be useful to bear in mind Fetter's observation that for the earlier years the figures for the Southern Region were more reliable than those for the other regions, an observation corroborated by Kuczynski, who states that "these returns leave no doubt that the population of the Northern Province had been understated even in 1931."[23]

Despite the apparent unreliability of the regional data, the more rapid increase of population in the Southern Region during the colonial period seems confirmed by the 1966 census, which gives 1945–1966 increases of 71 percent, 96 percent, and 105 percent, for the Northern, Central, and Southern Regions, respectively. The corresponding figures for the 1966–1977 period are 30 percent, 45 percent, and 33 percent—the higher figure for the Central Region being understandable in view of the relocation of the national administrative capital there and the contemporaneous unprecedented increase in estate tobacco production.

Population Density and Distribution

With the relatively rapid increase in population, Malawi has maintained its position as one of the most densely populated countries in Africa. Using the current officially accepted land surface area of 94,280 km^2 (the area was taken to be 97,370 km^2 during the 1926 and 1931 censuses and 95,390 km^2 in

TABLE 8.2 Intercensal Population Increase by Regions 1911–1945 (%)

Region	1911–1921	1921–1926	1926–1931	1935–1945
Northern	25	1	−3	30
Central	7	6	36	21
Southern	28	15	23	33
All Regions	24	8	24	28

Source: Based on population data from census reports.

1945), the population density increased nationally from about eight to twenty-three persons per square kilometer between 1901 and 1945, reaching, if we accept the estimates of population for these years, nearly thirty in 1956 and forty in 1963. The 1966 and 1977 censuses put the population density at forty-three and fifty-nine persons per square kilometer, respectively, thus maintaining the upward trend.

Notwithstanding any inaccuracies in the data, there is little doubt that during the colonial period the population was unevenly distributed, with many parts of the Northern and Central Regions sparsely populated, while the Shire Highlands districts of Blantyre, Zomba, Chiradzulu, Thyolo, and Mulanje were the most densely populated. The distributional pattern that emerged during this period is largely maintained today, as a quick comparison among the population distribution maps of 1928 by F. Dixey, 1957 by G. Trewartha, 1965 by Pike and Rimmington (all reproduced by Fetter), N. D. McGlashan's population distribution map based on 1966 census data, and Map 8.1 will confirm.[24] Particularly conspicious in all these maps are the exceptionally high densities shown for the Chiradzulu area. This district had densities as high as 115 persons per square kilometer by 1931, a figure several times higher than the current densities of all the Northern Region districts and the majority of the Central Region districts. In 1977 Chiradzulu District had an overall density of 240, with the area of traditional authority Mpama having a density of nearly 500 persons per square kilometer. In this part of the country pressure on land resources is acute, and for a long time it has been the cause of major concern to government.

The land problem in Chiradzulu District—and indeed in the Shire Highlands as a whole—has been exacerbated by the fact that a large proportion of the land had been alienated to non-Africans (more specifically, Europeans) at the start of the colonial era. Throughout the colonial period the Shire Highlands accounted for 60 percent to 70 percent of the country's European and Asian population, with the Southern Region as a whole accounting for more than three-quarters. Reflecting its relative lack of economic opportunities (partly resulting from relative inaccessibility), the Northern Region invariably accounted for less than 5 percent of the non-

African population. The pattern is slowly changing; but so far the Central Region seems to be gaining an increasing proportion not only of the non-African population but also of the African majority. Table 8.3 shows how, till 1977, the slightly better developed Southern Region accounted for an ever-increasing percentage share of the country's population at the expense of the other regions.

TABLE 8.3 Distribution of Population by Regions, 1911–1977 (%)

Region	1911	1921	1931	1945	1966	1977
Northern	19	18	14	14	12	12
Central	40	39	39	37	37	38
Southern	41	43	47	49	51	50
All Regions	100	100	100	100	100	100

Source: Based on population figures from census reports.

Demographic Factors Affecting
Population Growth and Distribution

By the the early 1960s many African countries were beginning to have reasonably reliable statistics on vital rates, but in Malawi such statistics were still lacking. Up to 1973 the only vital rates reported in the UN population bulletins were for 1953, and they were admitted to be either "an incomplete coverage or subject to considerable irregularity of registration." With the vital statistics registration system rendered virtually useless because of the serious deficiencies in coverage and demographic sample surveys almost nonexistent, it was difficult to estimate vital rates by direct methods during the colonial period. The crude manner in which the population was broken down by age groups in the censuses equally made it difficult to estimate vital rates through indirect methods. Thus, it is difficult to isolate natural increase from immigration as factors in population growth for this period. Such vital statistics as are available for the pre–World War II period have been critically examined by Kuczynski, who concludes that they are so deficient that they cannot justifiably be used to support the prevailing views of the time in official circles regarding the contribution of natural increase to growth. According to him, if any conclusions are to be drawn from the statistics, they are that during the first three decades of colonial rule births probably did not exceed deaths; that the next two decades may have been characterized by only a modest natural increase; and that for the entire first fifty years, besides improved counting methods, net migration could well account for the bulk of the recorded increases.[25] The country is believed to have received several hundred thousands of net migrants during the period, and Coleman[26] reckons that immigration accounted for 50 percent of the increase in population between 1901 and 1911.

Interestingly, although the isolated examples of vital statistics available for the colonial period vary irregularly among areas and over short time periods, they are generally in line with the (hopefully) more reliable statistics of the postcolonial period. For both periods the crude birthrates are generally high, commonly exceeding 48 births per thousand persons. The crude deathrates and infant mortality rates are equally high, with the former averaging about 25 per thousand and the latter generally in excess of 140 per thousand. There are signs, however, that while fertility rates still remain constantly high, mortality rates may be slowly declining and that an excess of births over deaths may be accounting for an increasing proportion of the modern rapid increase in population. In 1966 and 1977 persons born outside Malawi accounted for only 7 percent and 5 percent, respectively, of the total enumerated population.[27]

Labor Migration

If the available data leave no doubt regarding the importance of immigration in the growth of the total population prior to 1945, they equally highlight the massive scale of adult male emigration to neighboring countries in search of job opportunities. The exact level of labor migration will continue to remain a matter of conjecture; but there is little doubt that the whole colonial period—and indeed the postcolonial period up to 1974, when the government banned the recruitment of labor in Malawi for South African mines—has witnessed large-scale labor migration. Based on census and other data, Coleman estimates that by about 1910 approximately 10 percent of the country's adult males were working abroad; and since about 1921 this proportion has probably been in excess of 20 percent at certain times.[28] In 1966 as many as 266 thousand Malawians, mainly adult males, were recorded as being temporarily out of the country. Regrettably, the 1977 census made no attempt to collect data pertaining to migration.

The 1966 census confirmed earlier findings that the Northern Region, although contributing a smaller proportion (28 percent in 1945) of the total labor migrants, was suffering the greatest loss of adult males. Male migrants represented 28 percent of the region's total adult male population, compared with 20 percent for the Central Region and 18 percent for the Southern Region. Lack of cash-earning opportunities in what was known as the "Dead North" may account for the region's overrepresentation in the supply of migrant labor. (In 1966, although losing only about 18 percent of its adult male population, the Southern Region was actually contributing 47 percent of the total number of migrants.)

Population Composition

Since earlier colonial censuses were on a de jure basis, while all the post–World War II censuses (except the officially unrecognized "census" of 1963) have been conducted on a de facto basis, the data regarding population composition is not always comparable, but the patterns are clearly discernible. There is clear evidence of the effects of vital processes.

Immigration has significantly affected the ethnic and (to a much lesser extent) the racial composition of the population. Particularly notable is the fact that the Lomwe, who were a small minority ethnic group at the beginning of the colonial period, were in 1921 the fifth largest group, accounting for 9 percent of the population; and by 1945 they were the second largest group after the Chewa (including Chipeta) and were accounting for about 19 percent of total population. In 1966 Chilomwe was the second most widely spoken language at home after Chichewa, the national language. The Sena and Nkhonde are other immigrant groups who gained in terms of their percentage share of the total population at the expense of the more-established groups such as the Tonga and Tumbuka. In any discussion of the ethnic compositon of the population it is, however, important to bear in mind (as rightly emphasized in the 1931 census report) that the ethnic groups are not pure, homogeneous divisions of the African population.

In racial composition the population has remained predominantly African; but the non-African component did, nonetheless, increase from less than .1 percent in 1901 to .6 percent in 1956 before declining to .5 percent in 1966 and .3 percent in 1977. Prior to World War II Europeans composed about two-thirds of the non-African population, and Asians the remaining third; but during the 1945 and 1956 censuses Asians composed a majority, a position they still maintained in 1966 when they numbered 11,300 compared to 7,400 Europeans. In 1977 Europeans were slightly more numerous than Asians.

Reflecting the selective nature of labor migration, Malawi's population has consistently been characterized by a sex imbalance since the turn of the century. The unfortunate position of the Northern Region in terms of labor migration is clearly reflected in the sex ratios given in Table 8.4. Perhaps most intriguing about this table is that the sex imbalances for the pre-1945 period are about the same as those for the post-1945 period in spite of the fact that the figures for the former period are supposedly de jure and should therefore reflect the selective nature of labor migration to a lesser degree than the de facto censuses of the post–World War II period. This may suggest that males absent from the country during the earlier period may have been grossly underestimated, a point that seems to be corroborated by the fact that if estimates of population abroad in 1945 and 1966 are added to the de facto population figures, the male population accounted, respectively, for 49 percent and 50 percent of the total (compared with 46 percent and 47 percent of de facto population).

TABLE 8.4 Sex Ratio (Males per 100 Females) by Region, 1911–1977

Region	1911	1921	1926	1931	1945	1966	1977
Northern	73	80	82	83	76	85	90
Central	79	88	83	85	75	88	95
Southern	82	89	91	94	91	92	92
All Regions	79	87	87	89	86	90	93

Source: Population figures from census reports.

The preponderance of females over males only applies to the African population of course. For Europeans and Asians the sex imbalance has always been in favor of males, as was particularly true in the early part of the colonial era, when the country was much less developed and many non-African immigrants were male and traveled alone. In 1911 nearly 70 percent of all Europeans and over 90 percent of all Asians were male; but over the years the imbalance has more or less disappeared, and by 1966 the corresponding figures were only 53 percent and 52 percent.

The problems of age determination and the crudeness of population breakdown in the colonial censuses have already been stressed. It is interesting to note, however, that if we take marriageable age in the colonial censuses to correspond to age fifteen in the postindependence censuses (it was variously assumed to be between fourteen and twenty in the censuses), it is evident that for both periods we are dealing with a youthful population with 40 percent of its members below fifteen years of age. The population under five years of age ranged between 27 percent and 29 percent during the censuses of 1921, 1926, 1931, and 1945, compared with about 19 percent for 1966 and 1977. As expected, the non-African population presents a different picture. In 1911 over 80 percent of both the European and Asian population were between fifteen and forty-five years of age; and although this proportion has declined over time, reaching 46 percent in 1977, it has tended to be higher than the corresponding proportion for Africans.

The recent data also largely confirms patterns discerned or suspected during the colonial period as regards marital status. For instance, in 1977 only 18 percent of persons above fifteen years of age remained single, which to some extent confirms earlier findings that few Malawians of marriageable age remain single; in 1931, 10 percent of those considered to be of marriageable age were single. The data for 1977 also confirm the view widely held during the colonial period that more females married at an earlier age (below fifteen) than males. The recent data also confirm the finding in earlier colonial censuses that more females tend to be either widowed or divorced than males. These patterns are, of course, not unique to Malawi.

Socioeconomic Characteristics of the Population

Although not providing conclusive evidence, the colonial census data is suggestive on a number of socioeconomic indicators. It is fairly obvious, for instance, that during the entire colonial period the level of urbanization remained low. In 1945 there were only three centers—Zomba, Blantyre, and Limbe (now part of Blantyre)—recognized as being urban, which together had a total of 13,900 Africans, representing only about .7 percent of the total African population. This situation did not change significantly during the later part of the colonial period, and by 1966 only 5 percent of the country's population could by any definition be considered urban, a proportion that still remained below 10 percent by 1977. The country's low level of economic development and the safety valve provided by labor migration to neighboring countries must largely account for this low level of urbanization.

Unlike neighboring countries, Malawi has had to rely on agriculture for the economy; and although the colonial census data failed to show in detail the economic characteristics of the African population, there is no doubt that an overwhelming majority of the Africans were engaged in agriculture, a fact confirmed by the 1977 census, which showed that nearly 80 percent of the economically active working population aged over ten years were self-employed farmers (*mlimi*). The importance of agriculture extended to Europeans, too. In 1945 over a third of the Europeans were engaged in this industry, most of them concentrated within the Shire Highlands. Asians benefited from agriculture only indirectly, over 80 percent being engaged in commerce.

One of the indicators of social development for which some census data is available is education. As on other characteristics, this is inconsistent in terms of the measures used. However, whatever its inherent weaknesses, it reveals patterns that can be substantiated with other and more recent data. For instance, the 1911 census indicated that there were about a hundred thousand Malawians receiving some form of secular education offered by a number of missions, over 70 percent of whom were males. This sex imbalance continued to be a characteristic feature of school attendance in Malawi during the entire colonial period, and it continues to be a conspicuous feature today; during the 1983/1984 school year 63 percent of total primary school enrollment was of boys.[29] The 1945 census revealed another feature that has come to characterize the Malawian educational scene. It showed that literacy—however it was measured—was much higher in the Northern Region than the Southern and Central Regions. Both the 1966 and 1977 censuses have shown a similar geographical imbalance, thus confirming that in Malawi the more economically developed parts of the country do not enjoy a higher level of educational attainment.

CONCLUSION

Any census data is bound to have its limitations, and Malawi for both the colonial and postindependence periods is no exception. These limitations can, however, be more severe in some data than in others; and the colonial census data in Malawi definitely have severe limitations. Indeed, they are so crude that even such methods as advocated by A. J. Coale and P. Demeny for estimating demographic measures from incomplete data cannot be applied to them.[30] But I hope I have demonstrated in this brief survey that the data has a lot to offer as long as one is interested in studying general patterns and trends, rather than specific detailed measurements. In the past many users of the data have been interested mainly in direct or indirect measures of the level of labor migration, but surely more information can be extracted from them. The other supplementary sources of demographic information should not, of course, be overlooked.

NOTES

1. Malawi, Department of Census and Statistics, *Malawi Population Census 1966: Final Report* (Zomba, 1969); Malawi, National Statistics Office, *Malawi Population Census 1977: Analytical Report*, 2 vols. (Zomba, 1984); idem, *Final Report*, 2 vols. (Zomba, 1980).

2. Malawi, National Statistics Office, *Malawi Population Change Survey February 1970—Final Report* (Zomba, 1973).

3. R. R. Kuczynski, *Demographic Survey of the British Colonial Empire*, vol. 2 (London, 1949); G. Coleman, "International Labour Migration from Malawi, 1875–1966," *Journal of Social Science* 2 (1973), 31–46; idem, "Regional and District Origins of Migrant Labour from Malawi to 1966," *Journal of Social Science* 6 (1977), 44–59.

4. For a comparison, see Kuczynski, *Demographic Survey*, and papers in K. M. Barbour and R. M. Prothero, eds., *Essays on African Population* (New York, 1961); S. H. Ominde and C. N. Ejiogu, eds., *Population Growth and Economic Development in Africa* (London, 1972); and J. C. Caldwell, ed., *Population Growth and Socioeconomic Change* (New York, 1975).

5. S. Agnew, "Factors Affecting the Demographic Situation in Malawi in Precolonial and Colonial Times," in *African Historical Demography* 1 (Edinburgh, 1977), 373–400, esp. 387.

6. Nyasaland, *Report on the Census of 1921* (Zomba, 1921); idem, *Report on the Census of 1926* (Zomba, 1926).

7. J. R. H. Shaul, "Demographic Features of Central Africa," in Barbour and Prothero, *Essays*, 33.

8. Nyasaland, *Report of the Census of 1931* (Zomba, 1932); idem, *Report of the Census of 1945* (Zomba, 1946).

9. Federation of Rhodesia and Nyasaland, *Census of Population, 1956* (Salisbury, 1960).

10. J. G. Pike, *Malawi: A Political and Economic History* (London, 1968), 22.

11. United Nations, *Demographic Yearbook* (New York, 1962), 1.

12. W. Peterson, *Population* (New York, 1975), 20.

13. B. Fetter, *Colonial Rule and Regional Imbalance in Central Africa* (Boulder, 1983).

14. E. van de Walle, "Characteristics of African Demographic Data," in W. Brass et al., *The Demography of Tropical Africa* (Princeton, 1968).

15. R. W. Stephens, *Population Pressures in Africa South of the Sahara* (Washington, 1959).

16. J. G. Pike and G. T. Rimmington, *Malawi: A Geographical Study* (London, 1965); R. R. Kuczynski, *Demographic Survey.*

17. J. C. Mitchell, "An Estimate of Fertility in some Yao Hamlets in Liwonde District of Southern Nyasaland," *Africa* 19 (1949), 293–308.

18. Shaul, "Demographic Features," 61.

19. Mitchell, "Estimate of Fertility," 309.

20. M. Read, "Migrant Labour in Africa and Its Effects on Tribal Life," *International Labour Review* 45 (1942), 605–631.

21. *Malawi Population 1984 Analytical.*

22. Ibid.

23. Fetter, *Regional Imbalance*, 51; Kuczynski, *Demographic Survey*, 536.

24. F. Dixey, "The Geographical Distribution of Population in Nyasaland," *Geographical Review* 18 (1928); G. Trewartha, "New Population Maps of Uganda, Kenya, Nyasaland, and the Gold Coast," *Annals of the Association of American Geographers* (1957), 53–55; Pike and Rimmington, *Malawi*, 65; N. D. McGlashan, "The Distribution of the Population and Medical Facilities in Malawi," in McGlashan, ed., *Medical Geography Techniques and Field Studies* (London, 1972).

25. Kuczynski, *Demographic Survey*, 638.

26. Agnew, "Factors," 387.

27. *Malawi Population 1984 Analytical*, vol. 1, 30–31.

28. Coleman, "Regional and District Origins," 46.

29. I. C. Lamba, "The Nyasaland Post-War Development Plan: A Historical Examination of African Education Development Strategies Up to 1961 with Particular Reference to the Primary and Secondary Sectors," in *Malawi: An Alternative Pattern of Development* (Edinburgh, 1984); Malawi, Ministry of Education, *Educational Statistics* (Lilongwe, 1984), 2.

30. A. J. Coale and P. Demeny, *Methods of Estimating Demographic Measures from Incomplete Data*, manual 4 (New York, 1967).

9

A Demographic Approach to Colonial Burundi, from Administrative Documents, 1896-1960

DANIEL NYAMBARIZA

BELGIAN ADMINISTRATION AND POPULATION CENSUS

The earliest administrative instructions regarding population date from the Belgian military occupation of the western part of what was then German East Africa. The Belgians were motivated by the need to know the numbers of adult and healthy male Africans so as to gather information on numbers of people to be taxed. The royal commissioner of the territory occupied by Belgium, who resided in Kigoma, asked in his letter #2559 of 1920 that the Belgian occupiers in Burundi draft a bill imposing a cattle tax and urged them to register taxpayers.[1] Taxpayer records had been set up for this purpose as early as 1918. A letter of the Rutana administrator dated 15 September 1918 gave the number of Mpinga taxpayers.[2] The documents we have at our disposal in Burundi give only fragmentary figures that will not allow us to obtain an overall estimate.

Until 1924, although this population was judged to be very dense, a census could not be conducted for lack of personnel: the whole European territorial staff consisted of thirty people. However, in 1924 the report on the Belgian administration of Rwanda-Urundi was able to conclude that "partial censuses carried out in some areas indicated a total population figure not less than 3 million inhabitants."[3] Taking prior estimates into account, I believe that this figure is too high. The colonial administration justified these data by the fact that no epidemic occurred in 1924 and that medical care for young children had intensified. The authorities were rejoicing because "due to the density of the population, there was an abundance of manpower at all stations." Beginning in 1925, population studies were undertaken in all territories of the mandate. Still, it is impossible to draw final conclusions from this preliminary work, which was carried out on small groups in various regions. The results fluctuate to such an extent that it is difficult to admit the accuracy of some (if not all) of them. For instance, the 1925 estimate was identical to that of 1924.[4] It should be noted that popular mistrust made the counting process extremely difficult.

The people could not accept the idea that such research was not founded on fiscal concerns.

Even supposing that the reported data were rigorously accurate, the demographic picture of a population on any given date, its breakdown into men, women, adults, and children cannot be itself give an idea of the population change. Essential elements would be missing: number of births and deaths and age of death. Definite conclusions can be drawn from these statistics only if they could be compared to the state of the same population examined at an interval of some years. Results that at first appear to be the most favorable could in reality be the sign of an alarming situation. A very high proportion of children could mean either a very high birthrate or a regrettable decrease in the male population. Consequently, every figure supplied has to be examined with care.

The only groups on which precise data were gathered were the Christian communities, where records of baptisms, marriages, and deaths constituted an embryo of a registrar's office. But here, also, these communities were too new. It was impossible to reach conclusions applicable to the whole population from the demographic picture they presented.

Still, the 1926 report[5] was able to draw the following conclusions:

1. In the mountains, the birthrate is extremely high: a census carried out in Rugori (Ngozi) noted 288 children alive aged 3 years or less, for an adult female population of 202. Thus the birthrate was 47 children for 100 women per year.
2. New born mortality is low; it can be compared to the European experience.

   The Vicar Apostolic of Urundi mentioned an 8% rate for the first year of life. Later childhood mortality, however, is much higher than in Europe.

(Note that women interrogated on the number of their children provide valuable information; but the age of the mother should be taken into account when interpreting each figure. Similarly, individuals interrogated about the number of children their mothers had give very different figures as regards birthrate and survival, according to the age of the individual interrogated, and give no information on the number of barren or unmarried women.) In 1926, the population decreased and was evaluated at 2.5 million inhabitants.[6]

The same method of sample hills was followed for 1927. In each territory demographic surveys were carried out on a number of groups felt to be representative, and findings were applied to the whole population. The choice of representative samples, on which the value of the surveys rested, was the result of an examination to determine "typical regions" in each territory.

The reports indicate four typical regions:

- Pastoral regions
- Agricultural regions
- Mixed regions
- Extracustomary regions

A government specialist addressed a number of issues:

- Verification of "typical regions" and analysis of possible variations between similar typical regions of different territories
- Analysis of the hills chosen in each territory to constitute a "typical region"
- The study of variations in the numbers of inhabitants from one hill to the other
- The periodical and detailed analysis in the course of time of chosen "typical regions" and hills
- The detailed analysis of variations linked to terrain, altitude, population makeup, diseases, marriage customs, emigration, and so on
- The review of samples before each specific survey to make sure that they could be used without modification
- The setting-up and interpretation of regular demographic rates: birthrate, mortality, reproductive, and specific fecundity rates

The number of taxpayers was then multiplied by a factor that was evaluated each year by sampling.

The 1927 census applied to eight sample hills. A total of 480,000 taxpayers were recorded, to which number a factor of 4.435 was applied; the resultant estimate extrapolated a total population of 2,128,000 souls for 1928.[7] During 1929 the population was recorded by the previous methods. The total number of taxpayers reached 414,000 *Hommes Adultes Valides* (HAV)—i.e., able-bodied men; the 4.435 factor was applied, as in the preceding year. This produces an estimated population of 1,836,090 souls, amounting to a decrease of 291,910.[8]

Available administrative reports attribute this decrease to famine. Shortages had caused many migrations from one region to the other and also to other countries. We do not have at our disposal a sufficient number of documents to verify whether famine had been the only cause of this decrease. However, we are tempted to doubt it, because Africans were in fact migrating to the country from neighboring parts of the Congo. In his letter CB #730, written in Costermansville (Bukavu) on 8 February 1928, District Commissioner van de Ghinste asked the governor in Bujumbura to send back to Kalembelembe the many Wabembe runaways installed in Burundi.[9] (See Map 9.1.) Agents cannot establish themselves in a region where people are dying of hunger. This request was executed by Governor Marzorati with his letter CG #359/A/15 to the resident in Bujumbura. Resident Ryckmans required the delegate in Bujumbura to act promptly on letter #359.[10] Later, a letter from the same delegate to the resident, written in Bujumbura, says that the "real causes" of this emigration are due to the fact that

1. "Bacinoni, brother of the great chieftain Baranyanka, took over the chieftainships of Nguco, Mweto, Bisakumbwe and Mobeya (we are at the beginning of the administrative reorganization of the territory). Before leaving their chieftaincies, the latter spread the rumor that Bacinoni would hoard their cattle to send them to Rwanda and to his brother Baranyanka." Many Barundi established themselves in the Belgian Congo at that time.
2. A railway company from Kivu, the Chemin de Fer Tanganyika Kivu (CFTK), used to pay 70–75 francs a month, while the Ruzizi Company, established in Nyakagunda in Burundi, paid its workers 35 francs per month. Naturally, the Barundi felt it more advantageous to work for a company that paid them a higher salary and was not far from where they lived.[11]

While this report mentions only clandestine emigration, Governor Voisin, in his letter of 28 May 1930 addressed to the Burundi authorities, speaks of "forced labor recruitment for the Belgian Congo in }the center of a country which is considered as reasonably populated." He insisted, "It is urgent to know the exact population figures of the territory."[12]

There was intense activity that year in relation to population census. New methods were introduced: systematic methodological census through index cards and identification papers.[13] In his letter AIMO #62/C.7 to the resident, dated 6 October 1939, Governor Voisin insisted, "A serious effort should be made in order to end the uncertainty in which we live in relation to the population of our territories and the exact availability of the manpower they hold. Please send me a report, with numbers, on the situation by the end of the year."[14] Many census cards were sent by letter, dated 26 September 1930, to the territorial authorities, who began the nominal census: men, women, and children (boys and girls). Several African secretaries were hired to give the operation more chances of success. While waiting for complete results, the number of taxpaying men was still used as a basis to evaluate the total population.

It should be recalled that a number of people abstained from fulfilling their fiscal obligations. The figure thus obtained was far from being totally reliable. The administration claimed that the censuses undertaken on some of the hills helped to determine the percentage of adults who were not paying the tax, establish the total number of taxpayers, and give an estimate of the

MAP 9.1 Administrative Map of Burundi

SOURCE: Daniel Nyambariza

whole population by taking into account the proportion of women and children in relation to men. According to the preceding criteria, population estimates decrease from year to year.

Year	Population
1924	3,000,000
1925	3,000,000
1926	2,500,000
1927	2,128,000
1928	2,128,000
1929	1,836,090
1930	1,732,355

The real reasons for this decrease have not been studied, because of lack of documentation. The administration backs out with evasive explanations. It talks about evaluations based on "data that are too vague and often exaggerated" but does not talk about the exodus to neighboring countries or recruitment for the Belgian Congo.

Nonetheless, the nominal censuses ultimately showed an increase in the estimate population. On 31 December 1931,[15] the HAV population was estimated at 323,097; the 3.602 factor was applied, giving a total population of 1,163,795.[16] On 31 December 1932 this population had increased to 1,441,023.[17] During 1933 the administration continued the HAV census and kept the cards of the previously recorded individuals up to date. However, the administration estimated the total population by taking into account the HAV census, the study of the composition of the groups chosen in each territory, and the examination of the members of such groups in relation to the HAV. The total population was evaluated at 1,579,371.[18] Native authorities began to participate in census operations, and several native clerks had been assigned to this work.

Census by nominal fiche had already taken place in 1932 in the subchieftaincies for men, women, and children. Here is an example of the card that was sent to the territorial authorities:[19]

Urundi Residency   Month of——— 19—— ———Territory
             Censuses carried out:

a) during previous months _____
b) during current month _____
c) People recorded who have died or have left the territory _____
Difference _____
Situation at end of month ——— on ——— 19——

Identification cards were given to people who had been recorded.

In 1934 the number of HAVs was estimated at 400,349, the factor

4.3895 was applied, a trend indicating decline in population was again noticed.[20] The administration reported that 1934 was a bad year for agriculture, that even rainfalls were insufficient, that eastern Gitega and the town of Muyinga were badly hit. It even appears that in these regions many standing crops dried up, bean shoots were burned by the sun, and sowing had to be redone several times.[21] In 1935 and 1936 the populations were estimated, respectively, at 1,700,300 and 1,746,501 souls.[22] Here, a small decrease in the infant mortality, from 10.8 percent to 8 percent, was noted. But it should also be noted that the birthrate in relation to the number of adult women had decreased from 19.45 percent to 17.5 percent. Is this because many adult men went to work in the Belgian Congo mines, leaving the women alone, or for some other reason?

According to a study carried out in three customary groups, the 1936 report notes a diminished birthrate, 26.1 per thousand, against 30.93 per thousand in 1935.[23] The administration concluded that girls married late and that emigration was currently very strong. This migration to the neighboring countries was even characterized as very strong for Bururi and Rutana, though a total of 1,829,000 souls was recorded in 1937.[24] In 1938, one year before the war, Burundi population was estimated at 1,863,852 inhabitants[25] in spite of manpower emigration toward the neighboring countries. A definite increase in population was occurring.

While censuses were neglected during the war years due to lack of personnel (everybody had been conscripted for production), it was noted in 1944 that the population had decreased sharply. In his letter #334/A.1.12 dated 22 August 1944,[26] Denie, the Ruyigi administrator, estimated that the troubled political situation was causing a substantial population decrease; and old, handicapped people were forced to pay the tax. Cattle was also taxed. According to Administrator Denie, many Barundi left the country in order to take refuge in the English territories, where taxes were not levied. Many Barundi Christians were recorded during that year in Tanganyika's Catholic missions:

Mission Station	Barundi Christians
Kakonko	5,000
Nyabarongo	3,000
Mabamba	3,000

Since these numbers only applied to Catholics, one may suppose that the number of non-Christians who went to live in the English territories was higher than the number of Christians. The administrator commented,

In the English territories almost no war effort for the native. There is recruitment for the army, for which many of our natives showed enthusiasm; a good number of Barundi from the Ruyigi territory enlisted in the British army; with every post, many letters arrive from Ceylon, Egypt, Burma, etc., sent by Barundi soldiers to their families in the Ruyigi Territory.[27]

Let us hope that documents on this recruitment exist somewhere. But it should also be recognized that a devastating famine occurred during this period of the war.[28]

However, the difference existing between the reports of agents active in the territories and those of the Belgian Territorial Administration, which were prepared in order to be presented to the Belgian Chambers and to the United Nations Trusteeship Council, should be underlined. The first ones emphasize the real causes of migration or depopulation, while the others mention only causes that are often of secondary importance. As of 1945, the recorded population began to increase continuously until the 1960s.[29]

Year	Population
1945	1,910,953
1946	1,901,236
1947	2,027,339

Table 9.1 shows the increase in the number of young people.

TABLE 9.1 Increase in Number of Young People (%)

Year	Births	Deaths	Natural Increase
1945	3.59	2.58	1.01
1946	4.64	2.72	1.92
1947	4.13	2.05	2.08
1948	3.78	1.65	2.13
1949	4.29	1.95	2.31

Map 9.2 clearly shows the population density in 1949. In 1949 many changes occurred in government obligations, especially as regards labor. Compulsory roadwork was abolished and replaced by an annual tax. Offers of on-the-spot work were numerous; salaries increased. The decrease in emigration toward the British territories began to be felt in 1949. Starting in 1948, the reports spoke of an annual increase of 3 percent.[30] Until 1949 the exodus in the direction of noncustomary areas was insignificant, not reaching even 2 percent of the total population. The economic development of the country was too weak. European concerns played an insignificant role there. The density factors varied greatly, from 29.53 to 147.01 per square kilometer in Gitega, for example.[31] This appears in a striking manner on Map 9.2 on which population distribution is shown by a dot for every five hundred inhabitants.

A new method of population survey was under study as early as 1951.

MAP 9.2 Population Distribution in Ruanda-Urundi, 1949

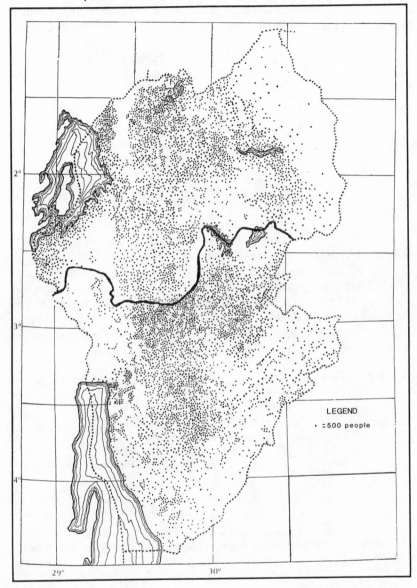

LEGEND

• =500 people

SOURCE: *1949 Decennial Plan for Economic and Social Development of Rwanda-Urundi.* Brussels: Ministry of Colonies, 1951.

Each able-bodied man's identification card included, together with his complete identification, the names of the members of his family and their own identification. This established that the total population was as follows:

Year[32]	Population
1952	1,092,060
1953	1,993,017
1954	1,934,737
1955	1,987,604
1956	2,041,259
1957	2,107,031
1958	2,137,918
1959	2,213,480
1960	2,234,141

Belgian Congo received natives from the border regions, while emigration from the other areas was in the direction of the British territories Uganda and Tanganyika (see Table 9.2). In Burundi the English territories recruited workers especially for the sugarcane and sisal plantations; this was made easier by the fact that forced labor still existed in Burundi, governed by the decree of 14 July 1952 for labor and public services. Burundi's population doubled in twenty years. The average density is over 150 inhabitants per square kilometer, one of the highest densities of the continent.

TABLE 9.2 Emigration Toward Belgian Congo and the English Territories

Year	Emigration Toward Belgian Congo	Emigration Toward English Territories
1949	3,379	16,543
1950	4,601	11,470
1951	4,470	10,182
1952	4,831	9,275
1953	610	13,298
1954	1,600	16,405
1955	1,086	28,113
1956	619	25,901[a]

[a]From *Report on Belgian Administration in Ruanda-Urundi During the Year 1956* (Brussels, 1957).

The exceptional density of this population and its numerical increase constitute the most disquieting demographic problem for the country, a problem that appears in all of its vastness if the figures conveying the overpopulation of the land and its insufficient productivity under the influence of soil degradation and unfavorable climatological conditions are compared to the preceding figures. Population displacements toward less barren areas occurred under the action of these various factors. The most urgent aspect of this problem is the food supply, of which it may be said that it dominates the economic and social development of the country.

NOTES

1. Archives Nationales, Dépôt Central (AN), Kitega, AA 138/1920/file 1.
2. AN, Kitega, AA 138/1920.
3. *Report on Belgian Administration in Ruanda-Urundi During the Year 1924* (Brussels, 1925).
4. *Report*, 1925.
5. Ibid., 47.
6. *Report*, 1926.
7. *Report*, 1927.
8. *Report*, 1928, 42–45.
9. AN, Kitega, AA 109/file 3.
10. AN, Kitega, AA 109.
11. AN, Kitega, letter no. 498/A.8.
12. AN, Kitega, AA/205/1930/file 1.
13. AN, Kitega, AA/186/1930–1964/file 1.
14. AN, Kitega, AA/186/1930–1964.
15. *Report*, 1929.
16. *Report*, 1930.
17. *Report*, 1931.
18. *Report*, 1932.
19. AN, Kitega, AA/1931–1956.
20. *Report*, 1932.
21. Ibid.
22. *Reports*, 1935, 1936.
23. *Report*, 1935.
24. *Report*, 1936.
25. *Report*, 1937.
26. AN, Kitega, AA$_4$/1944.
27. Ibid.
28. D. Nyambariza, "Les efforts de guerre du Burundi, 1940–45 et la famine de 1943–44 (Territoire de Bururi)," *Cahiers d'histoire* 2 (1984), 1–8.
29. *Reports*, 1945–1949.
30. *Plan décennal pour le développement économique et social du Ruanda-Urundi* (Brussels, 1951), 7.
31. *Plan décennal*, 9.
32. *Reports*, 1952–1960.

10

Catholic Missions, Mentalités, and Quantitative History in Burundi, ca. 1900-1962

GAËTAN FELTZ

Historical demography appeared as a full-fledged discipline of the Nouvelle Clio at the beginning of the twentieth century, especially during the twenties and thirties. Today, it would be useless to deny the importance of demography in societal evolution, especially where its growth becomes a social problem and requires recourse to a policy of birth control.[1] However, significant snags remain in relation to the historical dimension to be attributed to numbers. In what measure can statistical sources—whether total global or disaggregated—be trusted when we know that no structure capable of rigorously quantifying the demographic growth of a community or state existed during the colonial era?

Such was the case until recently in the African world for the greater part of these new nation-states. As a matter of fact, the rural population was never systematically recorded, either in the Belgian Congo or in Ruanda-Urundi Territory under the Belgian mandate (later *trusteeship*) until the 1970s. The map of population density in these three countries, drawn up by Pierre Gourou in 1950, relied essentially on statistics reported by the colonial administration on 31 December 1948, emanating from an evaluation of able-bodied adult males (HAV) by administrative subdistrict, multiplied by a "simplifying" factor of five, slightly overvalued.[2] At that time, the accepted average population density in Burundi was 82 inhabitants per square kilometer, that is, 1,990,000 inhabitants for an area of 24,273 km², discounting lakes, unused marshes, and forest preserves. For the Ten-Year Plan the corresponding figures were 1,978,355 inhabitants for 27,734 km², an average density of 71.33. These statistics came from two investigative sources: a census by index card of all male individuals and population surveys concerning, in each territory, a number of groups felt to be representative.[3] Present density in Burundi approximates 150 per square kilometer. According to the results of the August 1979 census, the density in Burundi reached 154 per square kilometer, with a population of 4,021,910 inhabitants for an area of 26,100 km². Together with Rwanda, Burundi (200 per square kilometer) appears to be one of the most densely populated countries of black Africa, contrasting with its neighbors Zaire to the west (12 per square kilometer) and Tanzania to the east (20 per square kilometer).

Nevertheless, during the colonial era, statistical sources were not absent. Colonial powers needed to quantify the population of their territories. There are many reasons for this, among them (1) the necessity of counting the labor force (HAV) (which would prove useful for determining the taxation level) and (2) the introduction of labor levies and forced cultivation (then necessary to establish political control over the whole population). These are the constituent elements of a system that permitted the evaluation of the actual political control over the populations under domination. But in fact, any authority feels the need to count its subordinates. This was especially the case for the Catholic missions, which wielded real power in the Belgian colonial ideology through their ascendancy over the school system.[4] They, too, quantified with an almost incredible rigor through the years of their expansion: from 1935 on, we know the exact numbers of catechists, baptized individuals, and catechumens; the sick cared for in dispensaries or hospitals; and Christians who died, not to mention the pupils of the various schools . . . nor the numbers of pagans, of Muslims.[5] Should anyone wish to exercise talents at arithmetic on such numerical data, it would be possible to obtain a global picture of the population of Zaire, Rwanda, and Burundi.

By reviewing the statistical sources of the Catholic missions, and by using as reference a basic source—the parish records—I believe that we may be able to retrace the local population history in several areas of the country. Some conclusions may corroborate the parameters used by historians in some recent studies[6] by analyzing both the demographic upsets caused by both political and crisis events (the war effort of 1941–1945 and the transition toward independence in 1960–1962) and natural calamities such as great famines and shortages. However, due to the still-significant influence of the Catholic Church in this part of Africa (especially that of the White Fathers Missionary Society, through the impression it left in the countryside),[7] we must make note of the social particularisms of the precolonial history of Burundi and of the influences born of the establishment of a mission in this or that place. Regional population history cannot be dissociated from social history or from the history of mental habits.

REVIEW OF SOURCES

If we disregard all the statistical data that may be found in school records, we have, in fact, four recorded missionary sources likely to provide information regarding the population of the region: the mission station diary, the *White Fathers' Annual Reports*, the parish records, and the *Annual Statistics of the Catholic Missions of Belgian Congo and Ruanda-Urundi*, published by the Apostolic Delegation in Léopoldville starting in 1935.

The Diary

In many respects, the diary represents a firsthand source. It provides day-by-day information on the station. This information is mainly of a religious nature but also contains social, political, and economic information: missionary penetration and ancient history; relations with the customary chief of the region, the populations, and the colonial power; and missionary accomplishments (Christianization, school attendance, economic and sanitation actions). The diaries of the first stations like Muyaga (1898), Mugera (1899), Buhonga (1902), Kanyinya (1905), and Rugari (1909) are extremely valuable because they contain data on the social history of the times. (See Map 10.1.) At times they give us commentaries on the population situation of the period. At the beginning of the century, the population of Mumirwa and Imbo contrasted with those of Mugamba and Bututsi. It appears that this was the main reason for creating as early as 1918 in the very heavily populated areas of Mwisale a branch of Buhonga—which would become the Rushubi station (1935).[8] Similar motivations seem to have encouraged the White Fathers to establish themselves in a peripheral area strongly opposed to the central authority: Kanyinya (1905) and Rugari (1909).

Certainly, this source reflects the missionary frame of mind, but it contains a large number of statistics relevant to ancient history. Such is the case for the regions of Burundi, Bugesera and Bweru with the two stations named above. These natural regions with high agricultural potential were not free from famines and shortages, to which must be added crucial political problems following the conquests undertaken by King Ntare IV Rugamba, who was succeeded by Mwezi Gisabo (1852–1908). Following rivalries before the king became of age, resistance broke out among the Batare chieftains of the region. Ndivyariye's heirs refused to submit to Mwezi Gisabo's authority, gave up the custom of *gusasa* (annual visit to the court), and did not attend the *muganuro* (annual sowing festival). After the Treaty of Kiganda (6 June 1903) and with the help of the Germans, Mwezi Gisabo undertook a bloody campaign against the rebel chieftains. Between 1904 and 1910 these heavily populated areas had to face simultaneously a significant drought and a war with all attending atrocities.[9] This critical situation reached a peak in 1908–1909 with the death of Mwezi Gisabo and the interdiction to cultivate fields until the new sovereign had been enthroned. An almost-similar situation occurred in the region in 1915: drought, the death of King Mutaga Mbikije, and insecurity due to the Belgian-German armed conflict in this part of East Africa.

While the Kanyinya and Rugari diaries mention a diversified agriculture (beans, peas, sorghum, eleusine, sweet potato, corn, taro, bananas), the use of the products of animal husbandry (milk, meat, butter, coagulated blood, and horn), exchange with Imbo and Buha (hoes to the west, salt to the south), this area of Burundi was subjected to periodical food crises. The 1910 famine caused numerous victims, but numbers are rather fragmentary: "1909

MAP 10.1 Catholic Missions in Burundi, 1898–1950

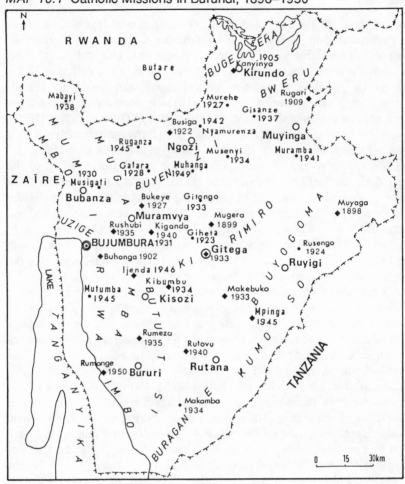

SOURCE: Gaëtan Feltz

- • Mission and date of foundation
- ◆ Projected mission
- ◎ Colonial capital
- ○ Administrative center
- *IMBO* Historical region

and 1910 were years of serious food crises. Many inhabitants left, abandoning their fields and banana plantations burned by the sun. On a hill where there had been 100 huts, for example, only 25 were left. Those who owned cows kept alive by drinking a little milk."[10] The inhabitants of Kanyinya got supplies from Rwanda, which had a surplus at the time. Other famines followed. We have mentioned the 1915 famine, which began with the death of the king. Three more occurred during Belgian colonization. In 1922, because of the drought, which attacked mainly Busoni, "entire families carrying their belongings and their work implements come by on our road, east of the mission. There are always Busoni looking for a more favored country."[11]

In spite of food relief to be reallocated by the missionaries, the situation did not improve, and they petitioned the colonial administration to obtain further relief, such as exemption from taxation.[12] Another similar request came during the famine of 1925.[13]

The last and most important famine occurred in 1943–1944, serious in that it affected several regions of Burundi as well as Rwanda. The number of victims was never expressed in figures; but according to some estimates, half of the Kanyinya population was forced to emigrate. It was referred to as *ruzagayura*. We shall see that it had a strong influence on the development of Christianity.

The consequences of these crises quickly affected evangelization, destabilizing Christian practice through a massive return to traditional religious rituals. Some statistics reveal that the process of Christianization slowed down considerably: between 1905 and 1910 only 127 Christians were recorded in Kanyinya, while in Mugera there were already 1,000 of them.[14] In order to stop the exodus during the famine of 1943–1944, the missionaries opened "camps for the hungry" to receive mostly children, women, the aged, and the sick.

Although the diary may appear more reliable in relation to regional social history and habits of thought, it is a chronicle of all the activities of the mission station, where the development of Christianity and education played a major role. The first diaries (1900–1920), are characterized by an abundance of information, which tends to decrease after the thirties, with the establishment of new administrative structures. Even later, however, they can be of considerable interest. The diary of the Mpinga station (1945) for the years 1956 to 1978 represents a major source, allowing us to follow the evolution of Christianity through contemporary events, from the country's independence until the advent of the Second Republic.

The White Fathers' Annual Reports
(Les Rapports Annuels des Pères Blancs [RAPB])

Starting in 1905, the annual reports replaced the quarterly chronicles (*chroniques trimestrielles*) of the Missionary Society of Africa, which had not been printed since 1878.[15] They synthesize all missionary activities of each station and are based on the diaries sent to Rome. But the statistical data are inconsistent: sometimes copious, sometimes nonexistent. They appear more tangible and more complete regarding school attendance, as shown in Table 10.1.

TABLE 10.1 Number of Schools and Student Population, 1906–1940

Year	Schools	Boys	Girls	Total
1906–1907	6	353	40	393
1907–1908	6	254	40	294
1909–1910	8	674	315	989
1910–1911	12	1,057	221	1,278
1911–1912	20	1,536	317	1,853
1912–1913	33	3,644	989	4,633
1917–1918	44	1,634	828	2,562
1918–1919	53	1,565	884	2,449
1919–1920	64	2,348	1,379	3,727
1920–1921	52	2,425	1,656	4,081
1922–1923	218	7,010	4,765	11,775
1923–1924	153	11,700	7,121	18,821
1924–1925	244	12,270	7,466	19,736
1925–1926	309	11,417	7,784	19,201
1926–1927	191	18,280	11,253	29,533
1927–1928	233	21,395	14,780	36,175
1928–1929	—	83,071	24,207	107,278
1929–1930	—	33,787	27,644	61,431
1930–1931	—	11,862	85,121	95,983
1931–1932	—	32,154	22,950	55,104
1932–1933	—	47,037	34,412	81,449
1933–1934	—	53,268	40,481	93,749
1934–1935	—	49,132	42,954	92,086
1935–1936	—	63,657	53,694	117,351
1936–1937	725	56,722	55,543	112,265
1937–1938	—	60,208	55,911	116,119
1939–1940	—	65,724	65,374	131,098

Source: Rapports Annuels des Pères Blancs, 1906–1940.

In reading this table, we note a constant evolution of school attendance in spite of two very apparent breaks: one during World War I, starting in 1917 (note that the years 1914–1916 and 1922 are missing), and one in 1932, apparently following administrative reorganization, the establishment of a system of compulsory cultivation following new shortages, and the introduction of corvée labor. (The economic crisis had less impact.) Recall that in Burundi attendance data encompass all schools, even religious reading schools (which were not subsidized by the colonial power), beginning with school regulations for 1925 and 1929. This may explain the very substantial increase in the school population in 1929, with later readjustments.

School attendance did not go beyond the primary level and subsidized schools were fewer than branch schools: 51 primary and secondary central schools comprising 338 classes with 11,641 boys and 5,275 girls, 655 rural schools (covering mostly the first year of education) with 31,322 boys and 1,555 girls, and   1,112 reading schools with a total of 55,139 boys and 71,921 girls,[16] making a grand total school population of 176,853 in 1946 (98,102 boys and 78,751 girls).

Parish Records

Parish records represent, of course, a firsthand source for everything that has to do with Christian social life: child and adult baptisms (*liber baptizatorum*), deaths (*liber defunctorum*), marriages (*liber matrimonium*), confirmations (*liber confirmatorum*), and family status (*status animarum*). However, two difficulties remain: (1) the birth date is not always reliable, especially for the adults prior to 1940, and (2) children deceased before baptism do not appear (and there was sometimes a long lapse between birth and baptism). On the other hand, the family index cards may be of great importance for the compiling of "survival tables."

Through quantitative evaluation of baptized individuals in seven parishes (see Table 10.2), we note three significant breaks or periods of decline— 1916–1919, 1937–1947, and starting in 1961—punctuated by short drops (especially in the 1950s, e.g., 1953–1955 and 1957–1959) mainly caused by redefinition of religious districts following the opening of new stations. If we take into account the population crisis of the years 1880–1910,[17] famines on the national scale in the country (1909–1911, 1925–1926, 1943–1944), and colonial constraints,[18] the first break (especially noticeable in the regions of Bugesera and Bweru) resulted from World War I and its immediate consequences, the death of Mwami Mutaga in 1915, and the ensuing famine. In spite of the agripastoral nature of this region, many calamities, both of natural and sociopolitical origins, beset it. The second break, much more significant in terms of time and space, began with a redefinition of missionary districts, which in turn altered the statistics. But as of 1941[19] the *manori* famine of 1943–1944, an exceptional drought, and biological and epidemic factors indicate a general decrease in the number of Christians in all recorded stations, which finally bottomed in 1944 except in Gitega, the country's second administrative center, which attracted the famished populations.

The third break begins in 1961 and its origin is mainly political. It appears that the events that precipitated the independence of the country are an immediate consequence of cases of regionalized famine due to a falling off of industrial and food crops. This is very noticeable in the statistical report for the Mpinga mission from 1962, especially in the number of children.

TABLE 10.2 Number Baptized in Seven Burundi Parishes, 1905–1966

Year	Kanyinya (1905)	Rugari (1909)	Makebuko (1933)	Gitega (1935)	Rushubi (1940)	Kiganda (1945)	Mpinga (1945)
1905	1	—	—	—	—	—	—
1906	11	—	—	—	—	—	—
1907	8	—	—	—	—	—	—
1908	45	—	—	—	—	—	—
1909	62	—	—	—	—	—	—
1910	148	—	—	—	—	—	—
1911	119	31	—	—	—	—	—
1912	129	41	—	—	—	—	—
1913	340	103	—	—	—	—	—
1914	226	63	—	—	—	—	—
1915	222	129	—	—	—	—	—
1916	124	105	—	—	—	—	—
1917	119	93	—	—	—	—	—
1918	170	54	—	—	—	—	—
1919	106	44	—	—	—	—	—
1920	175	101	—	—	—	—	—
1921	209	92	—	—	—	—	—
1922	197	106	—	—	—	—	—
1923	345	155	—	—	—	—	—
1924	381	126	—	—	—	—	—
1925	489	121	—	—	—	—	—
1926	182	206	—	—	—	—	—
1927	393	272	—	—	—	—	—
1928	448	346	—	—	—	—	—
1929	203	226	—	—	—	—	—
1930	441	298	—	—	—	—	—
1931	1,036	332	—	—	—	—	—
1932	982	437	—	—	—	—	—
1933	2,016	659	885	2,750	—	—	—
1934	2,254	1,069	3,566	3,226	—	—	—
1935	2,727	1,477	1,332	3,378	829	—	—
1936	4,488	1,480	1,491	4,549	1,613	—	—
1937	2,554	1,138	2,015	3,968	1,334	—	—
1938	1,714	983	1,238	3,916	964	—	—
1939	1,932	804	1,149	3,453	1,360	—	—
1940	1,796	946	1,549	3,237	1,725	1,118	—
1941	1,056	989	1,925	3,711	1,653	2,159	—
1942	1,311	707	1,678	3,763	1,677	3,314	—
1943	1,055	664	2,042	3,614	1,636	2,520	—
1944	896	549	1,778	3,747	1,311	1,027	—
1945	1,062	516	2,306	5,267	1,412	1,241	306
1946	1,071	776	2,713	5,405	1,729	2,051	575
1947	936	765	2,946	5,803	1,199	1,525	439
1948	1,033	961	3,395	6,721	1,625	1,888	604
1949	1,237	1,141	3,782	6,914	1,570	2,374	869
1950	686	1,275	3,151	6,949	1,780	2,467	859
1951	881	1,308	3,328	6,704	1,831	3,134	894
1952	884	1,589	2,042	5,699	2,082	3,502	1,121
1953	798	1,372	3,765	5,233	1,865	3,319	842
1954	792	1,309	2,941	5,013	1,998	3,608	1,000
1955	846	1,371	2,932	5,991	2,520	3,728	1,009

TABLE 10.2 continued

Year	Kanyinya (1905)	Rugari (1909)	Makebuko (1933)	Gitega (1935)	Rushubi (1940)	Kiganda (1945)	Mpinga (1945)
1956	791	1,399	3,491	6,140	2,299	3,001	1,193
1957	1,002	1,652	3,206	5,485	2,520	3,760	1,255
1958	1,080	1,747	3,167	5,331	1,737	3,624	1,246
1959	830	1,521	2,525	6,488	2,414	3,237	1,384
1960	—	—	—	5,689	1,970	2,287	1,441
1961	—	—	—	5,288	1,672	1,860	1,132
1962	—	—	—	6,826	1,112	1,642	743
1963	—	—	—	—	1,303	1,753	544
1964	—	—	—	—	1,126	1,308	547
1965	—	—	—	—	1,030	1,473	646
1966	—	—	—	—	970	1,337	454

Source: Registres de baptêmes: enfants et adultes.
Note: Falling incidence is shown by breaks between rows.

Annual Statistics of the Catholic Missions of Belgian Congo and Ruanda-Urundi (Les statistiques annuelles des missions catholiques du Congo belge et du Ruanda-Urundi)

This statistical source was recorded starting in 1935 by the Apostolic Delegation of Léopoldville (Kinshasa), based on data from each mission's "prospectus" on its status as of 30 June of each year. However, the years 1940, 1942, 1958, and 1960 are missing.

At first, this source appears to be very complete, as shown in Table 10.3. Right away, the importance of Catholicism in the Belgian colonial system is apparent. In numerical value the increase in the number of Catholics may prove credible, like the increase in the numbers of catechists and catechumens. It is true that proselytism soared after the administrative reorganization of 1929–1933, especially as of 1932–1935. The movement stabilized after 1940 at an annual increase of 8 percent to 9 percent (see Table 10.4). The consequences of the *manori* famine appear clearly, with the increase reversing brutally during 1945–1946.

However, this source becomes questionable when it applies to estimates of the Protestant, Muslim, and pagan populations—which, in a way, undercuts the credibility of the total population data. By comparing the rates of increase extracted from this source with those of the administrative census carried out by the colonial power, Table 10.5 reveals this unpredictable trend with a brutal decrease in population during 1937–1938 (certainly in relation to a typhus epidemic) and 1947–1948 (for which we have no data). Thus, if the *manori* famine is barely noticeable through this source (−1.71 percent), while it clearly appears in the administrative source (−5.42 percent in 1944, −2.89 percent in 1945), still we must acknowledge a curious fact: Burundi's population does not appear to have increased between 1935 and 1955 (just the

TABLE 10.3 Religion and Total Population in Burundi, 1900–1961

Year	Catholic Cathechumens	Catholics	Protestant Catechumens	Protestants	Muslims	Pagans	Total
1900	—	34	—	—	—	—	—
1905	—	292	—	—	—	—	—
1907	—	589	—	—	—	—	—
1909	—	1,157	—	—	—	—	—
1910	—	1,667	—	—	—	—	—
1912	—	2,865	—	—	—	—	—
1914	—	4,877	—	—	—	—	—
1916	—	6,922	—	—	—	—	—
1918	—	9,510	—	—	—	—	—
1919	—	14,217	—	—	—	—	—
1920	—	10,834	—	—	—	—	—
1921	—	12,219	—	—	—	—	—
1922	—	14,456	—	—	—	—	—
1923	—	15,474	—	—	—	—	—
1924	—	17,677	—	—	—	—	—
1925	—	20,379	—	—	—	—	—
1926	—	23,627	—	—	—	—	—
1927	—	27,874	—	—	—	—	—
1928	—	30,881	—	—	—	—	—
1929	—	36,910	—	—	—	—	—
1930	—	45,611	—	—	—	—	—
1931	—	58,560	—	—	—	—	—
1932	—	78,026	—	—	—	—	—
1933	—	107,000	—	—	—	—	—
1934	—	140,218	—	—	—	—	—
1935	585	176,076	217,233	1,500	4,000	1,600,000	1,997,809
1936	725	216,835	232,316	3,000	6,000	1,500,000	1,958,151
1937	828	253,665	227,395	4,000	6,000	1,400,000	1,891,060
1938	963	291,611	84,198	6,000	8,000	1,500,000	1,883,809
1939	1,167	326,027	234,680	6,500	8,000	1,400,000	1,975,207
1940	—	365,000	—	—	—	—	—
1941	1,398	400,005	255,208	9,000	8,000	1,325,000	1,997,213
1942	—	435,000	—	—	—	—	—
1943	1,715	465,015	222,642	11,000	8,000	1,275,000	1,987,657
1944	1,715	486,623	201,061	10,000	—	1,250,000	1,947,684
1945	1,722	497,252	204,612	11,000	10,000	1,240,000	1,962,864
1946	1,312	515,691	226,345	11,000	8,767	1,200,000	1,922,947
1947	1,387	540,704	241,635	27,803	8,999	753,600	1,572,741
1948	1,513	563,470	132,127	33,859	9,126	817,259	1,555,841
1949	1,562	609,077	239,711	34,170	10,912	822,333	1,716,203
1950	1,603	643,119	210,639	35,415	11,101	796,237	1,696,511
1951	954	693,911	223,859	37,129	11,609	822,806	1,788,360
1952	1,776	742,583	220,271	35,126	11,440	794,269	1,803,689
1953	1,889	790,194	224,697	44,832	13,589	780,629	1,803,941
1954	1,913	847,541	230,947	54,741	14,467	814,538	1,962,234
1955	1,926	906,366	228,668	53,342	15,192	788,927	1,992,495
1956	2,116	975,416	235,916	63,159	16,803	761,216	2,052,570
1957	2,280	1,058,679	135,023	68,996	18,932	730,205	2,017,835
1959	2,185	1,197,313	193,892	76,551	18,122	762,473	2,248,351
1961	2,260	1,337,373	148,003	99,308	6,929	787,920	2,379,533

Source: J. Keuppens, *L'Urundi ancien et moderne* (Bugasira, 1959). Délégation Apostolique, *Statistiques annuelles des missions catholiques du Congo belge et du Ruanda-Urundi* (Léopoldville, 1935–1961).

TABLE 10.4 Estimated Growth and Death Rates Among Burundi Catholics, 1936–1957

Year	Increase	Rate (%)	Deaths	Percentage
1936	40,759	23	4,864	2.24
1937	36,830	16.98	7,686	3.02
1938	37,946	14.95	8,142	2.79
1939	34,416	11.80	7,142	2.19
1940	38,973	11.95	—	—
1941	35,005	9.59	9,792	2.44
1942	34,995	8.74	—	—
1943	30,015	6.90	11,975	2.57
1944	21,608	4.64	13,975	2.87
1945	10,629	2.18	14,783	2.97
1946	18,439	3.70	19,457	3.77
1947	25,013	4.85	15,386	2.84
1948	22,766	4.21	12,601	2.23
1949	45,607	8.09	15,452	2.53
1950	34,042	5.58	15,410	2.39
1951	50,792	7.89	13,126	1.89
1952	48,672	7.01	9,396	1.26
1953	47,611	6.41	17,149	2.17
1954	57,347	7.25	14,840	1.74
1955	58,825	6.94	16,500	1.82
1956	69,050	7.61	14,319	1.46
1957	83,263	8.53	14,872	1.40

Source: Délégation Apostolique, *Statistiques annuelles des missions catholiques du Congo belge et du Ruanda-Urundi* (Léopoldville, 1935–1961).

opposite, –.26 percent), while between 1936 and 1949 official figures show an increase of 13.27 percent in absolute value. Administrative censuses mention brutal decreases that occurred in 1939, 1941–1942 (probably a result of emigration to East Africa),[20] and 1944–1945 (continued effects of the *manori* famine).

On the other hand, Table 10.4 seems more credible. In accordance with the nominal increase of the Catholic population of Burundi, we notice a decline in proselytization beginning in 1941, which would reach its lowest point in 1945 (2.18 percent), as a direct consequence of the great famine. Effects of recovery did not begin to be felt until 1949. These are elements that confirm the indicators cited above. The mortality rate of the Catholic population oscillated around 25 per thousand until 1950—noticeably lower than the figure shown in the *Reports on Belgian Administration of Ruanda-Urundi* (*Rapports sur l'administration belge du Ruanda-Urundi*), which reached 30 percent during the years 1931–1949. This may be explained by the sanitation effort undertaken by the missionaries through their network of dispensaries, which developed mainly after the 1950s.

TABLE 10.5 Population Change in Burundi, 1936–1959, Official and
Missionary Sources

Year	Official Sources			Missionary Sources	
	Population	Change	Percentage	Change	Percentage
1936	1,746,501	82,499	4.72	−39,658	−1.98
1937	1,829,000	34,852	1.90	−67,091	−3.42
1938	1,863,852	34,852	1.90	−1,251	−.06
1939	1,867,705	3,854	.20	85,398	4.51
1940	1,901,532	34,130	1.82	—	—
1941	1,923,821	21,989	1.15	22,006	1.11
1942	1,899,865	−23,953	−1.24	—	—
1943	1,961,087	61,222	3.22	−15,556	−.77
1944	1,854,670	−106,417	−5.42	−33,973	−1.71
1945	1,800,914	−53,756	−2.89	−15,180	.77
1946	1,910,953	110,039	6.11	−40,823	−2.07
1947	1,967,201	−56,248	−2.94	−349,300	−18.17
1948	1,987,551	20,350	1.03	−16,900	−1.07
1949	1,978,415	−9,136	−.45	−160,362	10.30
1950	—	—	—	−19,992	−1.16
1951	—	—	—	91,849	5.41
1952	1,902,060	—	—	15,239	0.85
1953	1,993,017	90,957	4.78	50,252	2.78
1954	—	—	—	108,293	5.84
1955	—	—	—	30,261	1.54
1956	2,041,259	—	—	60,015	3.01
1957	2,107,031	65,772	3.22	−40,678	−1.98
1958	2,163,708	30,887	1.46	—	—
1959	2,213,480	75,562	3.53	—	—

Sources:Plan décennal pour le développement économique et social du Ruanda-
Urundi (Brussels, 1951), 11; Rapport de l'administration belge au Ruanda-Urundi,
1950–1959 (Brussels, 1951–1960); Délégation Apostolique, Statistiques annuelles des
missions catholiques du Congo belge et du Ruanda-Urundi (Léopoldville, 1935–1961).

A PROVISIONAL GENERAL FRAMEWORK

In spite of gaps and of some conflicting trends reported in sources of this
type, the sources I mentioned do throw some light on the general trends of
Burundi's population history during the colonial period, all the more so
because the Catholic missions played a significant role in the contemporary
history of this part of Africa. Nevertheless, it cannot be denied that the lack
of a solid basis can be felt all the way through the analysis. We know that it
will always be possible to estimate birth, fecundity, and mortality rates in
the Christianized section of society; but we will have difficulty in
extrapolating this data to the whole population. Let us not forget that even
today only 60 percent of the population is Christian.

Apart from some fanciful statistical data, should the results obtained be
considered true? It is strange to note that the missionary sources tend to

underestimate Burundi's population. This is clearly evident prior to the 1950s, but it can still be seen today: while the 1979 general census evaluated Burundi's total population at a little more than 4,000,000 individuals, the Catholic Church in June of 1978 estimated it at 3,499,833. (In 1984 the church coincided with official estimates, that is, 4,340,312 inhabitants.)[21]

If we accept the colonial assessment from the beginning of the century, that is, one million people, Burundi's population quadrupled in the space of eighty years. Is such a spectacular population increase compatible with the "population decline and stagnation of the years 1880–1950" envisaged by researchers interested in Burundi?[22] Actually, we do not lack for data. First, we have quite a complete picture of famines and shortages (1889–1890 and 1904–1911, especially for the northeastern region; 1915–1916; 1922–1926; and 1943–1944) and epidemics (sleeping sickness in 1905–1910, Spanish influenza and smallpox in 1917–1918 and 1920, typhus in 1935–1936, and bacillar dysentery in 1956–1957.[23] Multiple causes have been well defined: natural, epidemic and microbial shock, and political and military causes and colonial intervention.[24] Second, we are also aware of the consequences of colonial policies—especially since 1930, with the introduction of new crops and the extension of seasonal crops in order to avoid famines[25] and monetarization of the Burundi society through poll tax and corvée labor. Even if the consequences of colonization were more rigorously examined, one direct consequence would result from the movement of manpower in the direction of the British territories. According to J. P. Chrétien, this migration peaked between 1937 and 1947, a period corresponding to unfavorable economic circumstances for the peasant: income stagnation and increase in taxation. In 1959 more than 500 thousand Rwandans and Barundi settled in Uganda (150 thousand of them Burundian), and about the same number settled in Tanganyika Territory (Tanzania).[26] Taxes, compulsory crops, and statute labor levies certainly contributed to the acceleration of this movement.[27] Financial reasons (taxes and dowry payment) often appear in the sources of the period: one goes away to "buy money": "The chieftains are pushing, pressing, they use violence to collect the tax as quickly as possible. This is in their interest since they receive a refund of 2 francs for each taxpayer, without including what they receive from the cattle tax. Francs, always francs, that's what we hear on all sides and, on top of this, always the days of compulsory labor."[28]

This decline and stagnation up to the 1950s is confirmed by colonial and missionary sources even if it is difficult to believe the administrative censuses based on the number of HAVs in each subdistrict.[29] Similarly, it is difficult to understand how the missionaries counted the total population in each of their stations prior to 1960. Could an evaluation of the total population of a missionary station based on baptism records and death records (less well kept) bring about new elements, especially for the colonial period?

On the other hand, a number of questions remain unanswered that are more related to social history and evolution of *mentalités*. While the Belgian and British administration had little difficulty counting emigrants when they crossed the border, administrative sources only *allude* to the movements of people to Rwanda to the north and to Buha in Tanzania, or, within the country, to the Bururi Territory in the South; "itinerant peddlers" were in constant touch with the Buha.[30] Also, regions such as Bweru in the northwest and Mugamba in the center were in a state of permanent movement: they suffered either from famines and shortages or from political events: people were looking for food. The Mugamba turned mostly to Mumirwa, the Bweru toward Kirimiro.

Lastly, while Burundi suffered from "chronic" famines and shortages, we know now that these never affected the whole country. This remark may apply in particular to the great famine of 1943–1944; Kirimiro suffered a lot less than Bweru, which is confirmed by the Mugera diary. The Bweru people came looking for sorghum, bananas, and beans, which existed in abundance in Mugera during the famines; these people came to work for the Banyamugera and were paid with provisions.[31] Immigration movements were felt in Buragane, especially from 1944: the colonial power had decided to displace part of the populations of Mugamba (territories of Kitega and Muramvya), who had suffered disaster, to the territories of Rutana, Bururi, and Usumbura.[32]

Thus, by studying cases founded on statistics of baptisms, marriages, and deaths in a station or parish, it is possible to uncover trends that are symptomatic of growth or decline caused by determinant factors such as an uninterrupted growth trend or the weight of a calamity. The contrast seems apparent in relation to two stations separated only by about thirty kilometers as the crow flies—Rushubi since 1935 and Kiganda since 1940—as evidenced by their statistical data shown in Figures 10.1 and 10.2. In Kiganda 1944 saw a high number of deaths (1,526, three times the yearly average), a noticeable decrease in the number of marriages (98, as compared to 235 in 1943), and a sharp decrease in the number of baptisms (1,027: 625 children and 402 adults). If we only take into account the adults, who are generally baptized in three phases, we have 204 in February, only 9 in July, and 189 in November. This leads to the supposition that at the peak of the *manori* famine, which strongly affected the Mugamba and thus Kiganda, the men left in quest of food. Did they die on the way to the Imbo, as recorded in the collective memory,[33] or did they simply emigrate, abandoning their women and children? I hope to resolve this question very soon.

Still, a careful analysis of these missionary data, which certainly requires a lot of patience, will allow us to confirm or refute at the regional and local levels the main trends of historical population history in Burundi during the colonial era.

FIGURE 10.1 Marriages and Deaths at Rushubi and Kiganda

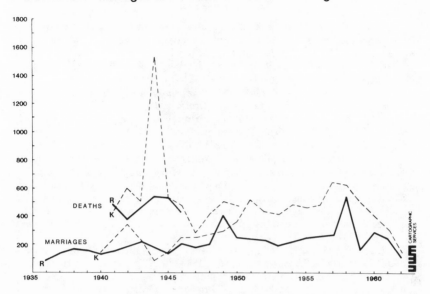

FIGURE 10.2 Baptisms at Rushubi and Kiganda

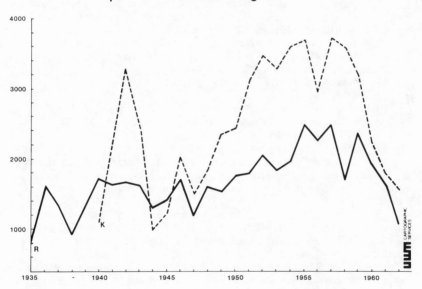

NOTES

1. C. Thibon, "Croissance et perceptions démographiques; une politique démographique intégrée: Quelques interrogations préalables," *Revue Tiers-Monde* 27, no. 106 (April–June 1986), 297–308.

2. F. Gourou, *La densité de la population au Ruanda-Urundi: Esquisse d'une étude géographique* (Brussels, 1953), 21–25.

3. Ministère des Colonies, *Plan décennel pour le développement économique et social du Ruanda-Urundi* (Brussels, 1951), 5–20.

4. G. Feltz, "Une introduction à l'histoire de l'enseignement en Afrique Centrale (XIXᵉ–XXᵉ siècles): Idéologies, Pouvoirs, et Sociétés," *Bulletin de l'Institut Historique Belge de Rome* (1981), 351–399.

5. Cf. Délégation Apostolique, *Statistiques annuelles des missions catholiques du Congo belge et du Ruanda-Urundi* (Léopoldville, 1935–1961).

6. C. Thibon, "Crise démographique et mise en dépendance au Burundi et dans la région des Grands Lacs, 1880–1910," *Cahiers d'histoire* (Bujumbura) 2 (1984); *Cahiers du Centro de Recherches Africaines* 4 (1984), 19–40; idem: "Un siècle de croissance démographique au Burundi (1850–1960), *Cahiers d'histoire* 3 (1985), 5–21.

7. J. P. Chrétien, "L'Afrique des Grands Lacs existe-t-elle?" *Revue Tiers-Monde* 27, no. 106 (April–June 1986), 253–270. Cf. also Roger Herremans, Annie Bart, and François Bart, "Agriculture et paysages rwandais à travers des sources missionnaires, 1900–1950," *Cultures et développement* 14 (1982), 3–39.

8. "Diaire de Buhonga," 1918, 27. J. Perraudin, *Naissance d'une église: histoire du Burundi Chrétien* (Bujumbura, 1963), 80.

9. "Diaire de Rugari," 7 July 1908 and August 1908. These data are corroborated by oral information. Cf. Antoinette Nijembazi (Master's thesis, Université du Burundi, December 1983).

10. *Rapport Annuel des Pères Blancs* (*RAPB*), 1910–1911, p. 85.

11. "Diaire de Kanyinya," 26 January and 2 February 1922.

12. Ibid., 24 February 1922.

13. "Diaire de Kanyinya," January 6, 1925.

14. *RAPB*, 1913–1914, p. 102.

15. L. Greindl, "Notes sur les sources des missionnaires d'Afrique (Pères Blancs) pour l'est du Zaïre," *Etudes d'histoire Africaine* 7 (1975), 175–202.

16. *RAPB*, 1945–1946, p. 220.

17. Thibon, "Crise démographique," 28–32.

18. Thibon, "Un siècle de croissance"; E. Ngayimpenda, "Déterminants de la croissance démographique en situation coloniale: L'exemple du Burundi, ca. 1920–1969," in *Questions sur la paysannerie au Burundi* (Bujumbura, 1987), 201–223.

19. Cf. the colonial sources found in the territory of Bururi analyzed by Daniel Nyambariza, "Les efforts de guerre et la famine de 1943–1944 au Burundi, d'après les archives territoriales en Territoire de Bururi," *Cahiers d'histoire* 2 (1984), 1–18.

20. J. P. Chrétien, "Les migrations du XXᵉ siècle en Afrique orientale: Le cas de l'émigration des Banyarwanda et des Barundi vers l'Uganda," in Commission Internationale d'Histoire des Mouvements Sociaux et des Structures Sociales, *Les migrations internationales de la fin du XVIIᵉ siècle à nos jours* (Paris, 1980), 643–680.

21. *Annuaire ecclésiastique: Burundi*, 1979 and 1985.

22. Thibon, "Un siècle de croissance," 10–16.

23. L. Kavakure, "Famines and disettes au Burundi traditionnel" (Master's thesis, Université du Burundi, 1982); cf. also, with respect to the 1922 famine in the northeast, Melchiade Bukuru, "Le Nord-Est du Burundi de Coya à J. B. Ntidendereza: Aspects politiques et sociaux (fin XIXe siècle–1960)" (Master's thesis, Université du Burundi, 1986), 53–61 (seminar paper of J. Gahama).

24. C. Thibon, *Techniques de recherche historique: La démographie historique* (Bujumbura, 1982), 46–52.

25. Cf. P. Ryckmans, *Dominer pour servir* (Brussels, 1931), 171–197.

26. J. P. Chrétien, "Les migrations du XXe siècle en Afrique orientale," 654–655.

27. P. Leurquin, *Le niveau de vie des populations rurales du Ruanda-Urundi* (Louvain, I., 1960), 76.

28. "Diaire de Muyaga," January 1927.

29. Ministère de la Coopération, *Atlas du Burundi* (Paris, 1979), pl. 13 ("Du mandat belge à l'indépendance," by J. Gahama and G. le Jeune).

30. Oscar Nibogora, "Evolution politique et économique du Buragane-Bukurira (environs 1930–1960)" (Master's thesis, Université du Burundi, 1986), 45–46, 153–154.

31. Oral surveys done by Anatole Bacanamwo on the Mugera mission from 1933 to date (G. Feltz seminar: Histoire sociale et Histoire des mentalités), 1985–1986.

32. Cf. of the governor of Ruanda-Urundi, E. Jungers, to the Belgian Congo Governor General, 13 October 1938 (no. 3424/A.I.); from the Urundi resident to the territorial agent of Bururi, 6 October 1944 (no. 2105/A.I.3), in *Archives de Bururi. Cités par Nibogora, O., Evolution politique et économique du Buragane-Bukurira* (D. Nyambariza seminar: Histoire des méthodes de colonisation), 1985–1986.

33. G. Feltz, "Mémoire, conscience collective, et mentalités au Burundi, ca. 1900–1962," *History in Africa* 16 (1989).

PART 2

INNOVATIONS IN METHOD

11

Demographic Estimation from Deficient or Defective Data

KENNETH HILL

The three processes by which a population develops over time are fertility, mortality, and migration. Fertility provides new members of the population as births at exact age zero. Immigration provides new members at any subsequent age, though predominantly at young adult ages. Mortality and out-migration remove members at all ages after exact age zero, mortality predominantly at older ages (and at very young ages in high-mortality populations) and out-migration predominantly at young adult ages. If the numbers involved in each process are exactly known, changes in population size can be followed; and if the numbers are known by age, the population age structure can also be tracked. However, such a wealth of data is very unusual, available only for a small number of countries with complete population registers. For all other countries or areas within countries, some degree of estimation is required to measure the three demographic processes, both the degree of estimation and the methods available for the estimation depending on the amount and accuracy of the data available. Developed countries, and a few developing countries, have records of births and deaths sufficiently complete to be used without adjustment, but we often have to rely on estimation to measure the migration component of population change. Other developing countries have records of births and deaths that require evaluation and possibly adjustment before use. Yet others, including most countries in sub-Saharan Africa, lack systems for recording births and deaths altogether or have systems whose coverage is so incomplete as to render them useless for the purpose of tracking population change.

I shall be concerned with methods for obtaining estimates of the three demographic processes from deficient or defective data. I shall review current practice in demographic estimation, as well as considering in some detail techniques of special relevance to the analysis of colonial census data. By introducing current procedures, even some apparently irrelevant to the analysis of the historical data generally available for Africa, I hope to alert demographers to the potential analytical value of data

133

that might otherwise go unconsidered. I would also like to stress that *estimation* is not something restricted to developing countries or historical studies. All data sets are defective, and most are deficient—always requiring evaluation, often requiring adjustment, and sometimes requiring the application of more elaborate estimation procedures. What varies, of course, is the amount, nature, and accuracy of the data available for analysis. As a general rule, the greater the variety and degree of disaggregation of the data and the greater the number of periods or time points for which they are available, the greater the potential for evaluation, adjustment, or estimation. The problem with studying the colonial populations of Africa is that the data are limited in type, limited in disaggregation, and available for only a limited number of observation points.

PRINCIPLES OF ESTIMATION

The basic principles of demographic estimation are evaluation, adjustment, and transformation. We *evaluate* by comparing the consistency of similar measures across sources or time, sometimes first converting dissimilar measures into similar ones using theoretical demographic relationships and sometimes comparing observed values with models expressing observed demographic regularities such as mortality or fertility patterns by age. We *adjust* when evaluation indicates a lack of consistency and we have reason to prefer one measure over another, a procedure that is particularly valuable when one of the two measures has been converted from some other, dissimilar measure, which can then be adjusted directly. We *transform* one measure into another generally on the basis of empirical regularities or theoretical relationships, partly to facilitate evaluation but also to obtain a measure of one of the three demographic processes from an indicator affected by more than one of the processes but readily available or easily collected in the field.

Our ability to estimate demographic parameters for developing countries has increased greatly over the last twenty-five years. A number of factors have contributed to this increase: the data available have increased in quantity (the number of observations), quality (no doubt partly as a result of better-educated populations and interviewers), and depth (the detail available); while at the same time new or improved estimation procedures have been developed, sometimes making more efficient use of existing data, sometimes requiring the collection of new types of information. I will outline the major existing methodologies for estimating measures of the three demographic processes and conclude by discussing what might be done with the very limited data for colonial Africa.

FERTILITY ESTIMATION

There are two broad approaches to fertility estimation, one being the evaluation and, if necessary, adjustment of specific fertility measures and the other being the transformation of a mixed indicator (an age distribution) into a fertility measure by allowing for the effects of mortality.

Specific Fertility Measures

Births in a period provide numerators for calculating the crude birthrate, age-specific fertility rates, and other fertility measures. Numbers of births can come from a vital registration system, census or survey questions concerning births in the previous year or date of most recent birth, or indeed a complete history of all births or pregnancies by data of outcome. Both registration and simple survey questions often fail to record all births, so evaluation is essential. Procedures have been developed[1] for evaluating births by transforming the implied fertility levels into different measures, either the average number of children ever born for a given age group of women or an age distribution measure such as the population under age five. Comparisons can then be made between measures from different sources (or at least different types of questions from the same source). By making assumptions about the likely effects of errors on the different measures, such comparisons can sometimes provide a basis for adjustment. For example, the Brass P/F (parity/fertility), ratio method compares average numbers of children ever born, often called *average parity* (as reported by women classified by standard age groups) with similar measures calculated by cumulating current age-specific fertility rates calculated from registered births in a year or from survey reports of recent births. By concentrating on the parts of the two sets of information thought to be most reliable—the age pattern of the age-specific rates and the fertility level indicated by the average number of children reported by younger women—the pattern of the former can be adjusted by the level of the latter to obtain an improved estimate of fertility. It should be noted, however, that assumptions are required about error patterns and that the comparison is between lifetime measures (children ever born) and period measures (cumulated current fertility). If the assumptions are not valid or fertility has been changing, the adjusted estimate may not be an improvement at all.

Average parities themselves can be used to obtain standard fertility measures. A model (for example the Brass Relational Gompertz fertility model)[2] can be fitted to average parities by age group, and age-specific fertility rates can be obtained from the fitted model. Total births and the birthrate can then be obtained. Again, however, period measures are being derived from lifetime fertility measures. This problem can be resolved if average parities by age group are available from two surveys. Intersurvey fertility can then be obtained from cumulated differences in cohort lifetime fertility from one survey to the next, a procedure that not only provides period fertility measures but also provides a sensitive consistency test for the two surveys.[3]

Birth or maternity histories (whereby a complete record of each woman's births or deliveries, with the date of each one, is made) have the potential for providing information about fertility over an extended period prior to the survey. Though errors of omission and misdating, selection effects, and any truncation effect make evaluation and interpretation essential, such histories can provide information about the past recoverable in no other way. A birth history survey conducted in China in 1982, for example, has provided useful information about fertility in China back to the late 1940s (though China is a rather special case, since ages and dates are known precisely and the survey included all women up to sixty-eight years of age). The more usual practice of including women only up to age forty-nine limits the period of study to some twenty years prior to the survey.

Age Distribution

The age distribution of a population reflects its history of fertility, mortality, and migration, with its more recent history (over the last twenty years or so) being more important for its present structure than its more distant history. The fact remains, however, that a population age structure is entirely determined by these three processes and that if we know any two of the three, we can estimate at least some summary measure of the third. In practice, the number of processes is often reduced to two by assuming the population to be closed to migration—often a reasonable assumption for large national populations, though a perilous one for some subpopulations such as the population of an urban area.

Assuming a closed population, there are a number of ways in which fertility estimates can be derived from age distributions. The most direct method uses estimates of mortality to project the population backwards in time. For example, reverse-projecting the population aged zero to four for five years and reinstating the children who have died provides the number of births in the five years preceding the reference date of the population. Reverse-projecting the population aged five and over for five years provides the population five years earlier. Dividing the births by some average of the actual population aged fifteen to forty-nine estimates a general fertility ratio. Reverse projection to ten or fifteen years earlier provides fertility estimates for two more distant five-year periods, but the further back the project goes, the more sensitive it becomes to the mortality assumptions made and to how the population is reverse-projected. Though reverse projection does not provide information about age patterns of fertility, the "own-children" development (whereby children are linked to mothers within households according to relationship and other information and both mothers and children classified by single years of age are then reverse-projected to the birth of the child) does provide estimates of fertility pattern.[4] Reverse projection makes few assumptions (normally only that mortality is known and migration negligible) and is widely applicable, but its results are affected by age misreporting or differential survey coverage by age, especially for the child population.

A second approach matches the observed age distribution to that of a stable population chosen to have either a level of mortality or a rate of population growth similar to that of the study population. A stable population is the population age distribution that results from the continued exposure of a population to fixed fertility and mortality conditions. Ultimately, the age distribution becomes characteristic of these fixed fertility and mortality conditions. Through the use of model age patterns of mortality such as those of the Coale-Demeny regional model life tables,[5] a stable population resembling the study population can be found by matching age structures with either the level of mortality or the rate of population growth; and the birthrate of the matched stable population can be taken as an estimate of the birthrate for the actual population. Matching by mortality level generally provides more stable estimates than matching by growth rates. The method makes fairly extensive assumptions, namely, that the age pattern of mortality is known (or at least known to be approximated by a model pattern), that either the level of mortality or the rate of population growth is known, that the birthrate of the matched stable population can be taken as an estimate of the birthrate for the actual population, and that the age distribution conforms approximately to that of a stable population. Data errors can also affect the results, through age misreporting or differential survey coverage by age, though to a lesser extent than in the case of reverse projection, since cumulated populations by age are used.

The third approach, using successive census age distributions and age-specific growth rates, has been proposed by Preston.[6] This method requires generalized expression for the age structure of a closed population, age-specific growth rates, proportions of the population passing through age group boundaries, and an assumed age pattern of mortality to estimate the birthrate and the level of the age pattern of mortality. The estimation procedure estimates these parameters by fitting a straight line to points for successive age group boundaries, and the behavior of these points by age provides a useful check on whether the assumptions are met. This method makes very good use of limited data (two age distributions by five-year age groups and an assumed age pattern of mortality) and, though effected by age misreporting, changes in enumeration completeness, and migration, shows the effects of these errors or deviations from assumption. Unfortunately, however, the method appears to be sensitive to the selected age pattern of mortality unless the level of mortality under age five is known.

MORTALITY ESTIMATION

There are four basic approaches to the estimation of mortality, the choice of which ones to use in a particular application being determined by the nature of the data available. The simplest in terms of data requirements is to apply stable population relationships to a single recorded age distribution. However, the simplicity in terms of data requirements is to apply stable population relationships to a single, recorded age distribution. However, the simplicity of the data needs is compensated for by the number of assumptions required, namely, that the population is both stable and closed to migration, that the age pattern of mortality can be represented by a selected set of model life tables, that some other demographic indicator (such as the population growth rate or birthrate) is known, and that the population age distribution is approximately correct. The normal procedure is to identify the mortality level implied by the proportions of the population under successive ages for stable populations of the given growth rate or birthrate derived from the selected set of model life tables. A final estimate is then obtained as some average such as the median of the different estimates from successive boundary ages. Though some sense of the reliability of the estimate can be obtained from the spread of the individual estimates around it, an estimate obtained in this way should generally be regarded as rough because of the potentially large effects of deviations from the underlying assumptions. Estimates of child mortality obtained in this way are particularly weak, since very different levels of child mortality combined with compensating differences in fertility produce essentially identical age distributions.

The second approach uses two census age distributions to estimate mortality from intercensal survival. In the traditional method cohorts identified by age at the first census are compared with survivors of the same cohorts, t years older (if t is the intercensal interval) at the second census, and the change in cohort size is taken to represent cohort attrition due to mortality. Recent developments of the method[7] use intercensal growth rates of age groups and an average intercensal age distribution (rather than cohort attrition) as the basis of estimation and are more convenient to apply when the intercensal interval is not a multiple of the standard age group width. These intercensal methods do not assume stability, but they do assume a population closed to migration. The results obtained are sensitive both to age misreporting and to changes in census coverage, and they provide little information about child mortality. The mortality element of the Preston method[8] described in the fertility section is essentially a form of intercensal survival. Despite its weaknesses, intercensal survival has been widely used (for example, forming the basis of India life tables from the late nineteenth century onward).

The third approach is to use survey questions about the survival or otherwise of close relatives of the respondent. The most widely used, most successful, and most important contributor to the improvement in our knowledge of the demography of the developing world is the range of techniques used to estimate child mortality from information on the survival of each surveyed woman's children. In its simplest form, information on the number of children ever born and the number dead of women classified by age group provides information on levels and recent trends of child mortality. First developed by W. Brass,[9] it has since been extended and refined by many others.[10] The basic principle of the methodology is that the proportion dead among the children ever borne by women of a particular age group is determined by the distribution of the births over time, governing their length of exposure to risk, and by the mortality risks themselves. By allowing for the time distribution of births, observed proportions can be converted into probabilities of dying by exact ages of childhood. Experience has shown the method to work well in a wide variety of conditions, and though the estimates are affected by any underreporting of dead children, they are remarkably robust to the assumptions and models inherent in the estimation procedure. Child mortality estimates have also been obtained successfully from maternity history data such as that collected widely by the World Fertility Survey, recording the date of birth and, if dead, age at death for all the births of each woman surveyed. Such data provide measures of levels, trends, and age patterns of child mortality without recourse to any major assumptions. Less successful have been attempts to estimate recent child mortality from information on the survival of the most recent birth: the mortality estimates obtained from such information seem generally to be too low.

Attempts have also been made to use data on survival of relatives to estimate adult mortality, though opinion is divided as to how successful these attempts have been. Methods have been developed to use information on survival of mother, of father,[11] of first spouse,[12] and of siblings[13] to estimate mortality levels; and Brass and Bangboye[14] have developed procedures for establishing reference dates, and hence trends, of the estimates obtained. The attraction of these methods is that they can be used in a single survey, but with the exception of information on survival of the mother, reporting consistency is poor, and the estimates obtained are suspect. Even estimates based on survival of the mother require careful interpretation.

The fourth approach is the evaluation and, if necessary and possible, adjustment of registered or recorded deaths by age. The evaluation is made by comparing the age distribution of deaths with the age distribution of the population. The original method, proposed by Brass,[15] assumed the population to be closed to migration and stable and the completeness of both death registration and population enumeration to be constant by age. Deathrates above a series of ages were plotted against birthday rates (the number of people having an ath birthday divided by the population aged a or over) at the same ages. A straight line fitted to the points estimates the stable growth rate as its intercept and the reciprocal of registration completeness as its slope. Methods replacing the assumption of stability by observed age-specific population growth rates (for example, from two successive censuses) but otherwise making similar assumptions have recently been developed.[16] These methods have greatly increased our ability to extract estimates from incomplete vital registration data, although they are of little use for estimating child mortality (since the registration completeness of child deaths may be quite different from that of adult deaths) and cannot be used with any confidence if the completeness of registration is really low (say, below 50 percent or so).

MIGRATION ESTIMATION

Migration has long been the Cinderella of demographic estimation, partly because it is often not very important at the level of national populations, partly because it is peculiarly intractable because migration flows are volatile and lack the regularities we expect in fertility or mortality rates, and partly because even in developed countries migrations are rarely recorded in the way births and deaths are.

The commonest approach to estimating migration is as a residual. The population observed at one time is survived forward using known or assumed mortality rates to a second point of observation, and the difference between the observed and projected populations is taken as being net migration. Application may be simplified by using an age-specific growth rate procedure,[17] and some consistency checking is possible if the age distribution of net migrants is known or can be assumed; but the estimates are fairly rough and require prior knowledge of mortality.

A second approach is to use commonly available data related to migration, such as information on birthplace, length of residence, or residence at some specified prior date such as five years earlier. Birthplace information is useful for immigrant populations, since residual methods can then be applied to a population of which the residual may be a substantial proportion, and emigration can be estimated from birthplace information collected in other countries or other parts of the same country. Birthplace information, of course, can show only one move a lifetime; but combining information from two sources referring to different time points can provide measures of flow during the period between the two points. However, evaluation and adjustment procedures have been used mainly on an ad hoc basis, without the development and systemization that have characterized similar procedures used in the study of fertility or mortality.

A third approach with a strong resemblance to the indirect procedures for estimating mortality has been tried on an experimental basis by asking survey respondents about the residence of specified relatives (for example, mothers about their children and all respondents about their siblings).[18] Though these methods are intriguing, it remains to be seen what their practical value will be.

CONCLUSION

The above outline is intended to provide an introduction to the sorts of methods used at the moment in demographic estimation. Many of these methods require information from special survey questions or vital registration or else require considerable depth of information in terms of detail and are simply not relevant to the task of developing demographic estimates for Africa's colonial interlude. However, it is surprising what information exists or can be constructed. For example, the 1948 and 1959 censuses of the Uganda Protectorate collected information on children ever born and children dead by age of woman on a sample basis. The data are remarkably consistent and suggest a steady and substantial decline in child mortality from the mid-1930s (with a probability of dying by age five of around 42 percent) to the late 1950s (with a probability of dying by age five of around 26 percent). Those working in historical demography should be aware of what can be done with census data that have not been fully used or with fragments of data that may be discovered. Such historical demographers or demographic historians should also be aware of the principles of estimation: of comparison, evaluation, while trying to use all the available information and fit it into a consistent and plausible overall picture. The data for Africa are often poor and always limited. Age distributions are distorted, totals are affected by coverage errors, and growth rates by coverage changes. However, it is essential to try to make use of all the available data, to disaggregate where possible in the hope of finding population subgroups less affected by error than others, to make as few assumptions as possible, and to use methodologies suitable for the task at hand. Finally, we must be suitably modest about our results and not make extravagant claims for counterintuitive conclusions.

NOTES

1. W. Brass et al., eds., *The Demography of Tropical Africa* (Princeton, 1968); United Nations, *Indirect Techniques for Demographic Estimation*, manual X, Department of International Economic and Social Affairs Population Studies, no. 81 (New York, 1983).

2. W. Brass, "The Use of the Gompertz Relation Model to Estimate Fertility," in *International Population Conference, Manila* (Liège, 1981).

3. United Nations, *Indirect Techniques*.

4. See, e.g., L. Cho, "The Own Children Approach to Fertility Estimation: An Elaboration," in *International Population Conference* (Liège, 1973).

5. A. J. Coale and P. Demeny, *Regional Model Life Tables and Stable Populations* (Princeton, 1966).

6. S. Preston, "An Integrated System for Demographic Estimation from Two Censuses," *Demography* 20 (1983), 213–226.

7. S. Preston and N. Bennett, " A Census-based Method for Estimating Adult Mortality," *Population Studies* 37, no. 1 (1983), 91–104.

8. Preston, "An Integrated System."

9. Brass et al., *Demography of Tropical Africa.*

10. For a detailed description of current methodology, see United Nations, *Indirect Techniques*, Manual X.

11. W. Brass and K. Hill, "Estimating Adult Mortality from Orphanhood," *International Population Conference* (Liège, 1973).

12. K. Hill, "Estimating Adulty Mortality Levels from Information on Widowhood," *Population Studies* 31, no. 1 (1977).

13. K. Hill and J. Trussell, "Further Developments in Indirect Mortality Estimation," *Population Studies* 31, no. 2 (1977), 313–334.

14. W. Brass and Bangboye, "The Time Location of Reports of Survivorship: Estimates for Maternal and Paternal Orphanhood and the Ever-Widowed," Working Paper no. 81–1, London School of Hygiene and Tropical Medicine.

15. W. Brass, "Methods for Estimating Fertility and Mortality from Limited and Defective Data," Carolina Population Center, Chapel Hill, NC.

16. E. G. Bennett, N. Horiuchi, and S. Horiuchi, "Estimating the Completeness of Death Registration in a Closed Population," *Population Index* 47, no. 2 (1981), 207–221; idem, "Mortality Estimation from Registered Deaths in Less Developed Countries," *Demography* 21, no. 2 (1984), 217–223.

17. S. Preston and A. J. Coale, "Age Structure, Growth, Attrition, and Accession: A New Synthesis," *Population Index* 48, no. 2 (1982), 217–259.

18. See, e.g., J. Somoza et al., *Barbados Experimental Migration Survey: Methods and Results*, International Union for the Scientific Study of Population Reprints Series, no. 4 (Liège, 1984).

12

Perspectives on Census Data for Migration Measurement

R. MANSELL PROTHERO

I have spent more than three decades of interest and involvement in the study of *migration* in Africa, using this term in an umbrella sense to involve all forms of population movement. I shall here draw on published sources (particularly those with which I have had a close association) in an attempt to provide some tentative and speculative perspectives on migration measurement from census data. More reference will be made to East and Central Africa, but example and illustration will also be taken from other parts of sub-Saharan Africa where these have seemed appropriate for comparative purposes.

The colonial authorities were in all places and at all times short of resources in money and men for the conduct of administration and for the promotion of economic and social development. But from the early stages of colonial rule the need for some quantitative evaluation of the size and composition of populations was recognized. Partial censuses in British territories in West Africa date back to the middle of the nineteenth century, though they were restricted in terms of areas and number of people involved.[1] With increasing acquisition of territory and of people, the need for enumeration was recognized. For Northern Nigeria, following the declaration of the protectorate in 1900, High Commissioner Lugard wrote in his second annual report:[2] "A census and a geographical survey, together with the collection of a mass of statistical information regarding products, area under cultivation, etc., are being effected in a rough and ready way; but the work of fully grappling with and completing so large a task remains for the future."

The first census of the protectorate was not taken until 1911, but over the previous ten years districts had been assessed and reported on, and annual provincial and divisional reports and provincial gazetteers were made, which were major sources of information presented in relatively generalized and unsystematic fashion.

Colonial administrators in Nigeria and elsewhere were concerned primarily with having population estimates, particularly for adult males, for the purpose of levying tax to contribute to the costs of administration and of the services that were being provided, albeit in embryonic form.

I. Masser and W. T. S. Gould[3] have distinguished three phases in the collection of census data in tropical Africa: (1) before World War II, an approach closely associated with the colonial administration; (2) after World War II, a more systematic approach with the setting up of specialist organizations (e.g., the East African Statistical Department and the Bureau of Demography in the Belgian Congo); and (3) further advance with postindependence recognition of the need for data to plan hoped-for social and economic development.

Our concern is with the first two of these phases. Censuses in the first phase were primarily estimated head counts, which did not involve *enumeration* in the conventionally accepted census meaning of the term.[4] These censuses were reviewed for British colonial Africa by R. R. Kuczynski,[5] who discussed in comprehensive fashion the range and reliability of the data, the problems encountered in obtaining them, and their many gaps. His conclusion with respect to the probability of substantial knowledge on the basis of the information then available were largely negative.[6] Censuses in the second and third phases have been wider-ranging in their content and their coverage, with the development of proper enumeration and increased reliability. They have been influenced by recommendations and advice from the United Nations through organizations such as the UN Economic Commission for Africa (UNECA) and the UN Fund for Population Activities (UNFPA).

Masser and Gould[7] also draw attention to what they call "two major traditions of data collection," which were firmly consolidated in the last decade of the colonial era:

- Conventional censuses relating to the whole population in anglophone countries
- Demographic surveys of varying intensity and coverage in francophone countries

These two traditions have produced differing results in respect to data relevant to the study of migration in general and particularly its measurement.

With this background, consideration may be given to what is available for the study of migration from official censuses and surveys in the colonial period, extending from the latter part of the nineteenth century up to the 1960s, when the majority of African colonial territories achieved independence.

COLONIAL CENSUSES AND SURVEYS

It may be stated very briefly and simply that the first phase of demographic data collection up to the end of World War II yielded very little that can be used for the study of migration. For tax assessment and payment colonial authorities were particularly concerned with the de jure residence of the people. In the earliest phases of administration it is also probable (though it remains to be verified) that colonial administrations either *believed* they were dealing with populations that were relatively immobile or *wished* populations should be stabilized for ease of administration and the provision of services. To take an extreme example—in the Horn of Africa (probably the part of the continent with the highest proportion of population consistently mobile) neither the British nor the Italian colonial administrations attempted a total census; and the first of its kind has been taken by the independent Somali government only recently.

Colonial governments became increasingly aware of movements of population, both movements of a long-standing nature and predating colonial rule and those that were more recent and occurred largely through economic development associated directly or otherwise with colonialism. They became particularly concerned with movements of migrant labor, which they both directly and indirectly initiated and stimulated.[8] These were made objects of study in themselves, but since labor migration primarily involved men only and since it was intended not to be permanent but temporary and circulatory, it is understandable that it should not—and indeed could not—be given particular attention in censuses.

Swaziland is a small territory where census experience may not be representative, but its 1966 census report conveniently provides a full review of the questions that were asked in censuses from the time when they were first taken in that country. There was variation in the nature and number of questions, reflecting the kinds of information deemed important at particular points in time, and also variation in the degree of realism entertained about the accuracy of responses that might be expected (Table 12.1). The questions relevant to migration were limited. The censuses that asked for place of birth (all except that for 1911) would have yielded information on lifetime migration, provided places of birth were cross-tabulated with the places at which respondents answered the census questionnaire. The following comments made on the various censuses and taken at random as examples are indicative of what needs to be borne in mind in considering the data:

- 1904: "Not all the data for every topic is, however, available for each census district and for each component."
- 1921: "The modified *de jure* principle, that 'all natives domiciled in Swaziland shall be enumerated as though they were in their homes,' was followed."
- 1936: "The census is not well-documented but it is clear that strict economy was observed; as the staff was limited so was the time taken to enumerate the population increase."
- 1946: "The modified *de jure* principle was again adopted because it

was thought desirable to follow practices in 1936. . . . A code list was published but no instructions were issued and concepts and categories were not defined. . . . The 1946 census was clearly one of Swazi residents in Swaziland only."

- 1956: "The census was clearly confined to enumerating Africans in Swaziland only. . . . The results of this census in particular, as well as those of previous years, are the subject of suspicion, the basic cause for which is the inefficiency of a census by assembly as a suitable method for controlling coverage and accuracy."[9]

TABLE 12.1 Swaziland: Comparative Summary of Census Topics, 1904–1966

	1904	1911	1921	1936	1946	1956	1966
Sex	X	X	X	X	X	X	X
Age[a]	X	X	X	X	X	X	X
Marital status	X	X	X	X	X	X	—
Literacy	—	—	X[b]	—	X	X	—
Languages spoken	—	—	X[c]	X[c]	X	X	—
Income	—	—	—	X[d]	X[d]	—	—
Occupation	X	X	X	X	X	X	X
Industry	X	—	—	—	—	—	X
Place of residence	—	—	—	X	X	—	—
Birthplace	X	—	X	X	X	X	X
Education	X[e]	X[e]	—	—	—	—	X
Fertility	—	—	—	X	—	X	—
Religious affiliation	X	—	X	X	X	X	—
Status of place of employment	—	—	—	X[d]	X[d]	X	X
Period of residence	—	—	X[c]	X[c]	X[d]	—	—
Nationality	—	—	X[d]	X[d]	X[d]	—	—
Home language	—	—	—	—	X[d]	—	—
Tribe	X	X	—	—	—	X	—
Sickness and infirmity	X	X	—	—	—	—	—
Ethnic group	X	X	X	X	X	X	X
Agricultural statistics	X	X	X	—	—	—	X
Mining statistics	X	X	—	—	—	—	—
Prison statistics	X	X	—	—	—	—	X

Source: Swaziland Government, Report on the 1966 Swaziland Census (Mbabane, 1968).
[a]In broad age groups for African except 1966.
[b]Africans only.
[c]Europeans only.
[d]Europeans and ONA only.
[e]School statistics.

It would seem that little can be done with the data from the majority of official censuses prior to World War II to provide even fragmentary or unreliable knowledge of overall migration patterns in any country of tropical Africa. The director of the East African Statistical Department wrote of Kenya, Uganda, Tanganyika, and Zanzibar for this period, "Information on the migratory movement of the non-African population is available, but very little can be gleaned on the African."[10]

Survey data were similarly fragmentary. In the Belgian Congo, by the mid-1930s, no regular census had been taken. Population data were obtained from a system of *recensement sur fiches individuelles*: people were registered in each administrative division, and *fiches* were transferred from one system to another for persons who changed their place of residence. In 1935 this system was claimed to cover 91 percent of the population. A further approach to the study of population movement was to select sample centers, typical of larger areas, in which counts were made each year; by 1935 they were estimated to cover one-sixteenth of the total population. However, doubt was expressed as to whether the statistical material "yet sufficient to enable an accurate estimate to be made of the character, or to determine the causes, of movement of population since the beginning of the European occupation."[11]

In the last two decades of colonial rule the situation improved variably in time and place, notwithstanding the number of censuses and surveys that were undertaken (Table 12.2). For example, review of the demographic features of Central Africa (Northern and Southern Rhodesia and Nyasaland) made no reference to movement of population.[12]

The postwar censuses were mostly de facto enumerations, though in many of the surveys and partial censuses there was a concern to establish small de facto populations to account for temporary absentees and residents, making possible some identification of population movement in the data. However, systematic comprehensive analysis of migration is only possible where there are questions that identify aggregate movement. These data provide two tools for analysis: *surrogate measures* (where migration is only implicit in the question asked) and *direct measures* (where information about individual mobility is explicit in the question).

Surrogate Measures

Measurement of migration from analysis of age and sex data is based on the assumption that migration is selective in terms of both of these characteristics and that overall levels of mobility can thus be inferred from regional variations in the age and sex of the population enumerated. For the more detailed analysis of migration at the national level such measures are only of limited value. Furthermore, any conclusions drawn from them must be treated with caution because of variations in the age and sex structure of the population that may occur as a result of regional variations in fertility and mortality rather than, or in addition to, migration. Analysis of these variations may also be complicated by inaccurate enumeration. Age misreporting is a well-known and serious problem in Africa and may vary substantially in extent within a population and between different parts of a

TABLE 12.2 Censuses and Surveys in Tropical Africa, 1945–1977

Country	Year(s) of Partial Census or Survey	Year(s) of Complete Census
Angola	—	1950, 1960, 1970
Botswana	1956	1972
Burundi	1952, 1965	—
Cameroon	1960–1965	—
Central African Republic	1939–1960	—
Chad	1964	1974
Congo (Brazzaville)	1960–1961	—
Dahomey	1960–1961	—
Equatorial Guinea	—	1950, 1960, 1970
French Territory of the Afars and Issas	1966	1961
Gabon	1960–1961	—
Gambia	—	1963, 1973
Ghana	1966, 1971	1948, 1960, 1970
Guinea	1954–1955	—
Ivory Coast	1957–1958	—
Kenya	—	1948, 1961, 1969
Lesotho	—	1956, 1966
Liberia	1969–1973	—
Malawi	(1945) 1970–1973	1966
Mali	1960–1961	1976
Mauritania	1964–1965	1977
Mozambique	—	1950, 1960, 1970
Namibia	—	1960, 1970
Niger	1959–1960	1977
Nigeria	—	1953, 1963, 1973
Portuguese Guinea	—	1950, 1960, 1970
Rhodesia	1953–1955	1962, 1969
Rwanda	1952, 1970–1971	—
Senegal	1960, 1970	—
Sierra Leone	—	1963, 1974
Somalia	—	1975
South Africa	—	1951, 1960, 1970
Sudan	—	1956
Swaziland	—	1956, 1966
Tanzania	—	1948, 1957, 1967
Togo	1953–1961	1970
Uganda	—	1948, 1959, 1969
Upper Volta	1960, 1961, 1968, 1969	1975
Zaire	1948	1957
Zambia	1950, 1963, 1974	1969

Source: I. Masser and W. T. S. Gould, *Interregional Migration in Tropical Africa* (London, 1975).

country. An analysis of the age and sex of the 1963 census of Northern Rhodesia stated that regional differences in sex ratios could be explained by rural-urban migration but that variations in age structure could be explained in some parts of the country "by factors affecting natural increase as much as by the effects of rural-urban migration."[13]

Surrogate measures of migration based on tribal data are dependent on the assumption that ethnic groups are spatially discrete and that all members of a tribe living outside the discrete tribal area are migrants. Using data from the East African censuses of 1948 (Uganda and Kenya) and 1948 and 1957 (Tanganyika), a simple but effective measure was devised to indicate the comparative tendency of members of different tribal groups to migrate away from tribal home areas.[14] The total number of each tribe enumerated in the home district was subtracted from the total number of the tribe recorded in the census, and the residue was then expressed as a percentage and termed the *emigration rate*. Differences in rates brought out very clearly the tendency of some tribes to provide more migrants than others, and in many instances explanations could be advanced for this varying characteristic. Applying this index to data for the male and female populations brought out some further interesting contrasts both within and between tribes.

It was possible to calculate the index because the East African censuses enumerated all major tribal groups in all enumeration areas. Such detailed ethnic enumeration was lacking in the Nigerian census of 1952–1953, where in the Northern Region, for example, only major tribes (Hausa, Fulani, Kanuri, Nupe, and Tiv) were enumerated in all provinces.[15] Apart from these, the selection of tribes to be enumerated was left to the discretion of the authorities in each province, resulting in a lack of uniformity, a degree of confusion, and only fragmentary data for other than the major tribes. With such data emigration rates could not be calculated in the detail that was possible in East Africa.

The Southall method of obtaining a migration measure might have been employed with the tribal data from the Uganda census of 1959 and the Kenya census of 1962. The major tribes were recorded in each of the enumeration areas, and the data were published at county level for Uganda and at district level for Kenya. The census data for Uganda and Kenya also included information on non-Ugandan and non-Kenyan African populations. Some non-Ugandan tribes represented in Uganda in considerable numbers were recorded separately (e.g., Banyarwanda and Rundi).[16] In addition, others from Ruanda-Urundi (the Belgian trusteeship territory) and Kenya who were not of these tribes were recorded in the category *unspecified*, one for each of these countries. This was done also for people from the Sudan and Tanzania. People from Egypt, Ethiopia, Somalia, and the Comoros Islands and Madagascar were grouped together as *non-Africans*(!); and those from other African countries not otherwise specified were classified as *other Africans*. In Kenya the classification for the non-Kenyan population was much less elaborate; and people were recorded as from Tanzania, Uganda, Sudan, Ethiopia, Rhodesia and Nyasaland, Ruanda-Urundi, or *other African countries*.[17] Thus, for Uganda and Kenya it was possible to have a measure of immigrants from other countries in eastern Africa.

Direct Measures

Data on place of birth and duration of residence were either completely lacking or were available only in general terms from colonial censuses. For example, a question in the 1948 census in the Gold Coast asked whether people were born where they were enumerated or in the South, Ashanti, the northern territories, Togoland, or *other British foreign country.* These data could provide some indications of migration, but only with reference to major areas into which the country was divided. Nevertheless, they were considerably more revealing than the 1952–1953 census of Nigeria, which included no question on place of birth.

In the 1960 census of Ghana (which was of course strictly postindependence in that country) the classification of place-of-birth data was similar to, but slightly more detailed than, that used in 1948. Population movements and growth in Ghana based on the 1960 census data were studied by E. V. T. Engmann[18] and by J. M. Hunter,[19] both of them drawing attention to the deficiencies of the data but nevertheless attempting to draw conclusions from them. Over two-fifths of the population were enumerated away from place of birth, indicating a high degree of mobility; but the limitations of the data precluded any study either of regional characteristics of migration or of seasonal movements.

In the 1963 census of African population in Northern Rhodesia place-of-birth data were recorded in two broad categories: *born in Northern Rhodesia* and *born elsewhere.* In the first category there was no further breakdown by district or otherwise, but in the second there was a breakdown by country of birth (Southern Rhodesia, Malawi, Angola, Mozambique, Tanzania, Congo, and *other countries*). However, these details were published only as totals for the whole of Northern Rhodesia. Further information was published showing the allocation of indigenous and nonindigenous (by country) population among three categories of land: *African rural areas, Crown Land farming areas,* and *urban areas.* Figures for persons born inside the country and outside the country (unspecified) were given for provinces and districts and also for the three land categories. For provinces only, numbers were given by sex in two main age groups (*born before 1942* and *born 1942 and after*) according to countries of birth. For example, the population of Barotseland was shown by sex and age according to place of birth in Northern Rhodesia, Angola, or *other countries.* Data such as these gave some indication of the patterns of immigration into Zambia but no indication of migration within the country (though the latter movements were in fact the larger).

Data for labor migration within Northern Rhodesia were given in the labor and population statistics in the *Annual Report of the Ministry of African Affairs* up to and including 1962. The numbers of taxable males were recorded in several categories: *living at home, employed but home on leave, at work locally within province, outside province but within territory,* and *outside territory* (in Southern Rhodesia, Malawi, South Africa,

Tanzania, Congo, or elsewhere). These data were collected by villages but were then aggregated and given by chiefs' areas in district reports and by districts in provincial reports, but even these details were not published. Figures were published only for provinces and territory in the annual report. Where they could be consulted for chiefs' areas and for districts, it was possible to plot the movements of manpower within and outside the country. No information was available on the movement of women and children.

In the Belgian Congo the demographic information for the 1950s was described as "rather extraordinary by African standards," being the result of

1. The evolution of a system of continuous registration, "with a higher level of accuracy than has been attained in any other African country";
2. The rapid extension through most of the country of birth and death registration, which was almost complete in some regions by the end of the decade; and
3. A Demographic Inquiry in the mid-1950s based on house-to-house interviews of a large probabilistic sample of the whole population.

The Demographic Inquiry interviewed 1.36 million persons in sample areas representing a population of about 12.8 million in 1956. It is difficult to comment on what the inquiry yielded on migration, though it included estimates of de jure and de facto population. In reviewing it, A. Romaniuk made little reference to migration but in an overall comment wrote, "Perhaps the most valuable product of this study is the set of estimated measures of fertility."[20]

COLONIAL AND POSTCOLONIAL CENSUSES

The ways in which place-of-birth data were treated in colonial censuses and in those since independence are distinctive. When questions on place of birth were included in colonial censuses, they were treated as subordinate to questions on tribal affiliation as indicators of migration patterns. The data were not used in published tabulations except to establish de jure populations for regions and to establish total numbers born outside the region of enumeration, thereby providing some indication of the extent of net migration. Examples are to be found in the censuses of Gold Coast (1948), Kenya (1948), Uganda (1948 and 1959), and Tanganyika (1948 and 1957). The report of the Uganda census of 1959 makes only three passing and highly speculative textual references to place-of-birth data, in contrast to giving very detailed data on tribal composition[21] for each parish in four volumes. Tribal data were given greater priority in analysis and tabulation than were place-of-birth data in the Swaziland census of 1966, and it was stated in the census report that a "question on ethnic group was regarded as essential and it was decided to elaborate this further and elicit the tribe to which each respondent acknowledged allegiance. As a check the birthplace data would be reintroduced and a correlation of the two fields obtained to provide a reasonable estimate, and incidently, useful information on migration and mobility."[22] The view that tribal affiliation was more meaningful than place of birth as an indication of movement persisted in the Southern Rhodesia census of 1969.

Apart from the special case of Swaziland (1966), tabulations of place-of-residence data were published in preindependence censuses only for Kenya (1962) and Gambia (1963), and these colonial censuses have greater affinity with the postindependence censuses in other countries. Tables 12.3 and 12.4 enable comparisons to be made between data on African place of birth from colonial and postindependence censuses. The principal differences between them were not in the questions asked but rather in the tabulations published. The emphasis changed to place-of-birth-by-place-of-residence data at the expense of detailed tabulations of tribal composition, even in censuses that included a question on tribal affiliation. The change was more apparent in Tanzania than in Kenya, for in the former the question on tribe was asked only of heads of household, and these data were used only in tables of household populations for each district by tribe of the household head. The postindependence censuses in Malawi (1966), Uganda (1969), and Ghana (1970), in common with those of many African countries omitted the tribal question altogether.

In the African censuses of the 1960s UN recommendations regarding questions on duration of residence and place of last residence were largely ignored. It is not clear why they were ignored, nor is this discussed in any of the published census reports. It could be argued that such questions were of less relevance in Africa than elsewhere; for many movements are temporary, and migrants often maintain a "home" residence to which they return frequently in circulatory, oscillatory, or pendular fashion.[23] However, a retrospective question on place of residence twelve months before was incorporated in the 1969 Zambia census to supplement the place-of-birth question asked in general enumeration.[24] Such additional information can be used to give a general indication of the time scales that might be associated with place-of-birth data and to check the validity of any assumptions made concerning the relationship between lifetime and recent movement. This accorded with the proposal that data on the place of residence at some time in the past should be collected in addition to those on place of birth.[25]

In postcolonial times the Population Programme of UNECA has come

TABLE 12.3 African Birthplace Data: Some Colonial Censuses

Census	Form of Enumeration of Birthplace Question	Number of Specified Birthplaces	Data Published	
			Number of Birthplaces by Residence Tabulations	Other Data
Kenya and Tanganyika	10% sample	—	none	de jure population
Uganda and Ghana, 1948	10% sample	7	none	none
Tanganyika 1957	5% sample	20	none	none
Uganda 1959	5% sample	17	none	none
Kenya 1962	all urban areas,	42	7	none
	10% rural sample	—	—	none
Gambia 1963	all	57	16	none
Swaziland 1966	all	4	6	disaggregated by 5-yr. age groups
Rhodesia 1969	10% sample	50	none	de jure population

Source: Masser and Gould, 1975.

TABLE 12.4 African Birthplace Data: Postindependence Censuses

Census	Form of Enumeration of Birthplace Question	Number of Specified Birthplaces	Data Published	
			Number of Birthplaces by Residence Tabulations	Other Data
Ghana 1960	all	7 + town or village	77	
Sierra Leone 1963	all	148	148	
Malawi 1966	all	24		
Tanzania 1967	all urban, 20% rural areas	19	67	5 -yr. aggregate groups born in district and elsewhere[a]
Uganda 1969	all urban, 10% rural areas	18	21	
Kenya 1969	all urban, 10% rural areas	41	8	
Zambia 1969	all	43	43	
Ghana 1970	all	9 + town or village	9	
Nigeria 1973	—[b]	—[b]	—[b]	

Source: Masser and Gould, 1975.
[a]Special tabulations of place of birth by age groups (0–14, 15–20, 30–44, 45+) have been made available to the present authors.
[b]Although a birthplace question was included on the enumeration, precise details of publication are unavailable.

to play a part in the planning and organization of censuses. Its function is essentially advisory; and its recommendations, like those from any UN agency, need not be followed by governments. But in practice, it is normally in a position to exercise very considerable influence. There are very few government officials in African countries with experience in planning and executing censuses, and there are very few population analysts. Consequently, the population experts of UNECA, have been called on at all stages: planning, organization, data processing, and publication. While the treatment of migration in the postcolonial censuses generally reflects UN recommendations, there are considerable variations in detail between censuses and some major departures from recommendations. These recommendations include the kind of enumeration used to collect migration data, the treatment of spatial differentiation, and the extent to which supplementary material is collected.[26]

The place-of-birth question is regarded as providing the most feasible single index of migration and should be given priority as part of the minimum census program for all countries. The limitations of this question are recognized, and where resources permit, supplementary material should be collected on duration of residence and place of previous residence at some specified time. Questions to elicit data on these are considered to be suitable for inclusion in a sample questionnaire, with a place-of-birth question in the complete enumeration of population. Further information on material that may be collected is given in the recommendations listed in Table 12.5, which indicate the degree of detail envisaged by UNECA. In the case of place-of-birth and duration-of-residence questions it is assumed that the tables will be prepared for each five-year age group and sex category and that the spatial units used in the analysis will distinguish between urban and rural origins. These indicate more what is desirable than what can yet be achieved.

The foregoing discussion has been concerned only with the nature of questions that will provide data for migration analysis. Attention also needs to be given to other important matters. While they could not be considered in colonial censuses, drawing attention to them further underlines the deficiencies of colonial censuses for the measurement of migration.

Where resources are limited, sampling can be very important in the collection of census data, but sample data should be planned carefully to supplement data collected in the main census. Even though the United Nations recommends that the place-of-birth question should be included in the general questionnaire for the whole population, this has not always been done. The use of sample data, rather than data from total enumeration, represents a problem in the analysis of the spatial structure of migration flows by recommended five-year age groups because of the small numbers involved and the large sampling errors likely. With

TABLE 12.5 African Recommendations for the 1970 Censuses

Tabulation Title	Population Included	Geographic Classification	Other Classifications
Ethnic Group[a] and Birthplace (other tabulations)	Total Population	Total Country and each major division, distinguishing urban and rural	ETHNIC GROUP: to be determined by local needs. BIRTHPLACE: locally born—each major civil or regional division and *not stated*; foreign-born—each continent, each country within continent that is the birthplace of a significant number of foreign-born persons, *all other countries* (combined) in each continent, and *continent not known.* AGE: under 5 yrs, 5–14, 15–24, 25–34 . . . 65–74, 75 and over, and *not stated.* SEX: male, female.
Duration of Residence (30 other tabulations)	Total Population	Total Country and each major division, distinguishing urban and rural, each principal locality	DURATION OF RESIDENCE IN LOCALITY: since birth resident for less than 1 yr, 1–4, 5–9, 10 or more, and *not stated*; and *transient or visitor* . DURATION OF USUAL RESIDENCE IN MAJOR CIVIL DIVISION: (as for *locality* above). AGE: 0–4, 5–9, 10–14, 15–19, 20–24, 25–34 . . . 55–64, 65 and over, and *not stated.* SEX: male, female.
Place of Previous Residence (31 other tabulations)	Total Population	Total Country	PLACE OF USUAL RESIDENCE: each major or other civil division in the country, *foreign country,* and *not stated;* for those who always resided in the same civil division, place of previous residence will be the same as place of usual residence; transients or visitors should be shown separately.

Source: Masser and Gould, 1975.

[a]Counties that wish to do so will substitute *citizenship* for *ethnic group* throughout.

the exception of Swaziland, even for countries where place-of-birth data for the total population exist, they have not been presented in the detail of age disaggregation suggested by UNECA. The full implication of this deficiency will arise when further censuses are taken and it is found that only the most general comparisons can be made between the two points in time. None of the methods suggested by the United Nations[27] for inferring time-specific data from place-of-birth data at two points in time can be developed without a detailed analysis in each age and sex category.

Other problems specific to migration analysis concern the spatial structure of the samples used in the collection of the migration and supplementary data. These data are particularly sensitive to the areas chosen for sample enumeration. There is a high probability of considerable nonmeasurable sample error when cluster sample procedures are followed— where the sample is areally, rather than demographically, constructed and is a sample of enumeration areas rather than of households and individuals. Since migration is highly structured in spatial terms and not randomly distributed either at source or destination, cluster samples of this kind are likely to produce biased estimates.[28] However, areal cluster sampling is easier and cheaper to organize than systematic individual or household sampling, and African countries have little prospect of the resources or administrative capacity to adopt systematic demographic sampling in the foreseeable future.

More thought also needs to be given to how spatial units should be treated as sources and destinations in migration questions. In many instances major administrative units are not appropriate for spatial analysis without subdivision. It may be difficult to distinguish between urban and rural origins in the place-of-birth question, and the urban destination may prove difficult to define in practice. Further differentiation of rural and urban destinations could be made from raw data where administrative definitions are inadequate, and the population of functional areas could be then derived. However, this would require access to data at a finer level of spatial resolution than is available in most censuses.

Lastly, there is the well-known problem of censuses that collect large amounts of data and then neither published nor analyzed. In the past, migration analysis undoubtedly suffered because the place-of-birth data, though collected, were not published. There is now the UNFPA, which a government with limited financial and technical resources can now call on to meet the costs of additional tabulations that would not be undertaken otherwise in the output from the census. Despite the availability of support from the UNFPA, there was still little evidence into the 1970s that governments had requested support for more detailed tabulations of place-of-birth data or cross-tabulations of these with other data. Census authorities need to be encouraged to undertake and to publish additional tabulations, and this is recognized in UNECA specifications for "recommended" and "additional" tabulations (Table 12.5). But in fact, systematic analysis of migration at the national level would require more tabulations than are "recommended" or "additional." The precise nature of these extra requirements needs to be indicated to census authorities, and to this end the requirements must be clarified by development planners and other scientific users of census data.

CONCLUSION

This is a tentative, partial, and largely descriptive review of available migration measures—or rather their limitations and the lack of data for them—in colonial censuses. Reviewing demography in Africa in the mid-1960s, F. Lorimer and colleagues wrote, "The measurement of migration in Africa is complicated by the heterogeneity of the patterns, which vary in relative importance between different regions and in the same region at different times." No one would dissent from this view. However, they went on, "There is no method of measuring migration that is both theoretically satisfactory and administratively feasible in Africa at the present time."[29] Nor did migration receive special study in the classic review of demography in tropical Africa in which these same scholars were involved.[30] While recognizing major difficulties, Masser and Gould[31] less than a decade later demonstrated what could be achieved in collating and systematizing a diversity of sources on migration from censuses and surveys, and maximized the analysis of data from the first postindependence census of Uganda (1969) to the present, and interpreted patterns of interregional migration in that country. It is unfortunate that their work has not received the widespread recognition it deserves; I have therefore drawn on it very substantially for this paper.

The majority of colonial censuses in Central Africa and elsewhere in sub-Saharan Africa either did not collect much in the way of useful data for the study of migration or, if they did, did not publish them. However, there has been a steady but slow improvement over time. Migration has always experienced a degree of neglect overall in the field of population studies in many other parts of the world besides Africa. It is conceptually elusive and theoretically difficult to determine and, for these and other reasons, technically difficult to measure. In view of the measures of, and insights on, migration in Africa that have been gained for the second half of the twentieth century, it must be a matter for regret that more is not known for the first half, and indeed for earlier periods.

NOTES

1. R. R. Kuczynski, *Demographic Survey of the British Colonial Empire*, 3 vols. (London, 1948–1949); R. M. Prothero, "Post-War West African Censuses," in K. M. Barbour and R. M. Prothero, eds., *Essays on African Population* (London, 1961), 7–15.

2. Colonial Office, *Annual Report for Northern Nigeria, 1902*, no. 409 (London, 1902), 111.

3. I. Masser and W. T. S. Gould, *Interregional Migration in Tropical Africa* (London, 1975).

4. C. J. Martin, "Population Census Estimates and Methods in British East Africa"; idem, "Estimates of Population Growth in East Africa"; and J. R. H. Shaul, "Demographic Features of Central Africa"—all in Barbour and Prothero, *Essays*, 17–30, 49–61, and 31–48, respectively.

5. Kuczynski, *Demographic Survey*, vols. 1–2.

6. F. Lorimer et al., "Demography," in R. Lystad, ed., *The African World: A Survey of Social Research* (New York, 1965).

7. Masser and Gould, *Interregional Migration*.

8. G. St. J. Orde-Brown, *The African Labourer* (London, 1933).

9. Swaziland Government, *Report on the 1966 Swaziland Census* (Mbabane, 1968).

10. Martin, "Population"; idem, "Estimates."

11. Lord Hailey, *An African Survey* (Oxford, 1938).

12. Shaul, "Demographic Features."

13. G. Kay, "Age Structure, Sex Ratios, and Migrations (1963)," in D. H. Davies, ed., *Zambia in Maps* (London, 1971), 46–47.

14. A. Southall, "Population Movements in East Africa," in Barbour and Prothero, *Essays*, 157–192.

15. R. M. Prothero, "The Population Census of Northern Nigeria 1952: Problems and Results," *Population Studies* 10, no. 2 (1956), 166–183; idem, "African Ethnographic Maps, with a New Example from Northern Nigeria," *Africa* 32, no. 1 (1962), 61–65.

16. Uganda Government, *General African Census 1959*, vol. 2, pt. 1 (Entebbe, 1960).

17. Kenya Government, *Population Census 1962*, vol. 2 (Nairobi, 1962).

18. E. V. T. Engmann, "Population Movements in Ghana: A Study of Internal Migration and Its Implications for the Planner," *Bulletin of the Ghana Geographical Association* 10 (1965), 41–65.

19. J. M. Hunter, "Regional Patterns of Population Growth in Ghana, 1948–1960," in J. B. Whittow and P. D. Wood, *Essays in Geography for A. Miller* (Reading, 1965).

20. A. Romaniuk, "The Demography of the Democratic Republic of the Congo," in W. Brass et al., eds., *The Demography of Tropical Africa* (Princeton, 1968).

21. Uganda Government, *General African Census 1959*.

22. Swaziland Government, *Report on the 1966 Swaziland Census*.

23. M. Chapman and R. M. Prothero, "Themes on Circulation in the Third World," *International Migration Review* 17, no. 4 (1983), 597–632; Prothero and Chapman, eds., *Circulation in Third World Countries* (London, 1985).

24. M. E. Jackman, *Recent Population Movements in Zambia: Some Aspects of the 1969 Census*, Zambia Papers, no. 8 (Lusaka, 1973).

25. United Nations, "Methods of Measuring Internal Migration,"

Population Studies 47 (1970). "Proposals for the Improvement of Internal Migration Statistics, Paper presented at the meeting of the UN Statistical Committee (E/CN/3/435), Geneva, 1972.

26. United Nations, "Methods."

27. Ibid.

28. C. Scott, "Vital Rate Surveys in Tropical Africa: Some New Data Affecting Sample Design," in J. Caldwell and C. Okonjo, eds., *The Population of Tropical Africa* (London, 1968), 163–171.

29. Lorimer, "Demography."

30. Brass, *Demography of Tropical Africa.*

31. Masser and Gould, *Interregional Migration.*

13 _____

Maps as Sources in Demographic Studies of Africa's Past, with Particular Reference to Zambia

_____ JEFFREY C. STONE

A carto-bibliographical search for relatively large-scale demographic maps of Zambia from the colonial period reveals only one item, a remarkable map of the African population of the entire territory of Northern Rhodesia as of 1956, a map compiled at a scale of 1:2 million.[1] The work of P. A. Penfold suggests that large-scale population maps do not exist for the colonial period.[2] Nevertheless, a recent suggestion that "the systematic use of colonial maps is original for most historians and does show up a source which has often been neglected"[3] is pertinent. Potentially relevant colonial maps do exist but they are not population maps: they are settlement maps. No more than inference can be drawn from most of them about aggregate populations or about trends in the growth or decline of total populations. On the other hand, all human populations distribute themselves spatially over the earth's surface. Admittedly, if African historical demography is to be considered solely in terms of fertility, mortality, and migration expressed as numerical abstractions, settlement maps are indeed scarcely relevant, but for anyone concerned to reconstruct past population distributions and spatial movements in any detail, extant cartographic sources are likely to be invaluable.

I shall demonstrate the utility of cartographic sources in African historical demography. I shall inquire why detailed maps of the location of human habitations were extensively compiled, particularly in the early colonial period, explore their consequent form and content, consider their utility as data sources by reference to a Zambian example, and outline their likely availability in some other African countries.

THE ORIGIN OF SETTLEMENT MAPPING

The subject matter of colonial maps derives from the purposes for which they were compiled. The exercise of European power and authority in colonial Africa brought about a massive increase in mapmaking, whose magnitude is probably not always appreciated because many of the maps were not published. Furthermore, the conceptual difference between an *imperial* relationship (scientific, commercial, and diplomatic, characterized by both historical continuity and European internationalism) and a *colonial* relationship (administrative rule, which is short-lived and nationalistic)[4] is evident in the content of the early maps of Africa.[5] It was the needs of colonialism, not of imperialism, that gave rise to carefully compiled maps of human settlement.

The cartographic divide between precolonial and colonial Africa is, however, less precise than the legal difference might suggest. There are two conceivable reasons why changing map content might not coincide with the formal dates of declarations of colonial authority: (1) nineteenth-century European explorers frequently made maps of their travels and observations, and (2) attributes of the imperialist attitude may have lingered in the mind of the cartographer into the colonial period. There is therefore a possibility that the colonial type of map may predate colonialism and that precolonial imperialist cartography may overlap into the colonial period.

R. C. Bridges has pointed out that evidence for a direct connection between the nineteenth-century European explorers and the imposition of colonial rule is often lacking. He goes on to demonstrate that in East Africa the connection was not really through the decisionmakers in London but was indirect, through what he calls the "unofficial mind" of imperialism, which was located in the commercial middle class of British society, in servicemen and officials, businessmen and missionary leaders. Bridges specifically mentions Livingstone and Stanley, who have particular relevance to Central Africa. The published narratives of Livingstone and Stanley remained in print for several decades and must have been a conditioning influence in Britain on public opinion on overseas affairs. Their travels gave rise to manuscript and printed maps. Livingstone's manuscript maps possibly assisted him in writing his published narrative and were objective field records for their own sake. The published maps helped the reader to comprehend the narrative, as well as imparting an aura of scientific objectivity. The maps were all part of the larger process by which, in Bridges' words, Livingstone's explorations provided "a respectable legitimation for European interference in Africa," but it does not follow that they contain the same information as maps compiled for the purpose of imposing or implementing colonial rule, and indeed they often have only limited utility for purposes of demographic study by comparison with colonial maps. They were compiled in the context of the "unofficial scramble" for Africa by the commerical and service classes, a precolonial imperialist process to be differentiated from subsequent direct intervention by European governments.[6]

There were, of course, other precolonial travelers to Central Africa, who also wrote extensively and compiled maps. Their maps were characteristically based on instrumental observation to a greater or lesser degree and add a scientific dimension to the travelers' records—an important element, as

Bridges points out, in legitimizing the penetration of Africa by European travelers in the unofficial mind. For example, travelers to Zambia include Alfred Bertrand,[7] C. Harding,[8] F. C. Selous,[9] A. St. H. Gibbons,[10] and J. M. Moubray.[11] They have their counterparts elsewhere in Central Africa, although their dates were not always precolonial in law in that their maps may have been compiled after the queen's protection had been declared over the area in question; but they depicted country where the writ of European law had still to be imposed. Their maps bear the hallmarks of precolonial imperialism, both in their origins and in their content. Their origins are internationalist, even in the last decade of the nineteenth century. There is no better example than Bertrand, a Swiss army captain who mounted a joint expedition to North-Western Rhodesia in 1895 together with the English traveler Gibbons. In his report, Bertrand describes himself as a member of the geographical societies of Geneva, London, and Paris. His report was published (with Royal Geographical Society map) in more than one European language. He clearly saw himself as a European and addressed himself to a European audience. As a Swiss national, he could have had little interest in promoting colonialism in Africa by his native land.

If the internationalist dimension of imperialism is apparent in the market and readership of explorers' maps, the free trade and accessibility ethic of European imperialism is apparent in the content of the maps. Perhaps the best known of Livingstone's maps accompanies his *Missionary Travels and Researchers in South Africa*[12] and was compiled by Arrowsmith from Livingstone's "astronomical observations, bearings, estimated distances, sketches, etc." In fact, Livingstone was later critical of Arrowsmith's compilation, claiming that his observations had been altered.[13] Clearly, Livingstone took pride in the precision of his observations. Debenham has drawn attention to the exceptional navigational skills exercised by Livingstone in constructing his maps in arduous conditions: there can be no doubt that the sense of scientific authenticity they conveyed was fully justified.[14] More relevant, when employed today as evidence of what existed in Livingstone's time, they must also command respect. Unfortunately, the widely available map of 1857 by Arrowsmith is not a major data source on past populations. For example, in the upper Zambezi valley above Victoria Falls, only some twenty settlements are located. A further ten settlements are located on the Batoka Plateau between Victoria Falls and the Kafue River. In part, the problem is that Livingstone was traversing. He was therefore observing and recording only a very narrow sample strip across the continent. More significantly, he was locating major physical features: principally rivers, but also cataracts, lagoons, lakes, hills, and springs. In total, there are over seventy named features (including settlements) in the Upper Zambezi valley and over thirty on the Batoka Plateau. By locating the prime landscape features he was affording access from Europe, a possibility that he himself was demonstrating. The map is in the imperialist mercantile mold; and because we do not know what causes a settlement to be included or excluded, its value as a map locating the contemporary population is comparatively limited. That is not to say that it is demographically worthless. It may permit a measure of qualitative assessment if read in conjunction with the text, which contains statements referring to parts of the Batoka Plateau, like "Leaving Kaonka we travelled over uninhabited . . . territory," "At Monze's . . . the people . . . are located all over the country in small villages," and "We passed through . . . country . . . thinly inhabited by man." May one infer three different degrees of population density? If so, the three sites can be located using the map.

Many of Livingstone's extant manuscript maps have not been reproduced, and they are deposited in several archives. Judging from the examples reproduced by Debenham and from an original in Livingstone Museum, Zambia, villages and other features were frequently inserted in characteristically the same proportions as on the printed map referred to above; but some of his manuscripts are at larger scales and do show greater densities of settlement. As Debenham shows, Livingstone's main purpose was to explore and map the drainage lines, and even as rigorous a field observer as Livingstone may have been less conscientious in recording the villages he sighted. No attempt seems to have been made to evaluate the *content* of Livingstone's maps, only their *accuracy*. To what extent do his village names serve as landscape features that help to differentiate watercourses? Or do they represent night halts? Does he locate villages along his routes in a comprehensive manner, or were some omitted? A major evaluation exercise awaits the cartographic historian; but given greater awareness of the determinants of content, there are sufficient maps over a wide enough area to afford at least the possibility of interesting comparisons of settlement density.

Later travelers sometimes possessed navigational skills of a similarly high order. For example, the extraordinary map *The Upper Zambezi Basin* published by Gibbons in the last decade of the nineteenth century to accompany his narrative is at an unusually large scale for the period and contains a great deal of detail.[15] Its content is not dissimilar to Livingstone's cartography, and its author describes the objective as the depiction of "the main physical features and tribal distribution."[16] The latter phrase is evident in the frequent and extensive ethnic names, but there are also many villages located and named. In fact, in the Upper Zambezi drainage basin, stretching as far east as the Hook of Kafue, there are over four hundred named settlements located on the map, often with latitudinal observations. In addition, there are occasional phrases such as *villages, small villages, many villages,* and *many small villages,* which indicate that the depiction of villages is incomplete. Nevertheless, the striking feature of the village distribution is the very dense clusters that are plotted, implying that the cartographer does more than show a random scatter of villages. There was a conscious effort to show what was known, even though all was not known. There may be the data for a historical study of the population geography of Bulozi in this map. On the face of it, this may seem surprising from an author whose lectures even as late as 1913 so characterized the imperial mercantile ethic of the precolonial period, but the application of science was a part of the "civilizing" role that justified reference to people, while the date of the map is within the colonial period.

There are other types of colonial forerunner maps containing elements of free trade imperialism and its attendant "civilizing" purpose, which also overlap into the early colonial period. The biennial reports of the British South Africa Company, entitled *Reports on the Administration of Rhodesia*, published in London between 1892 and 1902 and on sale to the public, contained maps toward the end of that period. The earliest maps, based in part on travelers' maps of both North-Eastern and North-Western Rhodesia, incorporated observations of company officers on the ground. Their very small scale (1:4–5 million) means that they contain little of demographic note.

A different type of map at a slightly larger scale (1:1 million) was even more clearly the product of, and directed at, the unofficial mind of imperialism, although not published by the chartered company. These were maps published by Edward Stanford of London depicting the territory "under the administration of the British South Africa Company," and they must have been compiled with the assistance of the chartered company. The maps were published in at least six editions between 1897 and 1906,[17] seemingly with an even earlier edition in 1895.[18] The map is full of economic optimism. The 1900 edition depicts a proposed alignment for the railway north of the Zambezi, by way of the Hook of Kafue and Serenje to Lake Tanganyika. Entries include *Good farming country running water and good feed all the year round, splendid country, Elephants abound,* and *water plentiful green grass all the year.* Here is a map with a purpose, that is, to convey the impression of economic potential awaiting exploitation by those of an adventurous mind—more a chartered company advertisement than an objective depiction of part of the landscape. The amount of settlement information is significantly less per unit of area than on Gibbons's map, although the total area shown is very much greater. The 1900 edition of the Stanford map shows less than half the number of settlements located by Gibbons in the comparable area, which suggests that imperial cartography immediately preceding the colonial period varies greatly in its utility for demographic reconstruction, depending on which of the two imperialist attributes predominates. Where the "civilizing" influence of the scientific mind is foremost, as in Gibbons's map, there may be much of value. Where mercantile access or rapid economic transformaiton is uppermost, as in Livingstone's or Stanford's maps, there may simply have been less settlement information available to Stanford's draftsmen.

The imperial cartography of Gibbons and Stanford in what is legally the very early colonial period shows that the change from the imperial to the colonial function was no more abrupt in maps than it was on the ground. There was a transition in Central Africa, at least north to the Zambezi, which is also apparent in the changing content of maps of the period, as internationally guaranteed free trade gave way to economic nationalism[19] and to exclusive access for the particular ruling European nation, the short-lived imperial aberration called *colonialism.*

The transition is completed in the maps constructed by the early company officials in the course of their duties. There are some notable extant manuscript maps that are a part of the evidence of how company rule was implemented on the ground. For example, Val Gielgud's *Sketch Map of the Hook of the Kafue* of 1901[20] was made on the ground by one of the men who had been dispatched at the instigation of the company's resident administrator of North-Eastern Rhodesia at Fort Jameson (now Chipata), preparatory to the extension of the western marches of North-Eastern Rhodesia. The map was drawn in October 1901, fifteen months after Gielgud entered the area, and shows the villages of "all chiefs who have been visited, made submission and who visited at my camp." The map was appended to a report by Gielgud to the administrator; and, indeed, two earlier pencil sketch maps, which were appended to previous reports, are extant. Gielgud's instructions were to report on the country and the conditions of the natives, and to pave the way for a peaceful occupation and administration of the area.[21] Clearly, an ancillary task in reporting on the country and preparing for company rule was to depict the settlement geography of the area. To administer an area it was necessary to know where people were located, including not only local inhabitants but also the mines and mission stations that had preceded Gielgud, as well as two Barotse Native Police Posts sited consequent on his arrival. The importance of the map as a tool in establishing an administrative presence is perhaps apparent from the careful manner in which this map was drawn, toward the end of Gibbons' stay but while living in camp conditions. Much of his time seems to have been spent on antislaving operations, but the fifty-nine settlements that he located are indicative of the energy he also devoted to the task of making contact with the inhabitants and of the extent of his travels from his base during some fifteen months.

A further significance of the Gielgud maps may be that the company had to be seen if it was to control the area that fell within its charter effectively. It had to have a visible presence to the administered people, of course; but it may have had to validate and legitimize itself in the eyes of its shareholders and political masters in London, too. The map helped the administrators demonstrate the company's active presence on the ground. The company could show that it knew the area better than anyone else did. (In addition, by drawing the map the company encapsulated the country and, in an act that was symbolic as well as utilitarian, took possession of it, a function that cannot be convincingly demonstrated, since the map probably remained on office files before eventually passing into archives: there is no evidence of its being displayed or even utilized in compiling later published company reports.) There was therefore good cause for it to be both as complete and as accurate as reasonably possible. As far as the settlements were concerned, the map was necessary to locate people for purposes of administration and helpful in advancing the company's claim to be in control.

There is evidence to show that Gielgud's work in compiling a map of an area about to become the subject of colonial administration was not unique. Indeed, it was typical, because it was a valuable tool in carrying out the initial functions of colonial government, namely, legal adjudication and the imposition of taxation, on the ground. The evidence of mapmaking as a prime task of early colonial administrators (in the absence of professional surveyors) in Northern Rhodesia has been drawn together elsewhere.[22] The importance of a map can be summed up in the words of the officers themselves. In 1908 an officer who was sent to Mongu to set up a local administration apart from the previously established office at the equivalent of the provincial level, writes of climbing a hill to make "a number of observations with a prismatic compass for the compilation of a district map which is of the utmost value to the district official."[23] Another serving officer has recorded that "initially the duty of the Native commissioner was to administer justice, compile a census, collect the tax, keep the mail paths open and organise the mail and make a map of the district."[24] The officer sent to initiate an administrative presence in the area that became Balovale (now Zambezi) District describes the work of his first long tour as "trying to make a census of the people and a map of the country."[25] Sometimes, the observations of these early officers were published in maps drawn in the style of the precolonial travelers and explorers, as transects across country, for instance, those of R. Codrington and P. H. Selby.[26] They were published by the geographical journals, which continued to publish substantial numbers of explorers' maps drawn in the imperial format. The requirements of the readers of these published maps were slower to change than those of the officials on the ground, whose urgent need was to know where all of the people were.

THE FORM AND CONTENT OF THE COLONIAL DISTRICT MAP

The maintenance of the district map became part of the normal duties of the administrative staff at every outstation. They were the subject of circular letters from territorial headquarters in the 1920s, they were inspected by senior officers on tour of inspection, their compilation is referred to by unofficial visitors, they are frequently mentioned or even lodged in district notebooks now in archives,[27] and they are mentioned in contemporary writing.[28] What is more important for their utility as sources of historical information, many survive in the manuscript original or in copies. The Livingstone Museum map collection includes thirty-eight district maps, covering thirty-one districts and ranging from 1904 to 1951. They are held in archives elsewhere in Zambia and the United Kingdom.

A fine example of an early Northern Rhodesian district map is illustrated in C. Fyfe and D. McMaster's *African Historical Demography*,[29] namely, J. H. Venning's map of Balovale Subdistrict (ca. 1911), which is characteristic of the content of district maps. Its prime subject matter is the settlement pattern of the populace. The map names and locates 264 settlements using the rivers as a reference framework and hence naming ninety-four rivers. Otherwise, a scatter of other physical features are also located, including hills, cataracts, plains, pans, islands, and so on, totaling only seventy-six items, thus emphasizing the express purpose of the map, which was to establish the whereabouts of the newly administered people.[30] The fact that villages were liable to removal did not deter, as it undoubtedly did with later official published topographic maps. In order to function the administration needed to know where people were, and the fact that they might relocate did not eliminate that need. Indeed, the effort that went into constructing maps of such impermanent features as rural settlement emphasizes the utility of the maps and the fact that they fulfilled an immediate and pressing need. This in turn implies that they tended to be as comprehensive as possible. In the case of what is now Zambezi District of Zambia, we have a detailed depiction of the settlement distribution some eighty years ago, at the outset of colonial rule, which can perhaps be interpreted with the help of anthropological and other sources to provide a pattern of *population* distribution.

District maps were revised and kept up to date in the course of the annual round of village-to-village touring, which resulted in separate maps to accompany tour reports. These show village distribution and are likely to be comprehensive, since they were drawn by the officers who had visited the villages named in their maps. They survive mainly in national archives, appended to copies of tour reports on secretariat files. At best, they provide detailed depictions of settlement distribution for precise dates.[31] Occasionally, maps were also compiled by administrative officers, incorporating settlements for particular purposes, such as the formulation of tsetse fly legislation, the recording of fishing camps, or the investigation of catchment areas prior to siting a school. In addition, maps were compiled by forest, agricultural, and livestock officers when carrying out their particular professional duties; and these, too, may incorporate settlements.

HUNT'S MAP OF MAPANZA: A CASE STUDY

I have referred to the maps by Gielgud and Venning to suggest the potential of the district map as a source of demographic information. (Strictly speaking, Gielgud's map of the Hook of Kafue is a forerunner of the true district map, since no district had then been established in the area portrayed.) I take the opportunity to examine and place on record another very early district map that may exemplify the potential of such maps for the detailed study of past populations.

The National Archives of Zambia possesses a map of an area north of Choma entitled *Sketch Map: Mapanza Sub-district* with the legend *Scale 4 miles to 1 inch, C. de Vere Hunt, Collector, 1.10.05*. Mapanza Subdistrict had come into existence by 1903, although the boundaries were still undecided in 1904, suggesting that its effective administration may have been delayed. The subdistrict was abolished in 1909. The area of the former subdistrict as shown on the map is now divided between Namwala, Choma, Monze, and Kalomo Districts: the northern third of the subdistrict falls in southern Namwala, a small area in the southwest part of the map falls in Kalomo, and a strip in the east part falls in Monze. Thus, the map extends from the Kafue Flats in the north to the state land of Choma District in the south, including at least a part of the areas of Muchila, Nalubamba, Siamusonde, Chikanta, Macha, and Mapanza, with the country around the Choma-Namwala road between Mbabala and Chitongo and the Munyeke River drainage basin at the center of the map. The surface area represented on Hunt's map is of the order of 7,000 km[2].[32]

The map covers an area whose demographic history has been the subject of discussion, mainly concerning the period immediately prior to the establishment of colonial rule north of the Zambezi and drawing on oral history and travelers' records. The reports of nineteenth-century travelers on the plateau, such as Livingstone, Holub, Gibbons, and Selous have been augmented by anthropologists and historians such as E. Colson, A. Roberts, and K. Vickery. The composite picture that emerges is one of "deserted uninhabited,"[33] plateau country,[34] prone to locust-induced famine[35] and epidemics, "a buffer zone and common raiding ground for two expanding states,"[36] which suffered depopulation in the late nineteenth century,[37] resulting in a small residual population of small widely scattered villages,[38] although with greater populations in a few refuge areas.[39] The fullest account by any of the early travelers is Holub's, who spent some time in 1886 at "Mo-panza" and estimated Mapanza's "subjects" as numbering about two thousand.[40] (Hunt's map almost certainly covers a much larger area than that occupied by any conception of Mapanza's people.) However, Holub suggests that the country of Mapanza could support twenty times the number, although the man Mapanza was one of a few Tonga leaders with authority,[41] and the Mapanza area was a population center at the time.[42] Hence, a variety of sources paint a late-nineteenth-century picture of a small population living in small scattered settlements (not inappropriate to an acephalous society), with large areas totally devoid of population, as well as pockets of relatively high density. Assuming that the situation had not changed markedly by the

MAP 13.1 Sketch Map: Mapanza Subdistrict

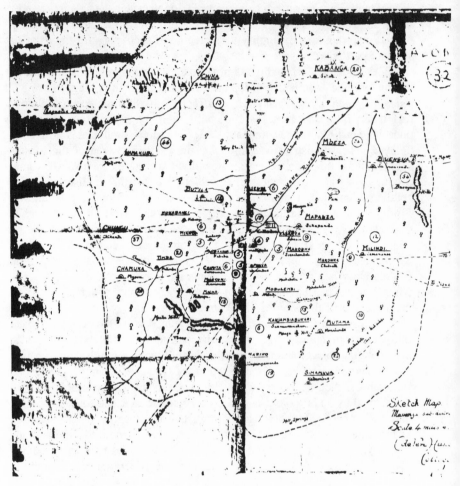

time that the map was drawn (that is, within two years of the imposition of colonial administration and long before the enactment of a reserve policy, which considerably changed the population distribution in the Choma area), does the map contribute in any way to the present state of knowledge of the population geography and the demography of the plateau in the past?

There is no key to the map, and much depends on whether the contents can be identified. The physical features present no difficulty since they are identified by the specific names. Thus, there are thirteen named rivers, seven named hills, seven areas of trees or scrub, two pans, hot springs, and pools. Routes, paths, or tracks are also self-evident from the directional entries at the periphery, of which there are eight. The subdistrict boundary is boldly displayed, although not closed to the east. An area of swamp is suggested by symbols in the northeast, and *Collector* (i.e., the headquarters of the collector) is very prominent. However, physical features, especially the rivers, serve little purpose other than to provide a reference framework within which to locate the human settlements, which seem to be indicated by a variation of a familiar "bowler hat" settlement symbol.

There are, however, problems in reading the map for its settlement data. The map displays nineteen settlement symbols. Names adjacent to settlement symbols occur in pairs, of which there are twenty-nine, that is, ten more than there are symbols. Moreover, every pair without exception has a numeral within a circle, ranging from five to fifty-four. For each pair of names, the first name appears in uppercase letters, underlined, and the second in lowercase letters, with an initial capital. What do the pairs of names and the numerals indicate?

The names assuredly refer to settlements. This can be demonstrated, in the absence of detailed local knowledge, by reference to a later manuscript map, *Mapanza District*, drawn by D. B. Hall to accompany Kalomo District Tour Report Number 2 of 1932 (National Airlines of Zambia file ZA7//39). Hall visited all 148 in chief's areas Mapanza, Macha, Mulindi, and Chikanta. All but twelve of the lowercase names on Hunt's map appear as villages on Hall's map. Three of the uppercase names also appear on Hall's map, namely, MAPANZA, MACHA, and MULINDI, that is, three of the persons who by 1932 had been designated by the colonial administration as *chiefs*, in the absence of local institutionalized foci of authority through which to maintain order.[43] Prior to the designation of chiefs in 1919, a large number of prominent men, usually ritual figures, were informally recognized as early as 1904.[44] Hence, a working hypothesis for the uppercase names is that they represent the tiny districts (*katongo*) coterminous with rain shrine communities and giving nominal allegiance to one man, the eponymous guardian of the rain shrine. Some 116 such districts had been recognized prior to 1919, a figure commensurate with their frequency on the map. Moreover, they were usually named from natural dominant features in the landscape,[45] as for example the name MARIKO on Hunt's map in the vicinity of the prominent Maliko Hill on the modern map (Zambia 1:50 thousand, Sheet 1626 D2). Similarly BUENGUA paired with *Samousondi* on Hunt's map, may be associated with the Bwengwa River, which is prominent in the vicinity of Chief Hamusonde. MUTAMA is also a river. To a person whose first language is ci-Tonga, the obvious linguistic difference is that the uppercase names are places (rivers, hills, chief's areas) and the lowercase letters are persons' names indicating chiefs or village headmen, some of whom are well known today (e.g., *Siamaundu* and *Nalubamba*):[46] villages were known by the names of their headmen, who had a nominal role in precolonial times,[47] even in an acephalous society.

The uppercase letters therefore seem to be *katongo*, that is, areal units, whereas the lowercase names seem to be villages. But unresolved problems remain. First, why is only one village named for each *katongo*? By the 1950s they contained perhaps six or seven villages, and it seems improbable that each contained only one in 1904. Indeed, the population may not always have been grouped into discrete village units, which were the product of colonial administrative action.[48] The symbols perhaps refer to amorphous settlement clusters rather than villages. Second, why do ten of the settlement names not have locational symbols? Is this deliberately indicative or is it cartographic inconsistency? Lastly, what is the significance of the numerals?

There may be a clue to the further interpretation of map content in the original purpose of the map—if this can be established. The date suggests that it was the product of the imposition of taxation. Taxation was proclaimed for North-Western Rhodesia in 1901,[49] but collection did not commence until 1904. However, in that year, the administration prepared to levy a tax of ten shillings on every adult (excepting unmarried women, widows, and first wives) resident in the Falls and Batoka Districts.[50] Mapanza was subdistrict of Batoka District as from 1903[51] and would therefore have been a likely subject area for the collection, which was initiated in Tonga country toward the close of 1904. The collection was conducted smoothly as a joint British-Lozi operation, with Lozi *indunas* accompanying the European collectors on their rounds. The Ngambela and Lewanika's son Litla observed the collection in the Mapanza area.[52] Hence, the map was drawn only months after the first tax collection. This suggests that the map may locate and enumerate the number of taxpayers in Mapanza Subdistrict in late 1904 or early 1905. The numerals within circles total 445. This figure could presumably be adjusted by whatever is seen to be the apppropriate factor to account for underenumeration. If a figure of this order is a plausible total for enumerated taxpayers and if no contrary interpretation can be placed on the subject of the numerals, the map locates twenty-eight areas within the subdistrict where stated numbers of taxpayers were enumerated. One further area, MAPANZA, has no numeral against it, perhaps an error of omission. Within each area, one village (or settlement cluster) headman is named, but not much weight should be placed on the exact location of the populace within each area, since ten of the personal names do not have settlement symbols. Also, there is the historical evidence to suggest that settlement was not yet nucleated without exception into villages and that more than one cluster or nucleation, where they did exist, may well have occurred in some areas. The map, then, should probably be read as portraying not a comprehensively nucleated population contained in twenty-nine villages but a more dispersed one, at least in part. The distribution of taxable population should probably be read at the level of area rather than point (village).

If this interpretation of map content can be sustained, an interesting distributional feature of the population of Mapanza Subdistrict emerges. The areas with large numbers are mostly widely spaced around the periphery of the subdistrict, whereas close to the center of the subdistrict both the areas and their numerals are relatively evenly and densely spaced, the periphery of the district contains some large but more widely dispersed clusters, that is, much more variation in population density.

If differentiation of population distribution and density is detectable in the map, the reason may in part be the differing ecological conditions and their associated agricultural systems. These were identified as long ago as 1936 in the classic study by C. G. Trapnell and J. N. Clothier, who recognized five different soil-vegetation associations within the area corresponding to Hunt's map. Three of them (alluvial floodplain grasslands, mixed species on transitional Kalahari sands, and mopane and mixed mopane lower valley types) occupy only a small part of the north of the subdistrict in country that is depicted as sparsely populated, with only two named areas (KABANGA and CHIRA). The phrase *mopani trees* and the grass symbols on the map confirm the approximate location of Trapnell and Clothier's limits on the subdistrict map, and the small population reflects the limited agricultural potential of these three ecological associations. The rest of the subdistrict falls within two further ecological associations (*Isoberlinia globiflora–Brachystegia* woodland on sandy loam and upper valley thorn and transitional soils). The second of these associations provides the environment for the operation of a distinctive "upper-valley thorn system" of agriculture, on soils of relatively high fertility. Trapnell and Clothier describe, in this context, the agriculture of the Nalubamba and Mbeza areas, utilizing the "rich Winterthorn alluvium of the Mbeza country," a name Hunt locates as a large population cluster in the northeast of the subdistrict. The same ecological association is coincident with the large population cluster of BUENGUA in the east of the subdistrict and also with the relatively densely settled center of the subdistrict, around the Mapanza-Macha axis. This leaves only the sparsely settled south and northwest of the subdistrict, where a stable variant of the "southern plateau system" of agriculture is recorded by Trapnell and Clothier; but the inherently infertile sandy loams seemingly did not attract or support the population numbers of more fertile upper-valley soils at a time prior to the alienation of land, designation of reserves, partial commercialization of agriculture, and consequent emergence of population pressure.[53] A distinctive pattern to the distribution of population suggested by Hunt's map seems to be in keeping with the ecology and agricultural history of the subdistrict as first described by Trapnell and Clothier, as is confirmed in more recent soil mapping.[54]

The interpretation of the content of the map as a quantitative statement of population total and distribution therefore tends to be confirmed by the ecology of the area portrayed. It may also be confimed, in the absence of field work, by what is already known of past social groupings in the area. Whereas Trapnell and Clothier refer to agriculture in the "Mbeza country" (located by Hunt) in 1936, E. W. Smith and A. M. Dale[55] offer almost contemporaneous confirmation of the existence of "the Bwengwa people," also located by Hunt and more recently known through the imposed institution of chieftainship by the name of Hamusonde (*Samousondi* on Hunt's map). Add to that the well-established, historical continuity in the name of Mapanza plus the other Tonga late-colonial combined chieftainship and village names that are among the settlement names on the map (e.g., MACHA and CHIKANTA); the use of a symbol normally associated with rural settlement in African colonial cartography; and the date of the map coincident with the imposition of taxation—and the principal feature located across the map is not in doubt, namely, the people of the subdistrict. Moreover, the characteristics of the distribution can be accounted for in broad terms. The map provides authentic demographic information unavailable from any other source.

Having looked to Hunt's map for evidence of locations and distributions, the question arises of the magnitude of planimetric error contained within the *Sketch Map*. Is distortion perhaps so great as to invalidate any attempt to extract locational information from the map? To some extent, the answer must be conditioned by the precision required in obtaining locational information from the map: a high order of precision has already been set aside as impracticable, because of how the settlements are portrayed. There are symbols apparently omitted; and it is not certain what sort of settlement form, whether nucleated or dispersed, is intended by the symbols. The pattern has therefore been interpreted only at a high order of generalization, comparing large parts of the subdistrict. Nevertheless, some assessment of the magnitude of error between points within the map is appropriate.

A difficulty in assessing the planimetric accuracy of Hunt's map is that the category of feature with the largest number of individual items is the settlement symbol. However, rural settlement locations on a modern and relatively accurate map (which in any event will tend not to show a rural settlement unless it includes a more permanent building such as a school, clinic, post office, or store) cannot be assumed to occupy the same place as they did in 1905. One settlement site on Hunt's map that can be located with confidence on a modern map is the perspective drawing labeled *Collector*, that is, Hunt's subdistrict headquarters. This is the "old government brick-built house" purchased by Bishop Hine as Universities' Mission to Central Africa (UMCA) mission headquarters in 1911[56] following the closure of the subdistrict at the end of 1909, and still the site of Mapanza Mission. The only other points on Hunt's map that can be reliably located on modern maps and therefore utilized as reference points in assessing the magnitude of distortion in the map are physical features, including three hills (*Namayawa, Mavooka,* and *Kalundu,* the latter assumed to be Kapili), two confluences (*Munyeke-Chamuka* and *Munyeke-Macha*), and *Chitongo Pools*—a total of seven points. Such a small array of comparable points means that the assessment must be tentative.

Techniques for the measurement of distortion on historical maps have been reviewed in relation to a district map of a part of Western Zambia.[57] While the literature has been expanded since then and new techniques devised, the present purpose of legitimizing the interpretation already placed on the settlement pattern shown on Hunt's map will be served by a simple technique appropriate to the paucity of the data and providing an assessment without a high order of precision. The assessment will be based on the comparison of adjusted linear distances, of which a maximum of twenty-one pairs can be derived from the seven known points. Employing the technique as previously described, the following are the percentage differences between comparable distances on Hunt's map and a modern counterpart, in order of increasing difference: 0, 0, 1, 2, 2, 3, 3, 4, 5, 5, 7, 9, 11, 14, 15, 15, 20, 24, 24, 51, 53. The two very high values are both over very short distances and are therefore the product of relatively small absolute differences. The range variation in scale on Hunt's map should more characteristically be thought of as ranging from nil to 25 percent. This is unusually large, even allowing for a majority of values below 10 percent, and would certainly cast doubt on any statements made concerning the precise location of individual places in relation one to another. It is not sufficiently variable to invalidate the very broad generalizations already made about the nature of the population distribution portrayed by Hunt.

In selecting a case study to demonstrate the utility of early and often technically rudimentary cartography in the demographic study of colonial Africa, I have consciously chosen an unusually difficult map to interpret. Many district maps locate many more places with much less ambiguity about content and much greater locational precision. I drew attention to the 1911 map of Balovale Subdistrict[58] (which locates 264 settlements in a map containing a much smaller range of scales) because it has been published in part, as have some samples of the district mapping of F. B. Macrae.[59] Some district maps were drawn not only with diligence but with enthusiasm and pride and are of a much higher quality than Hunt's work. The considerable problems in extracting precise demographic information from Hunt's map should not, therefore, be seen as typical; but if the map of Mapanza is now seen as a useful source, much greater potential exists in the many more detailed and accurate counterparts.

Administrative officers were not the only mapmakers whose work survives. Specialist officers were also occasional mapmakers for purposes as varied as tsetse control and forest conservation, and the maps sometimes located settlements. The reason why all of these officers made their own maps was fundamentally the same: professional mapmakers were too few, and their priority was primarily cadastral mapping. Indeed the first 1:250 thousand topographic series for Northern Rhodesia was a compilation series that drew heavily on traverses and sketch maps by administrative and other officers[60] rather than trained surveyors. Even when large-scale topographic mapping of a professional quality is published, the product is sometimes disappointing as far as rural settlement is concerned. Extensive coverage at a large scale was made feasible by means of photogrammetric techniques that cannot differentiate between the degrees of impermanence of rural dwellings. A cluster of thatched roofs may be seasonal shelters or a slightly more permanent village and in any case could rarely be named without ground control. Although rural settlement symbols may be shown on the finished map, they are probably less discerning than those on the district map, whose primary purpose was to locate settlement. This is a feature of post-1945 large-scale topographic mapping not only in Northern Rhodesia (and the federation) but in other parts of Africa. It is emphasized in the Mapanza area, where the late colonial (ca. 1960) 1:50 thousand scale locates much settlement but names very little. There are actually far more rural settlements named on the 1:100 thousand *Geological Map of the Mapanza Mission Area*.[61] Obviously, official topographic surveys should be checked as potential demographic sources; but they may occasionally disappoint. The presumed impermanence of much rural settlement seems sometimes to have been used as pretext for its omission in early published topographic mapping (e.g., GSGS 1764). Hence, the inadequacy (particularly of earlier large-scale official topographic mapping) for demographic reconstruction makes the work of the amateurs even more valuable.

THE DISTRICT MAP ELSEWHERE IN COLONIAL AFRICA

Do other former central African colonial territories have underutilized cartographic resources with potential in demographic study, compiled in the earlier years of colonial authority prior to professional topographic surveys, because of the imperatives of the translation of imperialism to colonialism? I have no knowledge of the situation in former Belgian or Portuguese Africa; but I can offer a few speculative comments about other former British territories, noting at the outset the first annual report of the Colonial Survey Committee, which in 1906 indicated that "the mass of available material consists of sketches made by travellers and explorers and by civilians and military officials when touring on duty or accompanying military expeditions."[62]

Malawi has been the subject of a cartographic history[63] offering evidence that district maps were compiled for administrative purposes. That being so, it is surprising that only two such maps are recorded. It is possible to suggest reasons why there is so little evidence of their existence;[64] but further archival searches are required before giving up the quest not only for the maps themselves but also for the accompanying textual documents, such as tour reports by administrative and specialist officers.

Zimbabwe, like Uganda, is fortunate in having an official history of trigonometrical survey[65] from its origins in 1897. A Trigonometrical Survey Section of the surveyor general's department was established in 1929 with the result that primary triangulation covered most of the country by a relatively early date. However, a program of 1:50 thousand mapping was not embarked upon until 1937,[66] which suggests that any administrative need for large-scale maps may well have been already met, particularly in Southern Rhodesia prior to 1922—whose administrative history is similar to that of Northern Rhodesia, with thirty-one "native districts" in 1912 administered by native commissioners who "should circulate constantly throughout the district."[67] This seems to be a situation conducive to the construction of tour report maps and to the maintenance of a district map, in which the most important category of information would be rural settlement.

Further north, in Tanganyika—and also in Kenya—there is some evidence of field mapping by administrative officers using prismatic compass and measuring wheel,[68] but the peculiar constitutional histories of Southern Rhodesia and Tanganyika during the colonial period might render plausible the suggestion that what were otherwise common British colonial administrative practices may not have been adopted in these particular countries. Is it even worth looking for unpublished cartography as part of the evidence of a common British colonial administrative policy of the type exemplified in Northern Rhodesia or Tanganyika? Possibly so, on the grounds of the administrative similarity between the two Rhodesias prior to 1922 and the Germans' extensive use of compilation mapping in Tanganyika prior to 1914, done largely in the spare time of government officers. There may be extant work, and there surely was a tradition of mapmaking established that may have influenced the subsequent British administration. However, there are further reasons for believing that it is worth inquiring after early unpublished topographic maps as demographic sources in colonial circumstances dissimilar from Northern Rhodesia's. First, the change in the nature of the relationship from imperialism to colonialism would be conducive to mapmaking wherever the new relationship was being established on the ground, even within the British colonial tradition of devolved authority and local autonomy. Second, Sudan under Anglo-Egyptian condominium represents a different colonial circumstance but was also divided into provinces and districts for administrative purposes. Henderson mentions "the district map on the wall" of the district office at Sennar in 1907, as though this was standard.[69] Third, there is some evidence from Botswana, whose colonial administrative history is yet a further variant, that for the man on the ground to map the administered peoples was compulsive.

The idiosyncratic administrative history of Bechuanaland, as one of the former high commission territories, initially employing an extreme form of indirect rule amounting to laissez faire in some respects,[70] was distinctively different from that of Northern Rhodesia in the degree of direct administrative and legal involvement. However, the protectorate was similarly divided into districts for the purposes of administration; and although rural settlement was much more nucleated than further north and although a system of tax camps rather than village-to-village tours was employed, maps were nevertheless drawn in the course of carrying out the minimal administrative function.

A particular enthusiast in this respect was Captain A. G. Stigand, who served as resident magistrate of Ngamiland and Ghanzi District for most of the period from 1909 to 1923. Over a period of some years he made extensive surveys of Ngamiland, in part out of personal interest and in part because of the inadequacy of existing maps of the area for purposes of orderly administration.[71] His work was good enough to be printed by the war office in 1925 (GSGS 2988) and to receive the acclaim of the Royal Geographical Society.[72] Stigand's work was incorporated into the first 1:500 thousand series of the protectorate (GSGS 3915) published in 1933 and reduced and republished in 1935 and 1984. The significant feature of the 1925 map for present purposes is its incorporation of much settlement detail in the Okavango Delta, including indications of settlement size and past settlement sites.

There is further evidence of nonprofessional mapmaking in Bechuanaland in the course of administrative and other duties, that is, of the colonialist rather than the imperialist function at work, regardless of administrative circumstances that might seem less conducive to compulsive mapmaking than, say, Northern Rhodesia. Hence, other former British territories in Central Africa and elsewhere, as well as perhaps the colonial territories of other European powers, may be expected to have a similar cartographic heritage, particularly from the early colonial period.

In the historiography of colonial surveys, much emphasis is justifiably placed on the Colonial Survey Committee[73] formed in 1905. This body was influential in the establishment of corps of professional surveyors in newly instituted specialist survey departments. Indeed, it was itself instituted to make available the sort of technical expertise that was not available within the colonial office staff.[74] Hence, it is not surprising that much recent writing on British colonial surveys tends to overlook the relatively ephemeral and less conspicuous cartography of the inexpert colonial officer. Nevertheless, it is the maps of the "amateur" surveyor—sometimes with other technical skills but often employed in administrative and legal rather than technical functions—that offer the greatest potential in demographic study. The district officer, native commissioner, or resident magistrate was the man at the sharp end in the replacement of imperial influence with colonial authority, that is, with implementing colonialism. The professional surveyor has the continuity that bridges the brief period of European colonialism in Africa. Although he did play his part in the implementation of colonialism, notably in the field of cadastral mapping, his geodetic techniques were applied to Africa prior to the advent of colonialism and are reflected in precolonial mapping. Arguably, with the passing of the colonial period and the return to a more imperialistic relationship between Europe and Africa, the geodetic, trigonometric, and photogrammetic skills of bodies such as Britain's former Directorate of Overseas Surveys are part of the evidence of an enduring imperialistic relationship. On the other hand, the amateur, large-scale mapmaker, who was relevant (if not essential) to the colonial function, is now totally absent. The ironic consequence is that we possibly have a poorer record of the rural settlement distribution of postcolonial Africa than we do for much of British colonial Africa and perhaps for other parts of colonial Africa.

NOTES

1. S. Williams, *Distribution of the African Population of Northern Rhodesia*, Rhodes-Livingstone Communication, no. 24 (Lusaka, 1962).

2. P. A. Penfold, *Maps and Plans in the Public Record Office*, vol. 3, *Africa* (London, 1982).

3. W. G. Clarence-Smith, Review, *Canadian Journal of African Studies* 19 (1985), 652.

4. J. D. Hargreaves, "The Berlin West Africa Conference, 1885: A Timely Centenary?" *History Today* 34 (1984), 16–22.

5. J. C. Stone, "Imperialism, Colonialism, and Cartography," *Transactions of the Institute of British Geographers*, n.s. 13 (1988), 57–64.

6. R. C. Bridges, "The Historical Role of British Explorers in East Africa," *Terrae incognitae* 14 (1982), 1–21.

7. A. Bertrand, *Au pays des Ba-Rotzi Haut-Zambèse* (Paris, 1898).

8. C. Harding, *In Remotest Barotseland* (London, 1904).

9. F. C. Selous, "Letters from Mr. F. C. Selous on His Journeys to the Kafukwe River, and on the Upper Zambezi," *Proceedings of the Royal Geographic Society* 11 (1889), 216–223.

10. A. St. H. Gibbons, *Exploring and Hunting in Central Africa* (London, 1898).

11. J. M. Moubray, *In South Central Africa* (London, 1912).

12. D. Livingstone, *Missionary Travels and Researches in South Africa* (London, 1857).

13. I. C. Cunningham, "David Livingstone and His Maps," in P. M. Larby, ed., *Standing Committee on Library Materials on Africa (SCOLMA)* (London, 1987), 14–20.

14. F. Debenham, *The Way to Ilala* (London, 1955).

15. A. St. H. Gibbons, *Africa from South to North Through Marotseland* (London, 1904).

16. A. St. H. Gibbons, "Northern Rhodesia," *United Empire* 5 (1914), 25–44.

17. R. A. Pullan, "A First Check List of the Published Maps of Northern Rhodesia 1890–1949," in *Zambian Geographic Association (ZGA) Bibliographies*, vol. 3 (Lusaka, 1978).

18. T. Campbell, *Catalogue 28: Admiralty Charts and Related Maps* (London, 1984).

19. A. J. Christopher, "Pattern of British Overseas Investment in Land 1885–1913," *Transaction of the Institute of British Geographers*, n.s. 10 (1985), 454–466.

20. J. C. Stone, "An Early Map of the Hook of Kafue," in R. C. Bridges, ed., *An African Miscellany for John Hargreaves* (Aberdeen, 1983), 93–95.

21. S. R. Denny, "Val Gielgud and the Slave Traders," *Northern Rhodesia Journal* 3 (1957), 331–378.

22. J. C. Stone, "The District Map: An Episode in British Colonial Cartography in Africa, with Particular Reference to Northern Rhodesia," *Cartographic Journal* 19, no. 2 (1982), 104–114.

23. E. K. Jordon, "Mongu in 1908," *Northern Rhodesia Journal* 2, no. 4 (1954), 60–72, esp. 66.

24. Stone, "District Map," 106.

25. J. H. Venning, "Early Days in Balovale," *Northern Rhodesia Journal* 2, no. 6 (1955), 53–57.

26. R. Codrington, "A Journey from Fort Jameson to Old Chitambo and the Tanganyika Plateau," *Geographical Journal* 15 (1900), 227–234; P. H. Selby, "Journey to the Kafue and Zumbo Districts," *Geographical Journal* 19 (1900), 605–607.

27. Stone, "District Map."

28. F. H. Melland, *In Witch-bound Africa* (Philadelphia, 1923); E. Bigland, *The Lake of the Royal Crocodiles* (London, 1939).

29. C. Fyfe and D. McMaster, *African Historical Demography*, vol. 1, (Edinburgh, 1977).

30. Venning, "Early Days."

31. See, e.g., Stone, "District Map."

32. J. C. Stone, *A Guide to the Administrative Boundaries of Northern Rhodesia*, O'Dell Memorial Monographs, no. 7 (Aberdeen, 1979).

33. D. Livingstone and C. Livingstone, *Narrative of an Expedition to the Zambezi and Its Tributaries* (London, 1865).

34. F. C. Selous, *Travels and Adventure in South-East Africa* (London, 1893).

35. Gibbons, *Explorations and Hunting*, 330.

36. E. Colson, *Marriage and the Family Among the Plateau Tonga of Northern Rhodesia* (Manchester, 1958), 8.

37. A. Roberts, *A History of Zambia* (London, 1976), 136.

38. E. Colson, *Life Among the Cattle-owning Plateau Tonga*, Rhodes-Livingstone Occasional Papers, no. 6 (Livingstone, 1949), 8.

39. Colson, *Marriage and the Family*, 25.

40. C. Johns, *Emil Holub's Travels North of the Zambezi 1885–6* (Manchester, 1975), 109.

41. Roberts, *History of Zambia*, 76.

42. K. Vickery, "The Making of a Peasantry: Imperialism and the Plateau Tonga Economy, 1890–1936" (Ph.D. diss., Yale, 1978).

43. Colson, *Marriage and the Family.*

44. K. Vickery, *Black and White in Southern Zambia: The Tonga Plateau Economy of British Imperialism, 1890–1939* (Westport, 1986).

45. E. Colson and M. Gluckman, eds., *Seven Tribes of British Central Africa* (Manchester, 1951).

46. Personal communication from Oliver Hazemba, 25 May 1986.

47. M. A. Jaspan, *The Ila-Tonga Peoples of Northwestern Rhodesia,* Ethnographic Survey of Africa, no. 4 (London, 1953).

48. Colson and Gluckman, *Seven Tribes.*

49. L. H. Gann, *A History of Northern Rhodesia* (London, 1964).

50. Vickery, "Making of a Peasantry."

51. Stone, "Guide to the Administrative Boundaries."

52. Vickery, "Making of a Peasantry."

53. C. G. Trapnell and J. N. Clothier, *The Soils, Vegetation, and Agricultural Systems of North Western Rhodesia: Report of the Ecological Survey* (Lusaka, 1937).

54. Federation of Rhodesia and Nyasaland, Department of Trigonometrical and Topographic Surveys, *Soils Map of the Federation of Rhodesia and Nyasaland* (Salisbury, 1960).

55. E. W. Smith and A. M. Dale, *The Ila-speaking Peoples of Northern Rhodesia* (London, 1920), 29.

56. P. D. Snelson, *Educational Development in Northern Rhodesia, 1883–1945* (Lusaka, 1970), 103.

57. J. C. Stone, "The Compilation Map: A Technique for Topographic Mapping by British Colonial Surveyors," *Cartographic Journal* 22 (1984), 121–128.

58. Stone, "Early Maps."

59. Stone, "District Map."

60. J. C. Stone, "The Compilation Map."

61. R. Taverner-Smith, *Geological Survey Report,* no. 10 (Lusaka, 1959).

62. His Majesty's Stationers Office, *Colonial Report,* no. 500, cd. 2684 (London, 1906).

63. C. G. C. Martin, *Maps and Surveys of Malawi* (Cape Town, 1980).

64. Stone, "District Map."

65. J. E. S. Bradford and A. C. Gauld, *The Geodetic Triangulation and Trigonometrical Survey of Southern Rhodesia 1897–1952* (Salisbury, 1952).

66. R. S. Cole, "Surveys and Mapping in Zimbabwe" (Harare, 1983, mimeographed).

67. H. Rolin, *Rolin's Rhodesia* (Bulawayo, 1978), 63.

68. Stone, "District Map."

69. K. D. D. Henderson, *Set Under Authority* (n.p., 1987).

70. T. Tlou and A. Campbell, *History of Botswana* (Gaborone, 1984).

71. National Archives of Botswana, DCGH 6/8.

72. A. G. Stigand, "Ngamiland," *Geographical Journal* 62 (1923), 401–418.

73. E. G. McGrath, "The Surveying and Mapping of British East Africa 1890–1946," *Cartographical Monograph* 18 (1976); C. I. M. O'Brien, "African Surveys 1890–1940," Paper presented at seminar of the Commonwealth Institute, London, 1985.

74. S. Constantine, *The Making of British Colonial Development Policy 1914–1940* (London, 1984).

14

Applications of Spatial Autocorrelation Analysis to Colonial African Census Data

FRANK C. STETZER

The field of demography has developed an extensive and impressive body of quantitative tools for the analysis of population change over time. Many of these tools are applied to geographically disaggregated data, such as data from the internal districts used in a census. Some demographic measures, such as internal migration rates, implicitly use this geographic framework; but few of these tools use the spatial structure of this geographic framework (in the sense that the *relative* locations of the places involved are not included). Yet spatial structure is certainly a factor in determining the migration patterns of a region, because the probability of a person's migrating depends in part on that person's location vis-à-vis potential migration opportunities. Occasionally, demographic measures are mapped in a search for patterns, and this is a good first step. I shall describe some methods for the spatial analysis of demographic data that start with, but go beyond, intuitively examining a map. These methods have not yet been extensively employed by demographers. I believe they can occasionally offer useful insights into the causes of demographic patterns, especially when dealing with census data like that from colonial Africa, with quality and quantity below the usual standards. Here, especially, it is unwise to ignore the additional bits of information spatial analysis can supply.

The rise of quantitative geographic analysis in the past three decades has stimulated the development of techniques for addressing various methodological problems in the analysis of spatial data. One of these problems is referred to as *spatial autocorrelation*. This is a property of geographic data in which the values of a variable measured at neighboring locations will tend to be more alike than values observed at widely separated locations; in other words, near places will be more alike than far places. I shall review two applications of this notion of autocorrelation and demonstrate their use in analyzing demographic change in colonial Northern Rhodesia and Nyasaland. These applications are *areal interpolation* (which makes data comparable between census periods when the district boundaries change) and *spatial modeling* (which incorporates autocorrelation in a regression model to account for patterns of fertility and migration).

AREAL INTERPOLATION

One of the many complications arising in research using historical census materials is the degree to which internal boundaries fluctuate between census years. Some definitional districts grew at the expense of others; districts were combined into larger, or split into smaller, ones. To compound the difficulty, the cartography is often uneven; and boundaries known to be stable show variation between successive maps due to cartographic errors, repeated tracing, and photocopying. These many irregularities make comparisons of demographic data between censuses frustrating. Unfortunately, there is no perfect solution to this problem. Any attempt to estimate population in an area whose boundaries are not defined at the time of the census will yield only a rough estimate. It makes sense, however, to produce the most reasonable estimate possible using the information at hand.

The simplest solution to this problem is to adjust the population to be proportional to the area of the district. If a certain district has forty thousand people at a census and an area of five thousand km^2 and at the next census the area has grown to six thousand kilometers, we can estimate the population of the larger area at the time of the first census as $(6,000/5,000) \times 40,000 = 48,000$. This figure can be compared to the census figure at the later time to estimate population change. The assumption, of course, is that any area added or lost has the same population density as the rest of the original district. This is simple and reasonable, but if maps of the districts at the two time periods are available, there is more information at hand. If the district grew at the expense of a very densely populated district, it probably gained more than eight thousand persons—and vice versa.

Areal interpolation uses the additional geographic information contained in the census maps to aid in the interpolation. There are several methods for incorporating this information,[1] but the most sophisticated is termed *pycnophylactic interpolation.*[2] It incorporates the notion of spatial autocorrelation by assuming that population density forms a smooth, continuous surface over the region, both within and between districts. This surface is estimated by an iterative process that is mathematically simple and easily performed on a computer but somewhat awkward to describe. Visualize a base map of the region at the time of the first census. On each district, place a piece of modeling clay with cross section matching the outline of the district and volume proportional to the population. Our initial map is covered with these clay steps (or prisms) of different heights. To smoothe this surface, we must remove clay from the upper edges of high steps and add it to the lower edges of low steps, while maintaining the same amount of total clay (population) in each prism. As this surface is sculpted in this fashion, it is gradually transformed from a set of steps to a smooth surface, representing the spatial autocorrelation assumption. To complete the interpolation we can carve out the districts corresponding to the definitions in the second census and measure their volume.

APPLICATION

The method of pycnophylactic interpolation was applied to total population figures by district from the Northern Rhodesia census of 1929 and the Nyasaland census of 1945. Between these census years and the next (1963 in Northern Rhodesia and 1966 in Malawi), several internal boundary changes were made. The first step in the process was to digitize the boundaries of the four sets of districts for input to the interpolation computer program. The computer-drawn boundaries are shown in Maps 14.1–14.4.[3] Some major changes in boundaries can be observed. For example, the border between Kasungu (District 4) and Momberas (District 3) in Nyasaland has been moved to the south significantly. In Northern Rhodesia the boundary between Mpika (District 4) and Serenje (District 27) shifts. There are many other apparent small changes.

The computer files containing the coordinates of the districts must be as comparable as possible for the areal interpolation to be done. To accomplish this, a computer program was used to scale and rotate the latter map to match the former map as closely as possible. Even after this, there were still many inconsistencies in the boundaries of the districts, even in locations where it is known that there was no change. This is due primarily to the element of human error in cartography and digitizing and cannot be avoided. To help resolve these inconsistencies, a ring of buffer district was added around each colony. These were assumed to have a population density equal to that of the neighboring ("parent") district.

Total population figures from the 1945 census of Nyasaland and the 1929 census of Northern Rhodesia complete the data requirements. Figures 14.1 and 14.2 display the smoothed population density surfaces for Nyasaland in 1945 and Northern Rhodesia in 1929. These were then "carved" into the new set of districts. Tables 14.1 and 14.2 show the results of the interpolation process. The workings of the process can be seen by examining Momberas-Mzimba (District 3) in Nyasaland-Malawi. Between 1945 and 1966 the district apparently gains significantly in size, but the estimated population change due to boundary change is quite slight. This is because most of the areal change came at the expense of Kasungu, which is sparsely populated. A similar example is observed in Northern Rhodesia, where Mpika gains territory from a sparsely populated Serenje.

MAP 14.1 Northern Rhodesia District Boundaries, 1929

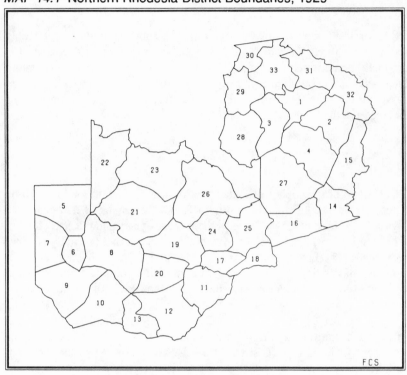

MAP 14.2 Northern Rhodesia District Boundaries, 1963

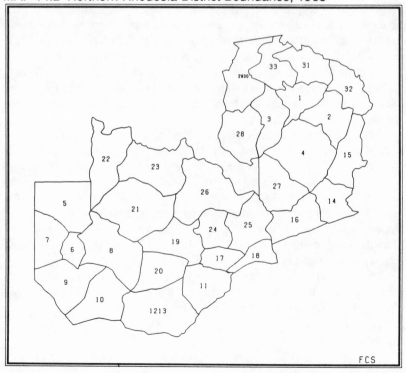

MAP 14.3 Nyasaland District Boundaries, 1945

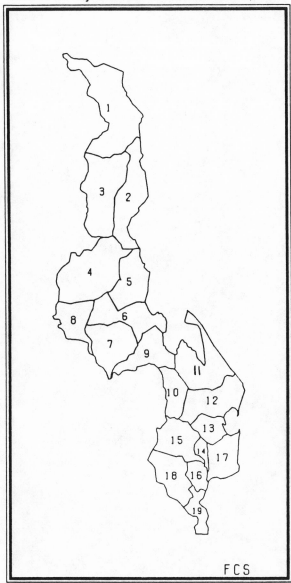

MAP 14.4 Malawi District Boundaries, 1966

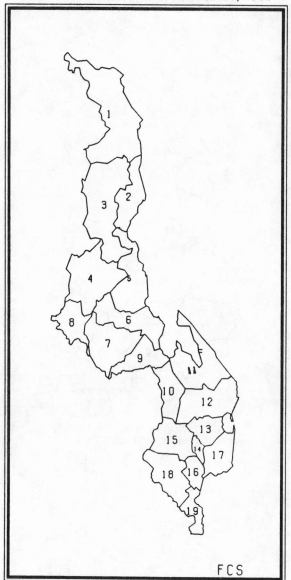

FIGURE 14.1 Nyasaland Smoothed Population Surface, 1945

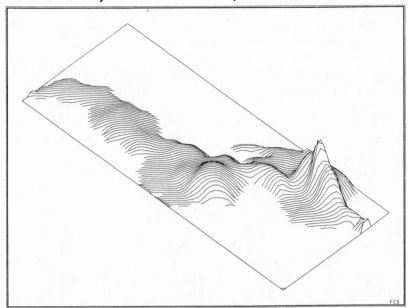

FIGURE 14.2 Northern Rhodesia Smoothed Population Surface, 1929

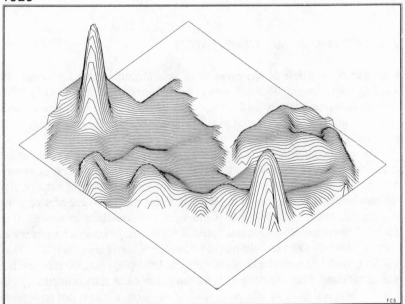

TABLE 14.1 Total Population by District in Nyasaland 1945 Interpolated into 1966 Districts of Malawi by Pycnophylactic Method

District Name and Number	Population, 1945	Population, 1966 Districts
1. North Nyasa–Karonga–Chitipa	82,508	104,208
2. West Nyasa–Chinteche	52,009	33,793
3. Momberas–Mzimba	156,208	161,059
4. Kasungu	40,197	42,333
5. Kota-Kota	75,522	91,353
6. Dowa	131,195	133,109
7. Lilongwe	230,891	232,703
8. Fort Manning	12,533	15,623
9. Dedza	142,324	104,102
10. Ncheu	87,690	85,220
11. South Nyasa–Fort Johnson	111,621	124,149
12. Upper Shire–Liwonde	87,682	97,796
13. Zomba	137,603	137,357
14. Chiradzulu	83,639	60,604
15. Blantyre–Central Shire	102,208	71,263
16. Cholo	119,746	127,689
17. Mlanje	209,522	228,758
18. Chikwawa	59,664	66,897
19. Lower Shire-Port Herald	66,746	71,464

MODELING SPATIAL AUTOCORRELATION

A second application of the concept of spatial autocorrelation occurs in building what geographers call purely spatial models. These models were developed on an analogy with time series models used in economics and engineering. They have replaced trend surface analysis as the primary method in the quantitative study of geographic data.

The most common time series model is the autoregressive model, which makes the value of a variable at a given point in time a function of one or more values at previous times. Similarly, the concept of spatial autocorrelation can be made into a formal model, specifying that the value of a variable at a certain place is a function of the values of variables at surrounding places. This notion of modeling the spatial dependency between variables has led to an extensive and still-developing literature within geography.

This model of spatial autocorrelation can be applied in three separate but related fashions. These include tests for the presence of autocorrelation, fit to a set of data, and used to interpret the residuals from a traditional regression model containing one or more independent variables. In any of these

TABLE 14.2 Total Population by District in Northern Rhodesia 1929
Interpolated into 1963 Districts by Pycnophylactic Method

District Name and Number	Population, 1929	Population, 1963 Districts
1. Kasama	39,886	39,485
2. Chinsali	25,814	24,317
3. Luwingu	49,473	49,387
4. Mpika	30,313	38,142
5. Balovale	54,157	52,413
6. Mongu-Lealui	85,400	80,384
7. Kalabo	79,541	81,068
8. Mankoya	27,534	31,408
9. Nalolo	44,272	44,984
10. Sesheke	24,764	24,721
11. Mazabuka-Magoya	70,364	70,880
12, 13. Choma–Kalomo	55,712	55,168
14. Fort Jameson	120,448	122,444
15. Lundazi	40,407	42,710
16. Petauke	62,787	61,871
17. Lusaka	18,764	17,833
18. Feira	16,400	20,335
19. Mumbwa	30,022	30,946
20. Namwala	23,288	22,263
21. Kasempa	18,798	17,545
22. Mwinilunga	21,055	21,433
23. Solwezi	21,429	21,380
24. Broken Hill	17,029	15,616
25. Mkushi	24,433	23,300
26. Ndola	38,255	37,975
27. Serenje	29,800	19,491
28. Fort Rosebery	61,267	63,350
29, 30. Kawambwa–Chengi	63,139	68,414
31. Abercorn	41,427	40,699
32. Isoka-Fife	36,346	37,439
33. Mporokoso	25,821	20,892

contexts, the presence of autocorrelation in a set of data or in the residuals
from a regression equation is given essentially the same interpretation.
Positive autocorrelation, in which the values of the variable at nearby places
are similar, indicates some process of contagion, averaging, or diffusion is
operating or that there is correlation between the variable of interest and some
other autocorrelated variable. Positive autocorrelation is usually apparent to
the practiced eye when examining a map. Negative autocorrelation, in which
nearby places are unlike (e.g., a checkerboard pattern, with alternating high
and low values) is relatively uncommon and indicates either a process of
competition or migration. It is difficult to detect visually. Autocorrelation in
the residuals of a regression equation indicates that the model represented by
the equation is in some way inadequate; whether there is more pattern to the
dependent variable than the independent of spatial autocorrelation in any
particular circumstance depends on the context.

The mathematical model of spatial autocorrelation most commonly used is due to A. D. Cliff and J. K. Ord.[4] Compared to the time series autocorrelation model, it contains two additional complexities. First, spatial data exists in a two-dimensional framework in which the observations are unevenly and irregularly spaced. Time series data, by contrast, consists of regularly spaced observations in a one-dimensional framework. This difficulty is circumvented by specifying the structure of the spatial system with what is termed the *weight matrix*. Second, the dependencies in spatially autocorrelated data extend in all directions; in time series data, only the past "causes" the present, not vice versa. This complication means that simple techniques for testing and modeling time series autocorrelation, such as least squares correlation and regression, cannot be applied in the spatial domain. The mathematics of tests for, and measures of, spatial autocorrelation quickly become complicated; however, the formulas needed are well known, and many computer programs are written and circulated among geographers.

The form of the purely spatial model is as follows:

$$Y_i = p_j\, w_{ij}\, Y_j + e_i,$$

where Y_i is the value of the variable Y at place i, p is the autocorrelation coefficient, w_{ij} is an element of a weight matrix w, and e_i is an uncorrelated error component. In words, this equation means that the value of a variable Y at place i is the sum of two components: the weighted average of the value of Y at surrounding places and a random, uncorrelated variable. The autocorrelation coefficient p ranges from -1 (perfect negative autocorrelation) through 0 (no autocorrelation) to 1 (perfect positive autocorrelation, a smooth surface). The error component e_i serves essentially the same function as the residual term in a regression equation: it mathematically represents the "unexplained variance." The weight matrix W is defined by reference to the spatial system being studied. Basically, a weight w_{ij} must be defined for each pair of places in the data. Two common ways of formulating W are by contiguity (in which w_{ij} is set to unity if places i and j are contiguous and zero otherwise) and by distance decay (in which w_{ij} declines with the distance between places i and j). I have experimented with several methods and found a combination of these two methods very useful. In this approach, weights are defined as

$$w_{ij} = \begin{cases} 1/d_{ij} & \text{if } d_{ij} < D_{max} \\ 0 & \text{otherwise,} \end{cases}$$

where d_{ij} is the distance between i and j, appropriately measured, and D_{max} is some distance cutoff. By varying D_{max} from small to large, it is possible to detect (positive) autocorrelation of corresponding to different spatial forms. If autocorrelation is found when using a small value of D_{max} but not when using a large value, the spatial pattern in the data is one of small clusters of high and low values. If the contrary occurs, the pattern is a broad trend or surface, with local variation or irregularities. In application, these weights are usually scaled to sum to unity for each place i.

This model for autocorrelation has led to several applications, two of which will be employed here. The first is a test for the presence of autocorrelation in a set of geographic data (a map). The most common test is the so-called I-statistic of Cliff and Ord. It is most often presented in standardized form as a z-score that can be interpreted as a test on the null hypothesis of no spatial autocorrelation. Second, this model for autocorrelation can be incorporated into a multiple regression equation with the autocorrelated variable as the dependent variable:

$$Y_i = p_j w_{ij} Y_j + b_0 + b_1 + X_{1i} + \ldots + b_k X_{ki} + e_i.$$

The rationale for this model is that in ordinary regression analysis one of the assumptions is that the errors (e_i) are independent of each other. The presence of autocorrelation, either temporal or spatial, directly violates this assumption. By incorporating a model for autocorrelation in the errors (residuals) two ends are accomplished: (1) the assumption of independence is again valid, which has some minor beneficial impact on the estimation of the model, and (2) since autocorrelation in the residuals indicates a spatial pattern beyond that in the independent variables, it makes sense to think of this pattern as something that has a cause and is therefore open to explanation. Although there is only one additional parameter p to estimate, the mathematics used to estimate this model are quite complex, and are described in Cliff and Ord's ninth chapter.

These two applications of the autocorrelation model—the test for its presence and the inclusion in a regression model—do not necessarily lead to the same conclusions. It is possible for a map of the raw data to reveal no autocorrelation; but when included in a regression equation with other independent variables, the spatial patterning in the data may become significant.

APPLICATION

On the basis of procedures discussed in the working paper I wrote with Bruce Fetter,[5] the rates of natural increase for Nyasaland (Malawi) in 1926, 1945, and 1966; for Northern Rhodesia in 1921, 1929, and 1963; and rates of net migration for the intervals 1926–1945 and 1945–1966 in Nyasaland and 1921–1929 and 1929–1963 in Northern Rhodesia were calculated. This data is displayed in Maps 14.5–14.14.

These maps were tested for spatial autocorrelation using the I-statistic of Cliff and Ord. The weighting scheme discussed above was employed, using

MAP 14.5 Natural Increase: Nyasaland, 1926

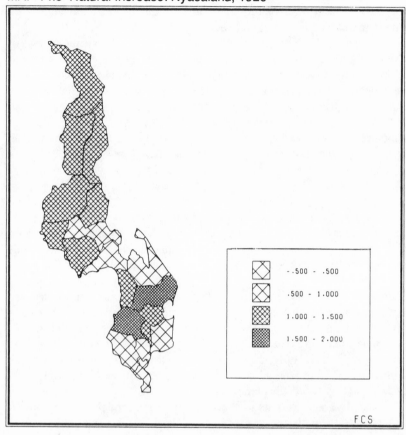

distance between district headquarters as d_{ij} and values of 100, 200, . . . , 600 km for D_{max}. The results of this test are presented in Table 14.3, with the test statistic converted to a z-score. A value outside the interval (–1.65, 1.65) can be interpreted as indicating spatial autocorrelation statistically discernable at the .1 (two-tailed) level. For Nyasaland-Malawi only the natural increase map for 1945 (Map 14.6) shows significant spatial autocorrelation, while for Northern Rhodesia, the rate of natural increase in 1963 (Map 14.10), reveals significant spatial scales (except 100 kilometers for Northern Rhodesia). This is not always the case.

These data were next employed as dependent variables in multiple regression equations and are displayed on Table 14.4. First, a standard stepwise regression analysis was performed. Then, a stepwise regression analysis incorporating an autoregressive component was performed for

MAP 14.6 Natural Increase: Nyasaland, 1945

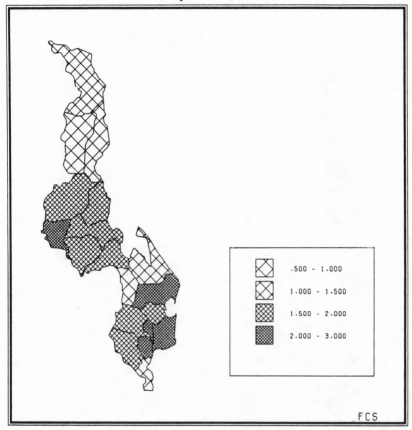

comparison. Since there are relatively few observations and moderate correlations between some of the independent variables, it was decided to employ a stepwise regression procedure to attempt to sort out the various factors into a parsimonious model while preserving degrees of freedom. A liberal significance level of .2 was used for retention of variables in the model, in keeping with the exploratory nature of this study and the lack of precision known to exist in the data.

In examining the causes of demographic change, three classes of external factors are considered: health (represented by the altitude of the capital of each district), wealth (measured by the sex ratio and the presence or absence of a railway and in the case of Nyasaland by the hut tax collected per adult woman in each district), and location (measured by the coordinates of the district headquarters and the presence or absence of a border with another colony).

MAP 14.7 Natural Increase: Malawi, 1966

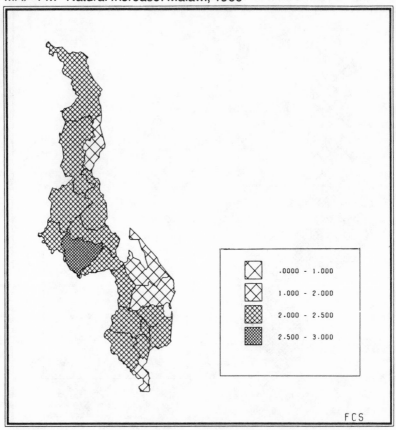

Some of these variables require a little elucidation. The relationship between altitude and health was early recognized by European settlers, who consistently preferred higher elevations in tropical areas. Africans also found higher elevations more salubrious; in particular, trypanosomiasis, which kills cattle and horses and produced sleeping sickness in humans, was not found there. The sex ratio also has an indirect significance. It is a good indicator of male out-migration, which in Central Africa was provoked by the hut tax. This money was crucial, in that men who could earn their money locally did not have to leave their homes. Borders with another colony may be a stimulus to migrate, and this migration itself may be a factor affecting natural increase. Northern Rhodesia shares borders with Belgian and Portuguese colonies, as well as other British colonies; while Nyasaland borders on British and

MAP 14.8 Natural Increase: Northern Rhodesia, 1921

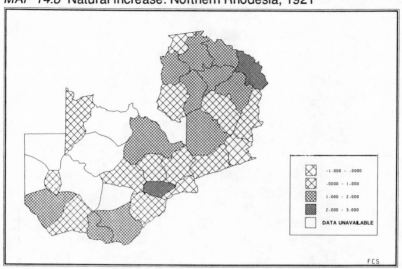

MAP 14.9 Natural Increase: Northern Rhodesia, 1929

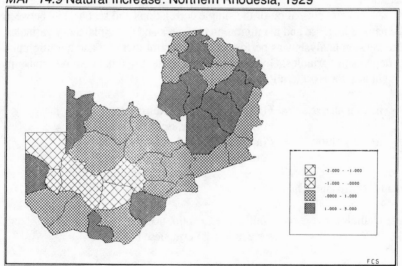

MAP 14.10 Natural Increase: Northern Rhodesia, 1963

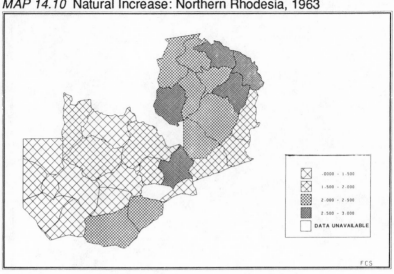

Portuguese colonies. These are represented in the analysis by dummy variables.

After an examination of the simple correlations and scatterplots between the natural increase and net migration measures and the explanatory variables, a regression analysis was performed with natural increase and net migration as dependent variables. Given the available data, the functional relationships sought are, for Northern Rhodesia,

natural increase   = f (altitude, sex ratio, railroad,
                      Portuguese border, Belgian border)
net migration   = f (altitude, railroad, sex ratio,
                      Portuguese border, Belgian border)

and for Nyasaland-Malawi,

natural increase   = f (altitude, sex ratio, tax rate,
                      early railroad, Portuguese border)

Table 14.4 presents the ten final models arrived at by the stepwise procedure. Eight of the ten regressions show an overall significance at the .1 level. Most of these, however, are quite weak, with R^2 values less than .4. In general, rates of natural increase are more closely determined by the independent variables than is net migration. The next paragraphs discuss the particular results from the regression analysis. In general, two classes of

MAP 14.11 Net Migration: Nyasaland, 1926–1945

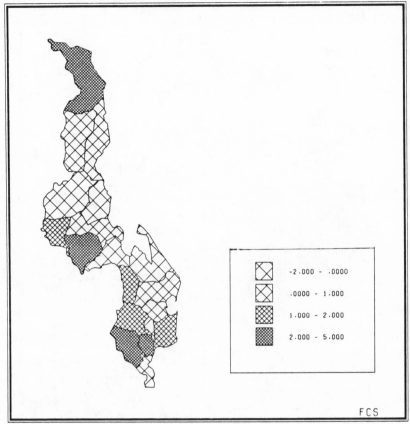

measures consistently affect the rate of natural increase: altitude and some measure of wealth (especially presence of a railway and the sex ratio). As far as Northern Rhodesia is concerned, both altitude and a railway appear in the significant regressions for 1921 and 1963, and the railroad is weakly involved in the regression for 1929. This leads to the conclusion that Africans living in districts of higher elevation and those living in districts crossed by the country's lone railway had more favorable vital rates than Africans living in other parts of the country. Altitude also seems to have affected the rate of natural increase in Nyasaland in the 1945 and 1966 censuses, making it the most consistent predictor of natural increase in our sample.

It seems that locational advantages were not necessarily permanent. Zambians living at higher elevations or in the railway belt in 1929 did not seem to enjoy significantly better conditions when the government was

MAP 14.12 Net Migration: Nyasaland, 1945–1966

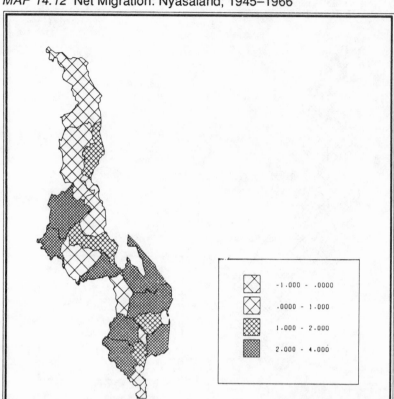

mobilizing the labor force for the development of the copper mines. Similarly, Malawians who lived in healthier or less peripheral districts enjoyed no particular advantage in 1926.

In Nyasaland a district's wealth also seems to have affected its fertility. Both the 1945 and 1966 censuses show a positive relationship between sex ratio and natural increase. Since the sex ratio was highest in the districts where men could earn their tax money locally, it might be assumed that these districts were better off from two economic standpoints: (1) more money was in circulation there, and (2) the labor force had not been denuded of its able-bodied men. The same appears true in Nyasaland in the 1945 and 1966 censuses. The tax rate as a measure of wealth, however, has a negative impact on natural increase in Nyasaland in 1926. And while railroads have a uniformly positive impact on vital rates in Northern Rhodesia, they appear to

MAP 14.13 Net Migration: Northern Rhodesia, 1921–1929

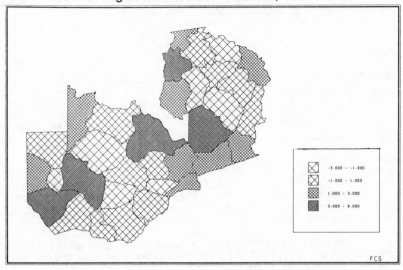

MAP 14.14 Net Migration: Northern Rhodesia, 1929–1963

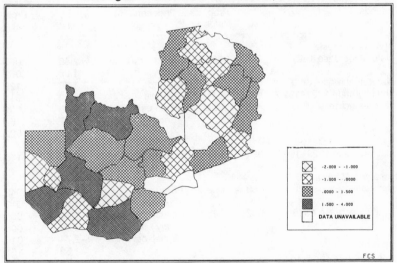

TABLE 14.3 Z-Score Test for Spatial Autocorrelation in Natural Increase and Net Migration Maps for Nyasaland-Malawi and Northern Rhodesia

Variable	D_{max} (km)					
	100	200	300	400	500	600
Northern Rhodesia						
Natural increase 1921	.400	−.075	.231	.096	−.076	−.051
Natural increase 1929	−.514	.067	−.008	−.425	−.305	−.215
Net migration 1921–1929	.173	.543	.957	.329	.425	.146
Natural increase 1963	.259	2.195	2.190	2.212	2.234	2.188
Net migration 1929–1963	.560	.470	.578	.097	.401	.518
Nyasaland-Malawi						
Natural increase 1926	−.404	−.619	−.452	−.511	−.483	−.545
Natural increase 1945	2.522	1.901	2.029	2.574	2.297	2.307
Net migration 1926–1945	.792	−.233	.164	.304	.267	.284
Natural increase 1966	.026	−.235	−.096	−.234	−.031	−.135
Net migration 1945–1966	−.193	−.877	−.854	−.726	−.795	−.802

Note: Based on the I-statistic of Cliff and Ord, author's calculations. Values of z outside the interval (−1.645, 1.645) indicate a spatial autocorrelation coefficient different statistically from zero at the .10 level (two-tailed).

TABLE 14.4 Stepwise Regression Analysis of Central African Demographic Data, 1921–1966

Dependent Variable	R^2	Prob. Value	Independent Variable	t-Stat.	Prob. Value
Northern Rhodesia					
Natural Increase 1921	.218	.009	altitude, railroad	2.98	.007
				1.95	.062
Natural Increase 1929	.075	.128	railroad	1.28	.128
Net Migration 1921–1929	.197	.011	sex ratio	2.70	.011
Natural Increase 1963	.423	.002	altitude, railroad,	3.68	.001
			British border	1.47	.152
				2.47	.022
Net Migration 1929–1963	.084	.113	railroad	1.64	.113
Nyasaland-Malawi					
Natural Increase 1926	.288	.066	Portuguese border,	−2.21	.042
			tax, rate	−1.37	.012
Natural Increase 1945	.632	.005	Altitude, sex ratio	3.38	.005
			early railroad,	3.30	.005
			British border	−2.74	.016
				−1.50	.151
Net Migration 1926–1945	.265	.084	tax rate,	1.73	.103
			British border	2.32	.034
Natural Increase 1966	.633	.005	altitude, sex ratio,	2.32	.036
			late railroad,	3.53	.003
			British border	−1.63	.126
				2.47	.027
Net Migration 1945–1966	.200	.005	sex ratio	2.06	.005

have a small negative influence in Nyasaland. This reflects the less significant role of the Nyasaland rail line in connecting the colony to other African markets and perhaps the expropriation of land along the rail line.

The pattern of net migration in Northern Rhodesia during the period 1921–1929 shows positive correlation only with the sex ratio variable, which is at least partially tautological. During the long period 1929–1963 only the railroad comes out as a stimulus to migration, and this relationship is very weak.

To recapitulate, these regressions reveal statistically significant coefficients of determination for eight of the ten models investigated. Altitude and some measure of wealth (usually either sex ratio or presence of a railroad) are often significant determinants, while the indicators of location are important in specific instances. This analysis demonstrates that these processes are not simple outcomes of one or two dominant forces, but are results of interrelationships that are complex but can be approached by careful analysis.

The spatial stepwise regression analysis was performed using the weight system discussed above. Distances were calculated between pairs of district headquarters, and maximum distance cutoffs of one hundred, two hundred, and four hundred kilometers were employed. For each distance the parameter p was estimated along with the rest of the regression parameters b, and the model that maximized the R^2 measure of fit was selected. The results of this analysis are presented in Table 14.5. To interpret the results, look first at the column containing the estimated value of p. This parameter is interpreted essentially as a correlation coefficient; it is constrained to the interval $(-1, 1)$, with zero indicating no autocorrelation. No significance test is valid in small samples, but a cutoff of plus-or-minus .3 can be employed as an arbitrary level. If the value of p is significant by this standard, its sign can be interpreted, and if the sign is positive, it is the value of D_{max} that gave the best fit. The R^2 value can be interpreted as the variance in the dependent variable accounted for by either the independent variables or the autocorrelation present in the dependent variables. It can be compared to the R^2 value from the aspatial equation only if the same independent variables are in both equations. There is no guarantee that the same variables will be selected for both equations since accounting for autocorrelation in the dependent variable changes that variable for the stepwise regression. The R^2 value for the spatial regression model will always be higher than for the aspatial equation.

Examining first the results for Northern Rhodesia, we observe that only one of the regressions had a value of p in excess of plus-or-minus .3. This is the regression for natural increase in 1963 (the same data that showed significant spatial autocorrelation above). The autocorrelation coefficient is .75, and the selected value of D_{max} is four hundred kilometers. These indicate a strong, spatially broad pattern of autocorrelation.

TABLE 14.5 Spatial Stepwise Regression Analysis of Central African Demographic Data, 1921–1966

Dependent Variable	R^2	p	D_{max}	Independent Variable	t-Stat.	Prob. Value
Northern Rhodesia						
Natural Increase 1921	.374	−.143	200	altitude,	3.24	.003
				railroad	2.04	.049
Natural Increase 1929	.145	.120	100	British border,	1.92	.064
				Belgian border	1.50	.144
Net Migration 1921–1929	.439	−.229	200	altitude,	−2.25	.032
				sex ratio,	2.24	.021
				Belgian border	2.30	.029
Natural Increase 1963	.582	.750	400	altitude,	2.31	.028
				railroad	1.95	.060
Net Migration 1929–1963	.092	−.069	200	railroad	1.66	.107
Nyasaland-Malawi						
Natural Increase 1926	.385	−.133	200	tax rate,	−1.80	.092
				early railroad,	−1.38	.186
				Portuguese border	−2.42	.028
Natural Increase 1945	.700	.190	100	altitude,	3.86	.002
				sex ratio,	3.23	.006
				early railroad,	−3.32	.005
				late railroad,	−1.62	.129
				British border	2.01	.065
Net Migration 1926–1945	.312	−.319	200	sex ratio,	1.98	.065
				British border	2.36	.310
Natural Increase 1966	.629	−.031	200	altitude,	2.34	.034
				sex ratio,	3.50	.003
				late railroad,	−1.62	.127
				British border	2.37	.032
Net Migration 1945–1966	.553	−.488	100	sex ratio	3.08	.007

Accounting for this autocorrelation boosts the R^2 value from .42 to .58 even though the British border variable drops from the equation. The interpretation of this is, most likely, that there is another factor working to cause the observed pattern of natural increase beyond the effects captured in the model.

The results for Nyasaland-Malawi show significant autocorrelation in the regressions for net migration in both time periods. In both cases the autocorrelation is negative.[6] (The test for autocorrelation performed above did not reveal any autocorrelation.) For the 1945–1966 data accounting for the autocorrelation raises the R^2 value from .20 to .55. This pattern of negative autocorrelation in net migration suggests that there are short-distance flows of persons that do not correspond to the patterns of the independent variables in our model—in other words, that the regression models are not very useful in capturing the pattern of net migration.

CONCLUSION

I have briefly described two applications of the concept of spatial autocorrelation, a concept that has received considerable attention among quantitative geographers in the past three decades. I have tried to demonstrate that the problems of areal interpolation and spatial modeling are useful in the analysis of demographic data, perhaps especially when the quality of data is low. Once the geographic aspects of demographic problems are defined, quantitative geographers can contribute their resources to a solution. I hope that the collaboration between geographers and demographers will be fruitful to both.

NOTES

1. See N. S. Lam, "Spatial Interpolation Methods: A Review," *American Cartographer* 10 (1983), 129–149.

2. W. Tobler, "Smooth Pycnophylactic Interpolation for Geographical Regions," *Journal of the American Statistical Association* 74 (1979), 519–530.

3. Unfortunately, the 1945 base map employed for Nyasaland proved to contain some major cartographic distortions (as well as a high degree of generalization). An effort was made to correct the most obvious distortions. In general, however, the results from the interpolation cannot be expected to be better than the base maps that are compared.

4. A. D. Cliff and J. K. Ord, *Spatial Processes: Models and Application* (London, 1981).

5. F. Stetzer and B. Fetter, "Determinants of Natural Increase and Migration in Central Africa 1921–1966," in *Studies on the Interrelationships Between Migration and Development in Third World Settings* (Columbus, 1984).

6. The autocorrelation coefficients in the net migration equations for Northern Rhodesia are also negative but do not meet our arbitrary standard of significance.

15

The Migration of Women in Colonial Central Africa: Some Notes Toward an Approach

SHARON STICHTER

The study of rural-to-urban and labor migration in colonial Central Africa would seem to be blessed with an abundance of statistical evidence, although (as others have pointed out) existing data are often of uncertain and uneven quality.[1] These difficulties are even greater with respect to women's migration, since those who left the rural areas were likely to be omitted from rural district censuses; and in urban areas the whole African population, male and female, was undercounted. Nevertheless, it is critical for demographic purposes that better attempts be made to assess the timing and magnitude of female out-migration from rural areas.[2]

There is also an exceptionally rich tradition of ethnographic and historical studies of migration in Central Africa; one need only mention the classic studies in the 1930s, 1940s, and 1950s of the Bemba, the Ngoni, the Barotse, the Tonga, the Plateau Tonga, and the Mambwe, as well as the later regional studies by C. Perrings and C. van Onselen.[3] Most of these studies make only passing reference to the migration of women, only in part because such outflow was a phenomenon more of the late than the early colonial era. A diligent review of all of these sources could, however, yield a much fuller historical picture of women's migration.

I want to turn instead to some of the theoretical issues surrounding the socioeconomic causes of female migration and in particular to discuss the interpretation of women's migration in terms of "household strategies," an approach that has become popular among some analysts of rural-urban migration in Latin America. I will suggest that this approach has certain pitfalls and inadequacies when applied to Africa but that despite these, it can be useful in making sense of what we do know about women's migration in colonial Africa and in indicating future areas of research. Finally, I shall briefly comment on some studies of women's migration in various parts of Africa, emphasizing individual as well as household-level variables.

THE HOUSEHOLD AND THE MIGRATION OF WOMEN

Studies of the economics of labor migration have generally been undertaken from one of two perspectives: the neoclassical microeconomic model (which focuses on the rational cost-benefit calculations made by individuals in the decision to migrate) or the political-economic structural model (which focuses on global economic forces emanating from the capitalist mode of production). The difference between these two approaches is not merely one of levels of analysis; but they have developed from opposing traditions in economic theory and therefore have posed themselves as mutually exclusive alternatives in the analysis of migration. There is no logical reason, however, why analyses at the individual and the structural levels need to be mutually exclusive.

In recent years analysis at the household level has been proposed as a way of linking individual and structural levels of analysis and has been shown to be an effective tool for so doing.[4] In most rural societies the effective unit of production and human reproduction (and thus of economic decisionmaking) has been and continues to be the household. There are many difficulties in defining the "household" unit, perhaps more in Africa than anywhere else.[5] Units of coresidence, kinship, production, and income pooling do not always coincide. Yet when a particular economic process (such as migration) is specific, the appropriate boundaries of the decisionmaking unit can usually be delineated.

The household is conceptualized as having various kinds of subsistence strategies or "survival strategies," such as home production for use or sale; petty entrepreneurship, wage labor, other kinds of labor exchanges, and human reproduction.[6] Migration is one such survival strategy. The choice of it depends greatly on the success or failure of other strategies, as do the various forms of migration (relay, seasonal, or permanent). The household operates, however, within the larger dominant mode of production, capitalism, which provides both opportunities and constraints. The household mediates between the larger structure and a myriad of individual decisions, such as migration, labor force participation, consumption, and fertility.[7] The patterns of these decisions are affected not only by the national and global political-economic pressures but also by factors specific to the household itself, which retains a certain degree of relative autonomy from the dominant economic and state structures.

The notion of *family survival strategies* has been applied to urban as well as rural households.[8] It is most apt in the case of poor households, since survival strategies ought to be distinguished from the kinds of upward mobility strategies (such as investment in education) likely to be pursued by better-off households. The concept of *strategies* is in fact quite vague; no goals have been specified or quantified, a wide range of behaviors is included under its rubric, and there is no unified or accepted theory of household behavior.[9] Still, the term has the merit of calling attention to the active role of individuals and families in shaping their own economic outcomes.

While the analysis of migration using the household approach has been carried out for the most part in Latin America, this approach would also be useful in the colonial and contemporary African context. I have argued elsewhere that neither male nor female migration in Africa can be fully understood without understanding its relationship to the rural household. The internal dynamics of the household particularly affect the age and sex composition of the migrant stream and its incidence among households.[10]

In explaining the migration of women in Africa, however, it seems to me that the notion of *household strategies* as it is usually employed can be quite misleading. In the rush to get away from the neoclassical focus on individual rational decisionmaking, the danger is that the notion of the household will become reified and that it, rather than the relations among its inhabitants, will become the sole focus of concern. Too often, the analysis begins and ends with the "needs" of the household, rather than with the needs of women. Household analysis should be used simply as a vehicle, a necessary step in the conceptualization of the multilevel forces that propel men and women into migration.

Economists in particular have tended to conceptualize the household as the proverbial "black box," a unified actor instead of a complex unit of interacting individuals with differing goals, resources, and power positions. Critics of the "new household economics," for example, have pointed to its tendency to treat household members as though they had identical "utility functions"—to assume that internal decisionmaking and income distribution is communal or egalitarian.[11] To come to terms with inequality, exploitation, and power differentials within households, we need alternative models, such as those put forward by Marxist feminists[12] and those of sociologists concerned with power and bargaining in the household.[13] The household has an internal structure that may or may not be—but usually is not—egalitarian; and patterns of migration, as well as other economic decisions, are the outcome of bargaining and struggle within this structure. This consideration is of particular importance for women's migration in Africa, since at least some of that migration has assumed the character of protest against oppressive family conditions.

There is, of course, a complex interplay between the household level of analysis and the analysis of individual motivations for migration. Household relationships and the sex division of labor may act to constrain women's migration as has been so often the case in Africa. On the other hand, households with differing land resources and a different sex division of labor might decide to send out women migrants, typically, in Asia and Latin America, unmarried daughters—who are expected to stay in paid employment and to support their parents and siblings until they marry. But such patterns are separate from the question of the women's own motivations for migration, which may, as mentioned above, include a desire (if not always a realistic one) to escape family constraints or oppressive household roles. In still other cases, such as those of female-headed households, the household configuration may be such that the woman's individual decision is actually synonymous with that of the household as a unit.

WOMEN'S MIGRATION IN AFRICA

For a complex of reasons having to do with the level of technical development of agriculture, the sex division of labor in most African households, and the preferences of European capitalist employers, the predominant pattern in colonial Africa was for men to migrate to work sites, mines, and urban areas and women to remain at home in subsistence production. Nonetheless, significant numbers of women did migrate to towns, particularly in East, Central, and Southern Africa, taking up roles as petty entrepreneurs such as food sellers, beer brewers, and prostitutes. In West Africa the colonial migration of women was more organically linked to traditional, precolonial patterns and was either for temporary commercial purposes or was part of family migration.[14] What follows will briefly review some of the findings as to the household-level causes of female migration in central and other parts of Africa.

Recent research has made it clear that female migration in Africa cannot be considered as merely derivative of male migration. While some women initially came to town in the company of, or at the behest of, their husbands, a good number did not. Further, when they got to town, even married women were not likely to be completely dependent on their husband's income. These generalizations have been fairly convincingly demonstrated for Zambia. H. Heisler has noted that many single women in Zambia migrated to the Copperbelt by themselves;[15] indeed, in the early 1950s half of the new female migrants were reported to be single. G. Chauncey, G. Wilson,[16] and others have documented the presence of many single women and "temporary wives" in the mines, in addition to "permanent" wives in traditionally sanctioned marriages. Chauncey points out that these customary marriages may have been contracted either in the rural areas or at the mines. He and others[17] have demonstrated the importance of gardening, beer brewing, temporary marriages, and prostitution as sources of economic support for urban women.[18]

Additional evidence from a neighboring country comes from the 1971 National Urban Migration, Employment and Income (NUMEIST) in Tanzania.[19] One-third of the urban migrants who arrived before 1950 were women or girls. Of those arriving in 1970 and 1971 a *majority* were women, indicating a sharp rise in the proportion of women in the migrant stream over those twenty years. Of the women migrants 13 percent of those arriving before 1952 and 33 percent of those arriving in 1970–1971 were unmarried on arrival.[20]

One cannot simply equate the unmarried-married dimension with economic-noneconomic motives for migration or with active-passive decisions to migrate (as R. J. Sabot and so many other analysts of large-scale surveys have). Unmarried women may have noneconomic reasons for migrating, and married women may have economic ones. For example, neither the NUMEIST study nor most other large-scale surveys are able to determine whether the married women actually arrived with their husbands and may have lived with them in the town or whether such women were running away from intolerable marriages or were widows; more detailed interviewing is necessary to answer such important questions. Even among women who in fact came to town with their husbands or other men, the women might not necessarily have been passive about the decision. C. Obbo reports that among Rwandan migrants to Kampala in the 1960s the wives, sisters, and other female kin had insisted on accompanying the men, since life in the village was increasingly difficult and the wage remittances insufficient.[21] E. P. Skinner reported that among Mossi migrants in the 1950s many young women had "run away to town with migrants" against the elder males' wishes.[22]

Whether women are married or unmarried, the economic and noneconomic causes of their migration are likely to be closely intertwined. Economic pressures, such as drought or lack of access to fertile land and agricultural inputs, may adversely affect women's ability to perform expected family roles: if they are young and unmarried or if they are widowed or divorced, they may come to be viewed by their poverty-stricken families as a burden. If they are married, they may be unable to perform the socially expected task of providing food for their children. Conversely, noneconomic crises of family status, such as divorce, desertion, widowhood, childlessness (failure to fulfill the role of generational reproduction), and marital conflict, may result in women's losing material support from their families even where there are few societywide economic pressures toward poverty. Access to economic resources in rural Africa is nearly everywhere structured through the family, especially for women. Access to land, for example, is contingent on satisfactory performance of family roles; hardly anywhere can a woman gain independent land ownership rights. Hence, family crises very often lead to out-migration by women.

The categories of rural women most likely to migrate are the young and unmarried, especially those with some education; those in unhappy marriages, particularly those who are childless or whose husbands oppose their economic activities; and divorced, deserted, or widowed women. The pressures of rural economic decline may intensify all these factors associated with family status to the point where, as in parts of South Africa today, many happily married women of any age, with or without children, attempt to migrate. Here, instead of economic pressures' being refracted through the household in such a way that some women become superfluous and are forced out permanently, it is rather the case that women's temporary migration, in addition to men's, becomes a strategy of household survival.

Some of the most interesting evidence as to the contemporary causes of women's migration comes from Obbo's 1971 study in Kampala. Of the 160 women interviewed 49 had come to town completely by themselves, and 15 had come to visit boyfriends or relatives, often in the capacity of housegirls. Those who had migrated on their own, apart from men, were from a variety of ethnic groups. Of these 11 gave as their primary reason seeking a job or education or "their fortune"; 8 came because of divorce, often coupled with childlessness; 15 came because of unsatisfactory marriages; 1 because of a sorcery accusation; 4 because of widowhood; and 12 because they were "tired of village life" or "tired of digging."[23] Closer examination often revealed a combination of reasons: some widows said they had migrated because they had no land or had never fitted in with their in-laws. Sorcery accusations were usually indicative of further problems: one woman had been bewitched by her husband's mistress, another had migrated to escape the stigma attached to a divorce triggered by a witchcraft accusation.

Barrenness was a reason for social stigma in the village and sometimes led to divorce and migration. But in one case a childless couple migrated because it was easier to remain married in the town. Unhappy marriages were reported to be an important cause of migration, and often this involved escaping polygyny. Some women felt it was better to live singly than to be dependent for support on a man who divided his time among several wives; they had chosen to leave rather than seek a divorce in the traditional way.[24]

Another factor of some importance among the migrants interviewed by Obbo was family opposition to women's economic advance in the rural area, including the jealousy of men and other villagers. The case of Lita, a successful Ganda shopowner, whose stated reason for coming to town was "to improve my business," is illustrative. She had begun by selling cigarettes and bananas in the village, then progressed to pens, books, and sodas. Finally, she expanded to sugar, salt, and beer. Although her in-laws lived twenty-three miles away, they were angry at her business activity. When her husband suffered an attack of malaria, she was accused of having used sorcery on him because she was allegedly jealous of the other woman her husband was seeing. At that point she left for town against her husband's protestations. Another case was that of Amina, a Lango woman, whose several ex-husbands had sabotaged her gin-distilling business in the rural area. She said she "did not ever want to remarry."[25]

The role of both economic pressures and marital conflict in women's migration to towns is also evident in R. Pitten's study of Hausa autonomous women migrants, most of whom support themselves in the urban area through the practice of *karuwanci* (courtesanship).[26] All of the migrants interviewed had been married at least once before migration—many several times—yet their migration was independent, a decision to leave the marriage and strike out on their own. The two major reasons for migration given by the women were (1) pressure from parents to enter or remain in an unwanted marriage and (2) hunger and poverty as a result, in this case, of drought. Women migrated to reduce the strain on family resources and, if successful in town, often contributed to the support of their natal families. A contributory factor was childlessness after a few years of marriage. Pitten is of the opinion, however, that these expressed "push" reasons are for the most part rationalizations and that many of the women had voluntarily chosen their lifestyle, which had several advantages and did not preclude remarriage.

The causes of migration indicated in such contemporary studies cannot be projected backward in time or to other areas of Africa without some qualification, yet they do have strong implications for the colonial era. Studies of the colonial period point to a quite similar range of precipitating factors. Muntemba has described how in Kabwe Rural District in Zambia, economic decline, congestion, and land shortage in the reserve led to women's traditional matrilineal inheritance rights' being challenged. Some widows no longer got the access to lands that they had before. And agricultural development, such as it was, bypassed women. Ox ploughs, handled by men, were necessary in many cash crop areas, and colonial extension services channeled new agricultural knowledge to men. Widespread migration of women to the mine compounds was the result.[27]

Escape from unhappy, exploitative family situations was also a factor in Zambia. According to Heisler, many of the earliest female migrants were sterile. Barren women could not produce the children needed to cement property rights and thus were less useful in the peasant economy. Whether from choice or social pressure, they were likely to migrate to town.[28] Divorce, however, was apparently less important in Zambia as a cause of women's migration than it was in areas of predominantly patrilineal peoples. Among the majority of matrilineal and bilateral societies of Zambia divorce was evidently an epiphenomenon and contributed little to the out-migration of women.[29]

Among the South African Xhosa, by the 1930s, B. A. Pauw reports that widows and young single women were particularly likely to migrate. What few land rights a widow might expect from her late husband's family became vulnerable to stiff competition from her own sons and from in-laws. Where rights could be claimed, envious relatives might still make life intolerable. Even a widow's natal family might become reluctant to accept her back, since she was yet another person competing for scarce land.

With the increasing incidence of premarital pregnancy, many young single women were also viewed as family liabilities, unlikely to bring in the traditional *lobola* (bride price). Girls themselves often acted to defy the system of arranged marriages and of polygyny, preferring to choose a partner on the basis of personal attraction. Running away to towns enabled them better to control their personal lives, particularly if they had had a few years of mission education and could thus qualify for domestic jobs.[30]

During the colonial period educational opportunities for women were few, yet many studies report the tendency of the few young single women who did receive some education to migrate to town. The small subgroup of educated female migrants has expanded in size in some areas in the postcolonial period: the "new women" of Lusaka described by I. Schuster, wage-earning white-collar workers, often single or separated and living on their own, are very much a phenomenon of the post-1960 years.[31]

While formal educational opportunities may have been thin in urban areas, Fetter's work suggests that such basic material conditions as health and nutrition were in fact better in urban and industrial areas of colonial Central Africa than in the rural hinterlands and that these are reflected in higher rates of urban natural increase (or lower rates of decrease).[32] The relative superiority of urban conditions and their improvement over time must have positively affected female, as well as male, in-migration.

Distance to urban centers, as well as ease and cost of transport, affected female migration patterns as well, perhaps even more than they affected male patterns. Case studies from several urban centers in Zambia, for example, indicate that women of local peoples were proportionately more numerous than men of those groups. The available evidence suggests that short-distance migration was favored by women and that the movement of women (and presumably children) was greatest near the main centers of employment.[33] The availability of cheap transport was also critical, and situation along a main transport route or line of rail clearly increased the likelihood of female migration. Finally, traditions of long-distance trade probably made it more likely that women, as well as men, would engage in migration.

Clearly, many of the causes of women's migration in the colonial era suggested here need to be corroborated by detailed ethnographic evidence from Central Africa, as well as assessed in terms of quantitative significance. It is equally clear that to focus, in such assessment, solely on whether women are married or unmarried at the time of arrival in town and, in particular, to assume that married women have migrated solely because they were brought by their husbands misses most of the complex dynamics behind women's migration decisions. Whether the women are married or unmarried, an in-depth analysis of their position in the household is necessary if their migration is to be understood.

CONCLUSION

The demand-side, or "pull," perspective on women's cityward migration has been persuasively argued for Northern Rhodesia in the important contribution by Chauncey.[34] He points out that the special situation of Northern Rhodesian mining capital in the regional competition for labor led mine managers to seek to localize the daily and generational reproduction of labor at the mines, with the result that women were allowed, even encouraged, to migrate and remain there. These policies ran counter to the wishes of rural male elders and of the colonial state, both of whom sought (though with little success) to control, restrict, or even prohibit the long-term movement of women to the compounds.

Elsewhere in Central and Southern Africa (for example, in Southern Rhodesia) a different policy toward the social reproduction of the labor force prevailed; mining capital's interest lay in keeping women in the rural areas and preserving the pattern of oscillating migrancy rather than in labor stabilization. In these areas the goals of mining capital, the state, and rural elders coincided. The classic statement of the "pull" perspective on migration in these areas is that by H. Wolpe.[35] It is striking, however, that despite the coordinated effort to restrict women's migration in these areas, substantial numbers of women still managed to establish themselves in towns and areas adjacent to mine compounds.[36]

Despite their differences, the accounts of both Chauncey and Wolpe share a nearly exclusive emphasis on the policies of capital and the state as determinants of women's migration. I have suggested that this approach is incomplete. A more interactive formulation needs to be adopted, one that recognizes that African rural patriarchal societies in themselves, especially those suffering colonially induced economic decline, contained conditions that could propel certain categories of women to migrate. Most of these "push" factors can be discovered by close analysis at the level of the household, the basic rural productive and reproductive unit.

NOTES

1. It is important to distinguish general country-to-city migration from specifically labor migration, particularly in the case of women. In colonial Central Africa most male migration was undertaken in search of income-generating activity in the capitalist sector, primarily wage work but also self-employment. The lack of wage opportunities for women meant that most female migration was in search of self-employment or support in the form of a husband or other male. Thus, the more general term is better in the case of women.

2. For example, B. Fetter has argued (in "Labor Migration and Infertility in Central Africa: A Regional Approach," presented at the meeting of the African Studies Association, 1983) that the adult female population in rural areas provides the most reliable available indicator of population increase since it was less affected by regional variations in out-migration than was male population. He has further argued that adult rural sex ratios are a good indicator of male out-migration ("The Long Arm of the Census Taker: Nyasaland Censuses and the Contours of Colonial Rule," presented at the

African Studies Association meeting, 1982). Both these relationships would be called into question for areas and time periods where it could be shown that female out-migration was substantial.

3. A. I. Richards, *Land, Labour, and Diet in Northern Rhodesia* (London, 1939); M. Read, "Migrant Labour in Africa and Its Effects on Tribal Life," *International Labour Review* 45 (1942); M. Gluckman, "The Lozi of Barotseland in North-Western Rhodesia," in E. Colson and M. Gluckman, eds., *Seven Tribes of British Central Africa* (London, 1951); J. van Velsen, "Labour Migration as a Positive Factor in the Continuity of Tonga Tribal Society," *Economic Development and Culture Change* 8 (1960), 165–278; E. Colson, "Migration in Africa: Trends and Possibilities," in F. Lorimer and M. Karp, eds., *Population in Africa* (Boston, 1960), 60–67; W. Watson, *Tribal Cohesion in a Money Economy: A Study of the Mambwe People of Northern Rhodesia* (Manchester, 1958); C. Perrings, *Black Mineworkers in Central Africa: Industrial Strategies and the Evolution of an African Proletariat in the Copperbelt, 1911–41* (London, 1979); C. van Onselen, *Chibaro: African Mine Labour in Southern Rhodesia, 1900–1933* (London, 1976).

4. C. Wood, "Equilibrium and Historical-Structural Perspectives on Migration: A Comparative Critique with Implications for Future Research," *International Migration Review* 16 (1982), 298–319; M. Schmink, "Household Economic Strategies: Review and Research Agenda," *Latin American Research Review* 19 (1984), 87–101; L. Arizpe, "Relay Migration and the Survival of the Peasant Household," in H. Safa, ed., *Towards a Political Economy of Urbanization in the Third World* (Delhi, 1982), 19–46.

5. See, e.g., J. Guyer, "Household and Community in African Studies," *African Studies Review* 24, 2/3 (1981), 87–138; J. Guyer and P. Peters, eds., *Proceedings of the SSRC/ACLS Workshop of Conceptualizing the Household: Issues of Theory, Method, and Application* (New York, 1985).

6. Wood, "Equilibrium and Historical-Structural Perspectives." In the African context, see W. Martin and M. Beitel, "The Hidden Abode of Reproduction: Conceptualizing Households in Africa," in Guyer and Peters, *Proceedings*.

7. Schmink, "Household Economic Strategies."

8. P. Pessar, "The Role of Households in International Migration and the Case of U.S.-bound Migration from the Dominican Republic," *International Migration Review* 16 (1982), 342–361; L. A. Tilly and J. Scott, *Women, Work, and Family* (New York, 1978).

9. Schmink, "Household Economic Strategies."

10. S. Stichter, *Migrant Laborers* (Cambridge, 1985).

11. E.g., N. Folbre, "Cleaning House: New Perspectives on Households and Economic Development," *Journal of Development Economics* 12.

12. J. K. Henn, "The Material Basis of Sexism: A Mode of Production Analysis," in S. Stichter and J. Parpart, *Patriarchy and Class* (Los Angeles, 1988). N. Folbre, "Exploitation Comes Home: A Critique of the Marxian Theory of Family Labour," *Cambridge Journal of Economics* 6 (1982), 317–329.

13. C. Safilos-Rothchild, "The Study of Family Power Structure: A Review, 1960–69," *Journal of Marriage and the Family* 29 (1967), 320–324; R. O. Blood and D. M. Wolfe, *Husbands and Wives* (New York, 1960).

14. N. Sudarkasa, "Women and Migration in Contemporary West Africa," *Sigma: The Journal of Women Culture and Society* 3 (1977), 178–189. Female migration in West Africa began to increase in the postcolonial era. J. C. Caldwell was the first to note this fact relative to Ghana: he found in the

1960s that equal proportions of men and women aged fifteen to nineteen planned to migrate to urban areas and that in some areas the female propensity to migrate was rising faster than the male ("Determinants of Rural-Urban Migration in Ghana," *Population Studies* 22 [1968], 361–377, esp. 369). More recently, K. C. Zachariah and J. Condé, (*Migration in West Africa: Demographic Aspects* [Oxford, 1981], 40) found that the sex ratios of interregional migrants in Ghana indicated the proportion of women migrating was still rising.

15. H. Heisler, *Urbanisation and the Government of Migration: The Interrelation of Urban and Rural Life in Zambia* (London, 1974), 63, 80, 130.

16. G. Chauncey, "The Locus of Reproduction: Women's Labour in the Zambian Copperbelt, 1927–1953," *Journal of Southern African Studies* 7 (1981), 135–164; G. Wilson, *An Essay on the Economics of Detribalization in Northern Rhodesia*, pts. 1, 2, Rhodes-Livingstone Papers, nos. 5, 6 (Livingstone, 1941–1942).

17. J. Parpart, "The Household and the Mine Shaft: Gender and Class Struggles on the Zambian Copperbelt, 1924–66," *Journal of Southern African Studies* 12 (1986).

18. A. L. Epstein (*Urbanization and Kinship: The Domestic Domain on the Copperbelt of Zambia, 1950–56* [New York, 1981]) suggests for the Copperbelt in the 1950s that men were more predominant in market trade, taken as a whole, than were women. Even if this were true, it would not necessarily contradict the findings of Parpart, Chauncey, and others as to the importance of trade as a percentage of women's incomes. More detailed studies of urban trade are certainly needed.

19. Analyzed by R. J. Sabot, *Economic Development and Urban Migration: Tanzania, 1900-1971* (Oxford, 1979) and in more detail with respect to women by N. Shields, "Women in the Urban Labor Markets of Africa: The Case of Tanzania," Staff Working Paper no. 380 (World Bank 1980).

20. Sabot, *Economic Development*, 89–98.

21. C. Obbo, *African Women: Their Struggle for Economic Independence* (London, 1980).

22. E. P. Skinner, "Labor Migration Among the Mossi of Upper Volta," in H. Kuper, ed., *Urbanization and Migration in West Africa* (Berkeley, 1965), 60-84.

23. Obbo, *African Women*, 76.

24. Among the Mossi in Upper Volta in the 1950s, Skinner reported ("Labor Migration," 66, 74) that marital difficulties likewise led to female migration, but here it was usually the married or soon-to-be married women's discontent with arranged marriages to elder men.

25. Obbo, *African Women*, 72, 79–80.

26. R. Pitten, "Migration of Women in Nigeria: The House Case," *International Migration Review* 18 (1984), 1293–1314.

27. M. Muntemba, "Thwarted Development: A Case Study of Economic Change in the Kabwe Rural District of Zambia, 1902–70," in R. Palmer and N. Parsons, eds., *The Roots of Rural Poverty in Central and Southern Africa* (Berkeley, 1977).

28. Heisler, *Urbanisation*, 75.

29. J. Gugler, "On the Theory of Rural-Urban Migration: The Case of Sub-Saharan Africa," in J. Jackson, ed., *Migration Sociological Studies* 2 (London, 1969), 134–155, esp. 139; Heisler, *Urbanisation*, 76.

30. B. A. Pauw, *Xhosa in Town: The Second Generation* (Cape Town, 1963).

31. I. Schuster, *New Women of Lusaka* (Palo Alto, 1979).

32. B. Fetter, "Relocating Central Africa's Biological Reproduction, 1923–1963," *International Journal of African Historical Studies* 19 (1986), 463–478.

33. J. C. Mitchell, *African Urbanization in Ndola and Luanshya*, Rhodes-Livingstone Communication, no. 6 (Manchester, 1954); G. Kay, *A Social and Economic Study of Fort Rosebery Township and Peri-urban Area*, Rhodes-Livingstone Communication, no. 21 (Manchester, 1960).

34. Chauncey, "Locus of Reproduction."

35. H. Wolpe, "Capitalism and Cheap Labour-Power in South Africa: From Segregation to Apartheid," *Economy and Society* 1 (1972), 425–456.

36. As Watson (*Tribal Cohesion*, 45–46) discovered among the Mambwe, "some women will go to extraordinary lengths to get to the towns," despite the opposition of the male elders. Another well-documented example is South Africa, where loopholes in the pass laws in the first half of the twentieth century made it possible for many women to migrate to towns: see J. Wells, "Passes and Bypasses: Freedom of Movement for African Women Under the Urban Areas Act of South Africa," in M. Hay and M. Wright, eds., *African Women and the Law: Historical Perspectives*, Boston University Papers on Africa, no. 7 (Boston, 1982), 126–150.

16

Labor Migration and Urban Child Labor During the Colonial Period in Zambia

KAREN TRANBERG HANSEN

My questions are not, strictly speaking, demographic; for age was an elusive variable hardly considered by colonial censustakers. Detailed information about urban children and their activities thus slipped between the established categories used in census enumerations. If age was a troublesome variable for censustakers, so (in the view of colonial administrators) were the children who kept appearing in the cities fresh from the bush. Lengthy debates about the problems presented by their presence in the towns and the enactment of formal rules and regulations to repatriate them to their villages give ample evidence of their presence in towns.

Much like women, children were among the missing migrants;[1] and their activities—just like women's often uncounted and unenumerated work—were not taken account of in employment statistics. I shall piece together a sketch of children's migration and the nature of their work in the towns based on colonial archival materials, comments on children drawn indirectly from the authorities' discussions about the problems women's urban migration entailed, and a variety of other sources. My argument is not with demography but rather with anthropology, particularly with those who continue to use the idiom of *kinship* when accounting for children's work, masking it as training or helping under the aegis of fostering. Such accounts need to be spelled out in their historical specificity, which I seek to do for the case of the colonial towns in Northern Rhodesia by asking questions about what role to attribute to children's work activities.

CHILDREN AND DOMESTIC LABOR IN THE COLONIAL SITUATION

Substantive evidence about children in Zambia's towns during the colonial period hardly exists, as only men in gainful employment were enumerated in the majority of that era's urban census records. The researcher has great problems finding more than scattered, isolated, and impressionistic comments on urban children's activities for most of the colonial period. More helpful for my subsequent discussion is a series of social surveys undertaken in the towns in the early 1950s under the auspices of the Rhodes-Livingstone Institute.

Till the mid-1940s it was colonial labor policy to recruit a migrant male labor force that returned to the rural areas after completing work contracts. Women and children were to reside in the villages, maintaining households and fields. But the reality was somewhat different, as most of the mining companies already since the 1930s had encouraged men to bring wives and children to town so as to increase labor productivity. Women and children also migrated on their own. In the official view of the time, such women were assumed to make their living by immorality, since there was no wage employment for them.[2] And the children were held to be unruly and without parental control. Colonial authorities cooperated with the rural native authorities in making a system of rulings to prevent unattached women and unaccompanied children from migrating to towns. Yet by the mid-1930s, the number of women and children in towns was increasing. By this time more than half of the able-bodied male population was working for wages away from home—as many outside the territory as within it.[3]

The fragmentary information I have collected from colonial records and culled from the literature on that era suggests that private householders and industry benefited from children's work, while children were considered a problem by colonial authorities, rural native authorities, and parents alike— but not for the same reasons. I shall address these issues in turn.

Women's and children's presence in towns was noted with much concern in the report commissioned after the first African strike on the Copperbelt in 1935: miners and other workers lay down their tools when tax increases were suddenly announced. To supplement the substandard food rations issued to husbands, many wives cultivated gardens on plots made available by the mines. Authorities sometimes regarded this practice as costly since some women "employ a boy to do the housework while they are on the plots."[4] "Children," wrote the compound manager at Roan Antelope mine in Luanshya in 1937, "are useful to parents in tilling the gardens, or in many cases obtaining additional revenue for the family by working for other natives or Europeans in the residential quarter."[5] *Piccannins,* as they then were called, worked for "single natives . . . to wash their clothes, clean their huts, and generally fag for them."[6] They also worked for African women, among whom the wives of clerks, according to the manager, "consider they are higher up on the social scale by the fact that they are able to employ a servant."[7]

Children worked in other towns as well. A 1937 report from Broken Hill Industrial Area noted that boys of about ten years of age and up migrated from other districts in search of work and adventure. Some arrived alone, others were brought by elder brothers "who subsequently move to some other centre, leaving the youngster behind. . . . They can rarely obtain regular employment, and what employment they do obtain is so poorly paid . . . that they cannot live without assistance. . . . They are not [usually] without relatives or friends to assist them, but when they are, they have to make up by dishonest means."[8]

Some of these boys had been brought to towns by relatives other than parents for the purpose of cooking for them en route and attending to their wants in the compounds. In 1938 children were employed in this way in the Broken Hill mine compound. Some of them worked for single men; but in Lusaka that same year more children were employed as servants by married African couples than by bachelors. In the official view such employment by Africans was considered an unnecessary luxury, either because cooked food rations were issued to workers in many industries or because workers had wives who ought to do the cooking.[9]

Children's employment was governed by the 1933 Ordinance on Employment of Women, Young Persons, and Children, which was framed in accordance with the International Labour Convention. The prescribed minimum age for employment of children in industry was fourteen years. The question of the age at which children were to be allowed to work brought about controversy in the Legislative Council.[10] In the Northern Rhodesian ordinance the minimum age was placed at twelve, with the stipulation that children under fourteen could be employed in industrial undertakings if the governor issued a license.[11]

Both mines and private householders benefited from this arrangement. While they did not do underground work, several boys were employed in the mining compounds to sweep, gather firewood, cut grass, and so on. There were 95 of them in the Broken Hill mine compound in 1938 and 166 in 1940.[12] The hiring of miners' children as *piccannins*, sweepers, and so forth on the Roan Antelope mine is also reported to have been widespread.[13] Because there were few schools, such activity was hardly considered work at all. The few schools available in the mining towns catered to a tiny proportion of the school-age youth. Thus, in Broken Hill only 750 out of 1,500 African children of school age went to school in around 1940.[14] Children were thought not to have any rival claims on their time, so work was held to be better than idleness and perhaps likely to inculcate habits of industry.[15] For work would keep children "out of mischief and under control" at the same time as it would subject them to "a certain amount of discipline."[16]

Time and again suggestions were made that children over ten years of age who did not reside with parents should be repatriated to their villages. Another suggestion discriminated between children in terms of their fathers' occupations: children of government servants, clerks, messengers, police, and those who had been born in towns might be allowed to stay, whereas children of unemployed fathers were to be repatriated.[17] Added concern about children's presence in towns was raised in the 1938 report on labor conditions in Northern Rhodesia, whose author stressed the likely rise of juvenile delinquency.[18] Another report from the same year put this squarely, pointing to "the serious danger of the production of a demoralised class of young hooligans who will become very dangerous elements later on."[19] Monies were appropriated for the repatriation of children, and the authority for moving them was found in the Juvenile Offenders Ordinance.[20] The perception of danger implicit in children's presence in towns was influenced by the assumption that "parental authority has largely disappeared in [the] unfamiliar surroundings and the trouble is accentuated by the large proportion of temporary marriages."[21] Although the extent to which urban children were "uncontrolled" (that is, not under parental authority) is not known, it is certain that Africans viewed the concept of *parental authority* far less exclusively than did colonial authorities: parental authority extended beyond the biological parents to classificatory mothers' brothers (in the region's matrilineal societies) and fathers' brothers (in the patrilineal groups) and revolved in general around seniority regardless of the specifics of descent. Rather than concerning parental authority per se, the assumption that children were uncontrolled highlighted another, more crucial issue; for the presence of both women and children in towns accentuated both the colonial authorities' fear of the rise of a proletarianized urban population in need of basic services and the rural native authorities' concern about the loss of tribal allegiance and the undermining of their own authority.

Officials expressed their fear about the growing numbers of children in the towns in terms of *detribalization*. Their concerns are summed up in the following annual report:

> More and more women are accompanying or joining their husbands in the urban areas, and while these women still visit the rural areas more frequently than the men and so keep a connection with tribal life, this state of affairs cannot be expected to last forever. A new generation born in the towns is growing up and presents an increasing problem. These children would under native custom be cared for and disciplined in most cases by grandparents and the maternal uncle, but these people have themselves often left the village to seek work and a livelihood in the towns, so the mother in the town has to look after her children entirely by herself and this she has in many cases still to learn to do. It is because in so many cases the customary guardians of children are not in the villages that schemes for repatriating children from the urban areas to their villages often break down. Children not under parental control may be sent home or fetched home by the native authorities but soon run away again to the towns because there is no longer anyone at home who is by custom primarily responsible for their care and upbringing.[22]

The question of how to control the migration of women and children was frequently on the agenda at meetings of the rural native authorities. If children grew up in town, new allegiances might arise and customary authority no longer be observed. To maintain the vestiges of such authority by controlling the young generation one chief suggested, "Our children should be well looked after and taught by ourselves in the villages. Then when they are of full age, they can go to town to seek work."[23] Among other suggestions were that "not more than two small children live in town with parents" (older children living "with grandparents according to custom") and that "schools be in rural and not urban areas."[24]

If the colonial and rural native authorities viewed children's presence in towns as problematic (though for different reasons), so did parents and guardians. Low wages, the rationing system, and lack of space made children in the compounds a heavy economic burden for their caretakers. Many parents found it expensive to support children in town, most had little room, and some felt that a rural upbringing was better for them. Until the mid-1940s family housing was not generally available to urban African workers. The previously mentioned policy of treating Africans as short-term urban workers who would return to their villages was built into the wage scales, the physical layout of compounds, and the regulations governing visitation practices. Wages hardly increased during the 1930s and many households had a hard time making ends meet. Most couples shared rooms with other couples. Where family housing was available, space was too scant to allow the customary separation of sleeping arrangements by age and sex. Godfrey Wilson has described how young children and visitors were present in all the compounds in Broken Hill around 1940 and how they slept either in the same room as their parents and hosts or in the open air. "The African dislike this necessity intensely, but cannot avoid it," he reported.[25] The arrangements for older children were that boys slept with adult friends in bachelor quarters, and girls in the homes of women whose husbands worked at night.[26] While the size of food rations depended on whether men workers were married, they were not influenced by the number of children and dependents. Since neither food nor room was directly provided for children, many urban parents allowed their sons to work for others in order to lessen the pressure on both household budget and space. This practice, according to Wilson, was "exceedingly common." Groups of single male workers sharing huts included young boys "who were not yet wage earners and who [did] the cooking."[27] Such young boys might be related to one of the men, having accompanied him to town or been sent to him by parents or relatives already in town: "A boy over six, who is with his parents, joins a group of single men in this way, whenever possible."[28] In addition, several youngsters worked as "young kitchen- or nurse-boys" in the European residential areas.[29]

During the last half of the 1940s the governing authorities finally recognized that large numbers of urban Africans were in the towns to stay. Copper prices had risen sharply in the world market in the postwar economic boom, and labor shortages were felt in all sectors of the economy. A more stabilized labor force was needed; and mines, local authorities, and private employers were charged with providing more housing for married Africans in addition to the usual bachelor quarters. Yet construction of houses for urban African workers was slow and could not accommodate the continuous rural influx, many of whom found shelter in squatter settlements.[30] The African population in wage employment in the country's main towns had grown from 37,527 to 68,214 between 1931 and 1946 and stood at 128,224 in 1956.[31] At a district commissioners' conference at the end of the war the compounds were described as "filling with youth, 16 years and under, attracted by the chance of a little money and freedom from village discipline. Indians, African clerks and messengers," the report continued, "employed them as servants and had them sleep in their kitchens." This practice, incidentally, was singled out for "its moral[ly] bad effects as wives of clerks, etc. were able to get cheap domestic servants."[32]

The migration from the rural areas had by then profoundly and adversely altered local productive systems so that most village societies had become dependent on urban wage labor. Children and youth had become more attracted to towns than ever before; for a system of compulsory primary education for children between the ages of twelve and sixteen had been introduced in the early 1940s, first in the Copperbelt towns and later in Broken Hill and Livingstone. It never included Lusaka, where the provision of school facilities was sorely lacking.[33] To make children attend school, the Employment of Women, Young Persons, and Children Ordinance was amended in 1949 to prevent the employment of young persons between twelve and sixteen in industrial enterprises without the permission of a district or labor officer.[34] Because of the urban school bias, more young siblings, nephews, and nieces came to town to live with uncles and elder brothers, hoping to get into school. But the number of school places was not sufficient, and young boys continued to find their way into jobs in private households. From Livingstone in 1944[35] and from Broken Hill in 1948 came complaints that the compulsory education scheme was being hampered by Europeans who hired African boys to work in their gardens and kitchens.[36]

Some of these children contributed to strained household budgets; for the cost of living for Africans had risen 100 percent between 1939 and 1946, far surpassing wage increases.[37] Other boys worked to get by on their own. According to a 1945 report, many schoolboys lived with friends and relatives, staying only three months on average and moving on when people tired of them. None got sufficient food from the people with whom they lived, and they had partly to fend for themselves. This they did by begging at the mine feeding store or the markets, earning money as golf caddies, and theft. Many lived in the mine bachelor quarters. They were allowed to sleep in the houses occupied by single men and were given the scraps left over after the men were fed. In return they were expected to keep the housing clean and sometimes to do the washing. They were seldom paid any wages, although they were sometimes promised five shillings or seven shillings sixpence per month.

They were usually told they had lost their pay because of bad behavior. Teachers felt that such boys should be sent home unless they had a parent or guardian approved by the headmaster of their school.[38]

Thus, some boys found school places but no relations. An article reporting on the compulsory education scheme commented that in the late 1940s at least half of the children in the Copperbelt schools were not living with their parents or any recognized guardian. "When the parents are present," the article continued, "their influence is too often weak or negative, due to inadequate housing—or indifference."[39] Some of these boys were taken into the country to camps in order to learn about the rural way of life. Others were brought there by force. Between 1941 and 1943 a total of 515 children had been repatriated from the Copperbelt towns. With a control agency—the school—now present in some towns, child repatriations initially declined and were reported to be negligible in 1943.[40] Yet the practice regained currency in the early 1950s when authorities, perhaps fearing the political mobilization that was sweeping the towns, once again became concerned about the "unfortunate increase in the number of young boys coming to the line of rail from the rural areas without guardians." In 1951 some were repatriated to their home districts.[41] In 1952 the government ordered the return of all "solitary" children from Broken Hill to their parents' villages,[42] and in that same year twenty-five Lozi children were repatriated from Livingstone.[43]

The repatriation of children was not particularly effective. Urban children not under parental control might well be returned to villages by urban authorities or fetched by rural native authorities. But they soon went to town again because their customary guardians in many cases themselves were residing in towns. People who remained in the villages were in many cases unable to produce sufficient food, and research carried out from the 1930s on has shown that villagers had less to eat than townspeople.[44] Bruce Fetter's argument that women who migrated were responding to the growing disparity between rural and urban conditions may easily be extended to their children.[45] Once back in town, African boys continued to seek work. According to a 1954 report, some European mothers were even content to entrust their children and babies to the care of youngsters (i.e., young boys). Other African boys worked as golf caddies, while grass cutting was popular with schoolboys during their holidays. The attraction to employers, the report ends, "is that their wages are relatively low."[46] Employers could hire juvenile workers from a growing labor supply because of the lack of school facilities.[47]

Judging from the records, it appears that girls rarely worked away from home and that they were not farmed out to relatives to the same extent as boys. In the earlier years parents found it difficult to socialize girls in the urban setting, which was held to provide many temptations.[48] J. Clyde Mitchell's 1951 Copperbelt studies reveal a definite inequality of numbers in the ten-to-fourteen-year age group, indicating perhaps that parents sent puberty-age daughters back to the villages. Some boys and girls lived elsewhere in towns, separate from their parents. More boys than girls did so, most of them attending schools but some working as domestic servants.[49] Merran McCulloch's 1952 survey of Livingstone also shows a disproportion between marriageable men disappeared to towns and the young women.[50] D. Bettison's 1954 survey of Lusaka's African townships shows an even proportion of young men and women residing with parents and the rest scattered across other parts of town, other towns, and rural areas.[51] Between 1954 and 1957 the proportion of children resident with parents in Lusaka had grown from 76 percent to 90 percent for both sexes.[52] In addition to resident children—and compensating, at least in terms of numbers, for those who had left—many urban households hosted live-in relatives. On the Copperbelt in 1951 Mitchell found coresidents in 3.5 percent of the households; McCulloch found them in one-fifth of Livingstone's married households and several others in the single quarters.[53] Approximately one-third of Lusaka's African households in 1957 hosted live-in relatives who were going to school, working elsewhere, looking for work or housing, doing the household work, or any combination of these.[54] Arnold Epstein's work on Ndola in 1950–1956 and Hortense Powdermaker's work on Luanshya in 1953–1954 offer rich details on the texture of African life in the rapidly growing Copperbelt towns, the new options confronting parents and children, and their problems and challenges in pursuing them.[55]

The information presented so far certainly shows that children were present in towns from the earliest colonial years and that many young boys worked, especially in private households, with or without pay. According to the 1956 census, three times as many juvenile boys as adult women were employed in all economic sectors in Northern Rhodesia's towns.[56]

But what do we make of this and the other bits of evidence about children's work? Did the role children's work played in the rural societies from which they came carry over, unaltered, into the urban situation? The ethnographic record provides evidence of the training and socialization function of rural children's work.[57] Young girls were first encouraged to imitate—and later expected to perform—much of adult women's work in and around the household, thus receiving education for adulthood in the homes of parents, guardians, or other relatives; they were rarely restricted to their individual family. Small boys would learn to do household tasks in similar contexts: sweeping huts, fetching water, keeping fires going, and cooking; at the time of puberty they were removed from the women's circle.

The functions of such activities tended to become transformed in the towns because of the growing dependence on the cash nexus. Due to the vagaries of urban living, strained household budgets, and lack of family housing, many such "helping" services were performed in return for support in the form of food, shelter, or money. Urban children's struggles for livelihoods in the Northern Rhodesian towns may have had much in common with those Suzanne Comhaire-Sylvain described at Kinshasa (then an African ward) in Léopoldville in the early 1940s. Reporting a "frightening . . . proportion of undernourished children,"[58] she noted avenues children pursued to get more food: finding someone willing to support them or share with them, stealing, or working. Some children would find a protector among relatives and in return for upkeep be obliged to work in the home or away from it. Groups of boys would get together, pooling whatever resources they had laid their hands on. Better still, they would find paid work. She found a good percentage of working children, almost all of them boys. Many schoolboys worked as part-time servants for Europeans, some sold newspapers, some carried shopping parcels, some hawked flowers and fruit, and some made handicrafts: paper flowers, string belts, baskets, and reed models of boats, trucks, or aircrafts. Some of the modelmakers formed an association of their own, trying to keep up a regular supply to satisfy their customers. Many of these boys had left school because they wanted to make a living on their own, and some were unable to go to school because they were orphans or their parents did not live in Léopoldville. Some of the boys without relatives would pool their resources and use a rotational system for dividing up their individual shares.

Children in Northern Rhodesia's towns are likely to have undertaken many more activities directed at economic survival than those mentioned in the scattered evidence from the colonial records. The pieces of evidence from those records may only form the tip of an iceberg, concealing a children's work culture and social organization of its own that to some extent provided the props that were missing in the cities: economic support and shelter. The information I have provided here suggests that although children in the Northern Rhodesian towns often provided services to kin, such work was not the result of the customary obligations that placed them at the beck and call of relatives. Young boys worked to lessen the pressures on their urban families' substandard household budgets and housing space, to provide alternatives to the lack of rural earning opportunities, or to eke out a living on their own. Although not all of them were paid, they all were units of labor. They worked cheaply and did the dirty work that—in ways so far largely unaccounted for—helped relieve the colonial administration of paying living wages and providing acceptable housing. They continued to do so on the eve of, and in the wake of, independence in 1964. The time slice 1963–1968 is the only one I have located that has employment statistics for domestic service categorized by sex *and* age.[59] Table 16.1 shows that juveniles (i.e., those under eighteen) were employed as domestic servants in larger numbers than adult women from 1963 through 1966. Their total number in this sector is likely to have been much larger, as the table includes only enumerated servants. After 1966 the number of enumerated juvenile servants dwindles, probably due to the expansion of the primary school sector after independence.

TABLE 16.1 Africans Employed in Domestic Service and Total Wage Employment

Type of Work	1963	1964	1965	1966	1967	1968
Domestic Service						
Men	27,240	26,800	31,500	31,231	31,508	36,491
Women	708	700	815	1,498	1,549	1,758
Juveniles[a]	1,090	1,037	1,839	663	60	80
Total Wage Employment						
Men	149,959	159,250	179,800	127,100	145,180	157,717
Women	3,125	3,303	4,389	3,803	3,742	3,911
Juveniles	3,437	2,736	10,313	11,312	4,017	1,069

Sources: Northern Rhodesia and Republic of Zambia: Annual Reports, Labour Department, 1963–1968.
Note: Excluding government employees; excluding North-Western Province.
[a]Young persons under 18 years of age.

CHILDREN AND DOMESTIC WORK AFTER INDEPENDENCE

At independence, the rules and regulations that had structured rural-urban migration and access to work and to housing were done away with. More people went to towns, especially women, anticipating new employment opportunities.[60] By the early 1980s half of Zambia's population lived in towns. The population had grown by more than 3 percent per year, and children below age fifteen now composed half of the country's total population. The educational system expanded rapidly in the immediate wake of independence; and more little children, particularly girls, were sent to school than ever before.

But not all children get school places. Of those who do, few qualify for entry into secondary schools. A new segment of children has entered the private household market. Today young girls can be seen in the sort of domestic work that tended to be done by boys in a previous era: some girls do service work at substandard wages, and others do household work in the homes of relatives in return for their upkeep. In Zambia *keeping relatives* means providing them with shelter, food, and occasional clothing. Some of the kept girls are town-born-and-bred, and others continue to arrive from the rural areas. "Children," says Elizabeth Colson for the Gwembe Tonga, "are exchanged freely between rural areas and city for a variety of purposes."[61] This must be explained against the background of the postcolonial economic decline, during which new pressures have been placed on rural and urban economies, housing stock, and private household budgets. In this situation everyone works at making a living, but fewer and fewer do so by being wage-employed.[62]

Among the many who do not pursue an occupation but still work, are young Zambian women below the age of eighteen who mind children and do household work in the homes of relatives. Other young women do the same kinds of work in the homes of nonrelated Zambians, in return for which they receive puny wages and are said to be members of the family. Most parents dislike to farm out their school-level girls in this way. Yet some will still do so, rationalizing their step by reckoning that domestic service will prepare their daughters' for their future roles as mothers. In contrast, parents say that young boys must be able to fend for themselves. They need skills different from those acquired in domestic service in order to be able to take care of future wives and children, as well as of parents in old age. If they can at all afford to, parents struggle to send young boys to special schools to retake failed classes, have them join formal or nonformal training workshops, or sign them up as apprentices with informal sector artisans.[63] Such opportunities are limited for young girls. Many young boys roam the streets, selling *michanga* (cigarettes) by the stick, checking passengers into minibuses, washing cars, guarding parked cars, doing any casual work they can find, and generally living by their wits. If boys can at all avoid domestic service, they do so.

CONCLUSIONS

Colonial authorities, alarmed at the prospect of a town-born generation growing up, considered children's presence in the towns to be a problem. Control over children's movements between villages and towns was a key to the administrations's attempt to delay the urban proletarianization process. Only by disciplining and training children at an early age in "tribal custom" in the villages could they ensure the reproduction of such customs. Children in towns without parents or guardians would never learn where they really belonged but would turn into hooligans and delinquents and grow up with no respect for tribal authority. By not improving the prospects for rural livelihoods and by for a long time retaining the illusion that African townspeople were temporary urban residents who did not need family wages and family housing, the colonial administration created the very problem it most feared: urban proletarianization. Increasing numbers of men and women—adults, young people, and children—migrated to the towns, where they all, in many different ways, contributed to the making of an African urban working-class culture and a social-organizational setup aimed at confronting the color bar restrictions of their day: substandard wages and substandard housing. Children's migration and urban work must be explained against that background.

To do this we must flesh out Elizabeth Colson's statement: certainly, children *are* exchanged freely between rural areas and towns in Zambia for a variety of purposes. But while such exchanges have been noted, they have neither been consistently described nor subjected to analysis. Writing about such practices generally, Ester Goody notes that because many ethnographers "do not enquire about the residence of children and [the use] of classificatory kinship terminology means that such information is likely to come to light only accidentally."[64]

As I have shown, rural-urban exchanges of children in Zambia have been noted from the early colonial days through the present. They were and are influenced by the different income opportunities in rural, as compared to urban, areas; the differential availability of schools; patterns of housing and lack of space; and crisis within families. The underlying assumption—and perhaps the reason why these practices have not been accounted for—has been that such arrangements reflected customary, shared rights in children within descent groups and that the placing of children with others therefore composed some sort of traditional responsibility system along the lines of fosterage.

While that might have been so in the distant past, it was not always the case in the towns during the colonial era; nor is it the case for all the children who today are kept in the households of others. The placing of children with kin, according to Goody, can only be effective within a system in which *claims* on kin have meaning.[65] The relationship gives rise to *reciprocal claims*, which have to be honored. When the claims are no longer reciprocal, the system ceases to be effective. She further suggests that "where differentiation and hierarchy are well advanced, there is little that poor relatives can do to reciprocate. At this point transactions become subject to calculations of equity. Masters take apprentices in exchange for a fee and the right to their labour for a fixed period. Mistresses pay housemaids; school boys pay boarding fees."[66] The Zambian situation I have described is approaching this point.

Although children placed with urban kin to do unpaid household work or with urbanites known to parents and guardians to work as servants for a pittance are recruited and controlled by personal relationships of kinship or quasi-parental authority, their work does not represent some lingering survival of primordial relationships belonging to a distant past. Such work, during the colonial period and at the present time, represents an *extraction of labor in a relationship merely cast in the familial idiom*. Whether exchanges of children between kin and nonkin were prevalent among Zambian ethnic groups prior to the rise of capitalist production or not is largely irrelevant to the question of what economic role the household labor of such children performs in the economy.

In the short term, children's work helps poor parents make a living, at least temporarily, by freeing them from the responsibility of support; and support in cases where a child worker's pay is remitted directly to parents, adults come in part to depend on their children's earnings. In the long term, children's work in private homes—like women's unpaid household labor and adult domestic servants' labor—helps produce labor power at little cost to the state. While all household members do this to some extent, children do it optimally for the state; for though *in* these households, they are not *of* them (since work, not familial affection or loyalty, is the reason for their presence) and can make no claim on them. Their role may continue to be spoken of in the language of kinship, but its functions have altered. Such children are units of labor whose work is consumed with little or no remuneration. Compared to adults, child workers have restricted control over the conditions of their labor and are more vulnerable to the whims of adults. And because they are more subordinated than adults in the labor process, they are subject to more invidious forms of exploitative relations than exist within the household.

NOTES

This is a revised version of a paper entitled "'Members of the Family': Paid Servants and Kept Relatives in Urban Zambian Households," presented at the annual meeting of the American Anthropological Association, Denver, 1984. In the present version, the discussion of the colonial period has been expanded and the sections on postcolonial developments have been almost eliminated. The information on which the paper is based is a by-product of my research on domestic service in Zambia, particularly of my sifting through files upon files in the National Archives of Zambia pertaining to women's migration. The research was funded by a grant from the U.S. National Science Foundation, no. BNS-8303507.

1. B. Fetter, "The Missing Migrants: African Seeds in the Demographers' Field," *History in Africa* 11 (1984), 99–111.

2. See K. T. Hansen, "Negotiating Sex and Gender in Urban Zambia," *Journal of South African Studies* 10 (1984).

3. A. Roberts, *A History of Zambia* (New York, 1976), 191.

4. United Kingdom, *Report of the Commission Appointed to Inquire into the Disturbances on the Copperbelt, Northern Rhodesia, July–September 1935* (Lusaka, 1935), 505.

5. F. Spearpoint, "The African Native and the Rhodesian Copper Mines," *Supplement to the Journal of the Royal African Society* 36 (1937), 49.

6. Ibid., 46.

7. Ibid., 18.

8. National Archives of Zambia (NAZ) SEC 1/1312: Administration of Native Labour, Investigations of Labour Conditions in Northern Rhodesia (1936–37). Central Province, 1937, 15–16.

9. NAZ/SEC/1349, Children in Industrial Areas. Repatriation (1938–1945). May 1938; September 1938; January 1938.

10. Northern Rhodesia, *Legislative Council Debates*, vol. 2 (1933), cols. 107–130, NAZ/SEC 1/1316: Labour. Employment of Children (1938–1945).

11. Large numbers of children below the minimum working age labored in the tobacco industry, and in subsequent years calls for the recruitment of children as farmhands were made when farm labor was short. Women were also recruited for such work.

12. NAZ/SEC 1/1316.

13. G. Chauncey, "The Locus of Reproduction: Women's Labour in the Zambian Copperbelt, 1927–1953," *Journal of Southern African Studies*, 7, n. 2 (1981), 142.

14. G. Wilson, *An Essay on the Economics of Detribalization in Northern Rhodesia*, Rhodes-Livingstone Paper, no. 5, pt. 1 (Livingstone, 1941), 32.

15. G. St. J. Orde Browne, *The African Labourer* (London, 1933), 109.

16. NAZ/SEC 1/1316: August 1938, April 1940.

17. NAZ/SEC 1/1348: "Native Education on the Mines," May 1938.

18. G. St. J. Orde Browne, *Labour Conditions in Northern Rhodesia.* Colonial no. 150 (London, 1938), 67–68.

19. *Report of the Commission to Inquire into the Financial and Economic Position of Northern Rhodesia*, Colonial no. 145 (London, 1938), 47.

20. H. Heisler, *Urbanisation and the Government of Migration* (London, 1974), 99–100.

21. *Report of the Commission to Inquire*, 47.

22. Northern Rhodesia, Labour Department, *Annual Report*, 1948, p. 7.

23. NAZ: Extracts from the third meeting of the Southern Province African Provincial Council, Livingstone, June 1946. Statement by Chief Musokotwane.

24. NAZ: Points raised by chiefs attending course at Chalimbana, 26 October 1946.

25. Wilson, *An Essay*, pt. 1, p. 25.

26. Ibid., pt. 1.

27. G. Wilson, *An Essay on the Economics of Detribalizaiton in Northern Rhodesia*, Rhodes-Livingstone Paper no. 6, pt. 2 (Livingstone, 1942), 75.

28. Wilson, *An Essay*, pt. 2.

29. Wilson, *An Essay*, pt. 2.

30. For the growth of squatting, see K. T. Hansen, "Lusaka's Squatters: Past and Present," *African Studies Review* 25, 2/3 (1982), 117–136.

31. Northern Rhodesia, *Report of the Census of the Population of Northern Rhodesia, Held on the 15th October, 1946* (Lusaka, 1949), 69; Federation of Rhodesia and Nyasaland, *Census of the Population, 1956* (Salisbury, 1960), 165.

32. NAZ/SEC 1/1316, August 1945.

33. NAZ/SEC 2/82: Annual Reports, African Affairs (1948). Central Province.

34. Northern Rhodesia, *Legislative Council Debates*, vol. 66 (1949), col. 460.

35. *Livingstone Mail*, 22 September 1944, p. 5.

36. NAZ/SEC 2/82.

37. Colonial Reports. Annual Report, Northern Rhodesia (London, 1947), 7.

38. NAZ/SEC 1/1338: Monthly Reports. Labour Department (1945). Western Province, Nkana.

39. H. Holmes, "Urban Schoolboys Go to the Country," *Rhodes-Livingstone Journal* 9 (1950), 31.

40. NAZ/SEC 1/1349, September 1943.

41. NAZ/NR 3/199, Annual Reports. Senior Labour Officer. Lusaka District (1950–1960), Midland and Southern Area, 1951.

42. H. Swanzy, "Quarterly Notes: Central Africa," *African Affairs* 51, no. 202 (1952), 20.

43. Ibid., 111–112.

44. A. I. Richards, *Land, Labour, and Diet in Northern Rhodesia: An Economic Study of the Bemba Tribe* (London, 1939); B. P. Thompson, *Two Studies of African Nutrition*, Rhodes-Livingstone Paper no. 24 (Manchester, 1954); B. Fetter, "Relocating Central Africa's Biological Reproduction, 1923–1963," *International Journal of African Historical Studies* 19 (1986), 473–474.

45. Fetter, "Relocating," 475.

46. NAZ/NR 3/199: Southern Area, 1954.

47. In a 1956 report the African Education Department pointed to the lack of school facilities for forty-five thousand African urban children: *Central African Post*, 29 July 1957, 7.

48. See D. Lehmann, "Marriage, Divorce, and Prostitution of African Women in a Changing Society," in Northern Rhodesia Council of Social Services, *Report of the Annual Conference, 1961, on Marriage and the Family* (Lusaka, 1961), 27–35; idem, "Lives of African Adolescent Girls in a Copperbelt Township," in G. J. Snowball, ed., *Science and Medicine in Central Africa* (Oxford, 1965), 645–653.

49. J. C. Mitchell, *African Urbanization in Ndola and Luanshya*, Rhodes-Livingstone Communication, no. 6 (Lusaka, 1954), 4, 6.

50. M. McCulloch, *A Social Survey of the African Population of Livingstone*, Rhodes-Livingstone Paper, no. 26 (Lusaka, 1956), 16. For a discussion of the problem of underreporting girls in their early adolescence, see Etienne van de Walle, "Note on the Effect of Age Misreporting," in W. Brass, A. Coale et al., eds., *The Demography of Tropical Africa* (Princeton, 1968), 143–150.

51. D. G. Bettison, *Numerical Data on African Dwellers in Lusaka, Northern Rhodesia*, Rhodes-Livingstone Communication, no. 16 (Lusaka, 1959), 29.

52. Bettison, *Numerical Data*, 32.

53. Mitchell, "African Urbanization," 7; McCulloch, "A Social Survey," 22.

54. Bettison, *Numerical Data*, 50.

55. H. Powdermaker, *Copper Town* (New York, 1962); A. L. Epstein, *Urbanization and Kinship* (London, 1981).

56. There were a total of 4,616 male juveniles compared to 1,594 adult females in wage employment in the towns of Northern Rhodesia in 1956. These numbers are abstracted from Federation of Rhodesia and Nyasaland, *Census of the Population, 1956*, table 80.

57. Among the ample studies of rural societies are two with special focus on childhood: M. Read, *Children of Their Fathers: Growing Up Among the Ngoni of Nyasaland* (London, 1959) and I. M. M. Mbikusita-Lewanika, "Zambian Society: An Oral History of an Unwritten Culture" (Ph.D. diss., New York, 1980).

58. Suzanne Comhaire-Sylvain, *Food and Leisure Among the Urban African Youth of Leopoldville* (Cupe Toron, 1950).

59. Republic of Zambia, Labour Department, *Annual Reports* (Lusaka, 1963–1968).

60. M. E. Jackman, *Recent Population Movements in Zambia: Some Aspects of the 1969 Census*, Zambian Papers, no. 8 (Lusaka, 1973). Regarding Zambian demography and the 1963 and 1969 population censuses, see also P. Ohadike and H. Tesfaghiorghis, *The Population of Zambia* (CICRED, 1975); Ohadike, *Demographic Perspectives in Zambia*, Zambian Papers, no. 15 (Lusaka, 1981).

61. E. Colson, "The Reordering of Experience: Anthropological Involvement with Time," *Journal of Anthropological Research* 40, no. 1 (1984), 10.

62. This situation is by no means unique to Zambia, yet few studies have been undertaken about children's work elsewhere in Africa. For some examples, see the work of Enid Schildcrout, e.g., "Age and Gender in Hausa Society: Socio-economic Roles of Children in Urban Kano," in J. S. La Fontaine, ed., *Sex and Age as Principles of Social Stratification* (London, 1978), 109–137; idem, "Women's Work and Children's Work: Variations Among Muslims in Kano," in S. Wallman, ed., *Social Anthropology of Work* (London, 1979), 69–86. In the aftermath of the 1979 International Year of the Child, more studies of children's work in developing countries began to appear. Among examples from this wave of studies are C. Mendelievich, ed., *Children and Work* (Geneva, 1979); G. Rodgers and G. Standing, eds., *Child Work, Poverty, and Underdevelopment* (Geneva, 1981); B. White, ed., *Child Workers*, special issue of *Development and Change* (vol. 13, no. 4 [1982]); R. Jolly and G. Cornia, eds., *The Impact of World Recession on Children*, special issue of *World Development* (vol. 12, no. 3 [1984]). Without discussing children's work at all, C. Mwanamwambwe and T. Zenebeworke describe shortfalls in education, health, and basic amenities in *Children in Zambia* (Stockholm, 1979).

63. Extensive research on youth training has been undertaken by W. Hoppers ("Youth, Apprenticeship, and Petty Production in Lusaka," *International Journal of Educational Development* 3, no. 2 [1984], 113–128).

64. E. Goody, *Parenthood and Social Reproduction* (Cambridge, 1982), 331.

65. Ibid., 278.

66. Ibid., 280.

17

Social Factors in Child Mortality in a Sample of Urban Women

J. CLYDE MITCHELL

Child-bearing histories were collected from some five thousand women during a social survey conducted in the line-of-rail towns of Northern Rhodesia (now Zambia) between December 1950 and May 1955. This survey, which was aimed at collecting data on the composition and degree of urban exposure among the African town residents at that time was conducted under the auspices of the Rhodes-Livingstone Institute. The survey was based on a 10 percent random stratified sample of all dwellings in which Africans were living at the time. The sampling strata were the different types of housing areas: those attached to the mining companies; those housing areas under the control of the local authorities; those controlled by the larger industrial concerns other than the mining companies; the housing on private, white, residential stands (on which domestic workers lived) and housing in the so-called unauthorized residential areas (i.e., squatter settlements). Details in respect of the child-bearing histories of women included, apart from the age of the women when children were born, the children's gender, and where they were then living or when they had died. Some estimates of fertility derived from this survey have already been published, but until now nothing has appeared about mortality estimates. The data published here are based on punch card tabulations made before the material was transferred to computer tape. In the process of transfer from punched cards to computer tape, it appears, that the data relating to the fertility and mortality data were lost. Although the original records still exist and the data could be reconstituted, the labour involved would be heavy and is quite beyond my resources. The analysis presented here is therefore an attempt to make the most of the material I have at my disposal.

THE FORM OF THE DATA

The original data relating to mortality were tabulated in the form of the age of death of children up to the age of five together with the number who were exposed to the possibility of death at that age. The period covered was the five years just before the date of interview in the sense that although data existed from older women of children born many years previously, the data presented here relate only to events in the five years just prior to the survey. From these data it is possible to compute age-specific deathrates between the ages of zero and five. The data were tabulated in terms of a number of variables that at the time appeared to have some possible bearing on levels of mortality. I shall analyze data relating to a set of social factors.

The rates have all been computed from the "raised" totals derived from the varying sampling fractions in the forty-one rates in the survey. The overall rates derived from these data are set out in Table 17.1. The urban infant mortality of 67.25 is lower than that of 182.00 estimated in the 1950 Sample Demographic Survey in Northern Rhodesia. As far as I am aware, there are no other estimates of the child mortality rates for the other ages.

TABLE 17.1 Overall Child Mortality Rates

Age	Deaths	Exposed	Rate/1,000
0–1	3,100.05	46,096.13	67.25
1–2	965.65	36,651.61	26.35
2–3	449.76	24,802.91	18.13
3–4	105.76	16,084.63	6.58
4–5	31.36	7,278.72	4.31

There were few differences in mortality by gender of the child as Table 17.2 sets out. There seemed to be slightly higher mortality among boys than among girls, but the differences were not great.

TABLE 17.2 Mortality Rates by Gender

Age	Deaths	Males Exposed	Rate/1,000	Deaths	Females Exposed	Rate/1,000
0–1	1,634.61	23,781.40	68.74	1,527.74	23,241.41	65.73
1–2	570.06	18,951.06	30.08	395.59	18,302.36	21.62
2–3	229.47	12,801.33	17.93	220.29	12,440.13	17.71
3–4	51.96	8,462.71	6.14	53.80	7,900.91	6.81
4–5	20.57	4,025.73	5.11	10.79	3,428.42	3.15

More striking differences were found between single and plural births. The mortality rates for single births as against twins are shown in Table 17.3.

TABLE 17.3 Mortality for Single as Against Plural Births

Age	Single Births			Twins		
	Deaths	Exposed	Rate/1,000	Deaths	Exposed	Rate/1,000
0–1	2,813.05	45,776.45	61.45	316.09	1,213.14	260.55
1–2	925.28	36,595.10	25.28	40.37	658.42	61.31
2–3	439.53	24,857.68	17.68	10.23	383.77	26.65
3–4	105.76	16,214.17	6.52	0.00	152.44	0.00
4–5	31.36	7,353.46	4.26	0.00	100.68	0.00

SOCIAL FACTORS

Tabulations were made of the mortality rates for a number of different background characteristics of the mothers of the children. Of the characteristics tabulated five have been selected for detailed analysis here:

1. *Age of the Mother*: Originally, the data were tabulated in five-year age groups; but for purposes of analysis here the data have been reduced to a dichotomy: *over the age of twenty-five* and *under the age of twenty-five*. This was at the approximate median point of the distribution of the ages of the woman.

2. *Socioeconomic Status*: Three characteristics of the mother were selected to be combined into a single indicator of relative socioeconomic status:

a. Whether the woman had had any education or not;
b. Whether the husband was in a semiskilled, skilled, or white-collar occupation or not; and
c. Whether the husband's wage was above the median wage or not.

The inconsistent patterns of attributes, on the assumption that the three characteristics were a Guttmann scale, were allocated to "perfect" scale types using image analysis. The patterns of attributes were then dichotomized at approximately the median point into those with generally high-status characteristics and those with low-status characteristics.

3. *Urban Exposure*: A similar procedure was adopted to divide the women into those with relatively high exposure to urban living and those with relatively low exposure. Three attributes were selected to form the basis of this classification:

a. The woman's expressed attitude toward living in town (Responses to the question what they thought about living in town were classified into nine categories—ranging from little sense of involvement in urban living and a sense of being locked into urban existence to complete satisfaction with living in town—and divided into generally negative and generally positive attitudes);

b. The length of continuous residence of the woman in town, divided roughly at the median point of the distribution; and

c. The proportion of adult life spent in towns as against rural areas. Once again, a cutting point was chosen so as to equalize the numbers in each category as much as possible.

As with the indicator of socioeconomic status, the inconsistent patterns were attributed to consistent patterns using image analysis on the assumption that the attributes in fact reflected a Guttmann scale. The patterns of attributes were then dichotomized at the point nearest to the median point of the distribution into those with a relatively high, and those with a relatively low, exposure to urban living.

4. *Religious Persuasion*: The women were classified simply into those who said that they belonged to any one of the Christian denominations and those who said that they did not. Since the number of Muslims in the towns at the time of the survey was very small, the non-Christians were in effect those who adhered to traditional religious practices.

5. *Parity*: The women were categorized at the approximate median point of the number of children they had had. The cutting point was between those who had had one or two children and those who had had three or more.

The mortality rates were then computed for the two categories for each of these attributes. Tables 17.4–17.8 set out the results. The findings in Table 17.4 suggest that the mortality of younger mothers' children is slightly higher than that of older mothers' children, the effect being more distinct in the youngest age groups. It is possible that this is a matter of maternal experience.

TABLE 17.4 Mortality Rates of Children Born to Women of 25 Years or Over and Women 25 Years or Less

Age	25 or More	25 or Less
0–1	64.69	69.73
1–2	24.68	28.04
2–3	17.44	18.87
3–4	6.03	7.24
4–5	5.00	3.34

Table 17.5 presents the mortality rates for those of higher and lower socioeconomic status. The results confirm the common finding of higher child mortality rates among mothers in lower socioeconomic circumstances. I lack the detailed ethnographic evidence to enable me to specify the particular causative factors underlying the mortality. Presumably, low incomes and consequent malnutrition would play an important part.

TABLE 17.5 Mortality Rates for Children of Relatively High and Relatively Low Socioeconomic Status

Age	High SES	Low SES
0–1	63.62	75.24
1–2	23.01	34.03
2–3	13.80	28.48
3–4	7.50	4.35
4–5	4.00	5.11

Table 17.6 sets out the mortality rates for children of mothers who have been more exposed, and those who have been less exposed, to urban conditions. The trends here seem to be irregular. The mortality rate of children aged one to two of mothers with low urban exposure seem to be somewhat higher than of mothers with higher urban exposure, but the trend is reversed for children aged two to three. The differences on the whole are small, and I am not sure that any substantial relationship is involved.

TABLE 17.6 Mortality Rates for Children of Mothers with More or Less Urban Exposure

Age	High Urban Exposure	Low Urban Exposure
0–1	67.92	66.75
1–2	20.13	31.01
2–3	24.24	13.27
3–4	5.92	7.09
4–5	5.90	2.80

Table 17.7 sets out the mortality rates of mothers who said that they belonged to Christian sects as against those who did not. It seems that mothers who did not claim to be Christian had, on the average, a somewhat greater probability of losing children below the age of three but not over that age. The mortality among infants aged zero to one for women who did not claim to be Christian was one-and-a-half times higher than that for women who claimed to be Christian. It is difficult to explain why this should be so. Presumably, if the phenomenon is real, it lies in the differing ways of life followed by women who had been introduced to practices in the mission stations relating to personal hygiene and to the care of children. The difference might be thought to be due to the possibility that women coming from the mission stations would presumably have been exposed to some education and were generally of higher socioeconomic status, but in fact there was only a slight preponderance of Christian women among the higher socioeconomic status groups (71.88 percent as against 67.99 percent). In the absence of detailed ethnographic information the cause must remain speculation.

TABLE 17.7 Mortality Rates of Children of Christian Mothers as Against Others

Age	Christian	Other
0–1	58.62	90.16
1–2	25.38	29.02
2–3	16.70	21.93
3–4	7.22	4.86
4–5	6.08	0.00

Table 17.8 sets out the mortality rates for women who have had three or more children as against those who have had either one or two. These results consistently suggest that the less experienced mothers in the sample tended to lose more children in all of the five age groups of children included in the analysis. Once again, without detailed ethnographic data it would be difficult to advance any causal explanation in which we might have any confidence.

TABLE 17.8 Mortality Rates for Women Who Have Had Three or More Children as Against Those Who Have Had Two or Fewer

Age	3 or More	2 or Fewer
0–1	61.30	72.30
1–2	21.73	30.10
2–3	13.65	21.41
3–4	3.32	8.98
4–5	3.44	4.90

A MULTIVARIATE ANALYSIS

The five background factors we have been examining, of course, if they have any influence at all, operate conjointly to exert this influence. In order to try to assess the effect of any one factor independently of the others we need to use a multivariate technique in which the effect of each factor on the level of mortality can be estimated while the effect of the others is held constant. The independent variables in this analysis are, of course, dichotomous; while the dependent variable—the mortality rate—is a proportion whose error distribution is taken to be a binomial.[1] The procedure adopted was to determine the goodness of fit when all five independent attributes were included together with one term that was designed to test the effect of the interaction between age and parity.[2]

In order to decide which of the attributes I have been able to include in this analysis have the greatest effect on child mortality, we may examine the decrease in the fit of the model when we exclude each attribute in turn. Table 17.9 sets out the proportional decrease when each of the attributes is excluded in turn. In order to estimate the effects of age and parity separately, the

TABLE 17.9 Proportional Decrease in Goodness of Fit When Attributes Are
Excluded from the Model

Attribute	Ages of Death of Children				
	0–1	1–2	2–3	3–4	4–5
Age	.001	.002	.020	.0114	.056
Socioeconomic status	.049	.124	.252	.026	.012
Urban exposure	.002	.118	.219	.001	.093
Religion	.382	.011	.018	.019	.309
Parity	.058	.072	.146	.145	.063

interaction term between age and parity is excluded from this analysis. The
mean effects over all child age groups are age .018 (1.8 percent),
socioeconomic status .093 (9.3 percent); urban exposure .087 (8.7 percent);
religion .148 (14.8 percent), and parity .097 (9.7 percent).

Surprisingly—to me at any rate—religious persuasion emerges as the
feature that on the average has most effect on the mortality of children. As I
have speculated earlier when considering the overall effect of religion on
mortality, since the connection between religious practices and the death of
children is hardly direct, it is not easy to interpret this finding.

The attribute with the second greatest effect on child mortality as a
whole is the parity of the mothers where the effect over all five child age
groups is .097 (9.7 percent). If we examine the effects in each of the five age
groups considered we see that the major effects seem to have occurred in the
two-to-three and three-to-four age groups. Once again, it is not easy to
explain why the effect should fall so heavily on these two particular age
groups. One possible explanation is that the mortality may be increased
when a new addition to the family takes place (though one would expect the
mortality to fall at a younger age than between two and four).

The next attribute to be taken into account in respect of overall mortality
effects is socioeconomic status, whose mean effect is a reduction of .093 (9.3
percent) in the goodness of fit when it is included in the model. The largest
effect seems to occur in respect to children aged one to two and two to three
(although we shall see when we examine the odds ratios in Table 17.10 that
the effects are in opposite directions). Certainly, the effects of socioeconomic
status seem to be minimal over the age of three.

Exposure to urban living had the next greatest effect, with a reduction of
.087 (8.7 percent) when this attribute was included in the model. As with
socioeconomic status, the major effect seemed to fall in the two-to-three age
group.

The attribute that had the lowest overall effect on child mortality was the
age of the mother, with a decrease of .018 (1.8 percent) in fit when age was
removed from the model. The effect over all five age groups was uniformly
low.

TABLE 17.10 Odds Ratios of Mortality Rates for Attributes for Age-specific Mortality Rates

Attribute	Ages of Death of Children				
	0–1	1–2	2–3	3–4	4–5
Base category	.054	.014	.014	.005	.007
Age (25 and less)	1.039	1.246	.355	.000	.000
Socioeconomic status (low)	1.174	1.476	2.261	.635	1.498
Urban exposure (low)	.969	1.464	.480	1.073	.379
Religion (non-Christian)	1.568	1.130	1.256	.682	.000
Parity (1 or 2)	1.259	1.647	1.679	2.606	2.143
Age + parity	.919	.667	2.768	2,067.303	1,674.048

The effect of the attribute as a whole on child mortality, however, obscures *how* the attribute has an effect on mortality. All we know is that excluding religious persuasion from the model leads to a 14.8-percent reduction in the predictive efficiency of our model: we do not know whether being a Christian increases the probability of mortality among the children or decreases it. In order to examine this feature of the model we need to examine the specific effects derived from the analysis. Table 17.10 sets out the odds ratios for the five attributes and the interaction term for the mortality rates for the five ages considered. The proportional improvement of fit contributed by these attributes varies between .384 and .207, the mean being .310. Odds ratios are an indicator of the extent to which the mortality rate of mothers in the category designated will be higher or lower than mothers in the base category. For example, in this analysis, the mortality rate for a non-Christian mother's children aged zero to one is estimated to be 1.568 times larger than a Christian mother's, other attributes being held constant. The analysis indicates, for example, that child mortality, holding other factors constant, is higher for women aged twenty-five or less than for women aged over twenty-five for children aged one to two but that the rates decrease systematically for children in the higher mother's age groups. With regard to mothers who said that they were not Christian, the relative rates of mortality seem to be steady for children under the age of three, with an appreciable decrease in respect to children over that age. When age is combined with parity, there is a general *increase* in mortality with age of child among women aged twenty-five and less as compared with women over twenty-five, the effect being particularly spectacular for children over three.

These results show that the tendency is for the mortality of zero-to-one- and one-to-two-year-old children to be higher for women aged twenty-five or less than for women aged over twenty-five; the mortality rate of children aged over two tends to be smaller among mothers aged twenty-five and less than among mothers of over twenty-five.

There were few other consistent results except that the deathrates in small families tended to be higher than those in the larger families, since the odds ratios were consistently larger than 1.0 across all five child age groups with a slight tendency for the mortality rates to be higher for older children.

CONCLUSION

This analysis has demonstrated one of the difficulties in using general survey data collected with different hypotheses in view if the purpose of the analysis is to seek specific explanatory relationships. The material has certainly thrown up some intriguing relationships, but they are not easy to interpret. A survey designed specifically to investigate child mortality could presumably have so focused inquiries so as to document characteristics that were considered a priori to have some bearing on the topic. As it is, however, the data analyzed here were collected in a general survey that was in fact directed toward other questions. The task of interpretation will need to be left to the historians.

NOTES

1. The NAG program GLIM377 written for the IBM-PC was in fact used in this analysis. I am grateful to Clive Payne, director of the Oxford Faculty of Social Studies Data Centre for assistance in interpreting the results of the GLIM analysis.

2. There are, of course, a large number of possible interaction terms that could be included. The interaction effect between age and parity was chosen because it seemed likely that mortality would be affected either if young mothers had large families or, alternatively, older mothers had smaller families.

18

Social and Organizational Variables Affecting Central African Demography

———————————————————————— PATRICK O. OHADIKE

I shall regard Central Africa as encompassing the old Federation of Rhodesia and Nyasaland (now Zambia, Zimbabwe, and Malawi). This definition clearly overlooks the broader geographical categorization of Central Africa, or Middle Africa, as including many more countries (which can be seen in UN publications, including those of the World Bank). The present grouping found also in the works of such distinguished scholars as Lord Hailey, J. R. H. Shaul, R. R. Kuczynski, J. Clyde Mitchell, and so on, embraces countries that possess common political, cultural, and historical links, especially if account is taken of their contact with the West. Also, the presentation focuses much more on the experience of Zambia (former Northern Rhodesia), because of a wish on my part for a more profound appreciation of its experience and because this will condense the analysis without loss of objectivity, meaning, or purpose. Besides, in view of the fact that Zaire (former Belgian Congo), shares common geographical, cultural, and linguistic configurations with certain parts of Zambia, aspects of its rich demographic experience can also be utilized.

There remains, however, the fundamental problem that the study of Central African demography, viewed from a historical perspective, has been befogged by the serious lack of reliable demographic data. The entire colonial era was one of enlightened guesses and estimates of the characteristics of the African population. In Zambia, while regular periodic counts of Europeans, Asians, and coloreds were carried out between 1911 and 1961, no efforts were made to enumerate Africans. R. R. Kuczynski has pointed out how unsatisfactory the estimates of the population were. The methods used were crude and could not have yielded valid and reliable measures. For instance, he observed in one of several of his monumental works that in Zambia (Northern Rhodesia) the earlier estimates were based on African tax returns. Later, they were based partly on enumeration and partly on estimates. The enumeration was done by counting the people visited by the district officers and then applying the observed variations proportionately to the unvisited areas. In some cases huts were counted, and population was estimated by applying fixed coefficients to arrive at the total population and its composition by age and sex. Clearly, the poor quality of the wildly fluctuating estimates, which varied according to the degree of care exercised by the district officers in charge and the accuracy of the coefficients employed from time to time, cannot be in doubt. The situation became chaotic by 1934.[1]

In Zaire, prior to the Demographic Inquiry of 1955–1957, report on the number of persons in the country were mainly summations of reports rendered by the administrative officials largely on the basis of the population registers maintained by the government agency in charge of labor supply and native affairs.[2] There is a large body of opinion that the underlying cause of the problem was the defeatist and nonchalant attitude of the colonial administration in easily assuming in advance, that the demographic situation was helpless and irredeemable without making any concerted effort to improve it. Indeed, year in and year out successive governments that consistently enumerated non-Africans discounted with facile levity the practicality of holding a complete count of Africans in Zambia. Even as late as 21 June 1945 the chief secretary to the government said in the Legislative Council that "while the desirability of carrying out some form of enumeration as soon as possible is fully realised, it is not considered that a complete census of the Territory is practicable at present due to the acute shortage of staff. It is hoped however to carry out an enumeration in a simplified form of the European and Asiatic population in 1946."[3]

Of course, it is equally true that there were major (though not insurmountable) problems, such as the acute shortage of educated and trained staff already mentioned and general lack of resources. The issue of inadequate number of educated personnel was clearly brought out in the analysis of the 1963 and 1969 census experiences as follows: "Reflecting postindependence improvement in the provision of education and training, the quality of staff employed in this census [1969] was higher than that used in 1963 . . . ; enumerators who then were of lower educational standard and were only expected to have had at least a standard six education, were required to have a minimum of form III education in the 1969 census."[4] Then there were the common but complex logistical problems. With poor transport and communciations, the remoteness and inaccessibility of many parts of this extensive territory (ca. 290 thousand square miles) defied colonial solution. In the first-ever complete count of Africans in 1963, it is significant that carriers and canoe paddlers were hired and used.[5] In a reference to the existence of similar problems in Zaire (Belgian Congo), A. Romaniuk remarked that "the size of the country and the low density of population in many regions hampered the development of an efficient network of vital registration offices. This resulted in considerable under-registration of events, especially deaths."[6] The defectiveness of the available data base has been so pervasive that we will be forced to consider it again and again in this analysis, for it is critical to the objective evaluation of any observed demographic patterns in the prevailing socioeconomic environment.

Postindependence effort at enumerating the population of Zambia has been kept up admirably. The 1963 census took place on the eve of independence in 1964 and was shortly followed by another, better planned, better organized, and better coordinated count with more comprehensive and rewarding results in 1969. The tradition of holding regular enumeration has not only been installed in Zambia but has been followed by organization of a national sample census of population in 1974 and a general complete enumeration in the decennial tradition in 1979.

A study of the social and organizational variables affecting Central African demography should basically recognize the fact that sociological and demographic inquiries are essentially complementary, a relationship that gives added meaning and significance to the present study. Invariably, one cannot understand any one of the two phenomena without reference to the other. Thus, the interpretation of demographic phenomena is greatly enhanced by reference to the sociological imperatives that influence behavior and have a critical bearing on the evolution of life processes, human adaptations, and the resulting demographic patterns. In the same way, the understanding of sociological events can be greatly enhanced by reference to their demographic correlates. Thus, the demographic variable *fertility* has certain patterns and attains certain levels in a society not only because of births as such but also, significantly, because of the social and cultural determinants of births as concerns their regularity, frequency, cultural significance, social and economic value, and so on. We can therefore understand demographic events better by reference to the social and cultural setting in which they occur. At the same time, the prevailing level of fertility—a demographic event—can generate new social forms of behavior: for instance, new practices could result from population pressure imposed by prevailing high levels of fertility. In the opposite direction, pronatalist policies could result from a felt need to increase the rate of population growth by inducing people to have more children.

The social and organizational factors that facilitate social, economic, and technological transition from traditionalism to modernization are the countervailing forces against the traditional status quo and precipitate new acculturation and adaptation processes in support of social change. These social forces inhere in the sociostructural and socioeconomic conditions in society. As explanatory variables they include, in the present case, kinship and social organization in relation to demographic factors such as marriage, fertility, and migration. Closely allied to this is the role of traditionalism and religion and the extent to which these admit of change. Finally, there are innovation variables such as education, literacy, and the monetization of the economy, which are at one and the same time important precipitants of change and barometers of the level and degree of change. Against this background, therefore, I shall examine the social and organizational factors in recording (1) the age and sex structure; (2) marriage and family formation; (3) fertility and infertility levels, patterns, and variations; (4) mortality levels, patterns, and variation; and (5) migration and the growth of the labor force.

SOCIAL AND ORGANIZATIONAL FACTORS
IN AGE AND SEX STRUCTURE

In this subregion, as in any other in Africa, unreliability of age reporting is a serious problem. Generally, ages even now are estimated by enumerators; and this is subject to serious biases in which the ages of respondents are either over- or underestimated. The situation was much more serious in colonial times, when *everything*—even the size of the population—was subject to guesswork. It was not even common to find clear references to the ages of the population in the earlier writings on the subject.

In the first complete census of Africans in Zambia in 1963 the scope and accuracy of the information on age was very limited. Data were collected mainly in three, broad age groups for persons born (1) before 1918, (2) between 1918 and 1941, and (3) after 1941. Apparently because of the influence of literacy and education, the years of birth for the youngest group were also recorded. Even so, there appear to have been gross distortions of the age distribution of this group—persons aged 21 1/2 years and below. It is curious that the distribution of age by single year of birth for persons born within Zambia and persons born outside Zambia was identical at every year of birth. Similarly, the same proportion of either sex was born each year in each birthplace category. This rather surprising coincidence further underlines the hazards of collecting age data in Africa.

The subsequent census of 1969 collected age data by single year of age for all persons in the population. A critical evaluation of the quality of the data generally showed that the age data for Zambia was highly inaccurate as measured by conventional indexes.[7] But in societies like Zambia, where there is a low level of literacy, one can hardly expect responses to questions on age to be highly accurate: people often do not know their correct ages; they have never kept written records of it or cannot remember it during the enumeration, or else the ages are wrongly given for them by others. Or enumerators have compounded the errors by resorting to estimation using various forms of benchmarks, such as the local calendar of events, the number of children born to a woman, and so on. These produce age data infested with heaping errors, digital preference, and other types of age misstatements.

Sex distribution of the population clearly excited greater interest in government and administrative circles in the colonial days. Hardly any discussion of demographic and economic change took place without implicating the exodus of males from the rural areas to employment and industrial centers within and outside the country. For instance, in 1921 the sex ratio of Zambia was 118.8 females per one hundred males based on figures that excluded absentees. Ten years later, in 1931, it was 123.1 females per hundred males excluding absentees. The preponderance of females is much greater still if account is taken of adults only. In this case the ratio was 144.2 excluding absentees and 129.8 including absentees. The major labor supply areas (Awemba, Barotse or Western Province, East Luangwa, and Kasempa) suffered from greater excess of females.

Subsequent census reporting appear to support the continued preponderance of females over males in the Zambian population. The total sex ratio in 1963 was 98 males per hundred females. That for persons born outside Zambia was expected, 121 males per hundred females. Theoretically, sex ratio levels are influenced by the initial preponderance of male births, lower female mortality, and greater migration. Any one or a combination of these factors must have helped to shape the observed sex ratio. In particular, evidence was adduced by the Central Statistical Office that more Zambian emigrant males than females of working age were domiciled in Zimbabwe, South Africa, and other neighboring countries.[8] This accords with the observation made above that there was a marked preponderance of males in a normally predictable direction among immigrants to Zambia. The immigrant masculinity ratio was higher in the European farming area (187 per hundred) than in the urban area (158 per hundred). In the rural area more female immigrants were reported. Discounting the chances of an undercount of males, it is likely that some immigrant wives were left behind in the rural areas by husbands in employment or seeking jobs in towns and in the European farming areas where houses for married persons were inadequately provided for. The effect of this is probably enhanced by the possibility of Zambian-born males of immigrant parentage marrying women born in their parents' places of origin, then leaving them in the rural area to go live in towns and other employment zones. It is also likely that immigrant women married to local Zambian-born males were left in rural areas.

Immigrants apart, the sex ratio for the total population shows that males predominate markedly in European farming areas and urban areas. Probably emphasizing the selective male migration pattern, rural male-female ratio at 90 per hundred was in favor of females, as opposed to 106 per hundred and 128 per hundred for the European farming area and the urban area, respectively. While the excess of females in the general population was further attested to in the subsequent census of 1969, it was also shown that males in any case predominated in the urban areas and other job centers. It should be expected that with the intensification and expansion of industrialization in the present climate of unbridled migration there would follow a gradual equalization of the sexes in urban areas as more and more females join the march and line up for work in towns and cities.

SOCIAL AND ORGANIZATIONAL FACTORS
IN MARRIAGE AND FAMILY FORMATION

Strictly defined, marriage is the contrary state to celibacy; it is not concubinage and not so-called free union. Marriage, from the point of view of marital stability and continuity of husband-wife relationship, entails greater exposure to the risks of childbirth and family formation, which is the essential demographic and sociological consequence of marriage in society. The family remains a highly valued social institution in Africa and seems to be resisting the inroads of rapid social change. Large families are still preferred. The desired average number of children in a 1969 Lusaka-based demographic inquiry averaged 7.1 children. The average for the most enlightened group was 5.8, almost twice as large as the average family size in the developed countries. This survey clearly reflected the continued survival of pronatal social values. Large family size apart, preference was shown for male children. It mattered very much to have children of both sexes, but (more often than not) more boys than girls was preferred. Only 11.5 percent of the surveyed females clearly approved of the establishment of clinics for family planning.

While the definition of marriage in a strictly legalistic sense is difficult, it is vital that any demographic or social inquiry in Africa should specify precisely the criteria used. Most studies commonly focus on the groups (1) married, (2) single, (3) divorced, and (4) separated. *Customary* marriage is the commonest in Africa; it involves the performance of traditional rites, including the payment of bride wealth and exchange of gifts.

In measuring the impact of marriage on family formation, it is essential to consider its incidence and timing in society—also the period that elapses between performance of traditional rites, the actual consummation of marriage, and the length and frequency of cohabitation. One serious problem of measurement of marriage in Africa is unreliability of age reporting. Generally, ages are estimated by enumerators, and the latitude of bias introduced in the results can lead to serious deviations from reality.

Despite the problems of definition and measurement, the married represent an overwhelming proportion of those who were ever married. In Zambia marriage is a normal and important part of life. It is ubiquitous. Permanent states of nonmarriage are rare, as shown by the low proportion of women who remain single after forty-five years of age. The result of the 1969 census shows that only 3.3 percent of females aged forty-five to fifty-four years were never married; the proportion was 2.9 percent for males. There is no doubt that marital structure and behavior affect the level and pattern of fertility in society. Not only the proportion celibate but also the proportion widowed and divorced affect fertility in a predictable way. Equally important is the fact that the size, tempo, and pattern of family formation can also set the pace and pattern of marriage in societies. We have tried to demonstrate this relationship in Table 18.1, in which selected marriage indexes were correlated with current and historical fertility measures. In a theoretically expected manner some of the indexes were positively or negatively correlated with fertility. Of major interest is the proportion of persons, male and female, who were never married, who were divorced, and who were widowed, which produced significant inverse relationships with current as well as historical fertility levels recorded in the 1969 census.

TABLE 18.1 Correlation of Fertility with Marital Status Indexes (Ages 15+) in Zambia, 1969 Census

Marital Status	Correlation (r)	
	Current Fertility	Historical Fertility
% males never married	−.1489	−.9591
% females never married	−.2830	−.8105
% males married	.1511	.9753
% females married	.4695	.2282
% males widowed	−.5697	−.2343
% females widowed	−.7209	−.2688
% males divorced	−.0304	−.8292
% females divorced	−.1768	−.5569

While these are interesting and significant relationships, note should be taken of the possibility that in Africa both widowhood and divorce are not always easy to measure. The criteria for divorce, given the different forms of union, are not easy to determine, especially in the case of free unions and consensual unions. Regular customary marriages and court and church marriages involved clearly defined procedures for divorce. For instance, in customary marriages, bride wealth is refunded or else some rites signaling the dissolution of marriage and of the bond established between the two kinship groups are performed. With regard to the effect of widowhood on fertility, some complications arise from the fact that among many African groups the death of a husband does not necessarily lead to the end of the relationship between the two kinship groups. This is because widow inheritance is practiced, and it enables a relation of the dead husband to put to use the woman's child-bearing capacity. All the same, inheritance may take place as a mere formality, in which actual cohabitation may not take place at all, or not regularly.

Although marriage is universal in Zambia, it does not appear, from records and estimates, that it took place as early as is commonly assumed. Certainly, according to J. A. Barnes, this has not been the case among the Ngoni, for whom the given age of first marriage has been traditionally very high.[9] While the practice among other ethnic groups in the country could be different, the fact remains that available data support the view that the age of first marriage in Zambia has not been generally very early, at least not soon after puberty for a majority of women. The estimated mean age of first marriage from the 1969 census result was 18.4 years for African females and 24.5 years for males. These averages compare favorably with those reported for other neighboring countries.[10]

Variations in age of first marriage among social groups is an important determinant of variation in fertility performance. While maternal age correlates more with the physiological maturity of the female, age of first marriage is more closely linked to the onset and periodicity of maternity. Within social expectations, age of first marriage regulates and sanctions unions, sexual intercourse, and reproduction on a continuing basis. The level of efficiency in reproduction can therefore be facilitated or impaired by early or late entry into marriage. The existence of an inverse relationship between fertility and the proportion of persons married has been indicated above. According to data from the Lusaka survey of 1969, a similar relationship was found to exist between the mean age of first marriage of wives and the mean number of children ever born to them. But there are other factors causally connected with the variation, and an important one of these is education. As a result of being positively associated with mean age at first marriage, it delays exposure to the risk of pregnancy and hence maintains an inverse relationship with fertility. The longer the time individuals devote to acquiring education and training, the greater the chances of postponing marriage and family formation. Indeed, controlling for the effect of education virtually wipes out the fertility variations by age of first marriage.

The relationship of marriage to fertility goes beyond considerations of early or late entry into marriage. Continuity and stability are important: the longer the duration of marriage, the higher the parity level attained. Again, in the Lusaka survey, this was generally true of all social and age groups.[11] This notwithstanding, instability and discontinuity of marital relationships tended to depress the fertility performance of some survey respondents. The negative impact of divorce and widowhood on the national level of fertility in Zambia has already been discussed elsewhere.[12] Besides, a little over 75 percent of the wives had married only once in their life; and they proved to be the most fertile. For example, 6.0 and 6.8 children were born to the once-married wives aged thirty to forty-four and forty-five or more years, repectively. The mean was 5.0 and 4.7, respectively, for those who had married twice. Such differences further underline the negative contribution of divorce and widowhood to fertility. Also of great significance is the possible reduction of fertility due to the temporary separation of spouses due to migration. The exodus of able-bodied males to job centers in and outside Zambia has been blamed for the prevalence of marital instability, although no clear proof exists in the colonial literature. Since unmarried women were not permitted in towns of colonial Zambia, single men living there could not find partners there. In Livingstone in 1952 married females represented 96 percent of females aged fifteen years or more.[13]

It has been claimed rather inconclusively that polygyny, as a result of the reduction of the rate of exposure to intercourse, tends to depress the level of fertility. Some studies have confirmed this,[14] while others have failed to confirm it.[15] Although the Lusaka survey tended, rather weakly, to support the view that polygyny impairs fertility, there still remain many imponderables about the operation of the polygyny variable. Issues involving definition and standardization of concepts and the degree and intensity of polygyny have to be clearly sorted out. It will be of special interest to demonstrate whether or not *la petite polygamie* found in Zambia (only 4.3 percent of the households were polygynous) depresses fertility as does *la grande polygamie* of some West African cultures. There would always be the need to discipline the data and eliminate the efforts of spurious correlations. For a long time to come, the incidence of polygyny—which exists much less in towns than in the rural areas[16]—will continue to engage the attention of scholars. Apparently, the practice has thrived, and will still thrive: polygynists can recruit wives because (1) differential mortality by sex, despite the excess of male births, tends to create an excess of females among adults; (2) polygynists tend to recruit females from younger ages into the married adult population; and (3) the delayed marriage of males, often considerably older than their wives, raises the ratio of wives to husbands. Added to this is the relatively small contribution to the pool of potential wives that permanent celibacy of males and differences in remarriage rates between males and females can make.

SOCIAL AND ORGANIZATIONAL FACTORS
IN FERTILITY LEVEL AND VARIATION

The data base for a historical analysis of fertility in Zambia has been very tenuous. Vital registration of African events as a major source of data was never pursued vigorously. There was a 1908 regulation providing for optional registration that was never put to use. The subsequent Proclamation of 1914, which supplanted the 1908 regulation, completely overlooked the voluntary registration of African vital events. The ordinances passed in 1930 and 1936 did not lead to the expansion of vital statistics registration services. The number of villages and the total population covered were significantly low. The Notification of Births of the Children of Africans Ordinance was passed in 1938; but its provision was not applied to the Livingstone Municipal Area, Lusaka, Kabwe (Broken Hill) Mine Township until February 1940 or to other African townships until December 1940.[17] Indeed, up till the time of independence not much had been achieved.

Progress was therefore very slow, which, as can be gleaned from various annual *Reports upon Native Affairs* (1929–1934), was attributable to a number of factors:

- The tendency that prevailed among administrators, medical officers, and European settlers to suspect that Africans resisted giving information because of superstition;
- The fact that Africans did not understand the purpose of an inquiry and resisted intrusions into their domestic affairs;
- Reluctance of Africans to talk about births and deaths and to report them (especially deaths);
- The method of inquiry was new to the African population and not well understood by them;
- Africans were extremely vague regarding the age of their children;
- The use of uninformed clerks of native courts as enumerators (the scarcity of qualified personnel was emphasized in 1945 when the director of medical services, in a Legislative Council debate, informed the bishop of Northern Rhodesia [Zambia] that "in 1939 an extremely experienced statistician . . . was on the point of sailing for this country on a tour organized by this Government, but the shipping facilities were not available and he did not come");[18]
- Illiteracy of the respondents, as a result of which data obtained suffered from misunderstanding of questions, ignorance of the necessary categorization, forgetfulness of events, and underreporting and overreporting of events occurring in a reference period. Closely related to all these is the fact that people have no clear knowledge of their exact age. Consequently, enumerators, using clues, resorted to estimates that often missed the mark, sometimes by very wide margin.

Thus, it is clear that no actual trend in vital rates can be established, particularly for the early days of colonial Zambia. However, the little and indeed very limited information that could be gleaned, points to the fact that Zambia's fertility has always been estimated to be very high. The annual birthrate fluctuated between fifty-six and sixty births per thousand population during 1931–1934. Until the 1950 demographic sample survey estimate of fifty-seven births per thousand, no other estimate seems to have been made. The level of the 1963 census estimate, which compares favorably with levels for other tropical African countries, can only pass as among the highest in the world. It was shown to lie between forty-three and fifty-two births per thousand population during 1953–1963. More detailed information was obtained from the analysis of the 1969 census results. The crude birthrate was around fifty births per thousand population; the corresponding total fertility rate was about 7.0, while the average number of daughters that could be borne by a woman passing through the reproductive life was 3.5. In general, the level of fertility in Zambia accords more with that of the East and West African subregion than with that of the Central African area, where a relatively low level of fertility prevails in places such as Gabon and East Cameroon, with estimated total fertility rate below 5.0.[19]

However, the subregions of Zambia are not homogeneous in terms of fertility levels and patterns. The existence of major variations among subregions and ethnic groups in the country—and indeed, in neighboring Zaire—have been known for some time.[20] Historically, administrative reports are replete with references to this phenomenon, which has been blamed (rightly or wrongly) on (1) the exodus of males to industrial job centers and their long absence from home and (2) physiological impairment associated with sterility and relatively high incidence of childlessness.

On the effect of the exodus of able-bodied males to work on the birthrate, we have to consider the surrounding conditions of the move. The impact will not be great if a married man chooses to go to work when he observes that the wife is pregnant. The duration of absence is also very critical in assessing whether the risks of pregnancy are seriously reduced. Also, if the male migrants are not of marriageable age, marriage will not be delayed. Where the wives accompany their husbands to work, fertility will not be reduced; besides, if single, unmarried women also go to the workplaces, this would enhance the possibility of marriage and sustain the level of fertility. It is probably because of these conditions that the 1931 *Report upon Native Affairs* states that although some provincial commissioners believed that exodus affected the birthrate, population statistics showed that the inhabitants were growing in number and the birthrate was satisfactory.[21] The 1932 report emphasized this point by stating, "No reliable evidence however has yet been produced to prove that the birth rate has materially altered as a result of large exodus of males to industrial centres."[22] In the same vein the 1937 report noted that the Bemba and Mukulu go abroad to earn money but showed higher birthrates than the Bisa and Unga. Only a minority of Bemba men remains away for long periods. Audrey Richards, in her work on Bemba marriage, has shown that to produce and possess children is one of the strongest ambitions of Bemba life. Writing about Northern Province, the 1938 report maintained that the effect of exodus on rural life was not great in the districts where labor moved out mainly for short periods. It was, however, more marked in Mpika and parts of Kasama District, where gradual depopulation was occurring, huts were in disrepair, and there was a decrease in acreage of land under cultivation. The cream of the manhood being away, the local labor supply was of the poorest, according to the district commissioner. In this connection, it was further noted that the Bemba space their births on a two-year basis; and as long as the period of absence was not longer than eighteen months, no great effect of exodus was felt.[23]

But if the impact of labor migration on the birthrate cannot be established firmly, the same is not the case with regard to health and pathological impairment on uniformly high fertility all over the country.

Clearly, there have been zones of pronounced relative infertility, that is, areas of the country where the birthrates have been so low that universal concern and apprehension have been generally expressed within government, medical, and even missionary circles. Thus, the famous Pim Commission *Report on Northern Rhodesia* in 1937 opined that it was still uncertain whether exodus affected fertility and the population. It emphasized, however, that venereal disease was a scourge in particular in Barotseland (Loziland) and Ila country. Noting that Livingstone remarked on its prevalence in Barotseland, the commission further observed that the disease was not of recent origin.[24] It was described as one of the plagues of Barotseland in 1875 by one Serpa Pinto, who thought it was brought there by the slave caravans from the West Coast.[25]

In Abercorn (Mbala) District a lady missionary, who for purposes of her own work made a census of two villages, was known to have observed with great surprise the absence of children.[26] In 1934 the Ila tribe in Southern Province was stated to be gradually decreasing in numbers as a result of promiscuity and venereal disease.[27] In the 1936 report R. R. Kuczynski pointed out that the conditions among the Ba-ila were discussed on 28 and 29 August 1945. Indeed, they had been raised and discussed several times in the House.[28] The situation has been described as most alarming. According to the bishop of Northern Rhodesia (a member of the Council for Native Interests), "As you visit village after village, great or small, you find but a handful of children. The schools in those parts have a struggling existence. The normal minimum number . . . is 20 but in the Ba-Ila country that regulation has to be waived."[29] Contributing to the debate, Colonel Sir Stewart Gore-Browne (Native Interests), while opposing the submission of the acting chief medical officer due to lack of services, insisted that "it is no new story, this story of the Ba-Ila. That is what makes me so bitter about it. . . . It has been known for years and years."[30]

In Balovale (Zambezi) District the average birthrate for 1929–1934 was thirty-two per thousand population, that is, lower than many other districts. Both venereal disease and the wide use of abortifacients were blamed for the low birthrate.[31] Attention was again focused on the low birthrate in Balovale District, the lowest in the territory, due largely to congenital syphilis.[32] As far back as 28 February 1887, François Coillard noted that "a very remarkable fact, which I can only indicate here, is that the *Barotsi* [Lozi] in general have small families. It is true though, that the mortality among children is very great." The 1937 *Report upon Native Affairs* dwelt on the situation in Barotse Province, noting that the birthrate was probably low owing to the high incidence of venereal disease. It further noted that the exodus of males to work in the province appeared to have had little effect on the agriculture but had tended to increase prostitution and to weaken marriage and other family ties and obligations. In these circumstances abortion was freely practiced.[33] Reference to lax morals as a consequence of the exodus of male labor to work have been raised in the reports for 1934, 1935, 1936, and 1938.[34]

But surely we are still treading on dangerous grounds. We cannot draw very firm conclusions on the overall spread and impact of the so-called pathologies implicated for lowering the birthrate (and indeed the growth rate) in certain districts of the country. The available records are limited in coverage, representativeness, and reliability. If anything, the birthrates ascertained, for example, for the period 1928–1934 suggest that fertility was very high. But we cannot confirm this with much certainty. However, it is possible that infertility was as strong as in neighboring Zaire, where it has been shown that sterility was usually high, with over 20 percent of the women past the age of menopause childless, as the following figures show:[35]

Age (Years)	30–34	35–44	45–54	55+
% Childless	22.4	22.3	20.3	28.40

In a society like Zaire, which places a high premium on fertility, the high incidence of pathological sterility and childlessness must excite critical debate. The phenomena are common notably among the Mongo-Nkundo in Equateur Province and the Azande in Orientale Province. The same is also true of the Azande in the Sudan across the border from Orientale Province. Like the various reports on Zambia, it is argued that the sterility is involuntary and physiological childlessness.[36]

More recent indications of subregional variations in fertility in Zambia are in tune with the pattern described so far for the colonial period. Using data from the 1963 and 1969 censuses of Zambia, an index of low fertility (relatively speaking) was worked out for each province. The index was simply a summation of the rank order score for mean number of children ever born to all females and to those aged forty-five to forty-nine years of age. The general rank order of scores beginning from the lowest to the highest for all provinces is shown in Table 18.2.

TABLE 18.2 Zambia by Province, 1963–1969

Province	Index of Low Fertility	
	Absolute Score	Relative
North-Western	16.0	100.0
Western (Barotse)	14.0	87.5
Southern	12.0	75.0
Central and Copperbelt	9.0	56.3
Luapula	6.0	37.5
Eastern	4.0	25.0
Northern	2.0	12.5

Attention has been drawn to Mitchell's findings, which further corroborate the results shown in Table 18.2. He found that women from Northern Province were the more fertile, while the lowest rate was recorded in Kabompo District followed by Balovale (Zambezi) District, both of which are in North-Western Province. He also inferred low fertility among the Tonga Ila of Southern Province and among the Lozi of Western (Barotse) Province.[37] These findings notwithstanding, the origins of the phenomenon remain a matter of conjecture. As can be seen from Mitchell's article, social status, urbanization, religion, diet, genetic inheritance, and disease—particularly venereal disease—have been discussed by various experts without much conclusive evidence. Clearly, not one of these variables operates or operated in isolation. There is therefore a crying need to bridge this hiatus in our knowledge about such subregional fertility differentials.

SOCIAL AND ORGANIZATIONAL FACTORS
IN MORTALITY LEVEL AND VARIATION

Mortality has and will remain the terra incognita of Central African demography. While much has been written about other variables, the study of mortality has been seriously handicapped by the greater dearth of reliable data, as a survey of the available literature will show. It is probably the one single variable about which analysis and evaluation have been forced to rely heavily on indirect statistical procedures. The poverty of mortality records has persisted all through the ages. Yet in talking about population growth, it is very clear that even with very highly reliable fertility data, the rate of growth cannot be measured without reliable index of mortality.

All through the ages, reliability of recorded mortality has been seriously plagued by the type of difficulties that surround the collection of vital statistics in Africa. In particular, it was found that Africans were reluctant to talk about deaths, especially those of children, and did not understand the motive for statistical inquiries. Besides, there was a general scarcity of qualified personnel in health and statistics. There was therefore inefficiency in measuring deaths—a feature made more serious by illiteracy and ignorance, omission of specific categories of death, and a general aversion to talk about dead relatives. *Colonial Reports upon Native Affairs* (1928–1940) are replete with references to the role of these factors in failing to promote the collection of reliable data on deaths.

Thus, historically and until recent censuses and surveys, the number of deaths in any location has never been ascertained with certainty. This fact notwithstanding, there was a consensus of opinion that the standard of health was poor. Undernourishment and disease were common afflictions. There were periods of grave undernourishment that amounted sometimes to actual famine, as has been the case in many parts of Africa, particularly the arid and semiarid zones. The Sahel, which was struck with drought during the later 1960s, early 1970s, and 1980s has suffered more than twenty droughts since the sixteenth century.[38] Given the prevailing environmental and climatic conditions, Africa will be experiencing more droughts in the future. There were also the yearly "hunger periods" coupled, in several places, with occasional severe food shortage.[39] Besides, there were common complaints about poor housing conditions even in mine locations. In 1940 it was noted that "much more urgent than the provision of increased welfare and recreational facilities is the provision of more and better housing for native workers everywhere."[40]

The inadequacy of medical services has also attracted a great deal of attention. Available services succeeded in reaching only the fringe of society, with large areas of country untouched and never visited by medical personnel, either government or missionary. A 1936 medical report stated that there were only twelve medical officers' stations in an area bigger than France, ten of which were devoted primarily to European interests. It further noted that the situation was not very greatly relieved by the maintenance of twenty-three rural dispensaries staffed by very imperfectly trained native assistants.[41] The need for improving the facilities for curative treatment for such debilitating conditions as venereal disease, ankylostomiasis, bilharzia, and other worms and malaria was emphasized by the director of medical services in the "Memorandum on Post-war Development Planning in Northern Rhodesia" submitted in 1947. The Pim Commission's report of 1938 was also highly critical of the unsatisfactory state of medical services, which it argued were monopolized by Europeans to the detriment of Africans in general.[42] The situation appeared to have deteriorated further during World War II, when there was a drastic depletion of medical staff by one-third. The paucity of curative services was very much matched by the absence of an efficient hygiene and sanitation scheme for the provision of preventive services.[43]

Against such a checkered background, is it any wonder that all the mortality measures, though roughly indicative, were on the high side? Infant mortality was generally felt to be considerably high. It has been estimated to be as high as seven hundred per thousand births, the major implicated causes being diarrhea and enteritis, poor living conditions and diet, and malaria.[44] In the seven years 1928-1934 the *Report upon Native Affairs* published infant mortality estimates that stood at 215, 210, 189, 232, 179, and 174. These figures would seem to indicate that about 20 percent of children born died while still under one year of age, as indeed the figures for Kalabo District (22 percent) for 1938 (which was considered a reasonable estimate) show.[45] But it is symptomatic of the rather confused state of affairs that Godfrey Wilson can state in his very useful study of three years later, in 1941, that the level of infant mortality was at least 50 percent.[46] Thus, the actual level or cause of infant deaths in those early years was not known with any degree of precision. Recent estimates by the United Nations put the current level for the country at 101 deaths per thousand live births. The world average for the same period, 1980–1985, was 81; it was 114 for Africa as a whole, and 92 for the less-developed regions. For the more-developed regions, the rate was only 17 deaths per thousand live births.

With regard to adult mortality in colonial times, information exists only for workers at the mines, at one of which, Roan Antelope, adult mortality was said to have declined from 34.6 deaths per thousand population in 1930 to 6.6 in 1938. This decline in so short a time appears very remarkable but cannot be said to apply to the generality of the population, which was still experiencing poor health, unsanitary living conditions, and highly deficient nutrition. There were figures indicating that cases of malaria at the mine had declined significantly from 142 in 1927 to 74 in 1929 and 50 in 1935. All the same, it is not easy to conclude that the decline of mortality at the mine was mainly due to lower incidence of malaria. Surely, a combination of factors must have been responsible, but we cannot tell precisely what these are because the diagnoses of the causes of death were rather grossly inaccurate.[47]

Based on the results of more recent censuses, the mortality condition prevailing in 1950 was estimated to be equal to a life expectancy at birth of thirty years only. Employing the 1963 census data, it was shown that the crude deathrate might lie between sixteen and twenty deaths per thousand population.[48] The results obtained from the 1969 census results were not radically different. Using different procedures, the range of the deathrates for Zambia was eighteen to nineteen deaths per thousand population; the median value was nineteen per thousand. More recently, the crude deathrate for 1980–1985 has been estimated to be fifteen per thousand; and the life expectancy at birth to be fifty-one years as against fifty-nine for the world and seventy-three for more-developed regions.

As with fertility, it has been claimed that the exodus of males to work centers has been associated with the level of mortality. We have already shown that mortality conditions were better in the mining centers of the Copperbelt than in rural areas, even though the statistics were questionable in coverage and reliability. However, the literature appears to support the view that those seeking work outside the country were on the whole more healthy than those who remained at home. The claim has been that the cream of the males migrated, leaving behind the weak, old, and infirm.[49] But how correct is this inference? Kuczynski believes that "all statements concerning the effects of internal and external migration are quite uncertain." Many observers have alluded to the evils of the practice. Unfortunately, statistics are completely lacking to show its full impact on population growth, food supply, health, mortality, and so on. We are left to speculate in confusion and uneasiness what these effects might be.[50]

But the fact that the mortality of immigrants from Zambia recorded in Zimbabwe has been all the time much higher than that of the local laborers would seem to suggest that the overall level of mortality in Zambia was, if anything, relatively high. As amply stated in the medical report of 1912 for Southern Rhodesia, "the death rate amongst the [Zambians] is out of all proportion to that of natives from [Zimbabwe] and the Portuguese territories, and is in excess, though not to the same degree of the deathrate amongst [Malawians]." Factors that tended to raise the deathrate among the Zambians were identified: it was shown that they came to their destinations usually ill-equipped and undeveloped for work in the mines; traveled much longer distances to the mines, arriving rather famished and debilitated; and were usually engaged for longer periods and were not able to terminate their contracts before they expired. On top of all this, they found themselves exposed to alien vicissitudes of life associated mostly with change of climate and the nature of work. These factors were believed to have contributed to the higher level of mortality among them. A comparison of their deathrates with those of persons at the mines in Zambia show, perhaps inconclusively, that the mortality of Zambian miners in Zimbabwe was lower than the mortality of miners in Zambia, but only in 1927 and during 1930–1934.

The social and economic gradations implied above in relation to subregional mortality differentials could also be illustrated by studying rural-urban differences. For example, in the 1955 study undertaken in Zaire by Romaniuk it was shown that the deathrate in the country was 26.1; it was 15.8 in urban areas and 28.3 in rural areas.[51] The implied variations have immense social and economic significance, even though the estimates for subdivisions of the country must have been subject to large degrees of errors. In a more recent 1978–1979 study in Zambia, it was shown that mortality, which was still very high, was considerably lower in urban than in rural areas. The general mortality level shows a crude birthrate of 20.7 for rural areas and a rather-too-low rate of 6.5 deaths per thousand population for urban areas. The infant deathrates were 120.3 and 36.5 for rural and urban areas, respectively.[52] The life expectancy at birth was estimated at 50.6 and 58.3 years for rural and urban areas. Among the three urban residential areas, children born to mothers in the squatter areas were the most disadvantaged. In general, children in low-density areas had the highest survivorship.[53]

SOCIAL AND ORGANIZATIONAL FACTORS IN MIGRATION AND THE GROWTH OF INDUSTRIAL LABOR FORCE

Both now and early in the economic history of Zambia the growth of an industrial labor force was very much linked to the migration of Africans from their traditional rural setting to urban and other industrial centers in and outside the country. To bring this about a change of the economic status and environment of Africans had to take place. But whatever stage the country has reached now in the process (particularly with respect to the type of flow and the resultant settlement pattern at the destination), there has been a combination of economic, social, and political forces at work.

The early economic development of Zambia rested very much on the growing number of immigrant European miners, farmers, and commercial men. This development was in turn responsible for the migration flows within the country and between it and the neighboring countries. The Africans in both Zambia and these countries provided a pool of cheap labor from which early industrialists (the miners in particular) obtained their work force. At first, it was not easy to attract Africans to offer their services. Therefore, they were *compelled* to work in order to find money to pay taxes, which the colonial administration imposed on them. Then there followed a period when recruitment agencies, such as the Native Labour Bureau in Southern Rhodesia (now Zimbabwe) were set up to recruit Africans for employment directly. Gradually, with changing economic circumstances, the African, under pressure to satisfy his expanded economic needs, voluntarily made his services available. So he moved to the towns, European farm areas, and other industrial sites in search of jobs. This voluntary migration began to develop about the time of the 1931 depression, during which the Native Labour Bureau stopped operating. Economic inducements triggered off by diversified wants ensured the supply of labor to industries, so much so that since 1931 the copper mines in Zambia succeeded in meeting their labor requirements from the free supply of labor, with few hindrances and demands imposed on them by recruitment procedures and rules. By then, wage earning was becoming an accepted social fact in the African's existence and survival.

Historically, it would appear that between 1919 and 1939 there has been enormous immigration from neighboring countries into Zambia, while only a few Zambians emigrated.[54] Indications are that alien Africans entering Zambia before the 1931 depression were numerous and were mainly from Malawi, Angola, and Zaire. Since 1932 the slump reduced their numbers significantly, as restrictions were also being imposed on their entry. Of 79,813 workers, 87.1 percent were Zambians, while 12.9 were not. Thus, alien labor appeared not to be highly relevant because the bulk of workers on the mines were Zambians.[55] Of those who emigrated, the bulk appeared to have migrated to Zimbabwe's gold mines and European farms and fewer to the Rand mines in South Africa, to which they were recruited by the Witwatersrand Native Labour Association, whose permission to recruit labor in Zambia and Malawi was withdrawn in July 1912. Other places, though not major destinations, included Mozambique, Tanzania, and the Katanga mines in Zaire.

While these estimates may be unreliable because of their poor quality base, the position thereafter was not more promising either, and it remained so up to the recent population censuses. This fact notwithstanding, it is necessary to bear in mind the possible impact of all these past migrations to job centers on the socioeconomic conditions of the sending districts in

Zambia. A lot has been written on the consequences of rural exodus occasioned by the migrations—its impact on marital stability, fertility, agricultural productivity, and so on. However, so much depends on the duration of absence from the districts. Obviously, short periods of absence would not have led to the destabilizing or disruptive consequences associated with rural exodus. But when the duration is long, invariably, it would have generated all the dislocations associated with it. Also, it was important to know whether some men moved to work centers with their wives and whether female migration of some sort was allowed to these centers. These possibilities would have helped to cushion the effects of exodus on both new and existing family formation. Old marriages will thus maintain their fertility, while new ones could be contracted.

It was already indicated that early colonial exodus to towns and work sites did not mainly lead to permanent settlement there or (therefore) to total loss of the male migrants to their rural districts. The situation was such that the males did not abandon their traditional roots but (as J. C. Mitchell had argued) circulated between town and country. Among the Bemba, for instance, the effect was severe; but among the Plateau Tonga, it was not.[56] But quite apart from rootedness in the traditional setting and the need to meet the implied obligations of the kinship group, the Africans also had to return home again and again because conditions at the labor centers and European farms to which migrants went were not conducive to permanent settlement. According to Lord Hailey, the colonial government was convinced that the African's normal and rightful place of residence was the tribal area and that only the need for job and money brought him to towns and the European farming areas.[57]

Thus, with inadequate housing and family accommodation and difficult conditions for land ownership, settled family life in the towns was not encouraged. Indeed, where such facilities existed (for instance, more married accommodations in Zambia than in Zimbabwe), married men had their wives with them.[58] This instability of residence therefore supported the circulation of labor, a situation much encouraged by the existence of a pool of surplus young workers from which new recruitments were easily effected. Thus, demographic, social, political, legal, and economic factors sustained the system. The reversal of the process to the current state of affairs has also been due to a complex set of interrelated factors. First, rapid population growth accompanied by rising expectation and standard of living encouraged further exodus to towns. Since the rural areas have limited opportunities for fulfilling expectations, people naturally gravitated to the towns. Then, of course, there followed improvements in housing conditions and the possibility of acquiring accommodation. Land rights were subsequently conferred on Africans in 1957 to allow them to lease plots in urban areas and build their own houses. At the same time, a housing loan scheme for Africans was also established. With the dawn of independence, more favorable legal and political actions have further enhanced African economic opportunities and speeded up the reversal process. But the turnaround is not total and complete; for while more permanent urban settlements have resulted, Africans, especially older ones, still maintain their links with their traditional kinship roots.

So since independence in 1964, migration has continued to be an important component of population growth and distribution in response to social and regional variations in employment and economic opportunities. As is clearly illustrated by the analysis of both the 1963 and 1969 population censuses, movements continued to take place as a result of differential job and economic opportunities, first between rural and urban areas and then specifically between industrial and nonindustrial locations. Thus, Copperbelt and Central Provinces,[59] which, broadly speaking, constitute the economic, commercial, political, and administrative nerve centers along the important rail line of Zambia, were the most important poles of attraction for most migrants. Copperbelt Province, in particular, continued to command economic and commercial supremacy, thanks to its rich copper mines, as well as the other industries drawn by the needs both of the mines themselves and the miners and their families. Taking all out-migrants in 1969, 52.6 percent ended up in Copperbelt (26.4 percent) and Central (26.2 percent) Provinces. North-Western (3.2 percent) and Western (4.1 percent) Provinces attracted the least number of migrants. The proportion for the remaining provinces were Southern (13.1 percent), Northern (10.2 percent), Luapula (8.8 percent), and Eastern (8.0 percent).

Between 1963 and 1969 the rural population grew by an average annual rate of .5 percent, while the urban population increased by an annual rate of 8.9 percent. This large disparity is apparently a function of the remarkable population gains through migration from the rural to the urban areas. Indeed, migration, very much more than natural increase, accounted for the marked variation in growth between regions and subregions. In Central and Copperbelt Provinces, 61.9 and 67.2 percent, respectively, of the total intercensal increase were due to net migration gains from other provinces in the period. The Copperbelt gained 89,427 persons through natural increase and 183,417 through net migration; the figures for Central Province were, respectively, 79,044 and 128,422 persons. The type of urban-directed migration under discussion has continued to be dominated by males, particularly, the young, able-bodied ones.[60]

Migration was also closely linked to educational and employment conditions and status. Not only had the urban areas attracted more educated migrants, they also had more and better educational facilities, so that migrants living in towns improved their education or acquired one. Indeed, the more urbanized localities had larger proportions of educated persons. Similarly, the urban and European farming areas, as shown by the census results, had a marked proportion of their males in paid employment. Of greater significance is the fact that the bulk of the urban wage earners (about nine-tenths, representing 53.5 percent of all male employees) were found in the ten major towns of Zambia in 1963. Two of the towns, Lusaka and Kitwe, had the largest pool, amounting to well over one-fifth of Zambia's wage earners. The main Copperbelt towns alone harbored 40.2 percent of all wage earners in Zambia and, in fact, 67.6 percent of all those in the urban areas.

Migrant destinations were not only those in the country. As in the past, international movement of labor between Zambia and its neighbors continued at the same time, as there had been significant inflow of refugees also from the countries bordering Zambia. In 1963 African immigrants born outside Zambia but in Africa formed 6.7 percent of the national African population. The proportion in 1969 was understood to be 5.1 percent and might have been lower because the group included some persons of other races. In 1963 Malawi (27.6 percent), Zimbabwe (23.4 percent), and Angola (26.2 percent) contributed over three-quarters of the total immigrants. Some 7.6 percent came from Mozambique, 7.3 from Zaire, and 5.4 from Tanzania. This pattern persisted in 1969 except that there was a decline in the numbers from Angola and Mozambique.

It has been clearly shown elsewhere that these African immigrants have been coming to work in the copper mines of Zambia.[61] However, it has also been indicated that they also came to work, and settled, in the rural area. The 1963 census showed that about 60 percent of the African immigrants were in the rural area, 7.7 percent in the European farming area, and 32.3 percent in the urban area.

The decline in the flow of immigrants is not unconnected with socioeconomic and political developments in the subregion. The promotion of national self-reliance, indigenization, and Africanization of jobs and the economy have been pursued successfully not just by Zambia but also by the sending countries. While this reduced opportunities for prospective immigrants to Zambia, it also simultaneously opened new ones for them at home. But the flow has only been reduced in volume and intensity. It will no doubt, with the passage of time, become more and more selective, depending on the extent to which indigenous labor can be readily used to substitute for imported skill.

NOTES

The views expressed in this chapter are not necessarily those of the United Nations Secretariat.

1. R. R. Kuczynski, *Demographic Survey of the British Colonial Empire*, 3 vols. (London, 1948–1949), 407–409.

2. A. Romaniuk, "The Demography of the Republic of the Congo," in W. Brass et al., eds., *The Demography of Tropical Africa* (Princeton, 1968), 242.

3. Northern Rhodesia, *Legislative Council Debates*, vol. 50, col. 21.

4. P. O. Ohadike, "Counting Heads in Africa: The Experience of Zambia, 1963 and 1969," *Journal of Administration Overseas* 9 (1970), 248.

5. P. O. Ohadike, "Demographic Measurements for Africans in Zambia: An Appraisal of the 1963 Census Administration and Results," Communication no. 5 (University of Zambia, 1969), 4.

6. Romaniuk, "Demography," 241–251.

7. P. O. Ohadike and H. Tesfaghiorghis, *The Population of Zambia*, CICRED Series for the World Population Year 1974 (Gap, France, 1975), 17–23.

8. G. Kay, *A Social Geography of Zambia* (London, 1967), 83–85.

9. J. A. Barnes, *Marriage in a Changing Society: A Study in Structural Change Among the East Jameson Ngoni* (London, 1951), 11.

10. E. van de Walle, "Characteristics of African Demographic Data," in Brass et al., eds., *Demography*, Table 5.7.

11. Ohadike, "Demographic Measurements," Table 3.9, p. 58.

12. See Romaniuk, "Demography," 229 for parallel results for Zaire. The study shows that the total fertility rate for women (single, widowed, and divorced) was 61.7 per hundred women aged fifteen to forty-four years; it was 143.9 for those in monogamous consensual unions and 217.2 for those in monogamous formal marriages. Hence, for those in monogamous unions as a whole, the rate was 120.9, as opposed to 140.7 for those in polygamous unions.

13. M. McCulloch, *A Social Survey of the African Population of Livingstone*, Rhodes-Livingstone Paper, no. 26 (Lusaka, 1956), 20.

14. H. V. Musham, "Fertility of Polygamous Marriage," *Population Studies* 10 (1956), 3–16; Vernon Dorjan, "Interrelations in Temne Society," *American Anthropologist* 60 (1958), 838–860.

15. Meyer Fortes, "A Demographic Field Study in Ashanti," in F. Lorimer et al., *Culture and Human Fertility* (Paris, 1954), 307–308; Romaniuk, "Demography," 229.

16. Romaniuk ("Demography," 226) indicates in his 1955–1957 study in Zaire that polygyny as a recognized institution has all but disappeared in the towns in Zaire, presumably due to economic conditions and to social and legal prohibition. It became illegal there to contract new polygynous unions after 1951. This precipitated a conflict between law and custom. The death of polygyny in towns without legal prohibition will follow naturally, since they no longer have important agricultural sectors in which polygyny retains its social value.

17. Kuczynski, *Demographic Survey*, 485–487.

18. Northern Rhodesia, *Legislative Council Debates*, vol. 50, 448.

19. Ohadike and Tesfaghiorghis, *Population*, 43.

20. J. C. Mitchell, "Differential Fertility Among Urban Africans in Zambia," *Rhodes-Livingstone Journal* 37 (1965), 1–25; Romaniuk, "Demography," 331–332.

21. Northern Rhodesia, *Report upon Native Affairs*, 1931, p. 32.

22. Northern Rhodesia, *Report*, 1932, p. 14.

23. Northern Rhodesia, *Report*, 1938, p. 54.

24. Pim Commission, *Report on Northern Rhodesia* (1937), pp. 7, 39, and 292.

25. Northern Rhodesia, *Report*, 1935, p. 91.

26. Northern Rhodesia, *Report*, 1933.

27. Northern Rhodesia, *Report*, 1934, p. 12; see also 1936, p. 30; 1937,

p. 41; and 1938, p. 32 (which describes the situation as nothing short of suicide).

28. See Northern Rhodesia, *Legislative Council Debates*, vol. 1, cols. 398, 441–442; vol. 46, cols. 400–401, 427–428, 535.

29. Northern Rhodesia, *Legislative Council Debates,* vol. 51, col. 41.

30. Northern Rhodesia, *Legislative Council Debates*, vol. 51, cols. 151–152.

31. Northern Rhodesia, *Report*, 1934, p. 13.

32. Northern Rhodesia, *Report*, 1936, p. 86.

33. Northern Rhodesia, *Report*, 1937, p. 101.

34. Northern Rhodesia, *Report*, 1934, p. 28; 1935, p. 8; 1936, p. 72; and 1938, pp. 75–76.

35. Romaniuk, "Demography," Table 6.47, p. 331.

36. Romaniuk, "Demography," 337.

37. Mitchell, "Differential Fertility," 8.

38. Food and Agriculture Organization and Organization of African Unity, *Famine in Africa* (Rome, 1982), 3–9.

39. Northern Rhodesia, *Medical Report*, 1941, p. 1.

40. Northern Rhodesia, *Labour Department Report*, 1940, pp. 2–3.

41. Northern Rhodesia, *Medical Report*, 1936, p. 1.

42. A Pim and S. Milligan, *Report of the Commission Appointed to Enquire into the Financial and Economic Position of Northern Rhodesia* (Colonial no. 145 of 1938), 288–291.

43. Northern Rhodesia, *Report on Health Services Development Plan, 1945–55*, 6–7.

44. Northern Rhodesia, *Medical Report*, 1926, pp. 16–17.

45. Northern Rhodesia, *Report*, 1938, p. 89.

46. G. Wilson, *Essays on the Economics of Detribalization in Northern Rhodesia*, pt. 1 (1941), 50.

47. See Northern Rhodesia, *Medical Report*, 1928, p. 24; also 1938, p. 4, and 1939, p. 2.

48. P. O. Ohadike, *Medical Report, Demographic Measurements* (1969), 9.

49. Northern Rhodesia, *Report*, 1938, p. 54; also 1936, p. 72; idem, *Legislative Council Debates*, vol. 28, col. 223.

50. Rita Hinden, *Plan for Africa* (London, 1941), 90.

51. Romaniuk, "Demography," Table 6.36.

52. UNECA, *Interrelationships Among Infant and Childhood Mortality, Socioeconomic Factors and Fertility in Zambia: A Case Study of Lusaka and Keembe*, E/ECA/POP/11 (Addis Ababa, 1984), 144–146.

53. UNECA, *Interrelationships*, 156–157.

54. Kuczynski, *Demography*, 442.

55. Kuczynski, *Demography*, 433.

56. J. C. Mitchell, "Wage Labour and African Population Movements in Central Africa," in K. M. Barbour and R. M. Prothero, eds., *Essays on African Population* (London, 1961), 236.

57. Lord Hailey, *An African Survey* (London, 1956), 565, 677.

58. Mitchell, "Differential Fertility," 238–240.

59. At the time of the 1969 census Central Province included present-day Lusaka Province.

60. Ohadike and Tesfaghiorghis, *Population*, 102–103.

61. P. O. Ohadike, *Development of, and Factors in, the Employment of African Migrants in the Copper Mines of Zambia, 1940–66*, Zambia Papers, no. 4 (Manchester, 1969).

Comments

OSEI-MENSAH ABORAMPAH

The demographic history of Zambia dates back to 1921, when the British colonial administration made the first attempt to count the people. This exercise was repeated with some regularity.

The quality of the returns of these preindependence censuses has remained suspect because of a multiplicity of problems that have plagued African resources: inaccessibility to some locations and age misreporting are a few examples that Ohadike points out. Consequently, it is difficult to use them to gauge past population trends accurately.

Postindependence Zambia has witnessed rapid improvements in censustaking. As discussed by Ohadike, the 1963, 1969, 1974, and 1979 censuses or sample surveys all improved on previous methods and scope of data collection. Even then, available data do not provide a sufficient basis to determine age and sex structure, marriage and family formations, fertility, mortality, migration, and growth of the labor force with the degree of accuracy that Ohadike would have required for analysis of the dynamics of Zambian population change.

In spite of these problems, Ohadike provides a fairly comprehensive picture of the social and organizational factors that affected these vital rates. In particular, he employs the pre- and postindependence census figures to portray the Zambian age and sex structure, in which there is a preponderance of males in urban and employment centers. Apparently, a normal age structure follows a typical pattern of large numbers in the youngest ages of each sex, with gradual declines in subsequent age groups. Precisely because of the inadequate nature of the Zambian age and sex distributions, a composite of the distribution of all, or selected, African countries would provide a clearer picture of the extent of distortions in the Zambian data.

Concerning marriage and family formation, Ohadike considers the traditional value placed on marriage and family and demonstrates statistically the relationship between marital status and fertility. The proportion married has a positive association with fertility, while the proportions never married, divorced, and widowed (i.e., single) are negatively related to fertility. The impacts of age at first marriage, duration of marriage, and polygyny are also discussed. The first two factors affect fertility in predictable ways. Evidence for the latter is inconclusive. Indeed, in my own work on the Yoruba of Western Nigeria, I found no significant relationship between the two variables. Interestingly, Ohadike suggests that the practice of polygyny will continue to prevail in Zambia, especially in the rural areas, because of differential mortality and age at marriage of the sexes and a related factor of recruitment of females from the younger ages. That is, no doubt, going to be the case for many African countries.

Perhaps another variable worth considering in the marriage-fertility relationship is the age of nubility. Given the matrilineal kinship structure of the Ila, Bemba, and other groups in Zambia, one would expect the likelihood of marriage to vary significantly with the age of nubility. Early or late age at marriage could be accounted for, in part, by the age of nubility.

Late age at marriage is also influenced by education, and the impact of education on fertility may be indirect through delayed marriage. While the inverse relationship between education and fertility cannot be doubted, it is important to note that the causal chain is complicated by a phenomenon I have called "education by installment." Many highly educated African women attained their educational level over long and interrupted periods of time. Certain parity levels were achieved long before the attainment of present educational levels.

In general, Zambia's birthrates have been high (fifty per thousand by 1969 count), and the fertility level is similar to those of East and West Africa. Regional, ethnic, and other differentials prevail due to the uneven developmental process, male exodus to industrial centers, and sterility in certain areas caused by venereal diseases. Ohadike calls for more multivariate analyses to disentangle the independent and joint effect of these factors.

Ordinarily, the incidence of death should be the easiest to measure, since the event occurs only once in a lifetime. However, the social organization surrounding death in Zambia—as elsewhere in Africa—in the sense of people's reluctance to talk about it has made it nearly impossible to ascertain the mortality level in Zambia. Nonetheless, many of the causes of death were known in the colonial era: disease, undernourishment, famine, poor housing for mine workers, and inadequate medical services. The high birth- and infant mortality rates have declined due to health and other improvements. Recent UN estimates place the Zambian deathrate at fifteen per thousand and life expectancy at fifty-one years, although considerable rural-urban differentials prevail.

According to Ohadike, a combination of political, economic, and social factors account for labor migration in Zambia. Early economic development was associated with European immigration. This development was also partly responsible for the migration flows (both voluntary and involuntary) within the country.

Colonial tax policies forced able-bodied, male rural workers to migrate to mines and other employment centers. Ohadike suggests that the impact of rural exodus on marital stability, fertility, and agricultural productivity depends on the duration of stay. He argues that migrants circulated between town and country because settled family life in town was discouraged, given inadequate housing and other conditions. Copperbelt and Central Provinces (the economic, industrial, political, and social nerve centers) have attracted the most migrants. Migration has been, and will continue to be, selective of able-bodied young males, as well as the educated and the highly skilled.

Bruce Fetter and others have questioned the assumptions of stable populations and constant fertility in colonial Africa by African demographers. The argument is that migration played a major role (rather than the assigned minor one) in the chain of factors that influenced vital events. To the extent that the zero migration and constant fertility assumptions do not approximate reality, it becomes even more important to understand the social and organizational variables that impinge on the intervening variables. To what extent did colonial tax policies influence migration decisionmaking, for example? What implications did the sex ratio imbalances caused by male exodus have for marriage, family formation, or fertility?

The high regime of reproduction in African societies continues to amaze observers. Yet efforts to understand the social and institutional factors that supported this regime have been minimal. Ohadike gives the impression that prolific childbearing was encouraged. One could expect that social, cultural, and other institutions made it not only possible but also desirable for women to bear children all through their reproductive years. Preferential marriages and public ceremonies of congratulations could be instituted to encourage reproduction, which in turn could ensure perpetuation of the lineage. The problem is that although high fertility levels may be sustained by the ideals and values implicit in the traditional social organization, we have very little knowledge about how these translate themselves into reproductive behavioral patterns. For example, the role of husband's and wife's lineages—the intricate system of decisionmaking and obligations that may extend far beyond the nuclear family—is often neglected.

Specifically, what fertility implications does one ascertain from what J. Caldwell calls the African "family morality and theology" or (in the case of Central Africa) what A. Richards calls the "matrilineal puzzle"? Of course, Ohadike has not addressed these problems; for colonial officers knew too little about African marriage and family life, notions of sexuality, and attitudes toward pregnancy and having children to be able to prepare demographically comprehensive reports.

Whether or not a couple brings forth many children depends, in part, on what K. Davis, J. Blake, and J. Bongaarts call the "proximate" variables, which are largely shaped by social and organizational factors. I suggest that whoever is engaged in such a delicate matter as family planning cannot do so without a clear insight into what people feel and think about procreation, which has its basis in traditional social organization. In this regard, whatever we can learn from colonial censuses and other demographic data can only be a step in the right direction.

PART 3

CASE STUDIES

19

Studying the Population of French Equatorial Africa

RITA HEADRICK

Interest in the demography of colonial Africa is part of an assessment of the changes the European takeover wrought in the lives of Africans. On the most basic level the important questions are whether or not people lived longer, had more children, were healthier, and were better nourished than before. On a global level the question is whether the population was rising or falling.

These simple questions are difficult to answer anywhere in colonial Africa; but data is particularly lacking for vast, underadministered French Equatorial Africa (AEF), a federation divided into the four colonies of Gabon, Moyen-Congo, Ubangi-Shari (now the Central African Republic), and Chad. (See Map 19.1.) The awkwardly shaped territory was described as a figure eight on the equator. It was one of the most sparsely populated colonies and had very little to offer France in the way of economic assets. There were neither minerals in AEF nor mines in neighboring territories depending on AEF's labor nor important agricultural products. A small timber industry confined to coastal Gabon generated most of the income from export products.

The French were more concerned about population size than were the other European colonizers. They easily transferred their historical preoccupation with population and low birthrates at home to their African colonies, more thinly populated than their rivals' territories. Even their language showed their engagement: regions did not just have low density or fertility indexes, they had "worrisome," "lamentable," "not brilliant," "unsatisfactory," or "dishonorable" indexes.[1]

Concern about the population, however, did not lead to demographic studies. French Equatorial Africa was governed from hand to mouth. A scientific study of the population, despite its obvious economic payoff, was an investment the colony could not afford. There was no manpower to count the dispersed population and no womanpower to investigate aspects of fertility or infant loss that might be hidden from men.

MAP 19.1 French Equatorial Africa Administrative Districts

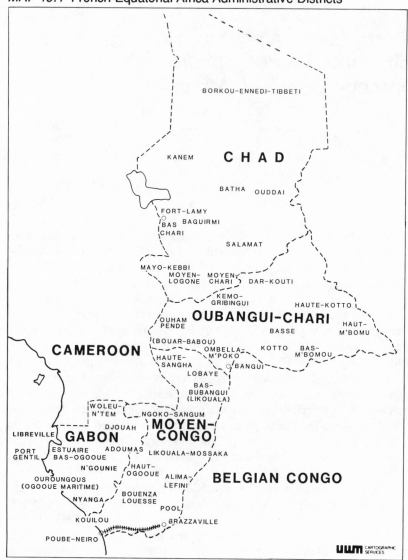

THE SOURCES FOR DEMOGRAPHIC STUDIES
OF FRENCH EQUATORIAL AFRICA

The history of demography in AEF followed a pattern found in most of Africa. The original estimates of population were grossly inflated for public relations reasons or through honest mistakes. Explorers took the denser populations along rivers to be characteristic of the whole territory, and the early administrators could not believe such a large territory contained so few people.

The first census rolls were compiled in the 1920s. As elsewhere in Africa, the primary motivation was collecting the head taxes that were gradually being imposed on the population. The censuses were rarely established after careful head counts. Rather, chiefs would report on the population of their villages; and administrators might follow with a cursory check, without careful inquiry as to those hunting, fishing, or working in the fields. There was a built-in bias against accurate counts of the nonassessed population: old people and, especially, children.[2]

The census rolls from the 1920s and 1930s can be found attached to local and annual reports and to the reports of the health service.[3] The latter are often more accurate than the administrators' counts, but they are available only for several years in the 1930s. Published lists of population by colony or circumscription appeared occasionally in *L'Afrique française*, a journal of the colonial lobby, and the *Annuaire statistique*.[4] Population figures are also given in the monumental demographic study of Gabon and Moyen-Congo by Gilles Sautter, *De l'Atlantique au fleuve Congo: Une géographie du sous-peuplement*.

There are familiar problems with much of this data. Population counts showed a continual growth in the population, but the crucial question is how much of this was due to the submission of new groups to French authority and taxation. Apparent population increases were often only a reflection of an extended fiscal apparatus. The raw data must also be used with great care because of frequent boundary changes between subdivisions, circumscriptions, and colonies, the three levels of local administration. (An ephemeral reorganization in the mid-1930s renamed the circumscriptions *departments*.) There are simply no shortcuts to carefully following the border shifts that appeared in the *Journal officiel* and adjusting the numbers accordingly. Finally, on the most mundane level, the data in this precalculator age is riddled with errors, both arithmetical and typographical. Errors got incorporated into the data and carried through from year to year. Censuses of a colony contained mixtures of circumscription populations from different years. Whole circumscriptions disappeared from the rolls because they had been dropped from the colony they used to be in (for example, Moyen-Congo) and not yet incorporated into figures from the colony they had just been transferred to (for example, Ubangi-Shari). Most seriously, the heavily-relied-on *Annuaire statistique* contains statistics for Ubangi-Shari in 1933 in which the population figures for five circumscriptions belongs to the circumscription one line above.

Any really sophisticated demographic work on colonial AEF must be preceded by searching the archives for all the data available and investigating how they were generated. The census rolls must be correlated with the presence and movements of administrators to determine whether it is likely to be accurate and whether increases only represented the extension of administration. Last of all comes the unromantic job of checking the series of figures for discrepancies, omissions, and errors.

Despite the difficulties with the data, these early censuses are not without value. Gilles Sautter believes that widespread attempts to evade the censuses were confined to crises periods, such as recruitment for the railroad from 1925 to 1930.[5] The census figures from 1920 in the three southern colonies show a regularity and consistency compatible with what we know about fertility and the extension of administrative control. For Chad, however, the census data remained irregular and unreliable.

In the years after World War II population figures for AEF were published in the *Annuaire statistique* and in several specialized articles.[6] However, there were no demographic surveys of the population at large. In fact, the first census designed by professionals was a study of Europeans and other foreigners, giving breakdowns by age, origin, profession, and residence.[7]

Professional demographers were not yet ready to tackle the population as a whole in the 1950s; but sociologists, geographers, and demographers employed either by the administration or by government-funded scientific organizations displayed an enormous interest in the ballooning urban centers of AEF. They studied Libreville, Pointe-Noire, Bangui, and the African sections of Brazzaville.[8] Though the studies differ in scope and emphasis, most were concerned with the rate of growth of urban centers and the source of immigrants; the age and sex structure of urban dwellers; their occupations, salaries, and rate of unemployment; and the ethnic composition of neighborhoods or occupations.

It was not until the year of independence that true censuses were attempted in AEF and its successor states. Professional censustakers using sampling techniques and interviewing undertook the first real study of the population as a whole. The results were published for the Congo in Service de Statistique, *Enquête démographique 1960–61: Résultats définitifs* (Paris, 1965); for the Central African Republic (formerly Ubangi-Shari) in Service de la Coopération, (Paris, 1964); for Gabon in Service National de la Statistique, *Recensements et enquête démographique en république centrafricaine 1959–60: Résultats définitifs* (Paris, 1965); and for Chad several years later in Service de la Statistique, *Enquête démographique au Tchad 1964: Résultats définitifs* (Paris, 1966).[9]

The census of Gabon covered the entire country. That of the Congo excluded the cities of Brazzaville and Pointe-Noire but included a detailed study of the third, far smaller, town of Dolisie. The census of the Central African Republic omitted Bangui and the sparsely populated eastern third of the country. Much of the data was grouped into three fairly homogeneous zones: the relatively densely populated west with its mixture of people; the center, almost exclusively Banda; and the people along the river, known for their low fertility. Chad's census excluded the desert and many nomadic groups in the Sahel, Kanem, and Fort-Lamy. Comparisons were made between north (actually the central band of Chad) and south. The former were Muslim herders and farmers in the six prefectures of central Chad. The latter contained Christian and animist farmers, half of whom were Sara, in the five southern prefectures.

Although these censuses were carried out in the early 1960s, they are very useful for the colonial period both because of their retrospective data and because they help explain some of the distortion in earlier population counts. Most interesting is the data on number of children and final parity of women of different ages and ethnic groups, which contribute greatly to a history of fertility in AEF. The censuses also confirmed the differential classifications of adolescent boys and girls. Many prewar tables showed more boys than girls but more women than men, figures that led also to low child-woman ratios. Adolescent girls, who matured earlier than boys and were often engaged or married, would be classified as women. Boys of the same age, however, would be counted as children, especially if their families misrepresented their age to avoid the head tax. The age pyramids from the censuses showed a clear contraction of the population at age ten or fifteen, as boys were retained in younger cohorts, and girls were pushed into younger or older cohorts depending on their marital status. (See Figures 19.1 and 19.2.) During the teen years boys outnumbered girls even where they were in the minority as children and adults. The censuses revealed consistent patterns of underestimating one-year-olds because they were often counted as babies if they were not yet walking or as two-year-olds if they were. Imprecision about age also came out in the improbable clustering of reported ages into years ending with five or zero.

In some respects, however, these censuses are less useful for colonial history. The new governments were more interested in the demographic results of modernization, urbanization, and education than of geography, environment, nutrition, or ethnicity. Thus, the censuses will compare fertility or marital patterns of those who lived in traditional villages with those in the new towns (*centres extra-coutumiers*) or those with different levels of education. It is much more difficult to compare the fertility of inhabitants of the forest with those of the savanna or those of regions more or less disturbed by colonialism. Especially disappointing is the lack of more precise data by ethnic groups. This was partly because ethnic labeling and

FIGURE 19.1 Central African Republic Census, 1959–1960

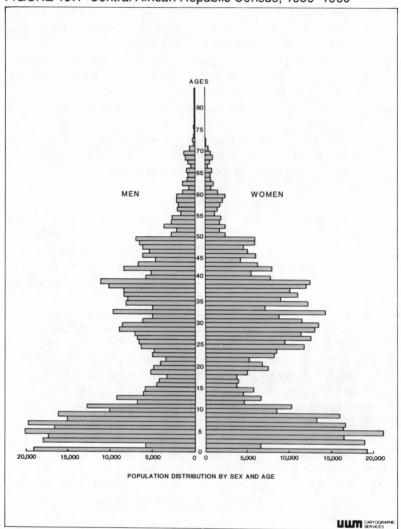

FIGURE 19.2 Congo Census, 1960–1961

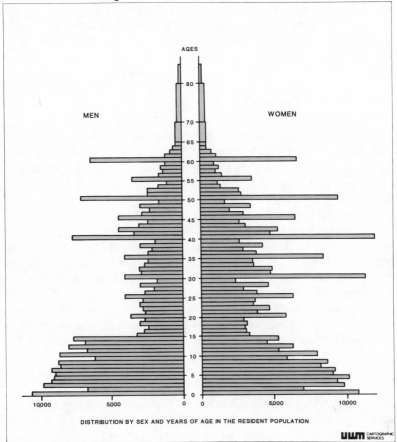

DISTRIBUTION BY SEX AND YEARS OF AGE IN THE RESIDENT POPULATION

grouping are delicate tasks and also because many of the groups were too small for the samples to be statistically significant. However, governments may also have feared that such data was potentially explosive, since ethnic tensions ran high in the late 1950s, as groups jockeyed for political power and came into conflict in crowded urban areas.

FERTILITY IN FRENCH EQUATORIAL AFRICA

Fertility was the most important determinant of population growth and density in AEF. Apart from localized epidemics or administrative exactions, mortality rates did not vary greatly by region or ethnic group. Birthrates, sterility rates, and final parity (number of live births per woman), however, were much less uniform.

Location correlated positively with fertility. Fertility in AEF increased with distance from the equator up to the Sahel, where it declined. A cause or effect of this relationship was that savanna dwellers had higher fertility than groups that inhabited the forest. Gabon was always the region of lowest fertility. Moyen-Congo and Ubangi-Shari have similar indexes, but this is because the highly fertile Bakongo people raise the average fertility of the southern colony. People from the south of Chad had even higher fertility than in Ubangi-Shari, but the numbers fell as you continued north to the middle belt between savanna and Sahara. (See Map 19.2 and Table 19.1.)[10]

Gabon

Gabon presents the clearest evidence in AEF of rising infertility during the colonial years. The colony was almost entirely rain forest; and despite differences among them, almost all ethnic groups suffered from high sterility rates.

The direct medical cause of sterility among women who were examined was blockages in the fallopian tubes due to scarring and lesion from infection.[11] Doctors suspected that the infectious agent was usually gonorrhea. Why gonorrhea or other infections should be so virulent in Gabon is unclear, but the rain forest environment in equatorial Africa was populated with low-fertility groups in Moyen-Congo and the Belgian Congo as well. Malaria may also have contributed to infertility because it can cause miscarriages, which lead to sterilizing infections. The poverty of rain forest diets may also have played a role. In any case, before the European presence could have touched more than a minute percentage of Gabonese women, sterility rates were high in comparison with other regions of AEF. Of Gabonese women born before 1890 20 percent had never had a living child, compared with 13 percent and 14 percent for the other three colonies.[12]

The percentage of sterile women in Gabon increased steadily during the

MAP 19.2 French Equatorial Africa Climate Zones

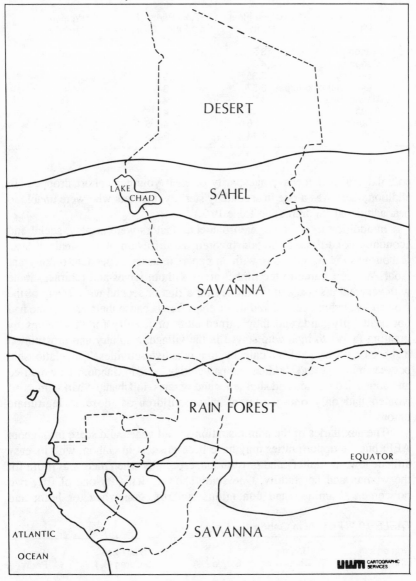

TABLE 19.1 Fertility of Women Born Before 1910

Place	Average Final Parity	Final Parity of Most Ethnic Groups	Women Sterile (%)
Gabon	3.20	2+	26
Congo	4.33	3+	15
Bakongo	5.35	5+	—
Other ethnic groups	3.57	3+	—
Ubangi-Shari	4.21	4+	14
Chad	4.48	4+, 5	12
South	4.86	4+, 5	13
North	4.14	3+, 5	11

colonial era, and the average parity of each younger cohort dropped. In addition, there was a rise in secondary sterility, mothers who were unable to bear additional children. (See Table 19.2.)[13]

In addition to whatever environmental factors were at play, social and economic conditions in Gabon favored the diffusion of venereal disease. Gabon was the only colony with an export industry dependent on migrant labor. Workers came to the timber areas without wives and returned home with venereal disease and the money for a first or second wife. Many of the women left behind considered themselves free because their bride-price had not been fully paid, and they earned cloth or jewelry for themselves by granting favors to men who stayed in the village. Adultery and prostitution had been transformed from culpable to productive activities. The relationship between marriage and children was particularly loose in Gabon, where married and unmarried women had similar fecundity rates. In Ubangi-Shari unmarried women had only one-quarter as many children as those in legitimate unions.[14]

The auxiliaries of the administration spread venereal disease throughout AEF; but the opportunities may have been greatest in Gabon, with its easy attitude toward adultery and prostitution, especially when there was profit for the woman and her family. One study showed that fifty-one of fifty-two policemen examined had contagious syphilis, gonorrhea, or both; and

TABLE 19.2 Fertility in Gabon

Women's Birth Year	Bearing Children	Sterile (%)	3 or More Children (%)	Final Parity
Before 1890	Before 1924	20	50	3.48
1890–1894	1905–1929	22	51	3.40
1895–1899	1910–1934	26	49	3.20
1900–1904	1915–1939	27	48	3.14
1905–1909	1920–1944	30	43	2.80
1910–1914	1925–1949	32	43	2.78
1915–1919	1930–1954	36	38	2.40

eighteen of twenty-four interpreters, guards, or domestic servants were contagious.[15] An investigation of fertility in the 1930s in Gabon showed what happened in "regions of intense traffic and prostitution." (See Table 19.3.)[16]

TABLE 19.3 Frequented vs. Isolated Regions in Gabon

Place	Number of Women	Sterile (%)	Children/ Woman	Children/ Fertile Woman
Near posts and on major routes	4,839	51	1.05	2.13
In the interior	5,984	34	1.64	2.48

Taxes also drove women to prostitution. "Taxes are so high," wrote one doctor "that in regions without commerce, women are obliged to come down to the commercial establishments on the banks of the river."[17] Women in prison were contaminated by the guards. Despite the administration's concern about venereal disease, its own auxiliaries and policies did more to spread them than its health service did to eradicate them.

The census data does not allow a complete investigation into the causes of low fertility. The ethnic categories of the census, for the most part, are umbrella terms that conceal tremendous variations and do not allow correlations with the natural environment, degree of contact with the colonial state, or participation in the export economy. Without that data all we can say with certainty is that sterility and infertility rose significantly in Gabon during the colonial period.

Moyen-Congo

Unlike Gabon, retrospective data from the Congo census of 1960–1961 indicated that fertility remained rather constant until after World War II, at which point the birthrate rose sharply. For women whose procreative years spanned the length of European colonialism, that is, for women born from before 1890 to those born before 1919, sterility rose only from 14 percent to 17 percent and final parity from 3.98 children to 4.14 children per woman.[18] This rise in final parity is more likely due to the better memories of younger women than to an actual rise in numbers of children born alive.

Unfortunately, the Congo census does not give retrospective data by ethnic groups or administrative division. This loss is acute because sections of the census and other studies suggest important differences between savanna and forest people and also suggest that the steady Congolese averages may conceal a rising Bakongo birthrate, while other groups' birthrates declined.

Throughout the colonial period the Bakongo were known for their large families. A Belgian inquiry in 1930 found that only 2.4 percent of women in the lower Congo born before 1885 had never been pregnant. The primary explanation for the fertility lay in a social structure that favored marital stability and discouraged divorce, as well as the marriage of girls too young for safe pregnancies. "The women are more reserved, the unions are more solid. The terrible sanctions against adultery have fallen into disuse . . . but marriage keeps its character and function."[19] An early report suggested the occasional cases of infertility resulted from infections, lacerations, or malpositioned uteruses caused by previous births, not by gonorrhea, as in chronically infertile groups.[20]

The people of the rain forest and northern marshes of the Congo, on the other hand, were declining. The "river races" had always had fewer children and kept up their numbers by incorporating in other groups by marriage or buying slave children. The region had been hard hit by sleeping sickness and was not recovering. As in Gabon, the money and family separation connected with export production (here palm oil and rubber gathering) favored the spread of venereal disease. This is also one region for which unambiguous evidence exists for provoked abortion and contraception by means of local plants as infusions or douches.[21]

The limited data extractable from the Congolese census on fertility over time also points to a decline among forest groups. Table 19.4[22] shows a definite drop in parity for women in three of the four forest groups—Kota, Sangha, and Makaa—and a slight rise for the M'Beti. The savanna groups have less dramatic differences, although the M'Bochi seem to suffer from lowered fertility.

TABLE 19.4 Fertility in Forest (F) and Savanna (S) Groups in Moyen-Congo

Ethnic Group	Percent of Population	Average Parity of Women Born	
		Before 1910	1911–1920
Bakongo (S)	47	5.35	5.30
Batéké (S)	20	3.65	3.84
M'Bochi (S)	11	3.64	3.21
M'Beti (F)	7	3.27	3.63
Bakota (F)	1	2.75	1.68
Sangha (F)	5	3.45	2.68
Makaa (F)	3	3.46	2.82
Echira (S)	4	4.47	4.57
Other	2	4.01	3.56

The social conservatism and economic adaptability allowed the Bakongo to profit from the European presence even in the 1920s. The Bakongo avoided demographic dangers such as venereal disease and recovered from the disasters thrust upon them, such as sleeping sickness and work on the Congo-Ocean Railroad. European demands for the export goods of the forest, however, were more disruptive to local societies than the demands for food crops from the Bakongo. The traditional forest economy was shattered by the installation of concession companies; and taxation forced the population to collect forest products, such as rubber, in ways disruptive to family life. The disposable income that remained served to inflate the bride-price and encourage prostitution and marital instability. All this suggests a drop in population and fertility in the forested half of Moyen-Congo during the 1920s.

Ubangi-Shari

The peoples of Ubangi-Shari had more children than the peoples of Moyen-Congo, however the presence of exceptionally infertile groups gave the colony an undeserved reputation for infertility. People in the west had the most children, despite turbulent histories in the colonial period. The central corridor, home of the Banda, had lower fertility than the west. The river region of the colony was the least fertile.

The predominant ethnic group of the river region is the Nzakara, the subject of Retel's classic works on infertility in Africa. Gonorrhea caused much of the sterility, and syphilis led to miscarriage rates of 35 percent to 40 percent and a stillbirth rate of 10 percent of all pregnancies.[23] Customs that encouraged easy premarital and extramarital sex and frequent divorce and remarriage facilitated the spread of venereal disease. "In principle a man is forbidden to force his wife to be a prostitute. But often the husband closes his eyes to his wife's activities if she brings him some of the money. . . . The mother looks for a generous lover for her daughter, and directs the negotiations."[24] This passage comes from a 1935 monograph remarkable for its topics: the right of a father to force his wife or daughters to be prostitutes, to sleep with his comrades, to serve as collateral for a loan, or to contract a temporary marriage with a European. In Nzakara society, as in Gabon, families would carry off their daughter from one husband to sell to a new candidate, while dragging their feet on refunding the dowry to the first spouse.

The Ubangi census presents some evidence that fertility was connected to diet. (See Table 19.5.)[25] The census data indicated that fertility declined throughout the years of colonialism until World War II. Apart from the small group born before 1890, there is a steady rise in sterility of successive cohorts from 7.7 percent to 20 percent and decline in average parity from 4.43 to 3.83 for women born before 1890 to those born from 1915 to 1919.[26] The most interesting trend is a rise in primary and secondary sterility in the low fertility regions. (See Table 19.6.)[27]

Fertility in Ubangi-Shari declined during the years of colonialism, but the decline is less marked than in Gabon and the causes are more difficult to pinpoint. The data do not correlate well with particular historical events or the imposition of export production. The Banda, forced to grow cotton, had mediocre fertility rates in AEF. Apart from the Nzakara, the people of Ubangi were more fertile than those of the southern colonies. The shocks to Ubangi society had a greater repercussion on age structure (in the lack of older people) than on fertility.

TABLE 19.5 Final Parity of Women Born Before 1910

Ethnic Group	Region	Staple Food	Final Parity
Sara	West	Millet	5.37
Mandjia	West	Millet	5.00
M'Boum	West	Millet	4.48
Baya	West	Millet and manioc	4.34
Banda	Center	Manioc	4.13
M'Baka (forest)	West	Manioc	4.00
River people	River	Manioc and fish	3.25
Nzakara	River	Manioc	2.30

TABLE 19.6 Women Having Fewer Than Two Children

	Region	
Age	Center	River
Over 70	17	25
65–69	24	22
60–64	22	29
55–59	28	30
50–54	32	37

Chad

The colonial occupation of Chad seemingly did little to change fertility patterns before World War II. The colony had fewer administrators in total— and many fewer in proportion to the population—than in the three southern colonies. The army was concentrated in the sparsely populated desert area and along the Sudanese frontier. Chad was spared the destruction or distortion of its traditional economy by concession companies, although the suppression of overt slave trading hurt some rules. When the first professional census was conducted in 1964, half a million new people were discovered; and disparities by prefecture between the administrative rolls and this survey ranged from − 24.9 percent to 40.8 percent.[28]

In the 1920s the Sara of southern Chad were recruited into the army and as laborers on the Congo-Ocean Railroad. Soon thereafter cotton production was introduced. The Muslim north remained less affected by colonialism because it was too remote to produce anything that could stand transport costs to Europe; and the people were not interested in European goods, education, or medicine. They did not volunteer for the army, and the French thought better than to draft them.

Doctors were few in Chad, and none carried out demographic studies. The general impression left by administrative report, however, was that infertility was not widespread; and the laments about declining and sparse populations were noticeably absent. Retrospective data from the 1964 census showed no trend up or down in sterility or final parity for each cohort of women born after 1894. The most pronounced distinction in data was between the homogeneous indexes of the south and the variety in the north. (See Table 19.7.)[29] Chad had the highest fertility rates in AEF, but these were lower than other countries in the Sudanic belt. Its average final parity of 4.5 children for women over fifty was surpassed by Mali, Upper Volta, and Niger, with final parities of about 5.5.[30]

TABLE 19.7 Fertility Among Women Born Before 1914

Ethnic Group	Final Parity	Percent Sterile
Northern		
Saharan, Kanem	4.0	4.6
Bas-Chari, Baguirmi	3.3	27.0
Fitri	5.0	6.6
Lac Iro, Melfi	3.1	17.2
Hadjari	5.1	8.8
Quadai	4.3	7.5
Arab	3.9	10.8
Southern		
South Logone	5.0	10.3
Sara	5.2	11.6
Lai	4.4	11.4
Quest	4.9	13.2

In the interwar period the European intrusion brought fewer shocks to the social systems, economies, and health of the population of Chad than the southern colonies. There is little evidence of inflated bride-prices, rising marital instability, or increased prostitution due to new monetization and wage labor. Syphilis was widespread before the European occupation, and colonial doctors did not note significant increases in venereal disease. The population was big enough, the administration small enough, and its projects modest enough that the population could absorb with less difficulty than in the south. Periodic famines in the Sahel were neither caused nor relieved by the administration. It is not surprising, therefore, that sterility and fertility did not greatly change among childbearing women before World War II.

THE IMPACT OF COLONIALISM ON FERTILITY

The changes in fertility during the colonial period resulted from the interaction between the demands of the colonial state and the social structure of African societies. This interaction determined what damage would be done by the sterilizing infections brought and spread by Europeans and their auxiliaries.[31]

Forest peoples were especially vulnerable to infertility for both ecological and economic reasons. While the reasons are unclear—perhaps nutrition, perhaps a milieu favorable to gonorrhea—women in forest regions have fewer children. To these biological factors was added the Europeans' demand for forest products such as timber, rubber, and palm oil, which were collected in ways that involved long family separations.

Wage labor and monetization contributed further to the lack of babies. Polygamy became "democratized" (in Sautter's words), and all men wanted two or three wives. The size of the dowries increased as increased wages allowed new means of accumulating wealth. Girls were married before puberty because their fathers were eager for the bride-price; and families began trafficking in their daughters, "buying" them back from one husband to "sell" to another at a higher price: "The fine for adultery loses its character as a reparation to be transformed into income. . . . Adultery itself is transformed into an industry."[32]

The general effect of colonialism on fertility in the years before World War II were negative. The infections and disruptions brought by colonialism were not yet compensated by increased standards of living, hygienic improvements, better medical care, or specialized care for women and children. These things would happen after World War II and bring with them, especially in the savannas of AEF, increased fertility and veritable baby booms.

INFANT MORTALITY IN FRENCH EQUATORIAL AFRICA

Data on infant mortality are scarcer and less reliable than even the limited data on fertility. Administrators, doctors, and missionaries gave fantastic figures, such as mortality rates of 50 percent to 80 percent in the first year of life. Some of these were honest estimates; but others were too quickly followed by comparisons with low mortality rates among their own patients or in Christian families or by diatribes on the ignorance of African mothers. The data are bad because doctors in AEF in the 1920s and 1930s did not have time or a special interest in obstetrics and pediatrics. Unlike the Belgian Congo, AEF had few religious or lay sisters running mother and child clinics.

Mortalité infantile was used to mean many things. Basic to all the confusion were the multiple meanings of *enfant*: "infant," "child," or "offspring of any age." Investigators were usually forced to use indexes that could be collected at one point in time—for example, when the doctor went through the village. The favorite index was percentage of children born who were still alive. Without the ages of the mothers and children, this will not yield infant mortality; but occasionally doctors got information on the age the children died. Some indexes included stillbirths.

The best statistics from the 1920s to the postwar period indicate that infant mortality in the first years was in the neighborhood of two hundred per thousand. (See Table 19.8.)

The demographers who conducted the postwar censuses were convinced that infant mortality was underreported, especially when a child died soon

TABLE 19.8 Infant and Child Mortality

Year	Place	N	Mortality (%)	Age
1920	Ubangi-Shari[a]		40	*première enfance*
1924	Kouilou, Moyen-Congo[b]	1,349	24	0–3
			6	3–12
1925	Woleu N'Tem, Gabon[c]	1,092	24	*bas âge*
192–	Sara, Ubangi-Shari[d]	719	31	*première enfance*
1932	Adoumas, Gabon[e]	14,911	16	before one month
			16	after one month
1936	Fang, Gabon[f]		16.5	0–1
			12	1–5
1937	Brazzaville[g]		16	0–1
1952–1955	Woleu N'Tem, Gabon[h]	2,469	22	0–1
			9	2–15
1954	Brazzaville[i]		12.8	
1955	Belgian Congo[j]	10% of population	16.5	0–1
1959–1960	Central African Republic[k]	11% of population	19	0–1
			3/yr	1–3
			2/yr	3–4
1960–1961	Gabon[l]	all	16.6	0–1
			2.7/yr	1–4
1964	Chad[m]	60% of population	18	0–1
			3/yr	1–4

[a]Ubangi-Shari, *Rapport annuel*, 1920, Archives Nationales Dépot d'Outre-mer, Aix-en-Provence (henceforth ANDOM) 4 (3) D27.

[b]Kouilou, *Rapports mensuels*, January–February 1924, ANDOM 4 (2) D38.

[c]Caperan, "Notes sur l'état sanitaire des populations M'Fang du Woleu N'Tem," *Bulletin de la Société des Recherches Congolaises* 12 (1930), 103–124; there are misprints and arithmetical mistakes in the tables, but I have assumed the raw data is correct.

[d]Muraz, "L'Alimentation indigène en AEF," in D. Muraz, ed., *L'Alimentation indigène dans les colonies françaises* (Paris, 1933).

[e]Afrique Equatoriale Française, Service de Sante, *Rapport annuel*, 1933, p. 479.

[f]F. Ledentu, quoted in Balandier, *The Sociology of Black Africa*, 100.

[g]Damien Laurent, "Les problèmes de l'enfance en AEF," *Revue de médecine et d'hygiène tropicale* 30 (March–April 1938), 58–86 and 30 (May–June 1938), 121–146.

[h]Estevé.

[i]Soret, *Poto-Poto, Bacongo*, 116.

[j]République du Congo, *Tableau général de la démographie congolaise: Enquête démographique par sondage 1955–57: Analyse générale de résultats statistiques* (n.p., 1961), 62.

[k]CAR-Census, p. 62.

[l]Gabon-Census, 97.

[m]Chad-Census, vol. 1, p. 153.

after birth. For that reason both in Gabon and Moyen-Congo they discarded their own data on infant mortality and gave expected infant mortality using model life tables. For Gabon this raised the deaths from 166 to 229 per thousand.[33]

Without birth- and deathrates, administrators and doctors used survival rates of children ever born to indicate if the population was replacing itself. Women of all ages were asked how many of their children were still alive at the moment of inquiry. Belgian doctors carried out a major survey in Kwango, interviewing twenty thousand women and finding a survival rate of 55.32 percent of all children born. A smaller inquiry in Woleu N'Tem in Gabon also found 55 percent surviving.[34] Comparable figures from the 1960 census showed rates of 61.5 percent in Gabon and 62 percent in the Central African Republic. These figures are, of course, as tied to the age structure of the female population as they are to mortality rates.

Children died in large numbers during their first weeks and months of life, primarily from digestive and respiratory problems. Malaria, which normally occurred toward the sixth month, may have accounted for one-fifth of the deaths. Intestinal parasites, a problem after the child began to crawl around, contributed to malnutrition and gastrointestinal problems.[35] There is no evidence of particular problems at weaning time, no descriptions of kwashiorkor, and no particularly high deathrates among two- and three-year-olds.

Colonial demands in the 1920s and 1930s may have contributed to infant mortality. It was primarily women who carried loads of manioc and other crops to provision cities, administrative posts, and railroad construction camps. A doctor who toured the Likouala region was worried about women involved in palm oil production:

> The women do the domestic work, clear the fields, and grow the food. On top of this, they carry the palm kernels to the presses, bring them home after the oil is extracted, crush the kernels and once again transport them to the trading post. . . . Pregnant women and young mothers take part in this work. The child, on the back of its mother, is exposed to rain, sun, mosquitos, and tsetse flies. He spends the nights out in the open and is poorly fed. He is subject to morning and evening rains without protection, without being dried off, without being covered. In these conditions the infant mortality has good reason to be excessive.[36]

The doctor observed that the price of the heavy work "which the men happily leave to the women," was paid for not in female mortality—for they continued to outnumber the men—but in the loss of children.

The increased demands put on women were not compensated for by specialized medical care for them. Mothers and babies were not considered important enough for the government to divert resources from other areas, such as the sleeping sickness campaign. Pediatrics was a fairly new specialty in Europe; and the young, usually unmarried, military doctor would not think to make efforts to attract women to clinics. French Equatorial Africa had very few medical missionaries, who would have been more family-oriented. Until the mid-1930s the only targeted maternity and child care was given by colonial wives, who sought diversion in distributing soap, blankets, advice, and Nestle's milk, donated by the company, to a few hundred mothers in Brazzaville and Libreville.

It is unlikely that infant mortality diminished until World War II, since medical care barely increased and sanitation was not improved. It is more probable that infant mortality increased as women were called on to do road work and porterage and provision towns. Doctors at the time certainly believed that this led to higher deathrates, but without careful studies we have nothing more than these impressions to go on.

THE POPULATION: GROWTH OR DECLINE?

The major problem in the demographic history of colonial AEF before World War II is to reconcile the censuses, which showed a rise in population, with the qualitative and anecdotal evidence, which pointed to depopulation. Some of the numerical increases reflected population increases; but many only resulted from better censuses, as the tax rolls were being transformed into reliable head counts. Likewise, some of the reports on depopulation were well founded, whereas others were based on small samples, showed population transfers rather than losses, or reflected despair at not being able to procure enough African labor.

To analyze the population of AEF after World War I, we must eliminate Chad, where the perfunctory administration produced totally unreliable census figures, and set boundaries so that the units remain comparable. Border regions were transferred back and forth for a variety of economic and political reasons, sometimes only as compensation for territory lost elsewhere. I have chosen the configuration that most accentuates the geographical distinctiveness of each colony and is closest to the actual borders for most of the interwar period:

- Gabon
    with Divenié
    without Haut-Ogooué
- Moyen-Congo
    with Haut-Ogooué, Lobaye, and Haute-Sangha
    without Bouar-Baboua
- Ubangi-Shari
    with Bouar-Baboua
    without Lobaye, Haute-Sangha, Moyen-Logone, and Moyen-Chari

Gabon

Gabon's censused population remained remarkably stable from 1920 to 1960. The census data in the annual reports reveals two anomalies: the unexplained peaks of 1926 and 1935–1936. These peaks are probably errors because their individual circumscription counts do not match those of the years before or after. The 1926 census was inflated for Moyen-Congo and Ubangi-Shari as well. The 1935 overcount came from a rise in the number of males in Estuary and Ogooué Maritime Departments. Perhaps timber workers, returning to their work camps in the postdepression recovery, were mistakenly counted in both their villages and the logging regions. The gain could certainly not have resulted from a growing population, because every medical report spoke of population decline. It is equally unlikely that better censuses uncovered twenty-five thousand new people, for administrative reports claimed Gabon was completely in hand. Furthermore, the rise was not accompanied by an increased percentage of children, a usual sign of increased administrative control.

Revised estimates indicated that the population slowly rose to 1931 and was stable thereafter. Gabon had a skeletal administration after the war and only by the early 1930s was effective control in place throughout the colony. Certainly, the rises in censused population came from having more administrators around to count more people. It is not at all unlikely that the real population was declining; for fertility was declining, doctors were sure the population was falling, and even the rises registered by the census were modest.[37]

Despite their imprecision, these early censuses reveal characteristics of the Gabonese population confirmed later. At every point there were many more women than men. Adult sex ratios were in the neighborhood of eighty men per hundred women, much lower than elsewhere in AEF. Labor migration cannot explain the disparity; all eight circumscriptions had more women than men and in 1932 only one of the twenty-six subdivisions—the timber outlet of Port-Gentil—had a male majority. The percentage of children, in comparision with the rest of AEF, was low and did not increase after 1929.

Moyen-Congo

Moyen-Congo's censused population rose much more sharply than Gabon's. The gains throughout the twenties were unquestionably due to more-thorough counting. The 1933 health service reported what was happening:

> The militia succeeded in arresting ninety-six Bakota living in the bush from hunting and fishing, counted them and installed them in regular villages near the post of Okangi. Another group of itinerants were made to choose whether they would stay in Gabon or Moyen-Congo. . . . The fight against these hidden camps has been carried out through the extent of the territory and

allowed us to discover numerous natives who had remained outside our authority. . . . In Carnot we found 2,102 natives who hadn't been inscribed in the rolls. . . . Comparisons of the 1932 and 1933 censuses shows a gain of 20,183 people. Really, however, this is due to closer control of the population and finding new people and finding fugitives.[38]

Moyen-Congo's censused population increased from 1921 to 1930 as the administration filled out, a jump from 1932 to 1933, following the manhunts described above, and a jump from 1933 to 1936. This last rise is more puzzling, for there is little change between 1933 and 1936 for most Moyen-Congo circumscriptions after adjustment for boundary changes. The jumps came first as Bas-Oubangui, rebaptized as Likouala Circumscription, rose from twenty-one thousand to thirty thousand, although this was an area of declining fertility, whose censused population in 1950 was back down to twenty-two thousand. The second puzzle is the Lobaye, transferred to Ubangi-Shari, which went from fifty-six thousand to sixty-six thousand people. This contained a heavily forested region with moderate fertility rates and a population considered "uncooperative." Since the 1950 census registered a population of seventy-seven thousand it is possible that more villages were found or that population was growing in the early thirties. Finally, the Haute-Sangha jumped from eighty-two thousand in 1933 to an improbable 106 thousand in 1935. Either a wealth of new people were found as the administration established serious control in areas disturbed by the Baya uprising or, more likely, new territory was temporarily added to Haute-Sangha from Ubangi-Shari. At some point in the 1930s the population began to grow in Moyen-Congo. However, the spurts registered in the 1950 census occurred not in the circumscriptions in the north but in the southern Moyen-Congo, where the Bakongo lived.

More important than the spread of administrative control after World War I was its penetration within the villages. The real gains in Moyen-Congo were registered not as new regions of undercensused circumscriptions were added to the rolls but as more children were counted. From 1920 to 1936 the number of adult men rose by only twenty thousand whereas a hundred thousand additional children were counted. Children rose from 31 percent to 39 percent. Since the retrospective fertility data does not indicate a rising birthrate for these cohorts, the higher number resulted from an increased attention to the nontaxed element of the population.

Ubangi-Shari

The censused population of Ubangi-Shari fluctuated more than that of the southern colonies. This resulted from the unevenness of administrative control, regional differences in demographic change, migration, and boundary changes between circumscriptions.

The initial rise in population from 640 thousand in 1920 to 762 thousand in 1924 was definitely due to better counting as a result of the replenishment of the administration after World War I.[39] The 1926 census, giving the largest population before World War II, reported high figures in all the colonies. The sharp drop in 1930 was statistically due to the failure to count Duham-Pendé, a newly created circumscription, either as a separate entity or as still belonging to Duham. The climb from 1931 to 1932 occurred two-thirds in Duham-Pendé, where an administrative report said, "We can evaluate at 15,000 the number of natives returned to our administrative control following military operations."[40]

Ignoring 1926 and 1930, the general picture that emerges is that new villages and previously uncounted children were being incorporated into the census until about 1932, after which the figures accurately reflected a real, though light, decline in the population.

The number of males rose as counting progressed in the 1920s but then (if we ignore fluctuations) seemed to fall. This is further evidence that the population was falling. The proportion of children rose only until 1933, a sign that most villages were now thoroughly counted. The rising percentage of children in the 1940s was a result of the baby boom in the Western circumscriptions, documented by the 1960 census.

Already in 1932 an inspection report pointed out that the eastern half of Ubangi had more serious demographic problems than the western half.[41] Inspectors directed concern at the low birthrates in the circumscriptions of Haut- and Bas-M'Bomou, noting that Africans on the Sudanese side of the border had the same problem. A further reason for population drops was migrations in frontier areas to escape French exactions. In addition to continuous movement across the borders, an exodus of twenty thousand people resulted when the French first forced Africans to grow cotton in 1927 and 1928. In the west, there was less infertility and emigration than in the east; however, the administraiton took several years to regain complete control after the Baya uprising.

The pattern of growth in western Ubangi and stagnation in eastern Ubangi is illustrated in Table 19.9.

TABLE 19.9 Populations from the Censuses (Thousands)

	1926	1930	1934	1936	1950
Western Ubangi-Shari	352.1	346.2	374.3	386.4	507.2
Eastern Ubangi-Shari	438.6	381.3	385.8	384.3	390.1

From 1926 to 1936 the western region showed moderate population increases due both to better counting and to the growth of Bangui, whose burgeoning population was very visible. In the east, if we ignore the suspect census of 1926, the population remained stationary. Here the inclusion of new areas could be making a real decline. After 1936 increased fertility in the west raised the population by 25 percent in 1950, whereas in the east population figures barely changed.

One curious aspect of Ubangi's population was the lack of old people; and the age pyramid from the 1960 census showed a sharp break, as if the cohort aged fifty to fifty-five was only half as large as the cohort aged forty-five to fifty (Figure 19.1). This impression is confirmed by Table 19.10.

TABLE 19.10 Senior Citizens in Adult Populations (%)

	Central African Republic	Gabon	Congo
Percent of adults over 50	9.2	20.8	22.0
Percent of adults over 60	3.3	10.0	8.4

Since the oldest women reported a higher parity than those giving birth later, higher mortality rates within the cohorts over fifty in 1960 must account for the small percentage of older people. In fact, it was the generation born before 1910 that suffered the most from the abuses of porterage, rubber collection, and railroad construction, and they probably suffered more than their contemporaries in Gabon and Moyen-Congo.

The population of Ubangi-Shari was probably falling until the mid- or late 1930s, when gains in population in the West overtook the losses in the rest of the country. The internal consistency of the figures and the peak in percentage of children imply that the census was fairly reliable by 1932.

Census and Population

Combining the raw census data from AEF's three southern colonies yields no surprises. A sharp gain occurred from 1921 to 1926 as control was established in many regions. The 1926 census, published in *L'Afrique française* amid articles justifying construction of the railroad, gave inflated figures for several circumscriptions, and the numbers dropped the following year.[42] Slight population rises are again registered in the early 1930s as the administration made new efforts to count everybody.

The trends become even clearer when we use the figures adjusted by eliminating the obvious errors. Gabon's graph is absolutely flat. Only the incorporation of new areas prevented the probably real decline from appearing in the census. The greatest gains were registered in Moyen-Congo due to tighter control of the population. Ubangi-Shari's numbers rose, then leveled off when there were no new areas to count.

Considering the extent of the increases in personnel and control, the population gains registered in the censuses were minimal and almost entirely due to the increasing inclusion of children. The tightened control did not produce gains in the total numbers of adults. This is strong evidence that newly incorporated regions were compensating for population declines in regions already counted.

The census data, after errors are corrected and adjustments made for the extension of administrative authority, support the views of contemporaries that AEF's population was decreasing until the 1930s. So, too, does the existing fertility data, scanty as it is. The period of decrease coincides with the establishment of European control. The causes include the large-scale disruptions to African life brought about by the military occupation of AEF, the demands of concession companies, and the building of the Congo-Ocean Railroad. Medical factors that contributed were the increase in venereal disease and the spread of sleeping sickness. Malnutrition likely increased as well, with European requisitions of food, labor demands that decreased food production, and occasional famines.

By the mid-1930s the situation had improved. The traumas of the occupation had ended, the Congo-Ocean was completed, and the concession companies were gone. Medical care had significantly improved, and the standard of living was higher. The results were a rise in fertility and, probably, lowered mortality in most of AEF. At this point the data from doctors, administrators, and others on the scene concur with the unaltered census rolls in signaling population growth.

NOTES

1. Such terms are sprinkled throughout Gilles Sautter, *De l'Atlantique au fleuve Congo: Une géographie du sous-peuplement* (Paris, 1966), as well as throughout administrative reports.

2. For an example of the undercounting of children and a discussion of the problem, see J. Schwetz, "Contribution à l'étude de la démographie congolaise," *Congo* (1923), 297–343.

3. These are available only in the archives in Aix-en-Provence and, for the health service, at Pharo in Marseilles. The archives of the Ministry of Colonies in Paris are now being moved to Aix-en-Provence. Only occasional census reports for the prewar years are in African archives.

4. Afrique Equatoriale Française, Haut Commissariat, *Annuaire statistique*, vol. 1., 1936–1950.

5. Gilles Sautter, "L'utilisation des documents administratifs pour l'étude numérique de la population au Moyen-Congo et au Gabon," *Bulletin de l'Institut d'Études Centrafricaines* (1954), 23–32.

6. Lotte, "Aperçu sur la situation démographique de l'AEF," *Médecine tropicale* 13, 304–319; J. Croqueville, "Etude démographique de quelques villages Likouala (Moyen-Congo)," *Population* 8 (July 1953), 491–510.

7. France, Ministère de la France d'Outre-mer, Services des Statistiques, "Les français d'origine métropolitaine et les étrangers dans les territoires d'outre-mer au recensement de 1946," *Bulletin mensuel de statistique d'outre-mer*, supplément série études, no. 18 (Paris, 1950); idem, "Le recensement de la population non-originaire des territoires d'outre-mer en 1951," *Bulletin*

mensuel de statistique d'outre-mer, supplément série études, no. 33 (Paris, 1956).

8. Guy Lasserre, *Libreville et sa région*, Cahiers de la Fondation Nationale des Sciences Politiques, no. 98 (Paris, 1958); Congo (Brazzaville), Statistique générale, *Recensement démographique de Pointe-Noire*, prepared by F. Ganon (Pointe-Noire, 1958); Marcel Soret, *Démographique et problèmes urbains en AEF: Poto-Poto, Bacongo, Dolisie*, Mémoires de l'Institut d'Études Centrafricaines (Brazzaville, 1954); France, Service de la Statistique Générale, *Recensement de l'agglomération de Bangui 1955-56*.

9. These censuses will be referred to as Gabon-Census, Congo-Census, CAR-Census, and Chad-Census.

10. Gabon-Census, 86, 89; Congo-Census, 46, 123, 125; CAR-Census, 95, 98, 241; Chad-Census (women born before 1914), vol. 1, pp. 121, 127, 134.

11. Camille Jeannel, *La stérilité en république gabonaise* (Geneva, 1962?). Jeannel found these blockages in 90 percent of the sterile women he examined: See also H. Moutsinga, "La stérilité féminine au Gabon en consultation gynécologique journalière," *Médecine d'Afrique noire* 20 (1973), 103–109. Gabon, Service de Santé, *Rapport annuel*, 1934, Colonial Health Service Archives, Pharo Marseilles (henceforth, Pharo).

12. Gabon-Census, 86; Congo-Census, 123; CAR-Census, 241; Chad-Census (women born before 1914), 94–95.

13. Gabon-Census, 86–89.

14. The best single source for social and economic factors in Gabon's infertility is Sautter, *De l'Atlantique*. Fecundity data from Gabon-Census and CAR-Census.

15. Gabon, Service de Santé, *Rapport annuel*, 1932, p. 65, Pharo; Afrique Equatoriale Française, Service de Santé, *Rapport annuel*, 1933, Pharo.

16. Ibid.

17. Gabon, Service de Santé, *Rapport annuel*, 1932, p. 75.

18. Congo-Census, 123, 128.

19. Sautter, *De l'Atlantique*, 482.

20. Duboccage, "La Natalité chez les Bakongo dans ses rapports avec la gynécologie," *Annales de la Société Belge de Médecine Tropicale* 9 (1929), 265–274.

21. Moyen-Congo, *Rapport annuel*, 1931, p. 21; ANSOM, Fond-Guernut, B-40; Robert Harms, "Competition and Capitalism: The Bobangi Role in Equatorial Africa's Trade Revolution" (Ph.D. diss., University of Wisconsin, 1978); Administrator in Stanley Pool, to lieutenant governor of Moyen-Congo, Brazzaville, 27 September 1917, Archives Nationales du Congo GG 440; Moyen-Congo, Service de Santé, *Rapport annuel*, 1931.

22. Congo-Census, 125.

23. Anne Retel-Laurentin, *Infécondité en Afrique noire: Maladies et conséquences sociales* (Paris, 1974); idem, *Infécondité et maladies chez les Nzakara, République centrafricaine* (Paris, n.d.).

24. Darré, "De l'organisation familiale chez les peuplades Nzakara," *Bulletin de la Société des Recherches Congolaises* 21 (1935), 61–92; quote from p. 67.

25. CAR-Census, 34, 98, 103, 245.

26. Ibid., 102, 242.

27. Ibid., 102, 142.

28. Chad-Census, vol. 1, p. 23.

29. Ibid., 127.

30. INSEE, *Service de la Coopération* (Paris, 1965–1967), vol. 1, *Vue d'ensemble*, 44.

31. This is not the place to discuss the heated issue of Europeans, Africans, and venereal disease. The earliest doctors and administrators in AEF were convinced that Europeans and their auxiliaries were spreading venereal disease, especially gonorrhea.

32. Sautter, *De l'Atlantique*, 954, based on George Balandier's study of the Fang in *The Sociology of Black Africa: Social Dynamics in Central Africa*, trans. Douglas Garman (New York, 1970).

33. Gabon-Census, 93, 94.

34. Schwetz, "Démographie congolaise," 325–340; Afrique Equatoriale Française, Service de Santé, *Rapport annuel*, 1935, pp. 152–159, Pharo.

35. Ibid., 6.

36. Moyen-Congo, Service de Santé, *Rapport annuel*, 1930, pp. 79–80, Pharo.

37. Woleu N'Tem, *Rapport trimestriel*, 1929, ANDOM 4 (1) D35; Gabon, *Rapport annuel*, 1933. Laments of depopulation were ubiquitous in reports from Gabon in this period.

38. Afrique Equatoriale Française, Service de Santé, *Rapport annuel*, 1933.

39. Ubangi-Shari, *Rapport annuel*, 1925, ANDOM 4 (3) D35.

40. Ubangi-Shari, *Rapports annuels*, 1931, 1932, ANSOM Fond-Guernut B-38; idem, "Situation financière
    de l'Oubangui-Chari," pt. 2, "Recettes budgetaires et capacité fiscale des indigènes," Boulmer Mission, no. 71, ANSOM AP 3131.

41. Ibid.

42. Georges Bruel, "La population du Cameroun et de l'AEF," *Bulletin du Comité de l'Afrique Française: Renseignements coloniaux* 37 (September 1927).

20

What Is Known of the Demographic History of Zaire Since 1885?

LÉON DE ST. MOULIN

Statistical data concerning Zaire's population since the 1920s abound, but the analysis required before they can be used has just begun. The available materials require recourse to divergent strategies. On the one hand, the lack of precision of the available data calls for a formulation with the help of population models. Bruce Fetter has demonstrated the possibility and the interest of such models in a pioneering article.[1] On the other hand, frequent changes to the administrative boundaries in which all population figures are set require a detailed knowledge of such changes if we are properly to appreciate the demographic evolution.

My plan here is to show the main features of the history of Zaire's population since the end of the last century—especially since 1935—such as they appear from work carried out at the Université Nationale du Zaïre for the past fifteen years.

To understand my analysis, let us begin with Zaire's administrative nomenclature. From 1912 until 1971, the largest of these was the province (four until 1933, then six until 1962, and nine since 1967). Provinces were subdivided into districts, which were in turn subdivided into territories (Map 20.1). Since 1971 the terms designating these units have changed to *region*, *subregion*, and *zone*. Towns may have the ranking of region (for the capital), subregion, or urban zone or simply be "centers" integrated into a zone. The administrative subdivision of a ranking lower than the zone was previously called *native circonscription* and is today called *collectivité*; it is strictly subordinate to the zone.

BROAD OUTLINE OF ZAIRE'S POPULATION HISTORY

Two facts are solidly established as regards the evolution of Zaire's population. The first is that the distribution of rural population has remained relatively constant, despite the development of urban areas. Moreover, this stability has been observed in most of the world's regions, sometimes since

MAP 20.1 Political Map of Zaire, 1988

classical times. The second verity concerns fluctuations in the total population. Zaire underwent a significant decline between 1880 and approximately 1920 and did not grow significantly until 1945, when the rate of increase accelerated rapidly.

Density Maps of the Population

Density maps of Zaire's population exist for 1970, 1948, 1938, and 1928 (see Maps 20.2–20.5). Moreover, there is another one, much more summary, for 1908 (Map 20.6, a revision of 1898 map); others, which are very detailed, for 1957–1959, published for four of the six provinces existing at the time; and an uncompleted one for the fifth province.[2]

I have personally drawn and analyzed the density map of Zaire's

MAP 20.2 Population Density, 1970

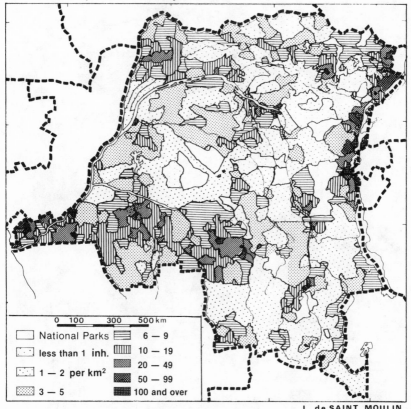

L. de SAINT MOULIN

population based on the 1970 administrative census. My analysis was largely confirmed by the scientific population census of 1 July 1984, the results of which, unfortunately, are only available at present up to the zone level. Data gathered by Pierre Gourou for 1948 led to the publication of a chiefdom-level density map and of an analysis with general features that still correspond to the 1970 reality.

The 1928 and 1938 maps only indicate the density by territory. There were 179 in 1928 but only 105 in 1938. The two main density axes of Zaire, from the Atlantic Ocean to Kabinda and from Lake Tanganyika to the Sudanese border may be identified, as well as a number of less important population nuclei.

On the 1908 map the relative emptiness of the central basin in relation to the regions of the Kasai, the Kwilu, and Bas-Zaire, and to the north and east of the country can already be noticed. A map of the Independent State of Congo in 1907, drawn at 1:1 million actually suggests more detailed

MAP 20.3 Population Density, 1948

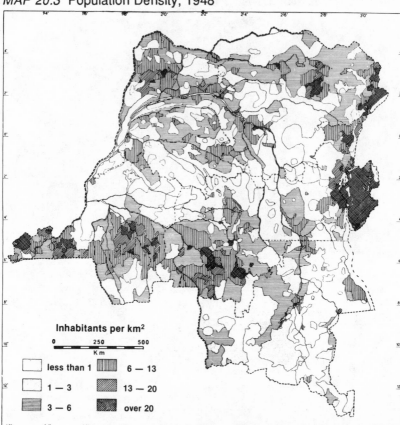

Inhabitants per km²

less than 1   6 — 13
1 — 3   13 — 20
3 — 6   over 20

SOURCE: Pierre Gourou, "Carte de la densité des populations," in *Atlas Général du Congo*. Brussels: Académie Royale de Sciences d'Outremer, 1951. Reprinted with permission.

similarities with the present population distribution in the swampy region south of the forest.[3]

It appears from these maps that colonization has not radically changed the distribution of Zaire's rural population. Moreover, some earlier indications allow us to take the origins of the present situation back to a far-away past. In particular, it is known that a high-density population already existed in the Upemba Depression at the end of the first millennium and that caravans going from Angola to the Lunda country at the beginning of the 1800s already regarded the Dilolo region as a population center.

Main Demographic Movements Since 1880

Arab and European penetration in Central Africa during the nineteenth century first brought about an important decline in population due to

MAP 20.4 Population Density, 1938

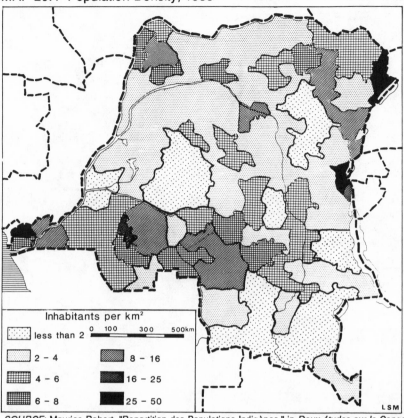

Inhabitants per km²

- less than 2
- 2 – 4
- 4 – 6
- 6 – 8
- 8 – 16
- 16 – 25
- 25 – 50

0   100   300   500km

LSM

SOURCE: Maurice Robert, "Repartition des Populations Indigènes," in *Deux études sur le Congo Belge*. Brussels: Université Libre de Bruxelles, Institut de Sociologie, 1945. Reprinted with permission.

dissemination of diseases, against which the population was defenseless, and the disruption of traditional agricultural organization. The ravages caused by the sleeping sickness sometimes caused the disappearance of 80 percent of the population, especially in the Bas-Zaire and the Maniema; however, details of its spread are incomplete and lack precision.[4] Mortality due to other diseases, especially smallpox and Spanish influenza is even less known. Official documents surmise that the 1918 Spanish influenza reduced Zaire's African population by 5 percent and the European population by 2 percent. Venereal diseases, also disseminated due to the Arab and European penetration, were at the origin of a serious fertility crisis, especially in the regions of Equateur, Tshuapa, the Ueles, and the Bafwasende.[5] This same situation exists in more localized fashion in some zones of the Kasai. The population declined for the whole of Zaire by at least a third, possibly by half.

On the other hand, it is generally recognized that this population

MAP 20.5 Population Density, 1928

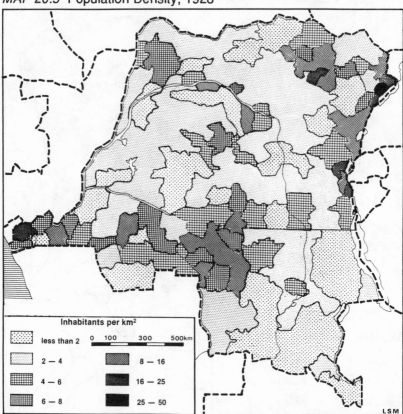

Inhabitants per km²

less than 2	0 100 300 500km
2 — 4	8 — 16
4 — 6	16 — 25
6 — 8	25 — 50

LSM

SOURCE: Based on a map of J. de Jonghe in *L'essor économique belge: Expansion coloniale.* Brussels, 1930.

increased considerably after 1945, according to a rhythm the acceleration of which has long been underestimated. In 1953 there was an attempt to adjust the data of administrative censuses since 1925 by assuming that the 1952 figures were correct and that the annual rate of population increase had gradually risen from 5.3 percent per thousand in 1926 to 10.2 percent per thousand in 1952. This last rate was certainly lower than reality, since the estimate of natural increase resulting from the 1955–1957 surveys is in the order of 20 percent per thousand. On the other hand, an uninterrupted increase in population since 1925 has not been confirmed. I believe it is more likely that it continued to decline until approximately 1930. Lastly, I believe that all population figures of the colonial period, including the 1952 figure, are underestimates. So I undertook a new adjustment by assuming a much faster growth rate (but only after 1930), starting from a population estimate by region done in 1975.

I resorted to population models for this estimate, which aimed at the

MAP 20.6 Population Density, 1908

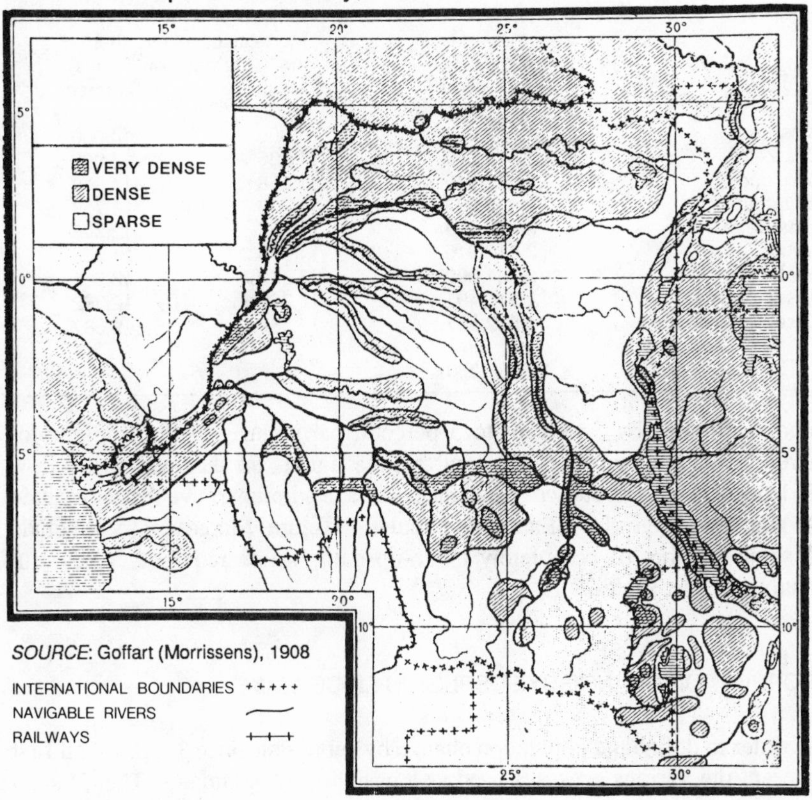

SOURCE: Goffart (Morrissens), 1908

INTERNATIONAL BOUNDARIES ++ +++
NAVIGABLE RIVERS
RAILWAYS ++ +

same time at establishing detailed age pyramids. For these models, relation-ships between age distribution, birthrate, and survival rates are known. Starting from an estimate of life expectancy at birth (I shall indicate the elements of this calculation later), and the proportion of individuals below the age of twenty found in administrative documents dating from 1970, 1975, or 1977, I have estimated the rates of natural increase by region from 1965 to 1975 by cross-checking for internal consistencies whenever possible. After some minor adjustments in order to take migratory movements into account, I then obtained estimates of the population by mid-1975, which are compatible with the present age structure.[6] (See Table 20.1.)

The new adjustment that I am presenting on this basis assumes that in 1938–1939 the administration was exercising a tight control over the population but that this control abated during the war years and was never completely reinstated after the war, due to the growing magnitude of the rural exodus. It seems to us that the official figures of the 1950s are mostly

TABLE 20.1 Population and Mortality Levels in Zaire 1975 by Region

Region	Mid-1975 Population	Mortality Level (Northern Family of Princeton Tables)	
		Men	Women
Kinshasa	1,679,091	14,000	14,000
Bas-Zaire	1,574,949	11,886	11,886
Bandundu	3,068,845	11,358	11,358
Equateur	2,619,693	11,758	11,758
Haut-Zaire	3,475,799	12,394	12,395
Kivu	3,812,815	11,375	11,338
Shaba	2,961,990	13,662	13,665
Kasai Oriental	1,516,491	12,362	12,362
Kasai Occidental	1,872,557	9,586	9,587
TOTAL	22,582,230		

underestimates by 3 percent to 5 percent, particularly in the fourteen-to-twenty-five age range. On the contrary, the figures for the years that follow independence are usually overestimates as each administrative district wanted to gain advantages by inflating its population figure. Moreover, they include a small number of completely made-up data, which require very careful analysis. (See Table 20.2.)

POPULATION CHANGE BY SUBREGION SINCE 1938

In order to define the population change by subregion since 1938, I shall first present the various censuses used as a basis for my estimates. Then, I shall comment on the general table obtained by showing the evolution of the number of inhabitants within the present administrative boundaries.

The 1984 Census

The scientific population census of 1 July 1984 was undoubtedly the most successful in the entire history of Zaire. However, in the form in which it was published, it does not yet allow for an appreciation of the importance and final results of the return of former émigrés, which occurred in a section of Eastern Kasai soon after independence (1960). The presumed increase due to the difference between the nine figures for this district and those for the end of the colonial period does not appear to be confirmed.

I am showing the results of this census for twenty-seven subregions and fourteen towns or centers holding at least zone status. In the tables, the centers of Boma and Kolwezi were separated from their rural subregions, which were included in the subregions of the Bas-Fleuve and the Lualaba, respectively, to which they belonged administratively until 1978. The figures of this census have not been corrected.

TABLE 20.2 Evolution of Zaire's Population: Results of Administrative Censuses and Adjustments

Year	Administrative Census Population	1953 Adjustments		Corrected Adjustment	
		Ns	Rate of Increase (%)	Ns	Rate of Increase (per 1,000 per year)
1925	7,692,573	9,564,990	—	10,303,932	—
1926	7,955,450	9,612,406	5.38	—	—
1927	8,121,194	9,669,886	—	—	—
1928	8,419,181	9,725,455	—	—	—
1929	8,674,086	9,783,142	—	—	—
1930	8,803,442	9,842,977	—	10,252,515	−.10
1931	8,880,881	9,904,992	6.30	—	—
1932	8,956,462	9,969,221	—	—	—
1933	8,872,283	10,035,699	—	—	—
1934	9,282,991	10,104,465	—	—	—
1935	9,775,191	10,175,559	—	10,381,314	2.50
1936	10,046,731	10,249,022	7.22	10,428,029	4.50
1937	10,217,408	10,324,899	—	10,485,384	5.50
1938	10,304,084	10,403,236	—	10,553,539	6.60
1939	10,328,409	10,484,080	—	10,632,691	7.50
1940	10,333,909	10,567,482	—	10,723,068	8.50
1941	10,507,549	10,653,493	8.14	10,824,401	9.45
1942	10,530,446	10,742,168	—	10,921,280	8.95
1943	10,486,291	10,833,562	—	11,013,565	8.45
1944	10,442,356	10,927,734	—	11,106,629	8.45
1945	10,508,449	11,024,743	—	11,206,034	8.95
1946	10,667,087	11,124,651	9.06	11,301,931	8.45
1947	10,761,353	11,227,523	—	11,430,140	10.45
1948	10,914,208	11,333,424	—	11,739,667	11.45
1949	11,073,311	11,442,422	—	11,739,667	14.45
1950	11,331,793	11,554,588	—	11,932,785	16.45
1951	11,593,494	11,669,993	9.98	12,141,012	17.45
1952	11,788,711	11,788,711	10.15	12,365,014	18.45
1953	12,026,159	—	—	12,605,513	19.45
1954	12,317,326	—	—	12,863,296	20.45
1955	12,562,631	—	—	13,139,214	21.45
1956	12,843,574	—	—	13,434,189	22.45
1957	13,174,883	—	—	13,749,221	23.45
1958	13,540,182	—	—	14,085,389	24.45
1959	13,864,421	—	—	14,443,862	25.45
1960	—	—	—	14,825,903	26.45
1965	—	—	—	16,975,580	27.45
1970	21,637,876	—	—	19,531,722	28.45
1975	—	—	—	22,582,230	29.45
1980	—	—	—	26,377,260	31.56
1984	29,671,407	—	—	29,992,348	32.52

Source: The official population figure for 1959 comes from Congo Belge, *Statistiques relatives à l'année 1959* (Léopoldville, n.d.). The 1984 figure comes from *Résultats provisoires du recensement scientifique de la population du 1er juillet 1984* (Kinshasa, 1984).

The 1970 Census

Results of the 1970 administrative census were published on 1 July of that year, without any indication of the precise date to which they corresponded. They are available by sex and in two age groups (in principle, individuals below the age of eighteen and the others), with some added information regarding nationality.[7] On that basis, there is no difficulty in establishing population figures that correspond to present administrative subdivisions. However, the figures of this census cannot be utilized in the calculation of growth rates without adjustment.

As explained, it was deemed necessary to reduce the total population of Zaire by almost 10 percent. I give here the totals resulting from my previous estimates by region for 1975 with growth rates established simultaneously for the years 1956–1975, with the following adjustments: for Bas-Zaire I changed this global growth rate from 30 percent to 25 percent; for Bandundu I retained the 1970 official figure; for Kasai Oriental the reduction is the result of the difference between Zaire's total population and the sum of the populations of the other regions. Table 20.3 shows the figures retained.

TABLE 20.3 Official and Estimated Population of Zaire, 1970, by Region

Region	Official Figures	Amended Figures	Difference (%)
Kinshasa	1,328,039	1,142,761	−13.6
Bas-Zaire	1,504,361	1,392,025	−8.1
Bandundu	2,600,556	2,600,556	—
Equateur	2,431,812	2,341,695	−3.7
Haut-Zaire	3,356,419	3,131,985	−6.7
Kivu	3,361,883	3,256,117	−3.1
Shaba	2,753,714	2,506,241	−9.0
Kasai Oriental	1,872,231	1,500,908	−19.8
Kasai Occidental	2,433.861	1,659,434	−31.8
Total	21,637.876	19,531,722	−9.7

The corrections I proposed were applied to all the subregions of the same region, except in the case of both Kasais. In Kasai Occidental, I first established the population figure for Kananga from the results of a good sociodemographic survey that gave an estimate of 277,934 inhabitants on 31 March 1976 and a growth rate of 55.8 per thousand (25 per thousand natural increase and about 30 per thousand from migration).[8] The factor proposed for the whole region was then applied to the Lulua subregion. Lastly, the population figure calculated by difference was attributed to the Kasai subregion.

In Kasai Oriental, where statistical data are especially inconsistent, the figures for the Mbuji-Mayi population were arbitrarily reduced by 20 percent, the Sankuru figure by 5 percent, that of the Kabinda subregion by 12 percent, and that of the Tshilenge population (calculated by difference) by 42.2

percent. In this last subregion and in the town of Mbuji-Mayi, the return of former émigrés was significant from 1960 to 1965; but it is also there that the 1970 census figures were especially inflated. In this way estimates for the subregions of both Kasai are reached. (See Table 20.4.)

TABLE 20.4 Official and Estimated Population of the Two Kasais 1970 by Subregion

Region and Subregion	Official Figures	Amended Figures	Difference (%)
Kasai Oriental			
Mbuji-Mayi	256,154	204,923	−20.0
Tshilenge	533,103	308,154	−42.2
Sankuru	497,352	472,484	−5.0
Kabinda	585,622	595,347	−12.0
Total	1,872,231	1,500,908	−12.0
Kasai Occidental			
Kananga	428,960	203,398	−52.8
Kasai	833,468	857,340	−21.1
Lulua	1,171,433	793,696	−31.8
Total	2,422,861	1,659,434	−31.8

As previously indicated, the proposed adjustments are based on a search for consistency between the proportion of individuals below the age of twenty recorded in 1970 or 1965 and a natural increase rate compatible with other data at hand. The first estimates established in this way were confirmed by the 1984 census, since they offer a better transition between the numbers of that census and those of the 1958 census. The estimates offered here have been partially revised according to the 1984 estimates in order further to improve this consistency.

The 1958 Census

The annual reports presented to the Belgian legislative chambers in the 1950s with respect to the administration of the Colony of the Belgian Congo (*Rapport aux Chambres*) include detailed population figures by territory and by center or agglomeration. These figures are slightly underestimated and do not include the non-African population. Nevertheless, I used them exactly as they were, endeavoring only to establish the number of inhabitants recorded within the present administrative divisions. This was easy in most cases. However, I had to resolve certain inconsistencies.

In 1958 most towns did not yet exist in the administrative sense. The population numbers taken for Boma, Bandundu, and Kikwit are those of the extracustomary center of the time. For Kolwezi I combined the figures of the extracustomary center and of the "other agglomerations," that is, the mining camps. For Mbuji-Mayi the figure of this same list of "other agglomerations" was retained. For Kananga I was able to establish a figure corresponding strictly to the present boundaries of the town by means of a thorough study.[9] The non-African population was included only in the Kinshasa figure.

Two special difficulties arise in the estimation of the population affected by the changes in boundaries that had occurred between the subregions of Kwango and Lukaya, on the one hand, and of the Lulua with those of Tshilenge and Kabinda, on the other. The first one was solved with precision, from detailed data published with R. E. de Smet's density maps. The second one was overcome through data by village collected by the same author in the Kasai region.[10]

The 1948 Census

The 1948 census is regarded as the first realization of the effort undertaken after the end of World War II to recover the censuses. However, I still believe that it underestimated Zaire's population by almost 6 percent. Lacking sufficient information to distribute this underestimation between the various subregions, I had to be content with adjusting the official figure of the time within the framework of present administrative divisions. In order to accomplish this, I had at my disposal population figures and collectivity maps (tribal circumscriptions) collected by P. Gourou for the publication of his 1948 density map.

For the towns I took the population of the corresponding extracustomary centers, with the exceptions of Kinshasa (where I knew the numbers, including the white population), Kisangani and Bukavu (where the figure for the territory corresponds exactly to the present boundaries of the town), Kananga (where the figure was set as in 1958 and also corresponds to present boundaries), and Lubumbashi and Likasi (where the reported figure shows approximately the same homogeneity in combining the population of the "town" and that of the extracustomary center, kept separate at the time). For Mbuji-Mayi and Kolwezi I kept the figures appearing in P. Gourou's notes.[11]

The calculation of population numbers by subregion within the framework of today's boundaries did not present any difficulty for Haut-Zaire and Kivu. In fact, the 1948 "territories" are totally integrated into one or the other present subregions, with very small differences, especially as regards Lubutu territory. On the other hand, I had to make some often difficult adjustments in order to determine the 1948 figures for the subregions of the Bas-Fleuve and Cataractes, Nord- and Sud-Ubangi, the Mongala, Equateur, Kabinda, Tshilenge, and the Lulua, as well as those of the Lualaba and of the Haut-Shaba. In the case of a transfer of one tribal circumscription to another territory, I could simply rely on the population figures at my disposal for that level. However, in six cases I had to follow a more complex method, first by defining precisely the boundary change that had taken place, then by calculating, from the very detailed 1958 density maps, the proportion of the population of the districts in question to be found at that time on both sides of the present boundaries, and finally by allocating in 1948 to each subregion the same proportions of the population recorded at the time.[12]

The 1938 Census

As mentioned above, the 1938 census is undoubtedly one of the censuses that most successfully reached the whole of Zaire's population. However, age definition was difficult at the time; thus, the analysis of the demographic structures of the time presents serious difficulties. It is all the more important to establish the direction of total population change as precisely as possible.

As regards the towns, the population change in Table 20.5 is, as is the case for 1948, the population of the extracustomary centers, with the exception of Kinshasa, where I used the population of the urban district, including the whites; of Mbandaka, where I used the population of the "native town"; for Likasi, where I added the population of the extracustomary center to the population of the urban circumscription;[13] for Lubumbashi, where I took my estimate from the 1940 population figure—at which time the boundaries of the territory practically matched the present boundaries of the town—and from the changes in the number of salaried employees of the Union Minière du Haut-Katanga in the camps surrounding the town from 1938 to 1940; for Kolwezi, where I subtracted 6 percent from the 1939 figure;[14] and for Kananga, where I kept the figure given in an official report for Lulua Gare.[15]

In order to determine the population existing within today's administrative boundaries, I had at my disposal population figures by district, population by territory for Kibali-Ituri, Tanganyika, and part of Kasai, as well as density figures by territory to one decimal place. I also had at my disposal some estimates of the districts' area established in 1940 and 1942. The 1938 administrative map is the one resulting from the ordinances of 18 March 1935 and of a slight enlargement of the urban district of Léopoldville that took place in 1936.

When the population of a 1938 territory was to be distributed among several present subregions, I first undertook to estimate the population of that territory based on the total of the district it was occupying and of the territory densities in that district and their estimated area. As was done for 1948, I then distributed this population according to a model that I was able to calculate on the basis of the 1958 data, which were extremely detailed. In the Kivu, where such data were not available, only the population of the Shabunda territory had to be distributed on a more summary basis, between the Maniema and Sud-Kivu.[16]

Table of the Evolution by Subregion Since 1938

Based on data established according to the indications described, Tables 20.5 and 20.6 show the evolution of the population within the boundaries of the present subregions since 1938.

The results obtained in this fashion show in particular that some regions have been tending toward demographic decline for a long time. Such was the case in Haut-Zaire, both Kasais, the Equateur and Tshuapa subregions, and even in Lualaba until 1948. During the course of the following ten years, migration to Kinshasa caused decreases in Mbandaka and Mbuji-Mayi and still continue in the subregions of the Lukaya, Equateur, and Tshilenge. Many subregions have an annual growth rate of below 1.5 percent. Between 1958 and 1970 Table 20.6 no longer shows a negative rate; but certain areas continued to decrease, according to official figures for smaller units. Such is the case for the zones of Bafwasende, Niangara, and Aketi (in Haut-Zaire), where birth and mortality rates measured in 1957 indicated a projected decline; for the zone of Gungu (in the Bandundu) and of Ubundu (in Haut-Zaire), which suffered greatly during the rebellion; and for the zone of Lusambo (Kasai Oriental), where the Baluba emigrated en masse after independence.

However, high growth rates already existed in some subregions between 1938 and 1948. This was especially the case in Nord-Kivu. Between 1948 and 1958 three regions experienced annual growth rates above 2.5 percent: Bandundu, Kivu, and Shaba. Accelerated growth occurred everywhere, converging at about 3.5 percent per year. Kwilu and Kivu first reached the 3 percent figure in the 1950s. Bas-Fleuve, the Mai-Ndombe, Sud-Ubangi, Mongala, and the whole of Shaba joined them prior to 1970, and finally Nord-Ubangi before 1984. These trends correspond to historical data at hand.

In the Equateur, the Ueles, and both Kasais the declines that continued in the 1940s are for the most part the result of the falling birthrate caused by venereal diseases disseminated during the Arab and European penetration. Moreover, the conditions in which corvées were imposed during World War I for the harvesting of rubber (vine or tree), porterage, road construction, and new mines should also be considered. They brought disruptions that compare with those imposed at the time of colonial penetration: some villages were unable to cultivate their fields at the proper time, which resulted in famines; others lost ecological control of their milieu by abandoning work previously done. In the Befale zone (Equateur), the population declined by 20 percent between 1940 and 1945.

In the Bas-Zaire the heavy increase that appeared between 1958 and 1970 in the Cataractes subregion is linked to the arrival en masse of Angolan refugees after the 1961 disturbances. In fact, during the 1970 census, 219,671 Angolans were registered in the region, 180 thousand of them in the Cataractes subregion.

TABLE 20.5 Population by Subregion and Present Region, 1938–1984

Region and Subregion	1938	1948	1958	1970	1984
Kinshasa	42,036	132,532	389,547	1,142,761	2,653,558
Bas-Zaire					
Matadi	12,488	25,811	61,661	102,189	144,742
Boma	7,390	11,590	30,292	56,495	88,556
Bas-Fleuve[a]	245,501	265,668	305,133	426,575	621,440
Cataractes	222,532	271,581	219,995	522,942	747,781
Lukaya	147,439	191,387	185,218	283,824	369,001
Total	635,350	766,037	902,299	1,392,025	1,971,520
Bandundu					
Bandundu	2,255	5,079	10,918	74,467	63,189
Kikwit	3,789	6,057	14,530	111,960	146,784
Kwilu	766,412	816,468	1,132,064	1,370,454	1,936,084
Kwango	398,205	403,873	469,296	614,210	847,876
Mai-Ndombe	215,228	242,930	292,200	429,465	688,912
Total	1,385,889	1,474,407	1,919,008	2,600,556	3,682,845
Equateur					
Mbandaka	8,641	10,137	56,622	103,911	125,263
Mongo[b]	—	—	—	—	18,072
Equateur	300,123	281,237	264,833	328,192	495,302
Nord-Ubangi	213,471	228,383	264,894	328,158	527,687
Sud-Ubangi and Mongo	345,662	398,494	483,446	661,851	991,891
Mongala	267,963	278,252	329,503	470,576	672,097
Tshuapa	428,099	402,223	402,334	449,007	575,200
Total	1,563,959	1,598,626	1,801,632	2,341,695	3,405,512
Haut-Zaire					
Kisangani	12,962	56,934	109,807	214,244	282,650
Tshopo	620,267	535,967	562,004	666,765	770,372
Bas-Uele	518,188	482,353	494,297	549,399	579,701
Haut-Uele	682,780	595,429	611,304	742,418	889,882
Ituri	507,489	576,854	697,421	959,159	1,683,464
Total	2,341,686	2,247,537	2,474,633	3,131,985	4,206,069
Kivu					
Bukavu[c]	—	18,835	48,269	130,618	171,064
Sud-Kivu	598,976	623,821	880,786	1,095,105	1,830,834
Nord-Kivu	369,065	532,175	891,648	1,427,027	2,379,471
Maniema	374,590	406,427	461,119	603,367	806,496
Total	1,342,631	1,581,258	2,261,822	3,256,117	5,187,865
Shaba					
Lubumbashi	26,077	89,658	168,775	289,422	543,268
Likasi	15,042	37,239	69,814	133,238	194,465
Kolwezi	8,365	21,700	52,203	75,921	201,382
Lualaba[d]	241,048	234,691	288,278	466,765	532,646
Haut-Lomami	269,497	296,222	363,446	548,234	881,046
Tanganyika	300,789	351,404	442,716	633,782	930,629
Haut-Shaba	174,630	211,320	268,944	358,879	590,583
Total	1,035,448	1,242,234	1,654,176	2,506,241	3,874,019

(continued over)

TABLE 20.5 continued

Region and Subregion	1938	1948	1958	1970	1984
Kasai Oriental					
Mbuji-Mayi[e]	—	11,064	39,829	204,923	423,363
Tshilenge	140,016	128,249	118,800	308,154	529,637
Sankuru	363,316	383,249	408,039	472,484	658,556
Kabinda	374,664	320,068	369,381	515,347	791,047
Total	877,996	843,103	936,049	1,500,908	2,402,603
Kasai Occidental					
Kananga	26,272	40,873	107,346	203,398	290,898
Kasai	423,367	440,582	497,098	657,340	1,019,787
Lulua	631,765	554,276	618,140	798,696	976,731
Total	1,081,404	1,035,731	1,222,584	1,659,434	2,287,416
Not distributed[f]	22,894	41,746	91,191	—	—
Grand Total	10,329,293	10,963,211	13,652,941	19,531,722	29,671,407

[a]Includes the zone of Moanda.
[b]Included in Sud-Ubangi until 1970.
[c]Included in Sud-Kivu in 1938.
[d]Includes the zones of Mutshatsha and Lubudi.
[e]Included in Tshilenge subregion in 1938.
[f]White population, mulattoes included, with the exception of the Kinshasa population.

Immigration to the Kivus was even more significant. Two groups of Banyarwanda were directed by the Belgian authorities to Masisi Zone in 1927–1945 and 1949–1955. The first one included 25,450 individuals and 2,800 head of cattle, not taking into account uncontrolled infiltration. Officially, the second one numbered more than 60,000 individuals, but it was estimated, as early as 1955, that these movements had resulted in the settlement of more than 170,000 Rwandese in Zaire. Official encouragement then stopped, but the movement continued.

The 1970 census reported 335,180 Rwandese in Zaire, most of them in Nord-Kivu.

In Haut-Zaire, the influx of Sudanese and Ugandans similarly explains a substantial increase in the population of the Ueles and Ituri in 1970 and of Ituri in 1984. In Aru and Mahagi Zones, the population grew from 131,166 and 166,280 inhabitants in 1958 to 392,214 and 416,058, respectively, in 1984.

In Shaba also, a foreign influx is necessary in order to explain the especially substantial growth rates from 1958 to 1970, but a good number of immigrants also came from the Kasais, especially Kasai Oriental.

I have explained, for both Kasais, why and in what direction I deemed it necessary to amend the official figures for 1970. In order to illustrate here the importance of migratory movements to Shaba, I add that in 1957 in the mining towns of Lubumbashi and Likasi 40 percent and 31 percent of the

TABLE 20.6 Annual Growth Rates per Thousand by Subregion

Region and Subregion	1938–1948	1948–1958	1958–1970	1970–1984
Kinshasa[a]	12.17	11.38	9.81	6.20
Bas-Zaire				
Matadi	7.53	9.10	4.49	3.52
Boma	4.60	10.08	5.57	3.26
Bas-Flueve[b]	.79	1.39	2.96	2.72
Cataractes	2.01	1.65	4.36	2.59
Lukaya	2.64	−.33	3.78	1.39
Total	1.89	1.65	3.84	2.52
Bandundu				
Bandundu	8.46	7.95	18.17	−1.17
Kikwit	4.80	9.14	19.43	1.95
Kwilu	.63	3.32	1.68	2.50
Kwango	.14	1.51	2.37	2.33
Mai-Ndombe	1.22	1.86	3.41	3.43
Total	.62	2.67	2.68	2.52
Equateur				
Mbandaka	1.61	18.77	5.42	1.34
Equateur	−.65	−.60	1.88	2.98
Nord-Ubangi	.68	1.49	1.88	3.45
Sud-Ubangi and Mongo	1.43	1.95	2.77	2.93
Mongala	.38	1.70	3.41	3.43
Tshuapa	−.62	−	.96	1.78
Total	.22	1.20	2.31	2.71
Haut-Zaire				
Kisangani	15.95	6.77	6.00	2.00
Tshopo	−1.45	.48	1.50	1.04
Bas-Uele	−.71	.24	.92	.38
Haut-Uele	−1.36	.26	1.70	1.30
Ituri	1.29	1.92	2.81	4.10
Total	−.41	.97	2.07	2.13
Kivu				
Bukavu[c]	−	9.87	9.04	1.95
Sud-Kivu	.71	3.27	4.17	3.72
Nord-Kivu	3.73	5.30	2.12	3.74
Maniema	.82	1.27	2.37	2.00
Total	1.65	3.64	3.22	3.38
Shaba				
Lubumbashi	13.14	6.53	4.80	4.60
Likasi	9.49	6.49	5.78	2.74
Kolwezi	10.00	9.18	3.31	7.22
Lualaba[d]	−.27	2.08	4.28	.95
Haut-Lomami	.95	2.07	3.64	3.45
Tanganyika	1.57	2.34	3.17	2.78
Haut-Shaba	1.93	2.44	2.54	3.62
Total	1.84	2.91	3.68	3.16

(*continued over*)

TABLE 20.6 continued

Region and Subregion	1938–1948	1948–1958	1958–1970	1970–1984
Kasai Oriental				
Mbuji-Mayi[e]	–	13.67	15.31	5.32
Tshilenge	–.06	–.76	8.54	3.94
Sankuru	.55	.62	1.28	2.40
Kabinda	–1.56	1.44	2.94	3.11
Total	–.40	1.05	4.19	3.42
Kasai Occidental				
Kananga	4.52	10.14	5.71	2.59
Kasai	.40	1.21	2.46	3.19
Lulua	–1.30	1.10	2.25	1.45
Total	–.43	1.67	2.69	2.32
Grand Total	.60	2.22	3.16	3.03

[a]White population included, that is, 2,135 units in 1938, 7,257 in 1948, and 21,566 in 1958.
[b]Includes the zone of Moanda.
[c]Included in Sud-Kivu in 1938.
[d]Includes the zones of Mutshatsha and Lubudi.
[e]Included in Tshilenge subregion in 1938.

inhabitants, respectively, knew the Tshiluba language. The corresponding percentage was 16 percent for the whole of the Likasi territory and 15 percent for the Kipushi territory.

THE SEARCH FOR POPULATION MODELS FROM 1938 TO 1984

In order to refine these first results even further, I attempted to complete them by resorting to population models in the form of the classic tables of A. J. Coale and P. Demeny. For the years 1958–1984, I took the conclusions of my previous work, set in reference to the North models of such tables.[17] For the earlier years, I adopted the reference to West models more commonly found in the work of U.S. researchers. The rates of natural increase reached in this way are slightly higher than they would have been had I kept the reference to the North models.

I used the proportion of females below the age of fifteen as entries in the population tables and an estimate of life expectancy at birth for the same sex. These figures (Table 20.7) have been determined for each of the nine present regions of Zaire.

In order to calculate the estimates for life expectancy at birth, I started from the results of the great demographic surveys of 1955–1957 as adjusted on 30 June 1956. I extrapolated these results for the years 1938, 1948, and 1958 by adopting the standard recommended by the United Nations of an

TABLE 20.7 Life Expectancy at Birth and Proportion of Females Below the Age of 15, 1938–1975

Region	Life Expectancy of Girls at Birth				Girls/All Females		
	1938	1948	1958	1975	1938	1948	1958
Bas-Zaire	30.615	35.615	40.615	47.215	474	474	484
Bandundu	29.296	34.296	39.296	45.896	419	437	448
Kinshasa	29.018	34.018	39.018	47.518	270	378	513
Equateur	32.796	37.796	42.796	49.396	342	360	382
Haut-Zaire	31.888	36.888	41.888	48.488	349	350	360
Kivu	27.346	32.346	37.346	45.846	399	421	474
Shaba	35.063	40.063	45.063	51.663	357	379	447
Kasai Oriental	31.806	36.806	41.806	48.406	330	359	396
Kasai Occidental	22.967	27.967	32.967	41.467	403	403	427
All	30.306	35.306	40.306	46.906	377	392	426

increase of 2.5 years for every five years. From 1956 to 1975, I assumed that all regions with the exception of the Kivu and western Kasai underwent a slightly less rapid growth of two years every five years. As a matter of fact, past a certain threshold, mortality is hard to reduce.

In order to determine the proportion of females below the age of fifteen, I adhered to the official figures for subregions or zones that best correspond to present boundaries. Taking into account expressed criticism regarding age determination during the colonial era, I made parallel calculations on the basis of a proportion of individuals below the age of fifteen obtained by relating the number of boys to the total of boys and adult women. However, these calculations led to less-satisfying results, suggesting overestimated rates of natural growth.

Based on the above two parameters, it became possible to calculate birth and mortality rates by region. They appear in Table 20.8 for the years 1938, 1948, 1958, 1958–1975, and 1975–1980.

The figures obtained in this way reflect in part the assumptions I adopted regarding the change in life expectancy at birth. However, these assumptions coincide with the increase in the proportion of individuals below the age of fifteen recorded in all regions. Actually, the combination of these data leads to an estimate of birthrates with a generally acceptable sequence. These rates are the lowest for Equateur, Haut-Zaire, and Kasai Oriental, as is known from other sources. Moreover, until today, the birthrate remains relatively low in Haut-Zaire: it began increasing in Kasai Oriental as of 1948 and in Equateur as of 1958. This also corresponds to recognized trends. The application of population models to the town of Kinshasa is unreliable; still, it indicates correctly that the birthrate was very low in 1938 and that it took its place among the highest in the country in all later censuses.

Starting from these birth and mortality figures, I compared natural increase with the intercensal total population increase in order to calculate net

TABLE 20.8 Birth and Mortality Rates, 1938–1984 (%)

Regions and Rate	1938	1948	1958	1956–1975	1975–1980
Bas-Zaire					
Birthrate	59.80	55.94	54.47	52.32	51.62
Mortality	35.23	28.69	23.55	19.30	16.81
Natural increase	24.57	27.25	31.02	33.02	34.81
Bandundu					
Birthrate	51.03	50.49	49.35	50.85	50.32
Mortality	35.48	29.45	24.31	20.76	17.96
Natural increase	15.55	21.04	25.04	30.09	32.36
Kinshasa					
Birthrate	28.31	41.32	60.58	54.90	55.83
Mortality	34.99	29.05	25.77	15.00	13.52
Natural increase	−6.68	12.27	34.81	39.90	42.31
Equateur					
Birthrate	36.60	36.91	38.04	42.39	42.09
Mortality	30.22	25.33	21.09	17.42	15.54
Natural increase	6.38	11.58	16.95	24.97	26.55
Haut-Zaire					
Birthrate	38.12	35.88	35.38	39.51	39.18
Mortality	31.24	26.19	21.96	18.14	16.34
Natural increase	6.88	9.69	13.42	21.37	22.84
Kivu					
Birthrate	49.15	49.11	54.79	52.29	51.86
Mortality	37.80	31.47	26.72	20.35	17.95
Natural increase	11.35	17.64	28.07	31.94	33.91
Shaba					
Birthrate	37.65	38.63	46.54	50.02	49.53
Mortality	27.86	23.27	19.28	15.68	13.46
Natural increase	9.79	15.36	27.26	34.34	36.07
Kasai Oriental					
Birthrate	35.37	37.19	40.38	47.59	47.13
Mortality	31.32	36.24	21.83	18.18	16.00
Natural increase	4.05	10.95	18.55	29.41	31.13
Kasai Occidental					
Birthrate	54.28	49.36	49.68	49.11	51.41
Mortality	45.57	37.01	30.83	24.66	24.07
Natural increase	8.71	12.35	18.85	24.45	27.34
All					
Birthrate	43.29	42.71	45.44	48.30	48.39
Mortality	33.27	27.73	23.18	18.85	16.83
Natural increase	10.02	14.98	22.26	29.45	31.56

migration. To this end, I assumed that the natural increase rate of the years 1938–1948 and 1948–1958 could be estimated by averaging the 1938 and 1948 rates on the one hand, and the 1948 and 1958 rates on the other. For an estimate of the demographic indexes from 1956 to 1970, I kept to the rates established for 1956–1975; and for 1970–1984, I kept to the rates established for the years 1975–1980. A comparison of the rates obtained in this fashion with the intercensal growth rates shown in Table 20.8 immediately appeared more consistent if corrections in terms of census trends are introduced in table. At the level of the total, I estimated that the censuses of 1938,

1948, and 1958 were on the average underestimated by 2.4 percent, 5.7 percent, and 3.9 percent. The result is an underestimation of the 1938–1948 annual growth rate on the order of .32 percent, approximately on the order of .17 percent from 1948 to 1958, and on the order of .34 percent from 1958 to 1970. If these corrections are taken into account, the growth rate of the total population of Zaire per year from 1938 to 1948 was .92 percent. It went up to 2.05 percent from 1948 to 1958, 2.82 percent from 1958 to 1970, and 3.03 percent from 1970 to 1984. This sequence appears more likely than the sequence of the numbers proposed previously. The question remains how to distribute the resulting adjustment between the regions.

Lacking more precise information, I restricted suggested rectifications in the total—for the African population only—to only those regions where change brought about a correction that tended to make the figure more credible. Thus, in 1938 and 1948 there was no correction to the population figures of Kinshasa, Kivu, or Shaba, where revised figures are more credible in light of historical knowledge. In 1958 the numbers for the same regions and for the Bandundu were not rectified for the same reason and also to avoid having to suppose a global increase rate higher than the natural increase from 1948 to 1958 for the Bandundu. The basis for these assumptions is the improvement of census quality rather than in higher population counts. It is like assuming either that the rate of census coverage had already reached its final level in 1938 (which might be the case for Kinshasa and Shaba) or that it did not go beyond the 1938 level in 1948 and 1958 (which might be the case for Kivu). For the Bandundu, where I recorded population numbers in 1938 and 1948 but not in 1958, I assume implicitly that total administrative control occurred in 1958.

After completing calculations and corrections as proposed, I arrived at intercensal natural and total increase rates. (See Table 20.9.)

TABLE 20.9 Intercensal Natural and Global Increase Rates, 1938–1984 (%)

Region	Natural Increase Rate				Intercensal Total Increase Rate			
	1938–1948	1948–1958	1958–1970	1970–1984	1938–1948	1948–1958	1958–1970	1970–1984
Bas-Zaire	2.591	2.914	3.302	3.481	2.354	1.484	3.326	2.517
Bandundu	1.830	2.304	3.009	3.236	1.081	1.917	2.678	2.517
Kinshasa	.280	2.354	3.990	4.231	12.176	11.384	9.810	6.202
Equateur	.898	1.427	2.497	2.655	.678	1.037	1.798	2.711
Haut-Zaire	.829	1.156	2.137	2.284	.046	.802	1.563	2.128
Kivu	1.450	2.286	3.194	3.391	1.649	3.644	3.219	3.383
Shaba	1.258	2.131	3.434	3.607	1.837	2.905	3.679	3.160
Kasai Oriental	.750	1.475	2.941	3.113	.051	.919	3.674	3.418
Kasai Occidental	1.053	1.560	3.445	2.734	.025	1.506	2.132	2.319
All	1.250	1.862	2.945	3.156	.918	2.048	2.823	3.032

The rates obtained in this manner could be compared advantageously with ones that could be calculated through an analysis of retrospective fecundity starting from contemporary data and those obtained from the 1955–1957 demographic surveys. However, the operation is not as simple as it appears, since there are no dependable contemporary data for the whole of Zaire's population. Even for the western regions of the country, where estimates of vital rates were done in 1975–1976, using these evaluations is awkward since they rest on obviously underestimated population figures. Thus, the proposed rates are not compatible with the census data that I have on the whole accepted. These estimates are shown in Table 20.10.

TABLE 20.10 Estimates of Edoza Survey for 1975–1976 (%)

Region	Birthrate	Mortality Rate	Natural Increase
Bas-Zaire	45.2	15.3	29.9
Bandundu	44.4	20.7	23.7
Kinshasa	54.9	15.0	39.9
Kasai Occidental	41.3	21.4	19.9

Retrospectively, the authors of the EDOZA survey are of the opinion that "a slight increase (in fecundity) has occurred during the last 20 or 25 years." This increase is estimated at 5 percent from 1956 until 1971 and "appears to have occurred mainly between 1956 and 1966."[18] My data show a tendency of the natural increase to stabilize after 1975, but they indicate that the most substantial natural increase occurred between 1948 and 1958 and is due essentially to a decline in mortality. It is possible to combine these historical trends but not to adopt estimates of the rate of natural growth increase so much lower than the intercensal growth rate that was retained. Thus, we are forced to limit ourselves to the results obtained from stable population models.

These generally consistent results allow us to assume that they represent a first approximation of reality. They acquire full significance when we calculate the balance of migration that they allow. I have done this by the method of expected population, that is, by the difference between the population figure created solely by the natural movement at the end of the period and the figure of recorded population, as I worked it out after various corrections were made.[19] For 1984 I increased the census figures by 1.08 percent, in accordance with overall estimates. The results of these calculations appear in Table 20.11.

For some regions, especially for the town of Kinshasa, the figures reached are a very good approximation of the already-well-known reality. The series I am offering is equally acceptable for the Bas-Zaire, the number of emigrants to Kinshasa being compensated for in 1958–1970 by the arrival of refugees from Angola. In Kivu, the migratory influx can also be easily

TABLE 20.11 Balance of Migration, 1938-1984

Region	1938-1948	1948-1958	1958-1970	1970-1984
Bas-Zaire	--19,256	-143,531	3,761	-254,634
Bandundu	-121,511	-74,195	-98,061	-338,970
Kinshasa	89,304	222,296	531,871	640,935
Equateur	-37,949	-75,035	-191,773	62,853
Haut-Zaire	-196,094	-93,647	-209,869	-45,062
Kivu	30,739	279,543	9,100	50,502
Shaba	68,900	120,339	67,252	-200,029
Kasai Oriental	-65,429	-59,481	117,545	123,214
Kasai Occidental	-120,023	-6,971	-49,768	-108,641
Total	-371,319	169,318	180,058	69,832

discerned, although the break in the external influx from 1958 to 1970 is unreliable. The balances of migration of Kasai are not understood as well. On the showing of my calculations, they had been relatively substantial with the outside; but the return of the Shaba's Baluba, which could serve to explain the high positive figure of 1958-1970, is not offset by corresponding departures from the Shaba region. It is possible that the positive balance since 1958 corresponds only to an overestimated population figure in 1970 and in 1984. At the national level, however, the totals obtained are credible. If they are confirmed, they would correspond to a net emigration of 371,319 individuals from 1938 to 1948, that is to say, for the most part, during World War II. This is B. S. Fetter's assumption and does not contradict my more detailed research.[20] Since 1948 external migrations show, in favor of Zaire, a positive balance until 1970 of 169,318 between 1948 and 1958 and 180,058 between 1958 and 1970. From 1970 to 1984 the figures shown should only be used with extreme caution, since they rely on estimates of natural movement that had been set at the source by assuming migratory movements differing from those proposed here.

If we continue to make similar calculations at the level of the subregions, we will probably come closer to reality. The estimates given here at the regional level demonstrate the possibility of proceeding to an extremely sophisticated reconstitution of Zaire's demographic history from 1938 at least, starting from the life expectancy determined in 1956 and the proportion of females below the age of fifteen. Our estimates by region also allow for an immediate understanding of the complex implications of the various assumptions about the history of Zaire's population.

CONCLUSION

I had planned to show the statistical data available since the 1920s for Zaire's population. I was not able to utilize the population figures of 1927-1928, since they are, on the average, underestimated by 20 percent; and their margin of imprecision leads to doubts about the growth rates from 1928 to 1938, which go beyond the scale of such rates. However, I was able to reconstruct the evolution of the population within the boundaries of today's subregions since 1938 and to offer estimates of birth and mortality rates and balance of migration by region. These estimates are not to be considered final, but they do offer a secure base for further research. As regards methodology, resorting to population models and supplying a cartographical analysis annexed to statistical study of population figures have been productive. In a large measure, they have already allowed us to propose a history of Zaire's population that is quite sophisticated.

NOTES

1. B. S. Fetter, "The Missing Migrants: African Seeds in the Demographer's Field," *History in Africa* 11 (1984).

2. L. de St. Moulin, *Carte de densité de la population d'après le recensement de 1970* (Kinshasa, 1978), 1:3 million and 1:5 million editions; P. Gourou, *Carte de la densité des populations*, in *Atlas Général du Congo* (Brussels, 1951), 1:5 million; M. Robert, *Considérations suggérées par l'étude du milieu physique centre-africain* (Brussels, 1945), inset map, 1:10 million; J. de Jonghe, Population density map for 1928, in *L'essor économique belge: Expansion coloniale*, vol. 1 (Brussels, 1930), 81; F. Goffart, *Le Congo: Géographie physique, politique, et économique*, 2d ed., ed. G. Morissens (Brussels, 1908), 94; F. Goffart, *Traité méthodique de géographie du Congo*, 2d ed. (Antwerp, 1898), 55; P. Gourou, *Notice des cartes de la densité et de la localisation de la population dans la province de l'Equateur, Atlas Général du Congo* (Brussels, 1960), 1:1 million; R. E. de Smet, *Carte de la densité et de la localisation de la Province Orientale* (Brussels, 1962), 1:1 million; idem, *Carte de la densité et de la localisation de l'ancienne Province de Léopoldville* (Brussels, 1966), 1:1 million; idem, *Carte de la densité et de la localisation de la population de la Province du Katanga* (Brussels, 1971), 1:1 million. The 1:200 thousand minutes and the corresponding demographic data were gathered by the same R. E. de Smet, who kindly shared them with us. I wish to express here my gratitude and my esteem. Thanks to him, I have also received a copy of the 1:1 million minutes and of the statistics gathered by P. Gourou for his map corresponding to the situation in 1948.

3. *Carte de l'Etat Indépendant du Congo*, 1:1 million in 12 sheets, Institut Géographique Justus Perthes (Gotha, 1907). Cf. L. de St. Moulin, "L'organisation de l'espace en Afrique Centrale à la fin du XIXᵉ siècle," *Cultures et développement* 14, nos. 2–3 (1982), 259–296.

4. Cf. P. Burke and J. Mortelmans, "Rol van België in de strijd tegen de slaapziekte en de dierlijke trypanosomiases en hun studie," *Bulletin des séances de l'ARSOM*, supplement, no. 1 (1980), pp. iii–135 and the bibliography in Sabakinu Kivilu, *La population du Zaïre: Un essai bibliographique* (Lubumbashi, 1982), 13–15.

5. Cf. A. Retel-Laurentin, *Infécondité en Afrique Noire: Maladies et conséquences sociales* (Paris, 1974) and the discussions that followed this publication.

6. J. Boute and L. de St. Moulin, *Perspectives démographiques régionales 1975-1985* (Kinshasa, 1978).

7. L. de St. Moulin, *Atlas des collectivités du Zaïre* (Kinshasa, 1976). Cf. also L. de St. Moulin, "La répartition de la population du Zaïre en 1970," *Cultures et développement* 6 (1974), 331-349.

8. SICAI, *Etude démographique de Kananga*, under the direction of J. Houyoux 18 and 101. This data is combined with my own estimate of the migratory movement.

9. Kayemba Mulumba, "Histoire de la ville de Kananga: Extension et aspects socio-démographiques des origines à 1970," Université Nationale du Zaïre (Lubumbashi, 1976), 95.

10. See n. 2.

11. Cf. Mulumba, "Histoire." Our thanks go to P. Gourou for this information.

12. Some 1948 census totals were distributed as indicated below:

Territory and Subregion	Population
Gemena	
Nord-Ubangi	62,059
Sud-Ubangi	172,694
Lisala	
Nord-Ubangi	5,524
Mongala	69,424
Bongandanga	
Equateur	15,485
Mongala	13,576
Tshilenge	
Kabinda	26,051
Tshilenge	118,625
Dibaya	
Tshilenge	20,688
Kabinda	5,017
Lulua	118,013
Luluabourg	
Lulua	43,362
Jadotville	
Town of Likasi (CEC)	15,290
Lualaba	20,356
Haut-Shaba	42,878

Moreover, a rectification appearing in later AIMO reports, maintained at the regional archives of Kisangani, led us to adopt as population numbers for the Isangi and Yahuma territories 125,613 (+273) and 39,313 (-602).

13. Kadima-Schipa, "Histoire de la population africaine de Likasi" (Lubumbashi, 1973), 34 bis.

14. Kazadi Nkola Lubilanji, "Monographie socio-économique du territoire de Kolwezi (1940-1958)" (Lubumbashi, 1977), 10.

15. Mulumba, "Histoire," 65.

16. Some totals from the 1938 census were distributed as follows:

Territory and Subregion	Population
Matadi	
Town of Matadi	12,488
Bas-Fleuve	11,277
Cataractes	23,345
de la Giri	
Sud-Ubangi	66,592
Equateur	17,351
Gemena	
Sud-Ubangi	109,361
Nord-Ubangi	46,801
Lisala	
Nord-Ubangi	5,303
Mongala	66,848
Bongandanga	
Mongala	16,259
Equateur	18,544
Buta	
Tshopo	12,900
Bas-Uele	110,717
Niapu	
Tshopo	11,373
Bas-Uele	42,044
Wamba	
Haut-Uele	153,536
Ituri	11,939
Lubutu	
Tshopo	4,938
Maniema	34,435
Shabunda	
Maniema	12,134
Sud-Kivu	76,901
Bukama	
Lomami	51,964
Lualaba	9,307
Jadotville	
Lualaba	38,844
Haut-Shaba	38,273
Tshikapa	
Kasai	185,199
Lulua	42,716
Luebo	
Kasai	66,062
Lulua	13,632
Dibaya	
Lulua	100,971
Tshilenge	68,525
Kabinda	5,015
Tshofa	
Kabinda	81,487
Sankuru	20,242

17. J. Boute and L. de St. Moulin, Zaire, in Groupe de Demographie Africaine IDP, INDED, INSEE, MINICOOP, ORSTOM, *L'évaluation des effectifs de la population des pays africains*, vol. 1 (Paris, 1982), 301–323.

18. République du Zaïre, Societa d'Ingegneria et Consulenza Attivita Industriali, Rome (SICAI) and Département de Démographie de l'Université Catholique de Louvain, *EDOZA, Etude démographique de l'ouest du Zaïre, 1975–1976*, vol. 1, *Mouvement de la population*, 65, 69; idem, *Synthèse des études démographiques de l'ouest du Zaïre 1974–1977*, 155.

19. Cf. G. Wunsch's calculation of balances of migration by the method of "expected population" characteristics and evaluation of slants, *Population et famille* 18 [1969], 49–61. Population numbers retained by region are shown in Table 20.12.

TABLE 20.12 Population Numbers Retained by Region, 1938–1984

Region	1938	1948	1958	1970	1984
Bas-Zaire	653,416	824,627	955,480	1,392,025	1,992,845
Bandundu	1,425,297	1,587,177	1,919,000	2,600,556	3,722,680
Kinshasa	42,036	132,532	389,547	1,142,761	2,682,260
Equateur	1,608,430	1,720,897	1,907,819	2,341,695	3,442,348
Haut-Zaire	2,408,272	2,419,439	2,620,486	3,131,985	4,251,564
Kivu	1,342,631	1,581,258	2,261,822	3,256,117	5,243,980
Shaba	1,035,448	1,242,234	1,654,176	2,506,241	3,915,922
Kasai Oriental	902,962	907,587	991,219	1,500,908	2,248,591
Kasai Occidental	1,112,154	1,114,949	1,294,642	1,659,434	2,312,158

20. Cf. L. de St. Moulin, "La population du Congo pendant la seconde guerre mondiale," in Académie Royale des Sciences d'Outremer, *Le Congo durant la seconde guerre mondiale* (Brussels, 1983), 15–50.

21

Population and Worker Mortality in Western Zaire, ca. 1900-1935

SABAKINU KIVILU

The analysis of population data produced in Africa during the colonial period is quite suggestive, in that these inquiries lead us to a number of fresh questions relating to not-so-distant times. Actually, their diversity, richness, and limitations not only are the occasion to perfect our knowledge (thanks to the important work accomplished in the field of African historical demography), but also constitute a basis for exploring various methodological approaches that can be used for different parts of the continent.

My approach, based on current technology in the field of population history, contains the following elements: (1) the assumption that level 4 of the South model of A. J. Coale and P. Demeny best describes the local situation,[1] (2) the willingness to test different stable population models,[2] (3) recourse to successive iterations for "which actual population evolution would be considered as an equation to be reconstructed—or more exactly as a group of complementary equations," and (4) the use of computerized simulation models.

However, these generalization models must coincide with specific African historical cases in order to validate their conclusions. There is, moreover, a risk that designs and indexes utilized in longitudinal analyses of demographic facts produce their own explanation, thus leaving aside historical and social realities. In the light of the tools and the methods put to use, this is to construct false evidence.

Actually, statistics—which express the ideology of the colonial power and are an instrument of domination, since they were the foundation for the planning of economic growth—produce "from actual materials, a fictitious reality presenting the appearance of an objective reality." To be able to function, the colonial state (or, simply, the industrial state) attempted to control the mechanisms of demographic regulation, especially as of the 1920s, a period during which obstacles were generated by African societies against the mechanisms imposed to produce men and lifestyles conforming to the needs of industrial societies. During this decade the colonial system of constraint began to traumatize the very milieu it was supposed to transform, working against the economic goals that its reproduction was intended to enhance.[3]

Thus, the manipulation of fecundity indexes would become a strategic area of *colonial demography*, for which a whole arithmetic system was devised not only to supply the demographic variables required for the formulation and the execution of economic policies but also to create mechanisms suitable for biological reproduction. Moreover, the religious missions, for their part, did everything in their power to create the same demographic constellations from a slightly different perspective. Their objective was to change the family structure and its ideology in order to enhance fecundity. Actually, they were attempting to impose a family code that would privilege the patrilineal line and monogamous marriage. Thus, Fr. J. van Wing was able to conclude, "The matriarchal clan is breaking down, and instead of producing a multitude of demoralized and sterile individuals, from its fragmentation appear monogamous and fecund Catholic families, where paternal rights are recognized, where the wife is honored and the children become the pole of affection and preoccupation."[4] As a result, demographic realities were found in indexes and in explanations of population phenomena constructed by colonial secular and religious bureaucracies.

This is why the statistics and analyses created by the discipline of colonial demography should be examined in the light of the effective operation of demographic regulation mechanisms rooted in the family production model. Such a perspective implies taking into account data and conclusions drawn from studies on the concern of the African societies for population problems and identifying ways of fostering population growth. This would allow us to really create a historical demography of African societies, distinct from colonial demography and *dependency demography*, which today keep us from going beyond the variables used in the demographic analyses of the industrial societies of Europe and the United States and to pose the problem of human reproduction correctly. These fundamental questions are examined in a collective study now in preparation.[5]

I shall turn to a more focused analysis of trends in total population and mortality among workers in western Zaire based on observations obtained from the colonial city of Matadi from 1900 to 1935. This period is of particular interest, because it is less known than more recent time.

The study comprises two essential parts: population formation and workers' mortality.

POPULATION FORMATION

Estimates and Trends of the Evolution
of the African Population of Matadi

Enormous difficulties appear when one attempts to know the rhythm of growth of the African population of Matadi before 1926. Data are irregular and heterogeneous. Only the narrative sources, in which are found numbers left by travelers, missionaries, journalists, and businessmen, together with their impressions, supply us with some information. This information is reproduced in Table 21.1, with the addition of some elements of appreciation.

Certainly, the estimates diverge in several areas, probably because of a different choice of basic estimates and multiplying factors. But judging from these estimates, one notes that the town of Matadi underwent some population increases, especially after World War I. At first, the growth rate of 6.7 per year between 1892 and 1925 that they suggest appears too big; but other data, especially those concerning the Catholic population, confirm the general increase in population suggested by these figures.

Ecclesiastical statistics are another source of estimating the evolution of the African population. They are contained in a register called "Etat religieux de la Préfecture Apostolique de Matadi" (Religious status of the Apostolic Prefecture of Matadi). This document, kept at the Bishopric of Matadi, gives statistical information concerning religious activities by year from 1904 to 1933 and by missionary station. It should be underlined that the total Catholic population includes baptized individuals as well as catechumens.

However, before using these figures, it is imperative to discuss their reliability and a determination of the limits of the population involved. Data exist that allow us to define their scope. We know that Matadi consisted of three areas: the first one in the center of the town, the second in the African quarter, and the third in the Kinkanda hospital. This distribution appears quite clearly in the source consulted. Besides, the numbers of catechumens from the villages surrounding Matadi are known. This allows us to exclude them. On the other hand, Matadi's immediate hinterland (the left bank of the river, at least) was less populated, and villages few. Moreover, the action of the Redemptorist fathers in Matadi was concentrated on the workers' population; while the surrounding villages were mainly in the orbit of the Protestant missionaries, who were established there since 1876.[6] Besides, I do not believe that the few differences observed between these estimates and those contained in some of the mission's reports impair the statistical series obtained.[7] Moreover, I feel that the 1922 figure is an overestimation of reality, since it deviates from the general movement suggested by the data obtained: thus, I shall not take them into account in my analyses.

Starting from such considerations, it can be affirmed that the recorded figures relate to the Catholic population of Matadi and reflect its movement to the extent that the missionaries were able to perceive it.

TABLE 21.1 Matadi's African Population from Travel Reports

Year	Estimates	Sources
1892	700–800	A. J. Wauters[a]
1894	±1,300	A. Thys[b]
1897	±1,550	P. Conreur[c]
1899	±2,000	L. Minjauw[d]
1901	±4,000	Baptist Mission Society[e]
1902	±3,000	G. Moulaert[f]
1908	2,300	F. van der Linden[g]
1910	±2,000	L. van der Dijek[h]
1920	5,000	S. Leplae[i]
1922	5,500	P. Despas[j]
1923	5,000	E. D. Chalux[k]
1925	7,000	J. E. Geil[l]

[a]General secretary of the Compagnie du Chemin de Fer du Congo (CCFC) and editor of *Le mouvement géographique*: "La population de Matadi," in *Congo illustré* (1892), 21.

[b]General administrative officer of the CCFC: *Conférence sur le Congo donnée le 15 janvier à l'établissement des Dames de la Sainte-Famille à Liège* (Brussels, 1894), 45.

[c]"La vie à Matadi," *Indépendance belge*, 19 May 1897. This article was written in Matadi on 11 April 1897. Some information concerning the author's biography is given in the present text..

[d]A Redemptorist father, responsible for writing the history of this congregation. He was able to access the first archival documents of the Catholic mission of Matadi: *Les Rédemptoristes, cinquante ans au Bas-Congo, 1899–1949* (Louvain, 1949), 23.

[e]BMS, *Annual Report* (1901), 86–87. The report notes that due to population growth in the city, "the chapel erected by the Coast people has been considerably enlarged and improved and new seats have been ordered from England."

[f]Sent to the Congo as a lieutenant of the police force in 1902 and detached to the fort of Shinkakasa. He completed the work on this important fort meant for the protection of the Lower Congo. On that occasion, he visited Matadi several times in 1902: *Souvenirs d'Afrique* (Brussels, 1945), 22; and Bibliographie Coloniale Belge (BCB) IV (Brussels, 1956), vol. 4, col. 232.

[g]A Belgian journalist sent on a mission by the dailies *L'Etoile belge* and *La Chronique* in 1908–1909: *Au Congo, les noirs, et nous*, 2d ed. (Paris, 1910), 59.

[h]Redemptorist father who arrived in the Congo in September 1909 and was detached successively to the missions of Tumba, Matadi, and Thysville. His letter was published in *Gerardusbode* 14 (1910), 315.

[i]The figure is supplied by Matadi, as for other important urban centers in 1920, in order to defend agricultural policies. Actually, the author was the general director of agriculture at the colonial ministry: "La politique agricole au Congo belge," in *Congrès National Colonial* (1920), 219.

[j]"Visiteur extraordinaire," in *Les Missions Redemptoristes*, ed. M. Dratz, 65.

[k]A journalist with the daily *Nation belge*, who stayed in Matadi in August 1923: *Un an au Congo* (Brussels, 1925), 30; see also "E. D. Chalux est mort, l'homme le plus extraordinaire que j'ai connu," in *Bulletin du Cercle Royal Africain du Centre* 47 (1950), 1507–1508.

[l]"The Year 1925 in the A.B.F.M.S.," *Congo Mission News*, July 1926, p. 17.

Two other elements appear important in this critique: the year of reference and the aim of the preparation of this statistical information. From 1903 to 1912 the ecclesiastical year began on 1 July, from 1913 to 1930 on

1 October, and from 1931 to 1933 on 1 June. In other respects these statistics were prepared in order to show the importance of missionary work and to encourage the generosity of the benefactors. Thus, they can only be considered as a scale of sizes. Figure 21.1 shows their evolution.

FIGURE 21.1 Evolution of the Population of Zaire, 1915–1984

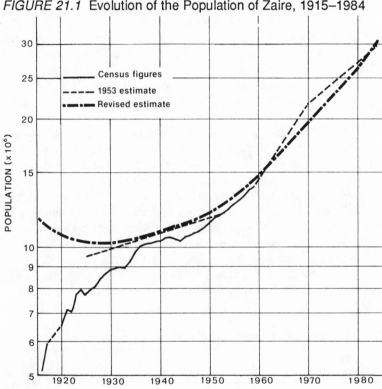

SOURCE: Gaëtan Feltz

On the whole, the tendency of the Catholic population is positive: 6.3 percent per year between 1904 and 1925. As an exponential model, the growth rate is 5.1 percent. For instance, fourteen years (i.e., till 1928) were needed to regain the level reached in 1913. Moreover, the progressive coming together of both curves—that of the Catholic population and that of the baptized individuals—is to be noted. This phenomenon is a sign of the improvement of statistical quality, as registration of baptisms was more systematic than registration of catechumens. This trend shows up rather clearly as of 1916 and lasts until 1933. However, the general movement of the Catholic population initiated prior to 1913 stops as of 1914. A decrease follows until 1929, except for increase in 1920–1921. World War I and the ensuing economic consequences certainly represent the main explanation for this. Actually, the decrease in external commerce limited manpower needs, which used to determine the population growth of Matadi. Other explanations may also be put forward. During the war missionary action slackened due to lack of personnel and financial means. Numerous catechists gave up their function for other jobs with the state—the CCFC—as the mission paid them little or not at all. This brought about irregularity in pastoral work.[8] The source that supplies us with statistical data gives us another explanation: the decrease in the Catholic population was due to the Angolans' going back to their country of origin.[9] The decrease observed in 1923 is attributable to the start of African resistance to Christian religion, particularly with the Kimbanguist religious movement. It must also be explained by economic factors.

Conclusions derived from this brief analysis of the Catholic population are certainly indicative of the main trends of the evolution of the total population. But one should not forget that the Catholic population represented only a part of the African population of Matadi. This is why one should question what fraction it represented in relation to the total Matadi population. This operation will allow us to reconstitute the numbers of African people based on the existing data. This undertaking requires knowledge of the mechanism of the problems under study. The following paragraphs initiate a reconstitution of the total population.

The "Registre de l'état religieux" (Register of the religious status) supplies estimates of the total population from 1931 to 1933, as shown in Table 21.2.

TABLE 21.2 Estimates of Total Population Based on Catholic Sources

Year	Protestants	Catholics	Muslims	Pagans	Total	Percent Catholic
1931	3,000	4,540	100	3,200	10,840	41.88
1932	3,000	4,355	100	3,208	10,663	40.84
1933	3,000	4,265	—	3,200	10,465	40.75

It stands out from the analysis of this table that the estimates concerning non-Catholics do not reflect reality. The same figures are recalled from 1931 to 1933. These years are years of great fluctuations in the workers' population because of the economic crisis. According to the source, the total population underwent a reduction of barely 3.4 percent; while the administration indicates 9.3 percent. Even supposing that the 1931 estimates are closer to reality, the result obtained deviates unduly from the result supplied by the administrative source (8,629) for the same year. This deficiency in the non-Catholic estimate leads us to use the data from administrative sources (since they appear to be closer to reality).

Based on these figures and those of the Catholic population, I calculated ratios and established an average. The Catholic population would, on the average, account for 44.14 percent between 1926 and 1931. However significant, this proportion cannot apply to the entire period under study. The birth of the Kimbanguist movement in 1921 was to bring about many defections from the Catholic church. If the Redemptorist fathers' statements are to be believed, this religious movement seriously hampered the action of the Catholic church in Matadi[10] and would justify the curve of baptized individuals, as was observed. In other respects, we have at our disposal another scale of size that allows us better to determine the ratio between Catholics and the total population: according to Fr. P. Despas, in 1922 Matadi's African population included 38.18 percent Catholics.[11] While I considered this estimate of Catholics undervalued, it represents a significant indication of the importance of the Catholic population. However, I find it difficult to specify the proportion of Catholics in Matadi's population. The absence of basic elements that could help with such a calculation[12] drives me to be content with approximative indications. I suppose that the Catholic population represented at least 50 percent, and the resulting population figures generally reach the same level as figures obtained from other sources. Table 21.4 regroups my estimates of the African population based on the Catholic population figures. Nevertheless, I adjusted them so that they correspond to the calendar year.[13] I also included population estimates obtained from African manpower data.[14]

TABLE 21.3 Ratios of Catholic Population and Numbers from the Administrative Census

Year	Catholic Pop.	Administrative Data	Percent Catholic
1926	2,363	4,841	48.81
1928	3,013	8,474	35.56
1929	4,367	9,313	46.89
1930	4,320	11,730	36.83
1931	4,540	8,629	52.61
Average			44.14

The main trends that appear are almost identical to those observed in the Catholic population. Generally, the population curve first progresses rather rapidly until 1912, then sags during World War I and increases again as of 1919. Even if we lack approximative indications to estimate population change in the years 1921–1923, there is no doubt that this change was affected by the economic crisis of 1921–1922, during which manpower figures show a reduction on the order of 30.6 percent. These precipitous declines were also observed in Boma and Kinshasa.[15]

Starting in 1926, the evolution curve of the fundamental structure of the Matadi population can be retraced more or less precisely. In order to get a

TABLE 21.4 Assumed Evolution of Matadi's African Population, 1905–1925

Year	Impressions in Numbers	Estimates Based on Manpower	Estimates Based on Catholic Population
1905	—	—	1,278
1906	—	—	1,530
1907	—	—	2,080
1908	2,300	—	2,760
1909	—	—	3,158
1910	2,000+	—	2,994
1911	—	—	3,380
1912	—	—	4,338
1914	—	—	4,782
1915	—	—	4,634
1916	—	—	4,150
1917	—	—	4,172
1918	—	—	3,864
1919	—	—	4,014
1920	5,000	4,731	4,678
1921	—	4,161	—
1922	5,500	3,279	—
1924	—	4,784	5,272
1925	7,000	4,902	4,890

better measurement and also to determine its rhythm, it is necessary to present the data in numbers, together with the critique that is called for prior to going ahead with the analysis and interpretation of the results.

The first administrative census at our disposal dates from 1926. It appears in the table "Modèle 1: Affaires indigènes et main d'oeuvre" (AIMO), annexed to the political report of the Lower Congo District. This document makes a very clear distinction between the rural population and the population of the extracustomary centers for each territory. The population is broken down according to age and sex. Matadi's population is evaluated at 4,841 inhabitants. However, it is difficult to obtain a true picture from this figure. Nevertheless, we know that the adult male population totals 68.69 percent of the whole population. This proportion appears to characterize the urban centers of the time: in fact, we find it again in the "Cité indigène de Léopoldville" (68.88 percent in 1926).[16] Thus, it represents an interesting indicator. Another element of the critique could apply to African manpower statistics; this segment appears to constitute 87.75 percent of the total registered population. This ratio does not greatly diverge from that of the adult male population. The difference corresponds to nonadult manpower and manpower living in the villages surrounding Matadi.[17] The 1926 figure, then, probably reflects reality. Matadi's economic function for exploiting the colony and the resulting administrative needs required a systematic enumeration of the population. The population volume of 1927 is unknown to us due to lack of documentation. However, it had to be higher than the 1926 volume. The important engineering works carried out in the harbor and on railway lines required large numbers of workers. Manucongo, for instance, which employed 720 workers in 1926, requested 800 for 1927. The increase in total population is partly confirmed by the economic report of Lower Congo District for 1927, which indicates that 4,738 workers were employed in Matadi. Therefore, assuming that the ratio noted in 1926 between manpower and population number is constant, the town of Matadi had 5,574 African inhabitants in 1927. One element leads us to take this into account: in 1928 manpower numbers counted for 86.62 percent.[18]

Starting in 1928, many indications appear in relation to total population. The yellow fever epidemic in Matadi at the end of 1927 and in 1928 was the occasion of a systematic census. Even individual dwellings were counted. The work was accomplished under the direction of Dr. A. M. Duren, public health specialist and associate inspector of the Public Health Service of Congo-Kasai Province. The figures that appear in the annual reports of the Public Health Service of Matadi Territory and Lower Congo District correspond to the figures of the report on general administration of Matadi Territory. I used them for the years 1928[19] and 1930. The importance of the medical service report resides in the fact that it breaks down the population according to type of dwelling. No such indications are included in any of the political reports that represent our only source of information for the years 1932–1933.[20] The AIMO report of 1934 is more precise. Population count is accomplished by type of dwelling. Its aim is mainly to supply information necessary to the creation of the extracustomary center in Matadi and to the political control of the population in this period of social unrest.[21] The 1929 and 1931 figures come from the economic reports of the district (1929) and Matadi Territory (1931).

The figures thus obtained relate to the African population of the "native towns" and urban district. In order to obtain a global picture of the population of this urban center, I have also taken into account the non-African population.[22] Table 21.5 describes the whole population from 1926 to 1934.

TABLE 21.5 Evolution of the Total Population of the Matadi Urban Center, 1926–1934

Year	African Population	Non-African Pop.	Total Population
1926	4,841	647	5,488
1927	5,922	661	6,583
1928	8,474	653	9,127
1929	9,313	659	9,772
1930	11,737	708	12,445
1931	8,629	592	9,221
1932	7,759	439	8,198
1933	7,821	430	8,251
1934	6,548	350	6,898

The picture emerging from the analysis of the total population curve is that of a rather rapid demographic growth. But a noticeable acceleration occurred between 1926 and 1930, together with an average annual growth rate of 12.3 percent. Thus, the population more than doubled in five years: from 5,488 in 1926 to 12,445 in 1930. A period of demographic recession then ensued. The movement, which started before the economic crisis of 1929, grew blurred as of 1930. In 1934 the population had declined by 44.5 percent, an average annual decrease of 13.7 percent.

However, some demographic characteristics, especially migration and mortality, deserve to be discussed in order to complete the population profile described in this fashion.

Evolution of Matadi's Human Hinterland

Our information concerning the origins of the population before 1926 is rather fragmentary. However, we can obtain some idea based on recruitment undertaken by the CCFC at the time of railroad construction.

At the start of the railroad construction, from January to May 1890, there were in Matadi 1,109 African workers of heterogeneous nationality, among them 32 Senegalese, 25 Sierra Leoneans, 535 Kruboys, 39 Accras, 19 Haoussa, 8 Kabindas, 51 Congolese from the surroundings of Matadi, and 400 Zanzibarites (arrived on 26 May).[23] These proportions changed progressively beginning with 1892. The areas of origin of the workers population present on CCFC's work sites are shown in Table 21.6.

TABLE 21.6 Areas of Origin of CCFC's African Workers on 1 February 1892

Recruiting Center	Number
Dakar	12
Bathurst	119
Sierra Leone	790
Various ports of the Kru coast	215
Monrovia	87
Grand Bassam	12
Accra	440
Wydah	180
Grand Popo and Petit Popo	128
Lagos	67
East Africa	200
Total	2,350

Source: Le mouvement géographique, 1892, p. 2.

Poor working and living conditions were the cause of heavy mortality and numerous desertions. Faced with the difficulties of continuing to recruit in West Africa because of that situation,[24] the CCFC decided to recruit their personnel in the Americas and China: 300 black Americans from the

Barbados and 540 Chinese from Hong Kong arrived in Matadi on 2 September and 11 November 1892, respectively. But these new recruits demonstrated very quickly that they were incapable of adapting to new working conditions, notwithstanding their good reputation and their long experience in railroad construction.[25] Working conditions began to improve after the opening of the Palabala massif. This brought about the resumption of recruitment in West Africa.[26] Also, during this period, the Congolese began to appear: 10 in April 1893, 300 in July 1894, and 419 on 31 August 1894.[27] In December 1897 the 8,207 railroad workers were distributed as follows: 1,128 Congolese, 70 Kabindas, 170 Loangos, 554 Lagos, 2,054 Accras and Elmina, 66 Kruboys and Sierra Leoneans, 1,700 Senegalese, and 175 miscellaneous.[28]

These various nationalities and ethnic groups were represented among the population of Matadi. In 1897 the journalist P. Conreur wrote, "The Niggers who live in Matadi are for the most part foreigners to the Congo. They all come from the coast and every point on the map from Bathurst up to Saint-Paul-de Loanda has representatives here."[29]

At the end of the railroad construction, Matadi's population had progressively become "Congolized." As a matter of fact, recourse to foreign African manpower was limited to the minimum. By circular letter dated 3 April 1898, the director of the CCFC asked for a complete stop to the hiring of West Africans.

Managing Engineer L. Goffin writes:

> In these conditions, we absolutely must have nothing but natives employed to the various activities on the date of first operation of the line. I don't have to insist on this point with the various department heads who will understand the crucial importance of the radical substitution of a staff of Native workers to the workers from the coastal areas who are employed at present.[30]

For the CCFC the important maintenance work on the railroad was to be accomplished without the help of the West Africans, except for specialized work (team and station heads, telephone operators, and clerks).[31] Replacement of the West Africans by Congolese occurred progressively; when the Belgian journalist F. van der Linden visited Matadi in July 1908, he found approximately two thousand Congolese and three hundred West Africans employed on the railroad.[32]

While the West Africans are easily identified, it is difficult, however, to define the areas of origin of the Congolese. In June 1897, 344 individuals originating from the Congolese coast and 1,334 from the Cataractes worked on the railroad sites.[33] In 1898 P. Conreur mentions the presence of numerous domestic workers from Loango and Kabinda in Matadi, while the police force was made up of Bangala and individuals originating from Maniema.[34] Those coming from the "Upper Congo" probably represented a significant portion of the population, to the point that the Catholic missionaries organized a separate Bakongo group during catechisms.[35] Moreover, in 1919 the CCFC had to call on people originating from the "Upper Congo" for the construction of the Matadi–Ango-Ango railroad segment.[36]

Many immigrants from Angola reached Matadi during World War I. Indeed, they had run away from the Portuguese reprisals against the revolt of the Buta, Zombo, and Sanza Pombo.[37] In the 1920s the African population already appeared to be of very diverse origins. This ethnic heterogeneity was perceived by Matadi's local administration as early as 1920, when it realized that the population came from all regions of the "Congo," both the French and Portuguese colonies; moreover, by 1921 the administration noted the arrival of many Angolans who for the most part had come from Makela de Zombo.[38]

Thus, Matadi's human hinterland went far beyond the present district of Lower Zaire and reached the North of Angola. It is difficult to study in detail the various ethnic subgroups who were there or to isolate them. However, immigration was not significant (even though demand was higher), because of the low salaries paid by CCFC and the surplus in male mortality (which I shall touch on later). However, starting in 1925, we can obtain some notion of scale from the statistics of the working manpower mobilized by the labor office responsible for supplying the manpower needed for the reconstruction of the Matadi-Kinshasa Railroad and the redevelopment of the Matadi harbor (1922–1932). They show that in 1925, 64.5 percent of workers came from the Lower Congo; in 1926 and 1927 this proportion reached 48.3 percent and 49.2 percent, respectively. In the course of the latter year 29.4 percent came from Kwango, and 21.4 percent from Sankuru.[39] There is no doubt that the same ratios were found in Matadi, which received a significant portion of the people recruited by the Offitra.

Moreover, the "Special Surveys of Native Manpower" (MOI) give us an exhaustive breakdown of the salaried population according to their area of origin. The result is that in 1928 out of 734 individuals employed in Matadi, 34.3 percent came from Angola, 37.4 percent from the Lower Congo, 2.9 percent from Kwango. The immigrants from Equateur Province numbered 6.4 percent, those of Orientale Province 6.7 percent, those of Kasai District 6.7 percent, and those from other African countries 2.3 percent. Thus, Matadi obtained its population from a very large "demographic basin" covering the whole of Zaire with the exception of Shaba, and this basin went way beyond the national frontiers. But it already appeared at the time that the largest numbers had been supplied by the near hinterland. As for people originating from the Lower Congo, four territories had supplied heavy contingents: of Luozi (30.8 percent), emigrants from Equateur came from the Ubangi District (75.6 percent); for those of Eastern Province, in the districts of Uele-Itimbiri and Uele-Nepoko (14.8 percent) and Stanleyville (30.6 percent) recruiting had occurred essentially in the Sankuru District (86.7 percent). This human hinterland will not greatly change during the colonial period. Notwithstanding reductions already noticed in 1930 among emigrants from Orientale Province and Kasai District,[40] it can be stated that the Matadi's human hinterland was defined during this massive recruitment of manpower, whose heavy mortality rate had become a major demographic phenomenon until the 1930s. Thus, it is fitting to examine the main characteristics before offering any explanation.

WORKER MORTALITY

Mortality Rates: Some Trends

Until the late 1930s, a mortality rate of varying intensity struck the labor force. We know for a fact that frightening mortality rates were recorded during the construction of the Matadi-Kinshasa Railroad: 25 per thousand in 1890, 41.4 per thousand in 1891. In 1892 the mortality rate goes beyond 88 per thousand and then falls back progressively: 50 per thousand in 1893, 31.3 per thousand in 1894, and 7.5 per thousand in 1897. In sum, the construction of this railroad appears to have cost their lives to 1,800 "colored" and 132 white men.[41] Undoubtedly, Matadi's population would have been affected in the same proportion. The heavy mortality rate the town suffered during the first third of the twentieth century confirms our assumption.

For that period we have at our disposal some data that relate not only to the town of Matadi but also to Kinshasa and the Union Minière du Haut-Katanga (UMHK). This allows us to enlarge our vision of the demographic situation prevailing at the time. However, these data only reflect reality within their own limits. Figures 21.2 and 21.3 indicate the importance and the intensity of this demographic phenomenon.[42] When contemplating them (and taking into consideration only the mortality rates higher than 49 percent) it becomes apparent that the curves diverge from the trend average, particularly in 1913–1920, for the UMHK recruits and in 1905–1906, 1910, 1912, 1915–1919, 1918–1920, and 1925–1931 in relation to Matadi's Catholic population. Apart from these geographic units, the same picture appears: at the labor office, the mortality rate remained above 40 per thousand from 1927 until 1930,[43] while it reached 44.6 per thousand in 1931 at the Compagnie Minière des Grands Lacs.[44] Thus, however diversified the sample, heavy mortality seems to us to be one of the most characteristic structural aspects of demography of the period; it even constitutes its dynamism.

Thus, it is advisable to question the seriousness and the intensity of this mortality crisis. Several methods are available: some cannot be applied to our data, others bring about results that show defects resulting from the methods.

FIGURE 21.2 Deathrate at the Union Minière du Haut-Katanga and at Kinshasa, 1913–1931

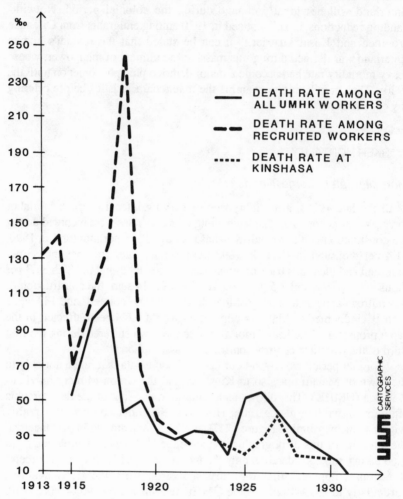

FIGURE 21.3 Birth- and Deathrates in the Catholic Population of
Matadi, 1904–1932

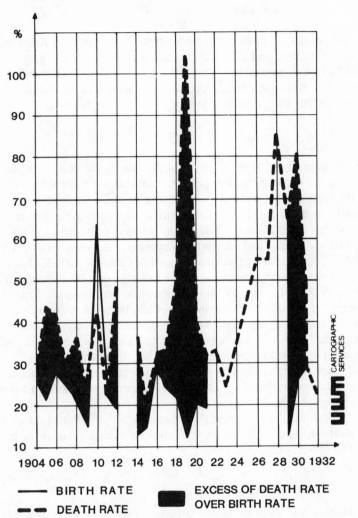

Hollingsworth's method[45]—according to which

$$I = q\ [q/(I - q)]\ (n2/3t - 2/3),$$

where I is the intensity of mortality, q the proportion of deceased individuals, n population numbers, and t the length of the crisis—was not adopted, because we have not found an $I > 20$ required by this method and because for the best results it applies to national populations. Faced with this obstacle, I chose Dupâquier's method, according to which:

$$I = (D - m)/\sigma,$$

where I is the intensity of mortality, D the deaths during the year, m the average of deaths for the ten preceding years, σ the standard deviation from this average. By applying this method to the data of Matadi's Catholic population, we have noted that the choice of reference years for the calculation of m has an influence on our results.[46] This is why we have considered the years 1914–1923 for the average and the standard deviation of the years 1904–1913; and 1924–1931, for the average and the standard deviation of the years 1914–1923. The following conclusions indicate the existence of a crisis of mortality in 1914, 1918, 1919, and 1927–1930, since indexes reveal it in both cases. The crisis peaked in 1919 and in 1928–1929. In fact, it is during those years that epidemics—the permanent cause of mortality—were the most deadly (as I shall show elsewhere). In 1919 mortality was significant and became a major obstacle to recruitment of manpower in rural areas.

In 1920, for example, the administrator of Luozi Territory had trouble finding the personnel required for the work of connecting the railroad from Matadi to Ango-Ango, following numerous deaths due to the Spanish influenza pandemic of 1919 among the Manyanga.[47] In 1928–1929 this elevated mortality rate hastened the execution of sanitation work in the elevated town of Matadi.[48]

Causes of Mortality

Such mortality is not linked to the age structure of the population. Matadi's population included more men than women; this population was generally young; the Manpower Commission in 1930–1931 for Congo-Kasai Province noted, "Many more men die among the workers who have been rigorously selected."[49] This implies the existence of factors that help to maintain the situation. I believe that two main causes explain this excessive mortality: poor living conditions and epidemics. The two factors are closely linked. Among these miserable living conditions, let us mention in particular mediocre material conditions, the lack of a public health service, and malnutrition.

Epidemics were the cause of considerable losses in human lives. The oldest one—which became permanent among African workers, since it was linked to rice, their main daily source of food—was beriberi. This disease caused a paralysis of the lower limbs, and death occurred because of a brutal cardiovascular collapse. The heavy mortality recorded at the CCFC from 1890 to 1894 is partly attributed to beriberi.[50] However, we know that in July 1898 a smallpox epidemic ravaged the African neighborhoods. Approximately sixty Africans died of it. In August of the same year, a new epidemic broke out in Matadi, which killed whites as well as Africans.[51]

Starting in 1900, epidemics became part of everyday life. The influenza epidemic that broke out at the beginning of May 1900 caused very few casualties. Other epidemics ravaged the population, notably smallpox in 1905[52] and yellow fever in 1911 and 1917.[53] In 1915, out of sixty recognized cases of typhoid fever thirty-two individuals died.[54] In 1919, Spanish influenza was more deadly, as noted earlier; this is confirmed in 1919 by a Kinshasa chronicler: "Very few deaths among the European population. The harsh stepmother found a better ground among the native population where death's crop was ample; will we ever know how many poor devils died during this epidemic. The ground was all the better prepared because famine threatened some regions like the Middle Congo and the Lower Congo, and the Mayumbe. There, many blacks died: because of malnutrition they were too weak to resist death! Some were seen falling in the streets, dying where they lay, after many hours of agony."[55]

It should be noted that the chronology of these epidemics sometimes runs parallel to subsistence crises, especially in 1911, 1917, and 1919. During those years drought and famine attacked Lower Zaire.[56] The extent and consequences of these calamities are still not well known. Further research will no doubt show their scope and depth.[57] In the meantime it may be reasonably stated that malnutrition resulting from famine made the epidemics to be more deadly.

Other diseases that regularly appear on the list of causes of death were added to the epidemics of smallpox, typhoid, and yellow fever, whose dissemination was made easier by the repugnant lack of sanitation. In 1921 the administrator of Matadi Territory assigns the heavy mortality rate that especially struck the Bazombo (Angolan) and the young recruits to the change in eating habits.[58] In 1922 the administration found that pneumonia was the main cause of death.[59] Dysentery and tuberculosis were also well represented. Causes of death are known for the year 1928: pneumonia, dysentery, beriberi, tuberculosis, and yellow fever appeared in 48 percent of cases.[60] Such diseases are generally exacerbated by poor nutrition and bad sanitary conditions. However, yellow and typhoid fever epidemics are essentially an indication of poor living conditions; tuberculosis is generally attributed to malnutrition; pneumonia to living and working conditions; beriberi and dysentery to eating habits. Thus, they are caused by socioeconomic conditions.

Such diseases took permanent hold in all industrial and urban centers of Zaire. In 1910–1911 typhoid fever and bacillary dysentery brought about excessive mortality in the labor camps of the UMHK in Lubumbashi.[61] It appears that up to 1917 these plagues had not yet been controlled; in 1917 antityphoid vaccination was made compulsory in Katanga because of about hundred deaths caused by typhoid fever.[62] Hygienic precautions taken punctually were not effective since they were not accompanied by improvements in the workers' condition. This is why the consequences of the "pandemic" Spanish influenza were catastrophic in 1918: it brought to the African workers of Katanga mortality and desertion of 503 per thousand and 208.7 per thousand respectively.[63] This epidemic raged without interruption in the whole colony; it is estimated that out of 61,040 individuals stricken, 2,937 Africans and 129 Europeans died of it that year.[64]

If we believe the results of surveys carried out by A. Duren, public health specialist of Congo-Kasai Province, dysentery and pneumonia caused 53.1 percent of deaths from 1925 to 1929[65] in Kinshasa. These two diseases, which appeared either in the epidemic or endemic form, undoubtedly found a milieu hygienically favorable, to cause 45.30 percent of deaths among the workers' population of Congo-Kasai Province during the period 1923–1927.[66]

The influence of the health service was weak because of the deficiencies of the health organization, which reflects the social policies of the colonial state: for the years 1910–1921 and 1924–1931 medical services represented 3.41 percent and 7 percent, respectively, of the regular expense budget of the colony.[67] Poor hygienic conditions affecting the workers' population compounded the deficiencies of the health organization. Nevertheless, this excessive mortality, a consequence of the operation of the mechanisms of primitive capital accumulation, did not affect the rural population areas in the same proportion: their dynamism was not affected.

NOTES

1. Cf. J. Thornton, "An Eighteenth Century Baptismal Register and the Demographic History of Manguenzo," in *African Historical Demography* I (Edinburgh, 1977), 405–515. The same author proposed a more ambitious vision in "Demography and History in the Kingdom of Kongo, 1550–1750," *Journal of African History* 18, no. 4 (1977), 506–530.

2. Cf. Bruce Fetter, "The Missing Migrants: Seeds in the Demographer's Field," in *History in Africa* (1984), 99–111.

3. Cf. Sabakinu Kivilu and Bogumil Jewsiewicki, "*La démographie coloniale, démographie historique et l'industrialisation ou comment manufacturer la réalité.*"

4. J. van Wing, "Evolution des coutumes Bakongo," *Congo* (1926), 2.

5. It should be noted that a good number of Noki's inhabitants worked in Matadi and had even been baptized. This is why the Redemptorist fathers wished to open a station in Noki. And in spite of the authorization granted

them by the bishop of São Paulo de Loanda on 8 February 1916 to practice their ministry in the surroundings of Noki, they were not authorized to administer baptism. M. Kratz, *Les missions des Rédemptoristes belges au Bas-Congo, période des semaines (1899–1920)* (Brussels, 1970), 77–79.

6. Kratz, referring to the report "Situation religieuse" and to baptism and marriage records, gives an estimate of six hundred Catholics toward the middle of 19, and puts the number of Christian families at eighty-eight, (*Redemptoristes*, 82).

7. Kratz, *Rédemptoristes*, 45, 84.

8. Religious status.

9. These Englishmen had arrived in Matadi in 1914, following the Portuguese reaction against the Buta revolt. Regarding this revolt, one may profitably read the autobiography of T. Lewis, *These Seventy Years* (London, 1931).

10. Cf. J. C. van Cleempt, "Mouvement prophétique au Bas-Congo," 26 October 1925, Tumba, Archives of the Matadi Diocese. Some useful information concerning the consequences of this religious movement may be found in the magazine *La Voix du Rédempteur* and the Kino weekly *L'avenir colonial Belge* of the time.

11. Kratz, *Rédemptoristes*, 84.

12. Estimates of the African population based on the 1926 figure according to the exponential growth rate of 8.4 percent from 1928 to 1958 does not allow the rate of demographic progression illustrated by all available statistical information to be uncovered. We recognize that the error comes from the fact that evolution did not occur uniformly during the period under consideration; for rationality's sake, the growth rate must be adjusted in order to adapt it to the context of each period.

13. Two procedures were used to adjust the data. From 1904 to 1912, the ecclesiastical year began on 1 July and ended on 30 June of the following year. For this year I took half of the numbers of each of the two years under consideration and added them together. As of 1913, the year started on 1 October: for that period, I deducted one quarter of the numbers of the year under consideration, and added one quarter of the numbers of the next ecclesiastical year. Through this process the year 1913 was eliminated.

14. Based on the proportion of the number of African workers for the years 1926–1930 and the resulting average, I made an estimate of the African population for the years 1920–1922 and 1924–1925, for which manpower figures are available.

15. Sabakinu Kivilu, "Histoire de la population et des conditions de vie à Matadi de 1890 à 1950," 2 vols. (Ph.D. diss., Université Nationale du Zaïre, 1981), vol. 1, pp. 104–105.

16. Cf. Congo Belge, Deuxième Direction Générale, Première Direction AIMO, *Enquêtes démographiques cités indigènes de Léopoldville*, vol. 1, (Léopoldville, 1957).

17. Lower Congo, *Rapport sur l'administration générale*, 1926; this manpower was estimated at 4,248.

18. I made my calculation based on 85 percent rounded down.

19. As of 1 September 1928, T. Heyse evaluated Matadi's population at 7,750. "Cession et concessions foncières du Congo," *Congo* (1929), 452.

20. The weekly *La Croix du Congo* of 9 July 1933 estimates Matadi's population at approximately eight thousand inhabitants. The assistant territorial administrator, F. Debognie ("Matadi, the Emerging Black City," *Le Courrier d'Afrique*, 11 February 1954) gives an estimate of six thousand.

21. Matadi Territory, *Rapport AIMO*, 1934.

22. Sabakinu Kivilu, "Matadi," vol. 1, pp. 133–148.

23. *Le mouvement géographique* 1890, pp. 39, 56.

24. Sabakinu Kivilu, "Matadi," vol. 1, p. 123.

25. R. J. Cornet, *La bataille du rail*, 3d ed. (Brussels, 1953), 229, 235.

26. Sabakinu Kivilu, "Matadi," vol. 1, p. 123.

27. *Le mouvement géographique*, 1898, p. 92.

28. Ibid., pp. 61–63.

29. P. Conreur, "La vie à Matadi," *Indépendance belge*, 20 May 1897.

30. *Le mouvement géographique*, 1898, col. 273.

31. Ibid., col. 45.

32. F. van der Linden, *Le Congo, les Noirs, et Nous*, 2d ed., (Paris, 1910), 63.

33. Cornet, *Bataille*, 336.

34. *Le Petit Bleu*, 20 and 18 September 1898.

35. Kratz, *Rédemptoristes*, 65.

36. Matadi Territory, *Rapports économique*, 2d semester, 1919.

37. Sabakinu Kivilu, "Matadi," vol. 1, p. 125.

38. Matadi Territory, *Rapports économiques*, 1920 and 1st semester, 1921.

39. Sabakinu Kivilu, "Matadi," vol. 1, p. 212.

40. Ibid., p. 213.

41. Ibid, p. 117.

42. For Matadi I used the statistics of the "Etat religieux de la Préfecture Apostolique de Matadi"; the statistics on Kinshasa and the Union Minière du Haut-Katanga Industriel come from the *Rapports aux Chambres*, 1925–1931; Colony of the Belgian Congo, *Rapport sur l'hygiène publique*, 1927, Archives Africaines (Brussels), rapp. An (82) 7; Union Minière du Haut-Katanga, Département Main d'Oeuvre Indigène, *Rapports annuels*, 1925–1930. A judicious utilization of statistics on mortality at the Union Minière du Haut-Katanga is to be found in Charles Perrings, *Black Mineworkers in Central Africa* (London, 1979), 83–85.

43. Colony of the Belgian Congo, *Rapport sur l'hygiène publique*, 1930; Office du Travail (Offitra), *Statistiques premier semestre*, 1929, Archives de la Sous-Région de Boma; *Rapports aux Chambres*, 1927–1931. In 1927, for example, a mortality rate on the order of 146.16 per thousand of recruits present in the workers' concentration camps was recorded; cf. Colony of the Belgian Congo, *Rapport sur l'hygiène publique*, 1927, p. 23.

44. *Rapport aux Chambres*, 1931, 24.

45. Cf. Thomas H. Holingsworth, "A Preliminary Suggestion for the Measurement of Mortality Crises," in Hubert Charbonneau and André Larose, eds., *Les grandes mortalités: Etude méthodologique des crises démographiques du passé* (Liège, 1979), 21–28.

46. Jacques Dupâquier, "L'analyse statistique des crises de mortalité, in Charbonneau and Larose, *Les grandes mortalités*, 83–87.

47. J. Dupâquier also recognized this danger: taking into account deaths that occurred in 1912 and 1919 as a basis for my calculations would have compromised my results.

48. Matadi Territory, *Rapport économique*, 1st semester, 1920, Archives de la Sous-Région des Cataractes dans Mbanza-Ngungu.

49. Sabakinu Kivilu, "Matadi," vol. 2, p. 555.

50. P. Ryckmans, *Le problème de la main-d'oeuvre au Congo Belge*

Rapport de la Commission de la main-d'oeuvre indigène 1930–1931, Province du Congo-Kasai (Brussels, 1931).

51. P. Conreur, "Epidémie de variole à Matadi," *Le Petit Bleu*, 18 September 1899.

52. P. Conreur, "Les travaux publics à Matadi," *Le Petit Bleu*, 26 May 1900.

53. Bas-Zaire District, *Rapport de la Commission d'Hygiène pour le 4e trimestre 1905*, Dos. H(840) VIII, H3, Archives Africaines (Brussels).

54. Remarks of Matadi's district commissioner, 6 January, Rapport trimestriel de la Commission d'Hygiène H(840), VIII; G. Deprez, "Cas de fièvre jaune constatée à Matadi (CB) en 1917," *Annales de la Société Belge de Médecine Tropicale 1920–1921*, 1, no. 1 (November 1929), 61–68.

55. *Rapport aux Chambres*, 1915, p. 184: Ninety-five cases resulting in twelve deaths were recorded in *bomas*.

56. Letter from Kinshasa in *La Tribune Congolaise*, 17 April 1919.

57. *Rapport aux Chambres*, 1912, p. 54; Bas-Congo District, *Rapports économiques*, 1918, 1919.

58. Matadi Territory, *Rapport économique*, 1921.

59. Ibid., 1922.

60. A. N. Duren, "Rapport d'hygiène du territoire de Matadi," in Colony of the Belgian Congo, *Rapport annuel d'hygiène* (Brussels, 1928).

61. *Rapport aux Chambres*, 1911, pp. 158–159.

62. Ibid., 1917, pp. 70–71, 94.

63. Perrings, *Black Mineworkers*, 82.

64. *Rapports aux Chambres*, 1918, pp. 100–129.

65. See R. Bruynoghe, "Les conditions générales de la santé," in *Essor Économique belge*, vol. 1 (Brussels, 1951), 159; Colony of the Belgian Congo, *Rapport sur l'hygiène publique*, 1927.

66. Colony of the Belgian Congo, *Rapport sur l'hygiène publique*, 1927, p. 24; I calculated this average.

67. Data relating to regular expenses of the colony come from *Rapport aux Chambres*, 1910–1931; those relating to the budget for medical services come from Bruynoghe, "Conditions générales," and *Rapports aux Chambres*, 1929–1931.

22

To Address a Common Problem

BRUCE FETTER

Though the contributing authors of this book differ widely in their approaches to the historical demography of colonial Central Africa, they share willingness to attempt to reconstruct it despite the paucity of "state-of-the-art" data—a willingness by no means shown by the majority of professional demographers. As K. T. de Graft-Johnson puts it, "Prior to 1960, the state of demographic data collection in Africa was very unsatisfactory."[1]

Should we abandon a scientific approach to the reconstruction of colonial demography in favor a more impressionistic one? Must we concede that our project is more an art than a science? The great molecular biologist, S. E. Luria, says that for him, "Science's path is essentially opportunistic. It aims at solving problems, not at doing good or bad experiments."[2] And for the contributors to this book, the reconstruction of colonial period patterns of fertility, mortality, and migration is a significant problem.

One important set of distinctions that can be made among our contributions is apparent in our chapter organization. The historians among us have been particularly concerned with assessing sources, which was the subject of Part 1. Other social scientists have provided the insights of their particular disciplines, which compose Part 2. Finally, three historians who have long worked in the field have, in Part 3, undertaken case studies at varying geographical scales.

This organization is not the only way to delineate the scholarly concerns that have brought us to study colonial demography. For some, it is a matter of affect: the emotional burr under the saddle that goads further action. For others, those concerns are a matter of research style; and for others, a tool to investigate a problem called by a different name.

The strongest emotions found in these pages belong to those born under colonial rule. Chapters 4, 6, and 21 in particular reveal the outrage of formerly colonized Africans: Djilali Sari, discussing Algerian censuses; Mwelwa Musambachime's account of factors affecting Zambian census counts; and Sabakinu Kivilu describing suffering and death in western Zaire.

None of our authors defends colonial practises, but some participated in them, and it is valuable to have the testimony of European actors of good will. Jeffrey Stone's narrative on how population counts were conducted in late colonial Zambia is most useful. Clyde Mitchell's analysis of infant mortality, based on materials collected during the Copperbelt survey of 1950–1955, shows how early work can continue to resonate in later research. Indeed, both Jean Stengers and Mansell Prothero, though not writing in these accounts of their personal experiences, were already engaged in ground-breaking research before the end of colonial rule.

Some of these authors live in Africa today, and come into daily contact with both contemporary conditions and the consequences of earlier development. These include David Beach in Zimbabwe, Justice Mlia in Malawi, Daniel Nyambariza, and, until recently, Gaëtan Feltz in Burundi, Patrick Ohadike in Ghana, and Léon de St. Moulin in Zaire. The rest of us, who view Africa from afar, are by no means indifferent to its condition—past or present.

Beyond our regional interests lie the currents in our respective disciplines. In this, of course, demography plays a central role, and our work would lack substance without the contribution of practicing demographers such as Kenneth Hill and the exposition by Patrick Ohadike and response by Osei-Mensah Aborampah.

For many others of us, demography has become a means of getting at other problems. Sharon Stichter shows the relevance of sexually differential migration patterns to feminist issues; Karen Hansen demonstrates how a very different kind of study can lead to an unprecedented mirror on the life of urban children.

In sum, our contributors come from a wide variety of disciplines and from an equally broad spectrum of motivation. What they have in common is concern for a shared problem: the reconstruction of the recent demographic past of the inhabitants of Central Africa. The relationship developed among these contributors, however, is stronger than that of people who would simply like to see their ideas published in the same book. We have come to constitute a community. By virtue of the interaction that began at the Milwaukee conference in 1986, a number of us have gone off in new demographic directions—enriching not only our own lives, but those of our disciplinary and regional colleagues.

This community-building is, for S. E. Luria, an important element in science. He writes that "science is an immensely supportive activity, which to me has been one of its strongest attractions. The support that science offers is both intellectual—the sharing of knowledge—and emotional—the sharing of purpose . . . membership in a segment of humanity that speaks and thinks in a common language. In fact, the world of science may be the only existing participatory democracy."[3]

The contributors to this volume cannot claim membership in a community as highly developed as that of the microbiologists—we have not yet even developed a common language! But we have deliberately joined to address a common problem, and we are, each of us, committed to the welfare of the African peoples whose lives we study. We invite others of like mind to join us in the task.

NOTES

1. K. T. de Graft-Johnson, "Demographic Data Collection in Africa," in E. van de Walle et al., *The State of African Demography* (Liège, 1988), 13.

2. S. E. Luria, *A Slot Machine, A Broken Test Tube: An Autobiography* (New York, 1984), 101.

3. Ibid., 117.

The Contributors

OSEI-MENSAH ABORAMPAH, a demographer of West Africa, is associate professor of Afro-American Studies at the University of Wisconsin–Milwaukee.

DAVID N. BEACH, author of two books on the history of precolonial Zimbabwe, teaches in the History Department at the University of Zimbabwe.

LÉON DE ST. MOULIN, S. J., has trained a generation of Zairian demographers and is currently vice dean of the Faculty of Catholic Theology in Kinshasa.

GAËTAN FELTZ, who has written extensively on Roman Catholic missions in Central Africa, teaches in the History Department at the University of Antananarivo.

BRUCE FETTER is a social historian of Central African and organized the National Science Foundation conference upon which this volume is based. He is professor of history at the University of Wisconsin-Milwaukee.

DAVID GARDINIER, editor of the African section of the American Historical Association's *Recently Published Articles*, is professor of history at Marquette University.

KAREN TRANBERG HANSEN has written extensively on women and children in modern Zambia and is associate professor of anthropology at Northwestern University.

The late RITA HEADRICK wrote a landmark dissertation on the demography of the former French Equatorial African federation, and taught at the University of Chicago Laboratory School.

DAVID HENIGE, editor of *History of Africa*, is the Africana bibliographer at the University of Wisconsin–Madison.

KENNETH HILL, a demographer who has worked in Uganda, teaches in the Department of Population Dynamics at the Johns Hopkins University.

J. CLYDE MITCHELL, who directed the pioneering social survey of the Zambian Copperbelt, is emeritus fellow of Nuffield College, Oxford University.

JUSTICE R. NGOLEKA MLIA is chair of the Department of Geography and Earth Sciences at the University of Malawi.

MWELWA C. MUSAMBACHIME is dean of the School of Education and past chair of the History Department at the University of Zambia.

DANIEL NYAMBARIZA has served as chair of the History Department at the University of Burundi.

PATRICK O. OHADIKE, who has written a number of works on the demography of Zambia, directs the United Nations Development Program's Regional Institute for Population Studies at the University of Ghana in Legon.

R. MANSELL PROTHERO, a pioneer on the study of migration in Africa, has recently retired as professor of geography at the University of Liverpool.

SABAKINU KIVILU has written widely on the population history of Zaire and is chair of the Demography Department at the University of Kinshasa.

DJILALI SARI, a leading authority on the demography of colonial Algeria, is director of the Sociology Institute at the University of Algiers.

JEAN STENGERS, a historical polymath, has retired from the Free University of Brussels, where he served as professor of history and dean of the Faculty of Letters.

FRANK C. STETZER, author of a number of articles on spatial autocorrelation, is a management information specialist at the University of Wisconsin–Milwaukee.

SHARON STICHTER, an authority on migration and women's studies, chairs the Department of Sociology at the University of Massachusetts–Boston.

JEFFREY C. STONE, an accomplished historian of cartography, lectures in the Geography Department and is secretary of the African Studies Program at the University of Aberdeen.

Index

About the Book

In essence a manual for reconstructing the demographic past of Central Africa, this is the first concerted attempt to recover the pre-1960 demography of an African region on the basis of colonial statistics. The authors begin by exploring the unexpected strengths, as well as the shortcomings, of extant records. They proceed to discuss how various social science disciplines can contribute to our understanding of Central Africa's recent demographic past, Finally, they examine case studies that synthesize a broad variety of approaches. The book can serve as a handbook not just for Africa, but for any part of the world where numbers are available, but not entirely reliable.

Bruce Fetter is professor in the Department of History at the University of Wisconsin–Milwaukee.